INDIA VIEWED THROUGH ITS NORTH EAST WINDOW

INDIA VIEWED THROUGH ITS NORTH EAST WINDOW

Editor

Rohini Kumar Baruah

GYAN

ISBN : 978-81-212-1226-7

Price : ₹ 1125

Published in, 2014

Published by

Gyan Publishing House
23, Main Ansari Road, Darya Ganj
New Delhi-110002
Phones : 23282060, 23261060
Fax : 011-23285914
E-mail: books@gyanbooks.com
Website: www.gyanbooks.com

Laser Typesetting: Gyan Print (AB-II), Delhi
Printed at: G. Print Process, Delhi

Cataloging in Publication Data—DK
Courtesy: D.K. Agencies (P) Ltd. <docinfo@dkagencies.com>

India viewed through its north east window / editor, Rohini Kumar Baruah.
p. cm.
Contributed articles.
Includes bibliographical references and index.
ISBN 9788121212267

1. Social change—India, Northeastern. 2. Economic development—India, Northeastern. 3. India, Northeastern—Economic policy. I. Baruah, R. K. (Rohini Kr.)

DDC 303.409541 23

Contents

Foreword

Senior citizens are the repository of experience and wisdom; they are the students who have learnt for a long time, in the schools of life. They have much to tell the youth, and the society can use their maturity and sobriety to enrich our surroundings, build bridges of harmony, trust and well being.

There are many an elderly people who still have fire in their belly and are committed to work selflessly for the good of the society. Many of them are pensioners and they are quite active; some of them had held important public offices and served the people and the country. Of them some were members of the All India Services that consists of the Indian Administrative Service, the Indian Police Service and the Indian Forest Service. These three services constitute the nucleus of governance in the country and symbolise the core functions of bureaucracy.

This volume has been brought out primarily by the retired members of IAS, IPS, IFS and ACS who had worked in Assam and outside and settled down in different places. Free from the yoke of bureaucracy they are able to take up new responsibilities and many of them are eminent opinion makers; they matter in social transformation, in recalibrating and fine tuning the machines of which they were components once. As ordinary citizens, now they live ordinary lives and share the common problems of every day existence.

The writers are from diverse experiences; the articles include nearly everything that is important in public administration, social development, economic growth and national security and many more. They are professionally informative, some are interestingly anecdotal, some even spiritually inspiring. All of them are the result of the authors' clear thinking based on their long innings in public service and their involvement with the issues discussed. They are objective, entertaining and engaging. I have learned much by going through these pages.

It is very rare that in one volume so many subjects are discussed and they are all relevant to the present situation. People who have written the articles are old but their memories are fresh, their elucidation and conclusions are coherent and contextual. Age is no bar to new ideas, they can still respond to the new challenges and many of them are involved in activities aimed at ameliorating the harshness of life of the fellow citizens.

There are three ages of man: First the chronological age tells how the old a person is by the calendar and the biological age is about how old a person is perceived in terms of critical life signs and cellular processes, which in other words is how old one actually looks. The third is the psychological age which is how old one really feels. Of these only the first one is fixed, yet it is the most misleading of the three. So, it will be an anachronism to say that after retirement people are old and useless. They are not; the authors in this volume have demonstrated that age is a matter of mind, if you don't mind it doesn't matter.

The great *Vaishnava* saint and social reformer of Assam, *Mahapurusha* Sankardeva wrote nearly half of his major works after he was over 95 years of age. He was a *Mahapurusha* – an extraordinary human being who continued to tirelessly fight obscurantism and social evils till his death at the unusual age of 119 years. The famous writer and journalist Mr Khushwant Singh continues with his prolific pieces and has published new books into his late nineties. The oldest person to get the Nobel Prize was Leonid Hurwicz at the age of 90 in 2007. Ageing is inevitable, being old is not.

In politics people do not retire at all. It may be because in this profession fight for survival is relentless and every day they have to remain alert. Sir Winston Churchill was awarded the Nobel Prize in literature when he was 79 years old and he was active in politics till in his eighties. Queen Elizabeth II is 87 years of age and there is no sign that she is going to walk into the sunset soon. Our Union Cabinet is virtually a geriatric ward with the oldest in his late eighties and more than half its members past their seventies.

The human intellect is ageless and it can remain sharp irrespective of how old a person is. The only condition is that it must be used regularly and like a knife it becomes sharper when it is used more. Ageing is a process of metabolism; it depends on how one metabolises one's experience and time, brings in experience. In the ultimate analysis therefore how one metabolises time is the most important aspect in the process of ageing because time is the most fundamental experience. Time well lived is time well used.

The senior citizens who have lived for longer time and who are still active and useful citizens are the ones who have used time to adapt themselves to new surroundings and challenges. They continue to be fresh and relevant. Their views are valuable and the youth must blend their energy with the learning of the age. The presumption that man stagnates with age is an old worldview. For some age brings in more maturity and greater perspectives and with modern medicine's great breakthroughs and upgraded health care facilities people all over the world are achieving higher life expectancy. The middle age now begins at mid-fifties and may well stretch up to mid seventies. When it is then that man becomes old? People do not grow old and useless; they become old and useless when they stop growing.

There is no point in creating a mind-set that one is old and helpless. Those of us who have worked for long in public administration are lucky because we have adequate income by way of pension and we are financially independent. We can still contribute without bothering about financial issues and I find great many of our fraternity is doing just that. Financial security at old age is a

liberating factor and it allows the senior citizens to live in dignity and freedom. In such a situation, there is no withering away in the departure lounge because one can work till the last day. Aging gracefully and healthily is the secret of an active life. I feel proud that the senior citizens are not idling away their time in the graying years.

This volume is a monument of their commitment to serve the society and change it so that the posterity can lead a better quality of life. I compliment the authors for their excellent articles and hope that they will continue to work for the betterment of the society.

22nd September, 2013 **Ranjit Shekhar Mooshahary**

Preface

Time creates and carries history of the contemporary human race but in its relentless march also tears and sweeps some of its pages to be deposited in to the sea of invisibility. Edmund Burke was right when he said, "History is a pact between the dead, the living and the yet unborn". A well written book patently forms a running cog in the wheel of history that retrieves and transmits some of the pages of the past and the present to the future and provides a Light House on the shore of posterity. And a book shaped and set in the mould of beauty and truth and reflected in the contemporary mirror is anointed to be a book, in the words of John Ruskin, 'a book of all time' as distinguished from a 'book of the hour'.

Such words of wisdom guided the All India Services Pensioners' Forum (AISPF), Assam to leave some footprints in the sands of time by opening their enormous storehouse of knowledge and experience, which they culled in their cherished service tenure in the States of Assam and Meghalaya. And memory being poignantly treacherous, the AISPF felt obliged to arrest its slip through time's escape route and consign the same to new pages of contemporary socio-economic history of the North East India to be stored in the Treasure Trove of posterity. Though enriched in their knowledge and experience, the members of the AISPF felt that the universe of knowledge is vast and boundless and that, that which they posses forms only a few particles of it. So, it decided in its wisdom to snatch some more from those who have them in abundance and are accredited scholars, intellectuals, litterateurs, journalists, educationists, technocrats, Professors of the University and justice of the Supreme Court, most of whom have earned their name and fame for erudition and prognosis in their respective fields of profession, research and investigation and honoured with the country's top literary and professional awards. I open out my heart to say that their invaluable contributions have added many a golden feather to the cap of our treasured book "India Viewed through Its North East Window".

I have given in the Introduction Chapter, an inkling of the nature and extent of the contents embraced in our book. Broadly speaking, the book is a collection of forty one essays written by eminent writers, litterateurs, journalists, professors, educationists, intellectuals and members of the All

India Services Pensioners' Forum. It traverses a wide range of subjects which reflect both the core problems and the rich natural beauty and resources of Assam and the North East India. The mystique turbulence of the mighty Brahmaputra, the magical charms of the blue hills and the red rivers with their maddening charms, the lure of the world famous one-horned rhino hideously showing up in and around its mystic abode of Kaziranga National Park, the extensive lush green tea gardens whispering the touching tales of sweat and sorrow of the tea tribes who momentarily sink their misery in the gleeful torrents of their colourful *Jhumur* dance , the sprawling virgin fields of the liquid gold and Asia's first refinery at the picturesque town of Digboi, *Majuli* the greatest river island of the world and the unique seat of the Vaisnavite culture with very many monasteries founded by Guru Sankar Mahapurusha and left by the poers-that-be in the lurch to be slowly consumed by the raging perennial erosion of the turbulent Brahmaputra, the incredible story of Assam being reduced to a dumping ground of millions of illegal Bangladeshi as also to a hub of multi-faceted terrorist outfits–in short, the hidden tale of riches and poverty making strange bedmates—all take the reader to an exotic sojourn never before experienced.

I cannot resist the temptation of reciting once more the refrain that most of the authors represent a select class of luminaries reposed in the prodigious store house of intellectuals, writers, litterateurs, journalists, educationist's economists and renowned administrators. While the former members of the All India Services have inked their treasured experiences accumulated in addressing the issues they were faced with in their active service tenure, the others represent a highly scholastic and intellectual class, who have made their name and fame in the fields of literature, journalism, teaching, authoring books and writing newspaper columns. Many of them have been honoured with top national awards in their respective fields including literature, journalism, science and technology and police and general administration. The facts culled and enumerated in the book qualify to be researched materials retrieved from the work fields as they were and, therefore, can be used with advantage by the researchers, the teaching and the learning community, writers and journalists alike.

I have no word to express my gratitude to all the benign authors who have helped us to fulfill our dream of producing this book with their valuable contribution, gesture and goodwill. I also thank all my colleagues including in particular the members of the Editorial Board who unfailingly stood by me through thick and thin which I had to encounter in forging ahead the project. Last but not the least, I express my unreserved gratitude to Messrs Gyan Publishing House, Daryaganj for their taking up the burden of publication of this book.

Dr. Rohini Kumar Baruah, IAS (Retired)
Editor
5, Pinaki Path, R.G. Baruah Road,

List of Contributors

Ranjit Shekhar Mooshahary, an IPS officer of Kerala Cadre, had retired in 2006. During his service career, he held many important positions under State and the Central Governments, including those of the Director General of Police, Kerala, the Director General of National Security Guards and the Director General of Border Security Force. Later, he became the first Chief Information Commissioner, Assam and adorned the position of the Governor of Meghalaya from 2008 to 2013. He lives in Guwahati and is leading an active public life.

Rohini Kumar Baruah, IAS (retired), is a noted writer and a columnist. After retirement he acted as an Editor of a local Daily, *Natun Dainik* for some time. Later, he was enrolled as an Advocate of the Gauhati High Court and has now taken to writing. He has so far authored twenty books including his Ph.D. Thesis and had received the Hem Baruah Memorial Asom Sahitya Sabha Award, 2005. He has founded and is associated with several socio-literary organisations.

Mrinal Kumar Barooah, IAS (Retired) is a short story writer in both English and Assamese. Until recently, he had also held the position of Member, State Consumer Disputes Redressal Commission, Guwahati.

Mr P.K Borah, is a retired IAS officer of 1966 batch. During his service tenure, he had held many important positions, including the prestigious post of Chairman, Tea Board, Kolkata. He retired as Chief Secretary to the Government of Assam. He is an avid reader of a wide range of books. Birds and forests are his subjects of special interest. Prior to joining the IAS, he had worked as a teacher in a local College of Guwahati, and used to write short stories in English.

Dangshi Barman, a retired Assam Civil Service officer, is an acknowledged expert on land matters. He writes articles in local Dailies which are read with great interest. He was also a Member of the Land Reforms Advisory Committee of the Government of Assam.

Harekrishna Deka, IPS (retired), is a prolific writer, a litterateur, a literary critic and an accredited poet. He writes on a wide range of subjects which include literature, reforms of the Police Administration and socio-economic problems of Assam. During his service tenure, he held many important positions including that of the Director General of Police, Assam. He has been honoured with many awards including the Sahitya Academy Award. After retirement, he worked as the Editor of an *English daily, The Sentinel,* and of a frontline Assamese magazine, *Gariyasi.*

N.C. Dutta, IAS (Retired), had been an able administrator. During his service career, he held many important positions under the State and the Central Governments. He also served in the Food Corporation of India and was the Director of Census Operations, Assam. He is a noted *writer* and used to write in *the Sentinel,* an English daily.

D.K. Gangopadhyay, IAS (retired), had been an able administrator. He held many important positions in both the State Governments of Assam and Meghalaya as also in the Government of India. Mr Gangopadhyay had ended with his career as Chief Secretary to the Government of Meghalaya. During his tenure as the Revenue Commissioner, Government of Assam, he compiled a very valuable book on Revenue Administration in Assam.

Jatin Hazarika, is a retired IAS Officer of Assam\Meghalaya cadre. He had been an able administrator and held crucial positions during the Emergency(1975) and six-year-long Assam Agitation on Foreign Nationals issue (1979-85). He was the Chairma of the Assam Administrative Reforms Committee and a recipient of 'PAUL APPLEBY AWARD' in Public Administration.

S.P. Kar, IPS (Retired) is a former Inspector General of Police, Assam. He is a writer on various subjects, particularly on matters pertaining to police administration and other matters of topical interest. He was awarded Indian Police Medal (IPM) for meritorious service by the President of India.. He has authored two books and is currently holding an assignment as Security Adviser to Oil India Ltd.

S.B. Medhi, IAS (Retired), is a known name in the Assam administration. An officer with an academic mindset, he is a noted writer and has authored several important books. He is associated with several socio-cultural organisations.

Hilary Pais, IAS (Retired), held various positions in the Assam Government as well as in the Central Government. He has several scholastic books and researched essays to his credit. He is an acknowledged authority on matters relating to labour movement and welfare and was an Adviser to the ILO.

Barada Charan Sharma, IAS (retired), was assigned to West Bengal cadre. During his service tenure, he held many important positions in both West Bengal and Central Governments. Retired as an Additional Secretary to the Government of India, Dr. Sharma had also served as a Member of the Central Administrative Tribunal, (CAT), Kolkata. Dr Sharma has authored several researched books.

V. Ramakrishna, IAS (retired), had worked in Assam and Meghalaya and held many crucial positions. He retired as the Chief Secretary to the Government of Meghalaya.

Bhaskar Barua, IAS (retired), held very crucial positions in both Assam and Central Governments. He retired as Secretary to the Government of India, Ministry of Agriculture and was also the Representative Member of the Food and Agricultural Organisation in Myanmar.

Mayur Bora, is an Assistant General Manager in the NABARD at Jorhat. A prolific writer, he is also a columnist and has authored several thought- provoking books on subjects varying from Vaishnavism to Marxism.

L.N. Bora, a retired Professor of the Assam Agricultural University, Jorhat, is a renowned name in the literary world of Assam and India. A former President of the Asom Sahitya Sabha, Dr Bora is a veteran litterateur who has authored more than 50 books including short stories, novels and essays on a wide range of subjects covering socio-cultural and literary arena. Dr Bora has received several national awards including the Sahitya Akademi Award, Saraswati Award etc.

Justice (Retd.) M.K. Sarma, Dr Sharma is a former Justice, Supreme Court of India and a renowned Sanskrit Scholar. An accredited exponent of Vaisnavite religion and culture, Justice (Dr) Sharma has been honoured with several awards for his Vaisnavite exposure.

Jishnu Barua, is an IAS officer of the Assam and Meghalaya cadre and is currently posted as a Principal Secretary to the Government of Assam. He is an avid reader and a noted writer. This article had come out in the Sentinel newspaper earlier.

Nishinath Changkakoti, is a former Director General of Police, Assam. Shri Changkakati is also a prominent writer and has written a good number of thoughtful articles on a wide range of subjects. After retirement he has been actively engaged in organising social and humanitarian activities. He is now the President of Karunadhara, a socio-humanitarian organisation rendering financial and allied assistance to distressed people.

M. Gopalakrishna, IAS (retired) has a glazing record of his services rendered in various capacities under Assam and Meghalaya governments. He was also on deputation to Government of India and finally retired as the CMD Rural Electrification Corporation (REC) of India. Settled now in Hyderabad, Shri Gopalakrishna is associated

with various socio-economic organisations. He also was the president of the Andhra Pradesh All India Services Pensioners' Association.

H.N. Das, IAS (Retd.), had been a brilliant IAS officer of 1961 batch. Known for his penchant for quick decisions, he held many crucial positions in the Government of Assam and rendered a glazing account of himself in whatever position he held. An accredited economist, the author had long experiences in matters pertaining to finance. Earlier, he was a Director in the Ministry of Finance; Government of India. He held the position of the Chief Secretary to the Government of Assam during 1990-95. After retirement, he held the position of Ombudsman, RBI, Guwahati and was also the Chairman of the Committee On Fiscal Reforms (COFR), Assam. He is a prolific writer and has authored several accredited books.

A.K. Neog, IAS (retired), had held various crucial assignments and is a former Economic and Statistical Adviser and Ex-officio Additional Secretary to Government of India in the Ministry of Agriculture, New Delhi. During his service career, he had represented Government of India in various international organisations and also obtained a post graduate diploma from Cambridge University. Presently he is engaged in entrepreneurship development work together with Dr. D.D. Mali and is a visiting Professor of the Gauhati University UGC Academic Staff College.

Paramesh Dutta, IAS (Retd.), had been a specialist in the matter of Small Scale industries and retired from service as commission and secretary in the Department of Education, Assam. After retirement, he has engaged himself in promoting educational institutions.

L.K. Barua, IAS (Retd.), is a respectable name in the Assam administration. Known for his academic mindset, Baruah is a committed litterateur and has made in-depth studies in the area of Folklore and cultural heritage of Assam. During his tenure as a faculty member in the Institute of Advanced Studies in Shimla, he had written several authoritative books and had carved out a *niche* in the literary field.

R.N. Ravi, IPS (retired), had been a Special Director, Intelligence Bureau., Government of India and a prolific writer specialised in insurgency in the NE Region. He is also a columnist and his facts-ridden articles on the subject written in various national and state level newspapers including the Assam Tribune have been highly educative and have been read with special interest by a wide range of readers.

Udayan Misra, is a former Professor and Head of the Department of English of Dibrugarh University and a National Fellow, Indian Council of Social Science Research Institute, New Delhi. A prolific writer, Dr. Misra has written many valuable essays and read many more in various seminars. He has authored several valuable books which have been acclaimed by a wide range of readers.

N.N. Barua, IAS (Retd.), had been a popular name in the Assam administration and had held crucial positions in various Departments of the Government of Assam. Mr. N.N. Barua had been a well-versed Professor of Mathematics – an interest that he retains even now.

D.N. Bezbaruah, a veteran journalist and was the Founder Editor of 'The Sentinel'. He is a prolific writer, a front-line columnist and writes regularly in local and national newspapers. His thought provoking articles are widely acclaimed. He is also a former Chairman of the Editors' Guild of India and has authored several authoritative books. He is currently engaged in a project of translating a series of literary works of crucial importance.

R.C. Borpatragohain, who was an Advocate of the Gauhati High Court, has now taken to teaching as a full time profession. He teaches law and is the Head and Dean of the of the Faculty of Law, Gauhati University. An expert on matters of immigration law, Dr. Borpatragohain is associated with several organisations where he acts as an Adviser or a Mediator.

M.P. Bezbaruah, IAS (Retd), a brilliant product of Delhi School of Economics as also of the London School of Economics, had held various crucial positions in both Government of Assam and the Government of India. After rendering accredited service

in the Ministry of Tourism, Government of India, he finally retired as the Secretary to the Government of India. Even after retirement, he held the assignment of the Banking Ombudsman, New Delhi, Chairman of the Fiscal Reforms Committee, Assam, etc. He is an Honorary Permanent Representative of WTO and currently has been a Member of the North-East Council, Shillong. He has authored several accredited books.

J.M. Bujor Baruah, was Resident Chief Executive of Oil India Limited at Duliajan, Director (Exploration and Development) of Oil India Limited at New Delhi, and Chairman and Managing Director of Bongaigaon Refineries and Petro-chemicals Limited at Dhaligaon, Assam during 1990-1997.

Hiren Gohain, a retired Professor/Head of the department of the Gauhati University, is an erudite scholar, a prolific writer, an eminent literary critic and an intellectual. He has made extensive critical and analytical studies on English and Assamese literature and is an accredited literary critic. He has authored, translated and prefaced many books and has been honoured with many prestigious awards at both State and national level, including the Sahitya Academy Award. Writing is his pastime and he is a social activist fighting against corruption, price rise.

A. Didar Singh, IAS (Retd.), a brilliant academic record holder, has retired from the IAS after serving in the governments of Assam and Meghalaya but had spent most of his period on deputation to the government of India. Known for his quality of head and heart, Dr. Singh had retired as the Secretary to the Government of India, and is currently holding the position of the Secretary General, FICCI, New Delhi. He has authored several valuable books.

K.K. Sinha, IAS (Retd.), had a long stint in Assam and Meghalaya. During the Bangladesh War of liberation (1971), he had played a pivotal role as deputy Commissioner Tura, Meghalaya in sustaining and coordinating the supply line of the essential commodities, Suave and sincere, Shri Sinha retired as the Additional secretary to Government of India, Ministry of Telecommunications.

Amal Kr. Borpujari, An academician-turned-professional, Dr Borpujari is a promising entrepreneur of Assam. An economist and an industrialist, Dr Borpujari is a serious writer with a fair degree of his flair for writing on issues relating to finance and investment. He attends and organises seminars and workshops both at national and international levels.

A.K. Bhagabati, is a Professor and an erudite scholar of the Gauhati University. His special fields of research interests include agriculture, bio-diversity and overall environment of North East India. He has so far written 23 books and is an accredited Research Guide leading to Ph.D. degree of many Research Scholars on the subject of Wetland. He has also produced several authoritative essays in national level seminars. He is associated with several socio-educational organisations of the state.

Dulal C. Goswami, is a former Professor of Environmental Science, Gauhati University. He obtained his Ph.D. degree from the USA in 1982 on Fluvial Geomorphology of the River Brahmaputra. His research interests include Fluvial Studies, Environmental Science of Geomorphology. He was the Chair Professor of Colin Mackanjy Chair, Anna University, Chennai. He is also a noted writer and writes particularly on the special areas of his investigation and research.

Arup Kumar Datta, a former Professor of J.B. College, Jorhat, Assam is a respectable name in the writers' world of Assam. An avid reader and a prolific writer, Mr Datta left teaching profession to dedicate himself to full time reading and writing. He is now an eminent writer, a columnist. He has authored about 30 books. He also held the coveted position of Indian Counselor, Indian Embassy, and has been honoured with several prestigious awards during 2004-2008. Hewrites for the Assam Tribune.

Col (Retd) Manoranjan Goswami, a resident of Lalganesh, Guwahati, is a retired Army officer. He has now turned in to a noted writer. He writes short stories and articles in local English and Assamese newspapers and magazines. He has authored several valuable books. He is also a social activist and is associated with several socio-cultural organisations.

1

Introduction

1. Rationale of the Book

The idea of producing a book by capitalising on and documenting the treasured knowledge and experiences of the All India Services Pensioners who wielded in the yester years of their life the wheels of administration and played custodians of progress and welfare of the society but in the evening of their life find themselves pushed to living on the latter's benevolence in the shape of pension, had rooted in and stemmed from the sense of obligation of the members of the All India Services Pensioners' Forum (AISPF) towards the society for redeeming their societal debt with whose loving care and nourishment they once made and have now ended their blooming career of the bye gone days, thanks to the inexorable march of time.

To take such a decision in the evening of their life when the light of their life had started slowly ebbing out like that of the evening sun, was undoubtedly a challenging task. But boosted, as they were, by emotionally surcharged care and concern for the societal progress and well-being, they accepted the challenge and plunged into the mission of leaving some footprints in the sands of time which they reckoned, would provide some beaconing light for the Governments of present or future, and more so, for the emerging generations, to whom the world the elders are preparing to depart from actually belongs, and, therefore, the elders of the current generation are obliged, morally and socially at least, to apprise them of the hidden hazards to the former's safe, secured and orderly life in the unseen future.

And, it is principally in that view, that the AISPF felt the need for reflecting at national level the burning problems of the North Eastern Region (NER), more particularly of Assam, with its location as the natural gateway to this vast tract of the landmass—a lush green landmass interspersed by rivers, hills and valleys—isolated from the mainstream of India, abundantly resourceful and characteristically backward. Of even far greater importance is the fact that with its strategic location, the region acts as an unflinching buffer between India and the mighty China, among others, and silently stands like a valiant vanguard to insure India's safety and security against assaults from its hostile neighbours.

The cruel irony is that the region, despite its munificent natural beauty, resources and strategic location, stands neglected and remains as one of the most backward regions of India, economically and socially, much to the mockery of her un-acclaimed epithet of 'Switzerland of the East' and ridicule of our Constitutional dispensation of equality of opportunity and treatment to all and further, pushing the Government of India's avowed policy of eradication of regional imbalances in development to nought. Such feelings do not just end with clamouring for a larger share in the national cake but penetrates deeper in to more fundamental aspects of protection of India's national security, territorial integrity particularly in the face of invisible threats from the mighty China, and her strange bedmate, Pakistan.

Of no less serious concern is the harsh fact that the feelings of neglect, exploitation and step-motherly treatment by the Rulers in Delhi, are disgustingly real in terms of facts rather than sham. The climate of despondency has generated revolt and boosted the mushroom growth of many terrorist outfits essentially and inevitably flourishing under the protective wings of, and nurtured by, India's hostile neighbours. Nor can the principle of equitable socio-economic development of all the regions of the country as enunciated in the Directive Principles of our Constitution under Article 38 be brushed aside capriciously. It is behind this shadowy background that the Government of India's credibility in estimation of the people of this region-pristine, gullible and simple as they essentially are stands smothered. They have long nourished an avalanche of grievances against the Rulers in Delhi—a fallout which flings unhealed wounds on India's unity, integrity and peace—that is, the India of Mahatma Gandhi's dream. The monumental words of farewell—'My heart goes out to the people of Assam'—that remorsefully dropped from the fractured lips of Jawaharlal Nehru when in 1962 China had plundered the Indian territory of Arunachal and advanced to Tezpur, are still green and indelibly imprinted in the minds of the people of Assam and Arunachal, only to resuscitate their grouse against the Union Government.

In fact, the region, benevolently blessed by Nature with, and possessed of bountiful natural resources provides an instance of a unique paradox of riches and poverty making disgustingly strange bed mates that while sleeping in the bed of riches; it is unable to wriggle itself out of the clutches of poverty, illiteracy and ignorance. And as if to add salt to the wound, Assam has been virtually converted in to a dumping ground of millions of illegal infiltrators from the erstwhile East Pakistan and now Bangladesh, the most productive human factory of the sub-continent, if not of the world. The combined effect of all this has been reflected in transforming the North East Region in to a disastrous breeding ground of terrorism, insurgency, social unrest, disbelief and disharmony threatening the territorial integrity and solidarity of the colourful Indian society. The AISPF felt that the nation must know about the dark horizon of the NER.

2. Paradigm

To delve deeper in to the heart of the problems and bring out the grave significance of leaving the core issues unaddressed and the people's grievances

unmitigated, it is necessary to take the reader along a wider spectrum of these problems reflecting, succinctly through, their inside view:

Lack of appropriate infrastructure—a *sine-qua-non* for economic/industrial development, stands as the perennially impregnable hindrance to the much-needed development that shatters the people's dream of living a reasonably sustainable standard of life matching with their natural resources of the State/ NE region. A storehouse of natural beauty and treasures, even the tourism industry which calls for less per capita investment and fetches speedy economic growth with spiralling boost to employment, languishes for want of the required infrastructures which the State governments cannot by itself build up. The mighty Brahmaputra, untamed and untapped, grows wild with fury and creates havoc taking in its sweep home and hearth, crops and cattle during its annual rituals of devastating flood, erosion, silting of agricultural land and not infrequently minor changes in course, thereby reducing the farmers to penury and bringing rivers of tear, while the Brahmaputra Board with its large paraphernalia remains a lifeless spectator. Thus, the State agriculture which is literally in primitive stage despite the ritualistic Five Year Plans, cannot sustain the poor agriculturists representing seventy-five per cent of the State's population. And to add salt to the wound, the State has been literally converted into a heaven for illegal infiltrators, almost wholly from Bangladesh. The ominous fallout has been that the encroachments on all classes of land—be they reserved forest or national parks, agricultural, marshy or hilly lands, Village Grazing Reserve (VGR) Tribal Belt /Block or National Park lands, '*Satra*' or '*Char*' lands—have gone to a 'free for all' encroachment stage and all have fallen under the inalienable grip of the swarms of ants—like infiltrators from the neighbouring districts which were once the parts of reconstituted Province of East Bengal and Assam, East Pakistan and now Bangladesh, in that order.

These land vultures lustily eye on and devour hungrily the vast landmass of the region in general and Assam the gateway of the region, in particular. The unabated encroachment on the landmass goes on at an alarming pace such that shrinkage of all classes of land, wanton poaching of the flora and fauna including the world famous one-horned rhino facing its imminent extinction and wanton felling of timbers with concomitant evils, ink a shocking story of imminent threats to the very identity of the indigenous people. But by far the most shocking of all maladies mentioned above relates to the invisible and not so invisible threats to the national security and territorial integrity of our country with most of the infiltration-dominated districts transformed into the hub of terrorists of all hue and colour, both imported and domestic brands. And reportedly they are receiving liberal patronage of Pakistan and China in particular with the inevitable result that certain infiltration-dominated areas have become the hub of crime, insurgency and spying particularly by Pakistan's ISI and the like.

No wonder that lawlessness, rampant encroachment, plundering of forests, poaching of rhino and elephants, polluted environment and ecological imbalance, and crimes like thefts, dacoity, killing, kidnapping for ransom, drug-peddling and even flooding the region with forged Indian currency notes

aimed at distorting the economy, have become a routine affair. All this has taken a toll on the State's law and order situation. Thus, with the lack of adequate economic development and dissipation of the natural resources on the one hand, and converting particularly Assam in to a dumping ground of millions of foreign nationals to derive political gains from the illegal vote banks made up of them, the people of the region are deeply anguished and enraged. They nurture their conviction that Delhi is interested only in exploitation of the natural resources of the region keeping it as an undeveloped buffer against China and using it as a dumping ground for the foreigners to be used as vote banks. All this incontrovertibly tells the sad story of mushroom growth of armed rebellion, insurgency, separatist movements, crimes and worst of all is the growth of terrorism with all their concomitant evils, gripping the region.

3. Empirical Investigation

To bring home the truth of what has been enumerated above, I need just to delve into one crucial area encompassing its background details loaded with highly surcharged fall out of even threats to the national security as vouched by no less an authority than the Supreme Court of India.

(i) During the early eighties, that is, in 1979, the vexed issue of millions of foreign nationals infiltrating into Assam ignited and captured the minds of the whole Assamese nation. The All Assam Students' Union (AASU), a massive student's organisation revolted and took up the cudgels to launch a unique, record breaking six years long massive agitation on foreign nationals' issue, demanding detection and deportation of the foreign nationals and deletion of their names from the Voters' Lists. Their names were enlisted as voters which is the violation of the provisions of the Constitution of India and the Citizenship Act of India, 1955. Of several other organisations that totally identified with and joined the agitation led by AASU were All Asom Gana Sangram Parishad (AAGSP), an organisation spearheaded by a firebrand intellectual named Nibaran Bora, and equally prominent student's organisation called the North Eastern States' Students Organisation (NESSO), among others. This agitation lasted for an incredibly long six years. The uninterrupted agitation was marked by violent protests with often anti-national slogans, frequent and recurrent Assam Bandhs, road and rail blocks, disruption of air flights, explosions, destruction of national assets and above all, diatribes against the Government of India who failed to check the systematic infiltration from Bangladesh, coupled with, sadly though, ill-feelings against Indian citizens from outside Assam.

During these six years of agitation, all government, semi-government and non-government offices remained mostly closed, often peaking up to uninterrupted four or five days. During the Bandh periods, which often were marked by violence followed by inevitable police action, all trading, industrial and economic activities came to a standstill. Business and industrial establishments faced threats to their life and property and shocked, they inevitably closed their firms with capital flights as its concomitant result. Supply of articles of daily consumption, bulk of which is imported from outside Assam was disrupted and prices of all commodities including articles of daily

consumption had sky-rocketed, much to the chagrin and sufferance of the common people. Normal office works and discipline were buried in the silence of the graveyard. All government programmes were stopped and elections to the State Assembly and Parliament were vehemently opposed by the agitators. However, in 1983, the Parliamentary election was forcefully held and completed with lakhs of foreigners' names in the electoral rolls—the vey issue on which the agitation was in its peak, as if to add salt after inflicting the injury. Amid protests of the mass people and large-scale violence, the governments at Delhi and Dispur had the satisfaction of completing the farce of an election with more than 90 per cent of the voters abstaining in almost in all Polling Booths of the State. Mercifully, this writer had the insipid memory of witnessing the farcical scenario as one of the election observers in the said election.

(ii) At a time when the agitation was at its peak and the social and political environment of the State of Assam was highly surcharged with emotion, tension, anguish and frustration and further, the divide between the people and the Congress Government led by Mr Hiteswar Saikia had gone to a point of no return, the Government of India at the behest of the State government of Assam did a very strange thing and that was to pass an equally strange legislation called the Illegal Migrants' (Determination by Tribunal), (IMDT) Act, 1983 which added fuel to the fire.

(iii) By resorting to such an unwarranted legal recourse, the government only triggered off the fire of agitation leading the State to a point beyond control. It became evident to all that the so-called IM (DT) Act was passed not to detect and deport the illegal Bangladeshi nationals but as a subterfuge to shelter and protect them in lieu of the illegal Vote Banks made up of the millions of non-citizen Bangladeshis as if to assuage their unquenched lust for perpetuating power by throwing the sanctity of law and the Constitution to the winds. The strangest thing was that while the indigenous people had launched the prolonged agitation with the sole purpose of compelling the Governments to detect and deport these foreigners, a Constitutional obligation of the Government, the people opposed, on the other hand, the IMDT Act tooth and nail for which there was no earthly reasons whatever, except that the so-called IMDT Act was nothing else but a shield devised for protecting the Bangladeshi foreigners. Even of greater surprise was the fact that for the purpose of detecting and deporting foreign nationals from any part of India, there already was an Act known as The Foreigners' Act, 1946 which was applicable and was effectively enforced in all the States of India including Assam and there was no earthly reason to single out Assam for enforcing another legislation nowhere else in force or applicable. The motive of the Government was unveiled by themselves that the only purpose of imposing an unwanted Act was to shelter and protect the millions of the foreigners dumped systematically over the decades in Assam as also other States of the NER. The Supreme Court of India, the highest Court of Judicature of the land, as would be seen in the later paragraphs, had unveiled the design vividly. Before the decision of the Supreme Court, a crucial development which took place was the Tripartite Assam Accord signed between the AASU on the one hand and the Governments of India and the State government of Assam on the other, gist of which is depicted below;

(iv) The leaders of the agitation with the solid support of the entire people intensified their attacks on the Central government offices and targetted their officers, establishments and enterprises such that the erstwhile Prime Minister Indira Gandhi and after her sad assassination her son and succeeding Prime Minister Rajiv Gandhi, lost their sleep and seriously thought of bringing this disgusting state of affairs to an end. Indira Gandhi made some genuine offers to the leaders of the agitation indicating a cutoff year/ date for the purpose of detecting and deporting the illegal Bangladeshis from the soil of Assam but the leaders of the agitation found it not acceptable and carried on the agitation with even greater vehemence. Six long turbulent years had already rolled by and agonies, anguish, frustration, social and economic instability, exhaustion and desperation had gripped the agitating organisations. It was Rajiv Gandhi who seized the opportunity and successfully concluded and signed with the leaders on the midnight of 14th August, 1985 a hotch-potch tripartite agreement known as The Assam Accord. This Accord was signed by the leaders of the agitation on the one hand and the State and the Central governments on the other. The terms were as follows:

(a) As per the terms of the Accord—(i) The foreigners who entered Assam after the cutoff date (25th March 1971) was fixed essentially in conformity with the date prescribed in the IM (DT) Act and also the date of the Indira-Mujib Agreement whereby millions of Bangladeshis displaced during the Bangladesh Liberation War were taken by and sheltered in India, mostly in Assam. Those who entered India between 1.1.66 and 24th March, 1971 were to be granted Indian citizenship after ten years of their registration by observing the legal procedure and formalities and those who entered after 25th March, 1973 were to be detected and deported. Under the IM (DT) Act, 1983, which virtually was enacted to protect the infiltrators (b) their names were to be deleted from the Voters' Lists (c) The Indo-Bangladesh international borders were to be sealed off. (d) Certain Constitutional safeguards and special economic packages were to be provided for removing the backlog in economic development and putting the state on the rails of speedy economic development etc.

(v) It is sad that even after the lapse of three decades of signing the Accord; the records of implementation of these terms of settlement, particularly detection, deportation and deletion of the foreigners' names from the Electoral Rolls are dismal. The Indo-Bangladesh international borders still remain open and infiltration, not unexpectedly, is going on unabated. The foreign nationals are yet to be detected and voter lists corrected, let alone deportation of the millions already growing in numbers and strength to prove their dominating presence in several districts, particularly in Lower Assam. The National Register of Citizens (NRC) is yet to be updated. The Supreme Court has very recently (October, 2013) while expressing its displeasure in this respect has given a time schedule for finally updating the NRC (December, 2013) with 1951 as the cutoff year. Though some economic development under the Special Economic Package clause has shown its elusive appearance, the issue of granting Constitutional safeguard is nowhere in sight.

(vi) Now let us go in to the judgment of the Supreme Court of India on the issue of legality and fall out of the IM (DT) Act, 1983. The Supreme Court of India had termed the same as illegal and *ultra vires* the Constitution of India and repealed the Act on 12th July, 2005 on a petition of Public Interest Litigation (PIL) filed by Mr Sarbananda Sonowal, the erstwhile leader of the AASU spearheading the six years long agitation on foreign nationals' issue. It was naturally unthinkable and shocking for the citizens of India to hear that a democratically elected government would enact a legislation that was declared unconstitutional by the highest judiciary of the land! Let us see how and why it was so:

(a) Disgustingly enough, this so-called IM (DT) Act, 1983 was passed by the Parliament when the indigenous people of Assam, by and large, had boycotted the farcical election infested with millions of foreigners as voters and there were barely few elected representatives from Assam in the Parliament. Quite expectedly and in impeccable tune with the design with which this legislation was brought to being, (i) there were few illegal Bangladeshis who were detected under the IMDT Act and far less deported. And amusingly enough, the few who were abandoned in the Indo-Bangladesh borders in the name of deportation, had crossed in to the Indian side soon enough to be back in to the pavilion, thanks to the loyalty of the Bangladesh Border Security force and the helplessness of the Indian Border Security Force (BSF). The fact is that without any arrangement made by the Government of India (GOI) with Bangladesh's to accept them as their citizens, there was no question of allowing the deportees entry into their original homeland by the Bangladesh authorities (b) Short of detection of the foreigners, the voters' lists remained contaminated and their numbers remained undetermined. In the meantime, infiltration continued with greater vehemence and their numbers increased further. (c) Various Census Reports had shown that their habitation was concentrated in several lower Assam Districts, mostly in the extensive '*Char*' areas and their growth rate of population was so high that it not only far excelled the national average growth rate but also radically changed the demographic pattern of the state with its inevitable outcome growing so disastrous that they have emerged as the majority in several districts. As per the Census report of 2011, they constitute majority in at least 12 districts with several other districts closely following them, much to the fear of losing identity of the indigenous people.

4. The Supreme Court on the IM (DT) ACT, 1983

(vi) It is behind this background that the Supreme Court of India, in its judgment dated 12th July, 2005 while repealing the IM (DT) Act, had observed thus:

1. "A deep analysis of the IMDT Act and the Rules made there under would reveal that they have been purposely so enacted as to give shelter or protection to illegal migrants who came to Assam after 25th, March, 1971 rather than to detect and deport them" (Para 28, 29, 39)

2. "The above discussion leads to irresistible conclusion that the provisions of the IMDT Act and the Rules made there under clearly negate the constitutional mandate contained in Article 355 of the Constitution, where a

duty has been cast upon the Union of India to protect every State against external aggression and internal disturbance. The IMDT Act which contravenes Article 355 of the Constitution is, therefore, wholly unconstitutional and must be struck down" (Para 67)

3. "The presence of such a large number of illegal migrants from Bangladesh which runs into millions, is in fact an 'aggression' on the State of Assam and has also contributed significantly in causing serious 'internal disturbances' in the shape of insurgency of alarming proportion making the life of the people of Assam wholly insecure and the panic generated thereby has created fear psychosis" (Para 28, 29, 39).

4. "The word 'aggression' is not to be confused with war". ......The unabated influx of illegal migrants from Bangladesh into Assam leading to a perceptible change in the demographic pattern of the State and a contributory factor behind the outbreak of insurgency in the State having dangerous dimension of greatly undermining national security is an act of aggression" (Para 32,37,38).

5. "The enforcement of the IMDT Act has no doubt facilitated to a very large extent the illegal migrants from Bangladesh to continue to reside in Assam, who on account of their huge number affect the language, script and culture of the local people (Para 71).

6. "The Foreigners Act and the Foreigners (Tribunal) Order, 1964 are applicable to whole of India and even to the State of Assam for identification of foreigners......It is therefore not open to the Union of India or the State of Assam or for that matter, any one to contend that the procedure prescribed in the aforesaid enactments is not just, fair and reasonable and thus violative of Article 21 of the Constitution. In our opinion, the procedure under the Foreigners Act and the Foreigners (Tribunal) Order, 1964 is just, fair and reasonable and does not offend any Constitutional provision" (Para 73).

7. "To sum up our conclusions, the provisions of the Illegal Migrants (Determination by Tribunal) Act, 1983 are *ultra vires* the Constitution and are accordingly struck down" (Para 83).

5. Discrimination against Assam

The most striking fact is that Assam was the only state which was picked up to introduce a strange legislation when another Act, namely the Foreigners' Act, 1946, remained effectively applicable in the whole of India including Assam. This incredible action of both Government of India and Government of Assam which resulted in discrimination against Assam and violation of the provisions of the Constitution of India was simply inexplicable and unthinkable. This unfortunate action, in confirmation with many other similar actions such as abandoning Assam to be included in Pakistan under Group C States of the Cabinet Mission Plan, Nehru's abandoning the States of Arunachal and Assam bidding farewell to the people of Assam on 20th October, 1962, the day when China entered upon Assam etc. shattered the confidence and broke the hearts of the people of not only Assam but of the entire NER. There was no other justification whatever in support of this strange and redundant Act than to

protect and shelter the millions of illegal foreigners with a design to garner political dividend by the ruling power.

6. Historical Background of Continued Infiltration

Assam has been a target of large scale migration of Bengali Muslims since 1905 when Bengal was partitioned and Assam was merged with a part of it to be formed into a new province called East Bengal and Assam with its capital at *Decca.* Top politicians, political parties like the Muslim League and the religious fundamentalists—all had eyed on the fertile land of Assam such that the Brahmaputra Valley has been a traditional and routine hunting ground for the infiltrators from the land mass now formed in to Bangladesh. Zulfiker Ali Bhutto, the Prime Minister of Pakistan wrote in his autobiography '*Myth of Independence*' that Pakistan had as much claim on Assam as on Kashmir. Shaikh Mujibur Rahman had very definitely articulated in his book: *East Pakistan: Its Population and Economy*' that Assam has abundant fertile land, forest and mineral resources which East Pakistan needs for its own development. This was the mind-set of the Bengali Muslim leaders of Bengal, Pakistan and Bangladesh since the early days prior to partition till now. The design of grabbing Assam has never abated since those days. Sir Mahammad Sadullah, the five times Chief Minister of Assam had brought large number of Bengali Muslims and settled them in the vast tracts of fertile land in the guise of "Grow More Food" campaign. This ominous trend provoked even the then Viceroy of India, Lord Wavell to remark thus in his book '*Viceroy's Journal*': "The Chief political problem is the desire of the Muslim Ministers to increase this immigration into the uncultivated Government lands under the slogan 'Grow More Food' but what they are really after is, 'Grow More Muslims' ". Mr. Mullan, the Census Commissioner of Assam, 1931 had only revealed the black truth when he cautioned in his Census report of 1931 thus "Where there is waste land thither flock the Mymensinghiyas ....the only thing I can compare it to, is the mass movement of a large body of ants .....It is sad but by no means improbable that in another thirty years, Sibsagar district will be the only part of Assam in which the Assamese will find himself at home". In making such a forthright observation, perhaps what the Viceroy General had in mind was the "Grow More Food campaign" launched by Sir Mahammed Sadullah, who as the five times Chief Minister of Assam had settled large number of Muslim peasants from neighbouring districts of Assam, now forming part of Bangladesh. And Lt. General (Retd) S.K. Sinha, the erstwhile Governor of Assam, in a detailed Memorandum to the President of India described how Assam was in the grip of millions of infiltrators from Bangladesh to the extent of losing its identity. Incidentally, this document filled with unassailable facts and figures formed a basis of the Supreme Court's judgment repealing the IMDT Act, 1983 delivered on 12th July, 2005, as mentioned in the earlier paragraphs.

7. The Age of Armed Rebellion/ Terrorism

It is behind such a despondent and frustrating environment that the youths of the NER have taken to armed rebellion seeking independence from India.

Assam in particular and the NER in general are faced with the ominous mushroom growth of terrorist organisations seeking either independence from India or separate states or some kind of autonomy.

Such uncongenial climates have induced India's hostile neighbours like China and Pakistan to collide with and aid and assist the terrorist outfits militarily and financially. The confidence of the youths of the region in the government of India has been shattered. The economic backwardness of the region despite the abundant natural resources has made them feel neglected, exploited and deceived.

They also feel that Delhi is out to exploit the resources and not interested in the development of the region. They have therefore, taken to armed rebellion demanding independence, autonomy, separate states and what not. This has created insurgency, unsettled social order and disaffection among the people and halt to development, much to the threats to our national security and peaceful living. And, to add fuel to the fire, the terrorist outfits like LeT, Indian Mujahidin, Jamatuddwa etc. aided and abetted by ISI of Pakistan and other reconnoitre agents are fishing in the troubled waters of the NER and perpetrating in subversive activities to create social instability. It is also sad to note that Assam has become a hub of terrorist outfits which not only resorts to explosion, subversion, destruction of public properties and killing of innocent persons thereby creating social instability and insurgency besides such crimes as drug peddling, killing and kidnapping, theft and dacoities and distributing forged notes to destroy India's, economy .The saddest part is that the nation remains in dark as to these grave dangers and disorders which affect not the NER and Assam alone but the entire nation.

8. Justification for Thrust on Infiltration

The purpose of discussing the problem of perennial infiltration from Bangladesh in such a great detail is two-fold: (i) it is a life and death question for the indigenous people of Assam and the NER whose identity is at stake. More importantly, even the very identity of the NER States is at stake. (ii) But, above all, the unabated infiltration puts India's national security and integrity at stake, as has been declared by the Supreme Court of India. Moreover, it is an area in which the judgment of the Supreme Court of India has laid bare the truth after detailed digging in to this crucial issue of large scale unabated infiltration of Bangladeshis methodically denied, or neglected by the Government(s) to take corrective action. The verdict of the Supreme Court has also put the final seal on the incontrovertibility of the issue of infiltration from Bangladesh.

Furthermore, the case of discrimination against Assam by the Central Government as reflected in their enacting a strange, redundant and discriminatory legislation exclusively for Assam even as another central Act was effectively enforced in the State as in all other States of India has been established before the nation conclusively. Finally, and sadly though, the nation at large remains in dark of the grave danger of the threats to national security, which the nation ought to know. We fervently hope that this would rouse the nation to face this menacing problem discussed in detail.

9. Conclusion

This is the story of the NER, a vast landmass—isolated, charming and resourceful, and yet neglected, discriminated and economically undeveloped. The problems are legion and the solution is elusive. The perennial problem of infiltration from Bangladesh and the Governments' tacit endorsement, if not patronisation, has been recounted above in meticulous details quoting from no less an authority than the highest Judiciary of the land, only as a means to bring home the truth about neglect and discrimination—a belief that has been nourished by the hapless, simple people of the region. And yet, ironically enough, the nation continues to be in the dark of the problems of which the menace of infiltration is just one, facing the region, grave as they are. The menace concerns not only Assam or the NER alone but the entire nation and every citizen of India for whom national security, integrity, unity and India's sovereignty matters. In fact, every citizen of India has a right to know the nature and quality of the governance that the custodians of India's destiny have dispensed. And, while the Governments have their Constitutional and custodial duty enshrined on them by the Constitution of India, the AISPF like any other formation and organisation as inseparable cogs in the societal wheel, and bound by the unbreakable thread of society, feels morally obliged to inform the nation of the grave problems that have confronted the nation through its neglected window of the NER. It is in this view that the AISPF had felt obliged and decided that the story be shared with the nation.

In pursuance of this decision, a Committee for Selection of Topics to be included in the book was formed with Mr H. N. Das, IAS as the Chairman, and myself, Mr S. P. Kar, IPS, N. N. Barua, IAS, K. N. Goswami, IFS, D. C. Barman, IAS and Paramesh Datta, IAS, as members and Mr L. D. Adhikary, IFS as the convener. The Committee selected 49 topics and as many as 41 writers including Justice of the Supreme Court, journalists, intellectuals, litterateurs, Professors and lawyer had responded positively and earnestly.

I take the opportunity of acknowledging our gratitude to all of them who, in deference to our request and in disregard of their preoccupation and aging strains, took the pains to be a part of our mission. The Editorial Board formed later on with H. N. Das as the Adviser, Dr Rohini Kr. Baruah as the Editor-in-Chief, Mr S. P. Kar, Mr N. N. Baruah, K. N. Dev Goswami and Dinesh Barman as Editors with L. D. Adhikary as the convener had followed it up. I am also thankful to Mr N. N. Barua, Mr S. P. Kar, Mr Dinesh Barman and Mr K. N. D. Goswami of the Editorial Board for their inspiring assistance in the process of compilation/editing of the book. It was touching to feel that Mr N.N. Barua kept his services open for the task brushing aside his ailing health.

We also express our heart-felt gratitude to Messrs Gyan Publishing House, Daryaganj, Delhi, for their kindly agreeing to publish our book, and particularly to Mr Amit Garg who has taken personal care to present the book to the esteemed readers within a short span of time.

The essays contributed to by the authors including eminent personalities outside the All India Services cadre, reflect the core problems as also the collateral issues stemming from them that the region, and Assam in particular,

is confronted with the object being to call the nation to its serious attention, because the members of the AISPF felt that they form as much a part of, and are committed to the cause of promoting the interest, of, the society at large through whose benevolent love and care, they have made and ended their flourishing career.

And, of course, the governments have their constitutional and custodial duty to address the issues detrimental to the citizens and to protect and promote the progress and welfare of the society they derive power from, to govern the State. In fine, if the AISPF is morally obliged to think about well-being of the society, the Governments are bound constitutionally, legally and morally, to ensure good governance. Because, whichever walk of life we might follow in our earthly sojourn, in the ultimate analysis, we all are products of and belong to the society, the soul of all. And, it is this eternal truth of man's inalienable bond of oneness with the society which takes me to Cowper and reminds me of his poem couched in fabulously fragrant words:

"Society, friendship and love/ Divinely bestowed upon man, / Oh, had I the wings of a dove,/ How soon would I taste you again!"

Dr Rohini Kr Baruah, IAS
Editor

2

Eradication of Corruption: A Challenge to the Society

M.K. Baruah, IAS (Retd.)

The twenty first century has witnessed a major techno-economic development in the World. However, such a scenario is often blurred by the wide-spread indulgence of many people in corrupt practices, particularly by swindling the funds earmarked for the developmental activities. Nowadays, it is regularly reported in electronic and print media that corruption has engulfed the society in a menacing proportion. Common people talk about it in different platforms and those who are in the helm of affairs and part and parcel in the delivery systems have shown serious concern. But the moot point is that how many people with unquestionable credibility in the higher echelon of public life can set glaring examples of honesty and sincerity amidst abundant opportunities and temptations. Though corruption in one form or the other was prevalent in the world in the ancient times, it is from the early part of the 20th century, that is, from the period from which the wheels of development moved faster in western countries in spite of the World Wars and other odds, the morality of the people have started dwindling gradually along with the on-going pace of economic progress and prosperity. Gradually, the vices of corruption have created such a situation that any idea in the direction of making a society totally free from corruption is generally considered as a utopian concept. Obviously therefore, any programme in respect of total eradication of corruption have become meaningless. Being faced with such a predicament the planners and the right-thinking people have now formulate plans and programmes for containing the menace rather than venturing its total extirpation.

For the common people the meaning of corruption is an evil or vice in which the public wealth is embezzled and siphoned off for personal gain. However, the Transparency International, (an international anti-corruption organisation) has defined corruption as the abuse of entrusted power for private

gain. Whereas, The World Bank's definition of corruption is "abuse of public office for private gain." The normal means of adopting corrupt practice is by theft, fraud, nepotism, abuse of power etc. Morally degraded people indulge in corrupt practices for the opportunities too tempting not to exploit. Corruption is normally indulged in a covert manner by one or more individuals entering into secret agreement or understanding. As such, it is very difficult to detect such practices of the corrupt people and dislodge the concealed agreement.

The Transparency International's Corruption Perception Index of 2010 lists the countries ranked from less corrupt to more corrupt. In such assessment Denmark, New Zealand and Singapore top the list of less corrupt countries. India ranks 95 out of 179 countries and Kenya, Cambodia and Russia ranked 154th. Somalia's position is in the bottom of the list as the most corrupt country in the World. In the last couple of decades India's policies and progammes for economic liberalisation, delicensing in several key sectors, cut down government subsidies, introduction of beneficial legislations, e-governance etc. have contributed in the overall growth of Gross Domestic Products. Such factors have significantly contributed in scoring higher rate of 3.1 in 2011 as against 2.7 of 2002 in corruption assessment reports. In 2008 study reports of the Transparency International it is projected that about 40 per cent Indians had first-hand experience of paying bribes or using a contact to get a job done in public office. This is an improved position from 62 per cent in 2005. With the days rolled on, corruption is spreading to new areas and now it exists everywhere. Whether it is from any need or greed to acquire more and more or it has become a culture or habit of the people to acquire more, the fact remains that people find corruption as a gifted opportunity of becoming rich or attaining a position too tempting not to exploit. For such an attitude people are falling easy prey to the available temptations and incredible desire to acquire more and more luxurious houses and cars, real estate properties, jewellery, fat bank balance and what not. The aspirations of the human being are unlimited in spite of the fact that huge property acquired by adopting corrupt means cannot give a new lease of life to the mortal being. For fulfillment of such crazy desire black money is required, as the known sources of income can hardy support such greed of the people. There are two possible sources of acquiring black money, such as by indulging in illegal activities like crime, drug trades, terrorism and embezzlement of entrusted fund; and the second is non-declaration of wealth lawfully acquired to evade payment of income tax. Though denied by the Swiss banker association, Indians have a huge amount of undeclared black money in the banks of Switzerland.

Unless the society becomes extremely vigilant, the government sponsored anti-corruption measures alone cannot check mental pollution, cultural contamination and ethical degradation of the people. A mass movement may help in raising consciousness of the people, as has been proved in the movements led by Jaiprakash Narayan and Anna Hazare, but for non-pursuing the follow up duties and responsibilities with all earnestness by the followers and for the undue influence of those people with vested interest, who have already carved a niche for themselves, the spirit of the movements are bound to die down before seeing the light of the day.

It is an established fact that in spite of displaying adequately the sense of patriotism in different critical times of the country, the Indians are generally less conscious about rendering their duties as against claim for their Constitutional rights. There are established mechanisms to assert their rights like Human Rights organisation, Information Commissions, Consumer Fora etc., but nowhere sanctity of their duties are emphasised by codifications. In fact, the whole world community is for getting about the duties of mankind and the real value of lives assigned to such duties. A lackadaisical approach of a person towards his duties is often proved as the beginning of adopting unethical practices like corruption. For an individual, ethics and morality play a vital role in his own behaviour in private and public life. For those who are steering the wheels of the nation these virtues are indispensably required in dispensation of justice and affecting a sound delivery system. The Indian Constitution begins with the words— "we the people of India", but within a few decades of the Independence India has unfortunately been divided on sectarian groups and classes on the basis of caste and creed, which was not at all the intention of the great architects of the Constitution.

The demography and some economic issues of India has unfortunately provided a fertile ground for exploitation of the 'Have-nots' by the 'Haves'. It is well-known that India suffers from the problem of over-population with an estimated 1.3 billion, out of which roughly one-third, that is equivalent to the total population of the United States of America, lives below the poverty line of subsistence. The World Bank estimates that 33 per cent of the global poor lives in India. The wealth distribution amongst the people is unjustifiably uneven, with top 10 per cent of the income group earning 33 per cent of the income. It is also estimated that one in every ten deaths in India is linked to poor sanitation and hygiene. Because of such inborn incapacity of the poor and illiterate sections there is hardly any resistance from them when the developmental fund meant for them is openly embezzled. In such misuse of money in petty corruption in basic services like education, health-care, public health and sanitation etc. a sizeable amount of the earmarked fund is wasted. Such a situation is aggravated by the lack of knowledge of the deprived sections and therefore they play a total indifferent role against the corrupt practices and misuse of authority in the implementation of benevolent schemes. The distinction between what is ethical and what is not, is projecting a confused picture before them. Amongst the common people the "*Dharma*" is often defined as religion, but the inner-meaning of "*Dharma*" is the code of conduct of human behaviour, which ensures morality and ethics of highest order. Many people do not bother to know, nor is any counselling available for them to know what is *Dharma*, as propounded by Gautama Buddha. The Indians are too conscious about their religion, but they are least bothered to practice "*Dharma*" in private as well as in public lives by performing their respective duties without insistence.

In a country like India corruption is caused by excessive regulations and authorisation requirements. Further, complicated taxation and licensing system, poor and multiple delivery system, lack of competitive markets, monopoly of

certain goods and service providers by government controlled institutions, bureaucratic delay, election expenses, non-punishment of the known corrupt officials and politicians, lack of transparent deterrent actions etc. are apparently responsible for prevalence of corruption. An effective and clean imaged bureaucracy with quick dispensation of their functions may immensely contribute in containing corruption level in the country. It is widely acknowledged that the Indian bureaucracy is not less efficient than their counterpart in the least corrupt countries, like Singapore, Japan etc. In spite of that since Independence, continuous chain of financial scandals, involving bureaucrats and politicians have made the country shameful and morally degraded before the World. Apart from that the vote bank politics has divided the people into various sectarian groups and classes. Money and muscle power are being liberally used in elections. Lack of transparency in public life, near absence of institutional accountability and absence of right to recall the elected leaders, collusion amongst politicians-bureaucrats-businessmen are some of the serious maladies requiring immediate attention of all the right thinking people.

Various successive governments in the country since independence have shown great concern in effectively addressing the problem. In spite of that, individual commitment of some of the politicians and bureaucrats, who are the main functionaries in the implementation of government programmes, are not always transparent. That lack of transparency confuses the common people to think that corruption has become a way of life in the higher echelon of the society. However, high powered Committees and Commissions are instituted to investigate the corruption cases and recommend for remedies. Public Service Commissions, Election Commissions, Information Commissions, the Comptroller and Auditor General of India, Vigilance Commissions, Anti-corruption Bureaus, *Lok Adalats*, Consumer Fora, Human Rights Commission etc. are functioning in regular basis to address, adjudicate or investigate the allegation and grievances against corruption. Besides these established statutory authorities Parliamentary/Assembly Committees, Judicial screenings, Magistarial enquiries, Civil Liberty organisations and number of other agencies deal with matters directly or indirectly relating to combating corruption in public life. Despite such measures taken by government the condition remains far from satisfactory. What is known in common parlance that "the wheels of administrative machinery is not moved without greasing and oiling every joint, nuts and bolts" has become the deep-rooted belief of the people.

Many remedial measures to combat corruption are taken at the initiative of the government. But, as it appears today, a long way is still to go to get some fruitful results. From the foregoing discussions it can be summed up that the words, "We the people of India" as inscribed in the Constitution should be understood with a wider meaning, that to keep the people united and solid to defend the Constitution, at any cost the citizens should be faithful to their duties rather than all the time asserting the Fundamental rights only. Similarly, measures like transparency in administration and socio-economic measures, like de-licensing, introduction of single window policy in granting government

clearances, restructuring income tax laws and election laws, electoral reforms to totally exclude black money, quick dispensation of justice in all levels, particularly against crimes relating to corruption, introduction of effective Lokpals free from any influence whatsoever, introduction of innovative incentive programmes for those who have proved honest and upright and so on, may contribute in formation of a strong ethical society in India. With adoption of such measures one can aspire to inhale non-polluted free air and devote himself in ensuring the good health of the society.

3

Assam-Nagaland Boundary Disputes: An Achilles Heel of Assam

Rohini Kumar Baruah, IAS (Retd.)

1. Introduction

Ironically, Assam from whose womb was born the State of Nagaland does not have good neighbourly relations with the *latter*. This is due to primarily because of its indeterminate boundaries *vis-à-vis* Assam since the inception of its birth as a Hills District of Assam —–no doubt, a legacy from the British Rule. The callous and inept handling by the Governments at Delhi and Dispur of the long lasting boundary disputes between Assam and Nagaland over the last six and a half decades after independence, and particularly after Nagaland became a separate State in December, 1963, has only added fuel to the fire, much to the tension, ill-feeling and animosity marked by recurrent armed clashes between the two States. This vexed imbroglio has further given vibrant encouragement to the Nagaland's insurgent outfits and authorities as well, to indulge in making more and more claims to and encroachment on Assam's peripheral lands. Absence of precisely defined boundaries, an unsavoury legacy from the British Raj, bolstered by adamant and expansionist attitude of the Nagaland Government as also by lack of firm action on the parts of both the Governments at Delhi and Dispur to effectively address this burning issue, has only anointed the climate for escalation of the soured relations marked by allegations, counter-allegations and armed clashes between the two States, pushing it almost to a point of no return. In the process, ominous threat to the security and safety of the innocent settlers living along the long boundary lines prevails showing its ugly face and their peace, progress and tranquility have suffered a serious setback. In addition, the tension-fed environment prevailing there has thrust undue strains on the police and paramilitary forces of both Central and State Governments including the Government of Nagaland.

It is in this view that this vexed problem needs to be addressed on an emergency footing. The questions naturally are: Who are these 'Nagas'? What is their origin? What do they need? The paragraphs that follow seek to answer some of these vital questions relevant to settlement of the protracted disputes between Assam and Nagaland.

2. The Naga Tribes: Ethnic, Socio-economic and Linguistic Background

(i) Settlement of the long lasting boundary disputes between Assam and Nagaland pre-supposes that the origin, social or tribal habits, custom, culture, dialects etc. of the various hill tribes inhabiting the land now called Nagaland, have to be clearly understood. The word 'Naga' is a generic name of more than 16 tribes variously known as—Ao, Angami, Zeme, Konyak, Lotha, Sema etc. They are pristine hill tribes living in the landmass now called Nagaland and the adjoining areas of Assam, Arunachal Pradesh and Manipur. There are divergent views on their origin, but they have inhabited the land perhaps from the pre-historic time. E.A. Gait in his celebrated work *"A History of Assam"* (page 313-314, revised edition.) says, "The people whom we call Nagas are known to the Assamese as 'Nagas'; they belong to a diversity of tribes, each speaking its own language and calling itself by a distinctive name. The collective designation by which they are known to the Assamese seems to be derived, as suggested by Holcombe and Peal, from *nok* which means "folk" in some of the tribal dialects. When strange parties meet in the plains, they are said to ask each other: *Tem nok e* or *o nok e*, meaning "what folk are you? Verrier Elwin's famous book "*The Nagas in the Nineteenth Century*" (compiled) *inter alia* records a note of Lieutenant Colonel R.G. Woodthrope who observes, "Various derivations have been given for the Naga, some supposing it to come from the Bengali word *Nangta,* in Hindustani *Nanga*-naked ...Other think that the Kachari word 'Naga'—a young man—a warrior, supplies the name; while others again derive it from 'Nag' = a snake".

(ii) On the basis of language, their origin is assigned by Grierson to the Tibeto-Burman group. P.D. Stracey, an IFS officer says in his book "*Nagaland Nightmare*" (page 9), "The biggest mystery is the origin of the various Naga tribes....But more remarkable is the fact that there are so many different Naga tribes, all speaking different languages which do not bear any resemblance to each other. This rigid comparmentalisation in the matter of languages can perhaps be explained by the isolation in which the tribes existed until very recently and the continuous warring with each other, in which head hunting was freely practiced".

(iii) There tribes carry behind them their distinct language, culture and practices. Most of the tribes kept the lower portion of their bodies almost naked and a strong section of the opinion thinks that the term Naga is derived from the word *Nanga* or naked. Head hunting was the practice or even a pastime of almost all of them, attributed, as it was, to be a sign of both revenge and heroism. It is said that girls and women are inclined to avoid marrying or living with such persons who have not hunted a single head. P. D. Stracy says, "Though in a popular parlance the term "Naga" is used as a generic name, the Nagas are actually divided into many tribes and sub-tribes inhabiting different

parts of the mountainous country.....speaking different dialect and having different manners and customs. Bitter feuds existed amongst the different Naga tribes and sub-tribes until very recent times". (Page 17) He further says, "Head hunting is a ritualistic practice considered to bring individual glory to a man and prosperity to his village in the shape of bumper crops, many children and good hunting....Raiding of neighbouring villages, ambushes and surprise attacks and even treachery provide the heads. These would ornament the walls of some of the houses, but nowadays the heads of animals,.....take the place of human heads".

(iv) Dr Lakshmi Devi in her thesis "*Ahom-Tribal Relations*" has stated, "Though in popular parlance the term 'Naga' is used as a generic name, the Nagas are actually divided into many tribes and sub-tribes inhabiting different parts of the mountainous country....speaking different dialects and having different manners and customs. Bitter feuds existed amongst the different Naga tribes until very recent times"' (Page 17).

(v) Isolation from other tribes is the hallmark of their characteristic features. As Stracy had observed, "The self-imposed isolation in which the Nagas for centuries have lived on their hilltops—an isolation in which monosyllabic languages like theirs grow apart from one another very rapidly has resulted in the people of even neighbouring villages being unable to understand one another" (Page 22). Thus, the barrier of language, as also the fear of each other became the unassailable barrier to inter-tribe intercourse amongst the various tribes. This follows that there has not been any concept of Naga nationalism, having anything in common with one another, one tribe not understanding the language, ethnicity, culture and habits of the other and involved in inter-tribe feuds with mortal fears of the less turbulent tribes for the more dreaded tribe like the Angamis, which kept them isolated from one another for ages.

(vi) *Trading in the Plains as Economic Activities and Social Contacts:* Interestingly, the only outside social contact which the Nagas could establish was with the Assamese living in the nearby plain districts of Nagaon and Sibsagar where they came down through the *Naga baat* for trading purposes with the Assamese. In the process they learnt and spoke a kind of Assamese language which in later days came to be known as *Nagamese* and which thus became a lingua-franca amongst the different Naga tribes. As Dr Lakshmi Devi says, "The Naga tribes bordering the plains were in constant communications with the plains for trade purposes during Ahom rule. They carried on trade in their hill products like cotton, betel leaves (or *pan*), ginger, Taro (or *Kachu*) and salt and in exchange for them carried back the articles in which their hills were deficient.

The method of trading was principally bartering, that is, exchanging their goods for the goods they needed to sustain life. Stracy also mentions that barter among different tribes was done often using oxen as the medium of exchange. The volume of trade, however, seemed to be very small, because, as S. E. Peal says, 'The tribes are too poor to be able to trade, and constant state of warfare renders commerce impossible'. The Aos and Konyak Nagas used to drag huge hollowed logs of woods with decorative ends to their hilltops to be

used for construction of *morungs* or dormitories which also served as war drums or for transmitting messages from village to village. Their principal economic activities comprised jhum cultivation, salt production and trading in the goods mentioned above by way of exchanging goods for goods.

3. Creation of the Naga Hills District, Undefined, Imprecise and Shifting Boundaries

(i) The Naga Hills District was created under orders of the Government of Bengal with the sanction of the Government of India on 15th November, 1866 comprising areas vaguely defined, with its headquarter at Samoogooting. As the Sundaram Committee had observed, "The description of the territories included in the new district of Naga Hills was very vague......... An attempt was made next year to rectify the defects and the boundaries were defined elaborately by the Government of Bengal in a notification dated 16th December, 1867, but the definition was far from being precise or accurate" (Para 34,35, Sundaram Committee Report). The Report also said that under this notification, "No part of North Cachar Sub-division lying to the west of the Dhansiri was included in the new district though that subdivision was abolished" (Para 34).

The report continued, "The imprecise and inaccurate notification of 1867 was thoroughly revised at the instance of Captain Butler, the Political Agent, Naga Hills in 1875". In his letter to the Chief Commissioner of Assam dated 26.6.1875, he characterised the boundaries as being 'either utterly wrong or so extraordinarily vaguely defined as to be commanded revised boundaries ...' Thus, the imprecise and inaccurate notification of 1867 was thoroughly revised at the instance of Captain Butler, the Political Agent, Naga Hills in 1875.

"The revised boundaries proposed by Captain Butler were accepted *in toto* by the Government and notified on 24.12.1875. However, under this revised notification, the eastern boundary of the District was not even indicated. Captain Butler had advised that it must obviously be left an open question until the whole tract of country along the Brahmaputra-cum-Irrwadi watershed has been thoroughly explored and surveyed – now a mere matter of another season or two" (Para 37, Sundaram Committee Report).

Based on these facts and developments, the Sundaram Committee observed, 'It appears, therefore, that in 1875 the tract of the country on the right bank of Doyang, lying to the north of its junction with. Harupani was not included in the Naga Hills district but considered part of Sibsagar district. The boundary between the latter district and the hilly areas to the south and east of it inhabited by different Naga tribes was not defined at that stage" (Para 38)

"There is a fairly large tract of low lands lying just immediately west of the Dikhu and south of the Line.......I propose to apply for the inclusion of this tract in Sibsagar. I do not know why it was not included before and why the Inner Line north of it was drawn so as to exclude it" (Quoted by Sundaram Committee, Para 43). The tract referred to was what some years later constituted the Geleki Reserved Forest. Pushing the Inner Line out to the foot of the hills, from Jhanzi to Dikhu, however, took place only in 1901. The notification of 1875 defining boundaries of Naga Hills district was revised in 1882 but as stated earlier, it still had left the eastern boundary undefined.

The Sundaram Committee had observed vide Para 48 thus, "The Naga Hills district attained the maximum extent in 1880. In fact, it was overgrown in size for proper administration. As early as 1891, the Deputy Commissioner of the district, (Mr Davis,) represented that its size had increased too much and it was physically impossible for him to look after the plains area and the Mikir-Rengma hills lying beyond it. His proposal to exclude these areas from the district, however, remained in abeyance for seven years. When it was renewed by the successor Deputy Commissioner, Captain Woods in 1898, the Chief Commissioner observed, "At present, the greater part of Rengma and Mikir Hills and the whole of the Nambor Forest Reserve are included within the jurisdiction of Naga Hills district and this arrangement was convenient so long as the head quarters of the district were at Samaguting". But it has become very embarrassing since the transfer of the head quarters to Kohima… So, as Sundaram Committee had observed, "the Chief Commissioner had no doubt (that) it is necessary to remove these tracts from the Naga Hills district without delay" (Para 48.3). About Dimapur, the Report quotes, "The Chief Commissioner does not think that there is any necessity for reserving Dimapur itself within the jurisdiction of the Deputy Commissioner of the Naga Hills district" (48.6).

"In accordance with the above proposals, the transfer of the large tracts of land from the Naga Hills district to the districts of Nowgong and Sibsagar was effected from the beginning of 1899. However, the notification issued by the Chief Commissioner on 9th December, 1898 also suffered from the usual defects of vagueness and imprecision which were subsequently corrected. (Para 49 read with Appendix 111, No. 6 and 7)

4. Introduction of Inner Line Regulation Not to be Confused with District Boundary

The 'Inner Line Regulation' was adopted and a notification to that effect was issued on 21st June, 1876 under the Bengal Eastern Frontier Regulation of 1873 "to prohibit all British subjects from going beyond the Inner Line without a Pass (issued) under the hand and seal of the Deputy Commissioner of Sibsagar". Thus, the Inner Line did not necessarily indicate the limits of the district as such. The survey (that is, cadastral survey) of the revenue paying lands of Sibsagar district was notified on the basis of the revenue survey as the Inner line of Sibsgar district. The notification of the Inner Line system made it very clear that "the mere fact of taking the Inner line from 'A' to 'B' instead of the roundabout way …. would not in the slightest degree preclude its being altered hereafter, should it be considered necessary, nor would it give the Nagas any claim whatever to the country between it and the hills". Thus, neither the Inner lines nor the Ladoigarh or other ramparts wherever they were constructed by the Ahom Kings purely on military and strategic considerations for the protection of the land and the people from the possible attack by outside forces or from the frequent raids of the Nagas, had anything to do with the boundaries between the Sibsagar and Naga Hill Districts.

The inner line so defined was changed by a notification dated 24th February, 1882. According to a note in the recorded proceedings of the GOI,

"the effect of this amended notification was to push the Inner Line to the foot of the hills and take in tracts covered with valuable forest, not in the actual occupation of Nagas."

5. Movement for Independent Nagaland by the Naga National Congress (NNC)

(i) The Naga National Congress led by Phizo was the first group to launch an armed agitation for an independent Nagaland in 1947. They resorted to large scale terrorist activities to attain their goal of independence and went underground in 1956. Then the National Socialist Council of Nagaland (NSCN) which sprang up later took hold of the movement and in the process itself stood divided in to the Isak-Moiva and Khaplang groups. This outfit had sustained the agitation for an independent Nagaland and of late, sticks to their demands for a Nagalim or a greater Nagaland characteristically with dreaded ferocity.

(ii) Highlights of the National Socialist Council of Nagaland (Isak-Moiva and Khaplang Groups)

The National Socialist Council of Nagaland (NSCN) was formed in 1980 to establish a Greater Nagaland, encompassing parts of Manipur, Nagaland and the North Cachar Hills of Assam. The NSCN split in 1988 to form two groups namely NSCN (IM) and NSCN (K). As of now, both the groups are in ceasefire with the Indian government. Though sovereignty/independence was their ideology initially, of late the Indo-Naga talks seem to centre around Greater Nagaland/ '*Nagalim*' which is being vehemently opposed by the Sates of Assam, Manipur and Arunachal Pradesh solely for the reason that it is nothing short of encroachment on their territories—a demand which continues to foment suspicion and ill-will in the North-east India. What is more serious is that they continue to be actively involved in illegal activities including extortion, kidnapping, inter-factional clashes, bootlegging and recruitment of the young generation to their cadre besides imposing various tax/duties on all types of commercial enterprises and establishments, much to the disaster of the peace and progress of the States, in addition to colossal wastage of human lives and resources. It is relevant to note here that the Khaplang group had opposed the Shillong Accord signed at Shillong between the NNC and the Government which resulted in its break from the Isak-Moiva group.

The NSCN of both the groups run parallel governments in Nagaland but perpetrate their repressive depredations on extensive areas of Assam bordering the districts of Sibsagar, Jorhat, Karbi Anglong and parts of Nagaon districts. Their *modus operandi* is repression. To run their so-called governments, in particular for purchase of arms and ammunitions from Pakistan, China etc., they need huge amounts of money. So, they extort from the innocent, poor people living on the Assam side of the Assam-Nagaland Borders by way of tax, tolls etc. They extort money from the Assam Government employees, tea gardens which they claim are theirs. They extort, kidnap and kill those who fail to meet their demands. They have converted the reserved forests to the habitats of the Nagas. To do this, they have made deep inroads on the forests, denuded them by wanton felling of valuable trees, sell them and then covert the forest areas

into Naga hamlets. They have also converted the forest reserved land into cultivable land after denuding the forests. For this, either the Nagas living on the top hills and practising *Jhoom* cultivation there have shifted to the newly-converted hamlets of the same name and resorted to wetland cultivation or a new class of agricultural labour mostly of the Bangladeshi Muslims have been engaged to do the cultivation on their behalf as also to train them about wet-land cultivation. Thus, an absentee landlordism amongst the Nagas as also certain extremist leaders has emerged and the lush green deep forests in those areas have become a past memory, yielding place to a cluster of new villages in the heart of the reserved forests. These encroachments, constructions, extortions and repressions have been taking place in the very presence of the so-called neutral forces pushing the situation to a point of no return.

And again, all this has happened in the very nose of the State Government who has lost their political will and courage to check these encroachments and destruction of the Reserved Forests of Assam. They have also displayed their profound callousness in taking up adequate border development programmes in the border areas. Most of the areas of the total areas remain almost untouched by roads, electricity, school, hospitals etc. and they live miserable life there. The people live in perpetual fear of the Naga extremists' repressive actions which have now become routine. BOPs seem to be inadequately equipped such that the armed police posted to protect the life and property of the people is themselves scarry of their own security, let alone that of the people for whom they exist. Nor are the Central Government security personnel doing their job of preventing encroachments, providing security to the people along the border areas of Assam. Eye witness account would suggest that the central security forces, far from being neutral show their inclination to be partisan largely because they themselves are dependent for maintenance of their dreary life in the hostile climate on the Nagaland authorities for their water, electricity and supplies but also partly because they want to eschew the wrath of the NSCN armed personnel, well-distended, ferocious and ruthless in their operation, as they are.

(iii) Endeavour of the Peace Mission

The demand for an independent Nagaland under the aegis of the Naga National Council (NNC) was marked by intensified armed violence such that it took a toll on the smooth governance of the State of Assam with the law and order as also the peace and development of the region becoming its first casualty. Thus while the people of the plains celebrated their freedom from the colonial British Raj, the Nagas were enmeshed in their struggle for their own independence from India. Significantly, the NNC observed Naga Independence Day on August 14, one day ahead of India's Independence Day. Viewing the Naga struggle through the eye of a psychologist or a humanist, it could perhaps be said that inherent in their secessionist movement was their goal for maximum autonomy to protect and promote their ethnic and tribal entity. Fortunately, this reality had dawned, belatedly though, on the Government of India who in its wisdom had decided to understand the Naga psyche and finally, appointed a Peace Mission led by Jayaprakash Narayan with Bimala Prasad Chaliha and

Rev. Michael Scott as members. The Mission made an in-depth study of the root cause of the Naga struggle taking cognizance of their political and social aspirations. Thus, the armed conflict of the Naga came to be tethered in the Pasteur of the civil society carving out a by-pass exit for armed hostility for the time being.

The Peace Mission's initiative was followed by ceasefire and a series of negotiation which built the foundation for, and ultimately led to the formation of, the State of Nagaland in 1963. The most remarkable outcome of this action of the GOI's creation of the sixteenth State of India was that a new Article 371A was added to the Constitution of India. Under the provision of this Article the Parliament's power to legislate on matters that related to (i) religious and social practices of the Nagas (ii) their customary law and procedure (iii) administration of civil and criminal justice involving decisions according to Naga customary law, and (iv) ownership and transfer of land and its resources was curtailed in that its power to legislate on the said subjects was made limited and subject to the approval of the Nagaland State Assembly.

This special Constitutional concession to the Nagas, for whom Jawaharlal Nehru, the then Prime Minister of India had an instinctive soft corner, should have been accepted as fulfillment, by and large, of the Naga hopes and aspirations. But alas! Peace and tranquility in that picturesque hilly land seems to have avowedly eluded. Their dream remains still unfulfilled and is the root cause of the Assam Nagaland unsolved boundary disputes is their goal of creating a Greater Nagaland, *Nagalim,* as they call it, by annexing large areas *inter alia* of Assam, Manipur etc. And short of this, the encroachment on Assam's reserved forests and adjoining lands continues unabated, thereby threatening the security, peace and development of both Assam and Nagaland.

6. Constitution of the State of Nagaland: Enactment of the State of Nagaland Act, 1962

At the commencement of the Constitution of India, the State of Assam had two administrative units known as the 'Naga Hills District 'and the 'Naga Tribal Area' inhabited almost entirely by the Naga tribes. These two units were combined to form a new unit to be called as Naga Hill Tuensang Area (NHTA) administered as Part B Tribal Area with effect from 1st December, 1957. The NHTA got restructured to be a full-fledged State called Nagaland with effect from 1st December, 1963 by an Act of the Parliament called the 'State of Nagaland Act, 1962'.

Section 3(1) of this Act provides that the new State shall comprise the territories which were previously comprised in NHTA. The boundaries of the new state were thus exactly the same as those of the combined Naga Hills District and the Naga Tribal Area before 1950. Its western boundaries form the border of the three districts of present Assam, viz., Sibsagar, Karbi Anglong and North Cachar hills District. As observed in the Report of K.V.K. Sundaram Committee who had gone in to the matter at length, "except for a short stretch of about 20 km at the northern ends from the Taokok Nadi to the Teok Nadi, this boundary was defined accurately and in great details in a Notification dated 25th November, 1925, and was not altered subsequently". The details of

the notification were based on Survey Operation conducted over a period of seven years between 1916 and 1923. The boundaries notified generally coincide with the natural boundaries like the hill ranges, rivers, streams, forests etc. Wherever this is not done, it refers to the boundary pillars set up and numbered chronologically making the boundaries legibly identifiable. Even where such boundary pillars now do not exist or have been deliberately removed by some miscreants or vested interests, they remain easily identifiable by reference to co-ordinates recorded in the Survey book. It would not be incongruous to mention here that it is now the common knowledge that many of such boundary pillars were deliberately removed with the motive of advancing their claims on Assam territory far beyond the original boundary pillars fixed by the Ahom Kings.

7. Nagaland's Claims on Assam Territories

It should be clearly understood that Nagaland has claimed vast tracts of Assam's territories comprising more 12,880 sq. km, or "about 5000sq miles" as observed by Sundaram Committee vide Para 4 of his detailed Report.

The area claimed comprises:

(a) the whole of North Cachar Hills District covering 1,888 sq miles,

(b) more than half of Mikir Hills District (present Karbi Anglong District) and a small part of Nagaon district, covering 2368 sq. miles; and

(c) about 718 sq. miles of Sibsagar district covering all the reserved forests adjoining Nagaland and also a number of (11) tea estates and villages clearly within Assam side of the Assam Nagaland border.

Induced by their above unfounded and imaginary claims on the vast tracts of Assam's territories, the Nagaland authorities have intensified their unabated encroachment spree-making deeper and still deeper inroads on the Reserved Forests of Assam, causing wanton destruction of valuable timbers, and after the cleaning operations, setting up new villages/hamlets with roads, buildings, schools, hospitals, offices etc, despite the facts that the so-called neutral Central Paramilitary forces are posted there to prevent such encroachments and destruction of timbers. Now, let us briefly review the nature of their demands.

8. NNC's Demand for an Independent Nagaland: A Greater Nagalim

On 26th June, 1947, the Naga National Council (NNC) presented an Address to the Governor of Assam at Kohima and while asserting their right of self-determination and demanding that the Naga people scattered in the adjoining areas be brought together, had also asserted that the ancient boundary of the Ahom Kingdom had been overstepped throughout its length and demanded that all the valuable forests which were previously parts of the Naga Hills District and later transferred to Sibsagar and/or Nagaon districts, should be restored to them. This point was amplified in an Appendix as follows:

"The ancient boundary with the Ahom Kingdom was the Ladoi Garh. It ran from the Dikhu River in the vicinity of Naginimora to Nakachari. The ancient boundary should be restored........" By this Memorandum, they claimed 10 Reserved Forests wholly and 11 tea gardens of Assam either partly or mostly.

No action on this Representation was taken, and the extent and shape of the Naga Hills district remained unaltered. But the agitation of the Nagas for a

separate State with extended boundaries continued. At a convention of the Naga people held in October, 1959 a Sixteen Point Memorandum was approved to form the basis of negotiation with the Government of India (GOI). Points No. 12 and 13 thereof demanded that "all the Reserved Forests and other Naga areas that were transferred out of the Naga areas will be returned to Nagaland with clearly defined boundary under the present settlement and that "the other Naga tribes inhabiting the area contiguous to the present Nagaland should be allowed to join Nagaland, if they so desire".

It is relevant to note that discussion on the Memorandum took place on July 27 and 28, 1960 between the Naga delegation led by Dr Ao and the Foreign Secretary to the GOI. The Foreign Secretary said that the Naga Hills District was constituted in 1866 and much the larger area of these forests formed part of that district only for 21 years from 1881. For the rest of the period, they have formed part of Sibsagar and Nagaon districts of Assam. It was clearly impossible for the Government of India to make any commitment without consulting the other State concerned. The Foreign secretary rejected in effect both the contentions of the Naga Delegation which was evident from the records of discussion reduced to writing. Needless to say that the Nagaland Government or other outfits clamouring for the Reserved Forests and the so-called contiguous areas inhabited by other Nagas to be included did never make any factual case based on unassailable evidence nor did they do anything to comply with the requirements prescribed by Articles 3 and 4 of the Constitution of India. The Foreign secretary referred them more than once to the provisions of Articles 3 and 4 of the Constitution which lay down the procedure for transferring areas from one State to another State. While the ultimate authority for this purpose is Parliament, the Bill providing for any such transfer has to be introduced on the recommendation of the President, and furthermore, the President has to obtain and consider the views of the Legislatures of the States concerned, before allowing the Bill to be introduced in the Parliament". (page 4). Curiously, the Naga leaders did not do anything to comply with the procedure laid down in the Constitution and as advised by the Foreign Secretary, nor did they adduce any unassailable evidence in support of their claims for inclusion in Nagaland the 10 Forest Reserves and inclusion of adjoining areas beyond Nagaland for the obvious reason that in most of those areas the Nagas were the microscopic minority while tribes/people other than Naga formed the bulk of the population of those areas.

The allegation that the Assam Government had demarcated the boundary as per the 1925 Notification in 1950 to 1952 without the knowledge of the Nagas is without any basis. The fact is that the Nagas by and large did not co-operate with the Assam Government's efforts to settle the boundaries amicably and in this instant case, they ignored and boycotted the call of the Assam Government to be present at the time of so fixing the boundaries. Again, the facts of history bears it out that the embankments or ramparts were constructed on the sole consideration of strategic or military importance to effectively prevent the Naga raiders from perpetrating ritualistic depredations as also to protect the land and the people from the outside enemies, whether Mohammedan or inter-

ethnic, and this had nothing to do with fixation of boundaries of the Naga Hills District by the Ahom Kings. Their shelter under 'Assam government's arbitrary fixation of boundaries' is untenable as the Naga encroachers making the reserved forests their hubs with overwhelming presence in all the disputed or sensitive areas along the entire border lines could not have been unaware of such fixation of boundaries under the 1925 Notifications.

About the missing boundary pillars along some sectors, it is well-known that the Naga insurgent groups including the dreaded NSCN have made the reserved forests their hub of terrorist activities, from where they operate and carry on their attacks on the Assam patrolling police and the innocent local people, raise tolls, and terrorise. They have denuded the forests in collaboration with the Nagaland Government, constructed roads and buildings and Government offices. It is unthinkable that they were ignorant of the fixation of boundaries as per the Survey Report and the Notification of 1925. In fact, the boot is on the other leg as should be evident from the large scale encroachment on the forest land and their demand for inclusion of large areas not only of Assam but also of Manipur and Arunachal Pradesh, to create a Greater *Nagalim* through annexation and expansion. As the Sundaram Committee says (Para 4), "It is quite frankly a claim to about 5000 sq. miles of Assam's territory on the ground that, in the last century, this area was included by the British for about thirty years in the Administrative Unit called Naga Hills District," and, what they call 'traditional Naga areas" are nothing but unauthorised occupation of those areas of Assam, and commands of law cannot be nullified by such unauthorised occupation. Because holding of these large territories are neither covered by the boundaries fixed by the Ahom Kings nor by the notification of 1925, nor by the extended Inner Line Boundaries shifted up to the foothills of the Naga Hills District, as the then Chief Commissioner made it clear that the Inner Lines did not form the boundaries nor did it give any rights over these tracts to the Nagas.

9. Unjustifiability of Nagaland's Claims on the Assam Territories: An Overview

(a) North Cachar Hills District

As mentioned earlier, Nagaland's claim sweeps the entire North Cachar Hills District and practically half of the present Karbi Anglong District. In support of their claim to North Cachar Hills District, the Nagaland Government claims that it is mainly inhabited by Zeme Nagas. As the Sundarm Committee observed, "This is not true today (as the Census figures of that district would show) nor was it true in the last century. This area was part of the Cachari Kingdom whose capital at one time was Dimapur....Despite their frequent fighting with the Ahom, Manipuri and Jayantiya Rajas, the Cachari Rajas were holding the hills and the plains of Cachar for the next two centuries......when the British annexed the Cachari Kingdom in 1832, the northern part was left by them under the control of Tularam Senapati and his son until 1854" (Para 51).

In his book *"History of the Government Relations with the Hills Tribes of the North East Frontier"* (1884), Alexander Mackenzie states that there were six district tribes in North Cachar and that the names and numbers as given in an official report of 1859, were: Hills Cacharis-6735, Hozai Cacharis 3260, Mikirs

5076, Old Kukis 3709, New Kukis 4763, and Aroong Nagas 5885. He describes the Aroong Nagas (also known as Zeme Nagas) as "an inoffensive tribe probably an offshoot of the Kacha Nagas. And as Sundaram Committee observed (Para 53), "Even in 1901, the Zeme Nagas were a small minority in the North Cachar Hills Subdivision of Cachar district. According to the census taken in that year, there were 8708 Cacharis and 5483 Kukis in the Sub-division as against 4141 Nagas". Moreover, the Zeme Nagas do not live in compact blocks and live in three different portions with Kuki or Cachari in the intervening portions.

According to the Census figures of 1961, while the Cacharis numbered 21,503, nearly half of the total tribal population of the district, and Kukis, Hmars and Mikirs numbered 13,691, the Nagas were only 6725 which were only 15.6 per cent of the total population of the district. Even as per the census figures of 1971, the demographic composition is not very different. Thus, out of the total population of 76,047 of the District, 52,583 (i.e., 69.15 per cent) are scheduled tribes and only 8321 (10.94 per cent) are Nagas-6423 being entered as Zeme Nagas and the rest as other Nagas. The above facts and figures absolutely leave no doubts that the claims of Nagaland on this large part of Assam's territories are without any substance and basis and that the Nagaland State Governments or the various insurgent outfits clamouring for such an absurd demand have not advanced any proof to substantiate their claims in accordance with the historical and legal facts nor have they taken any steps to place their demands in adherence to the provision of Articles 3 and 4 of the Constitution of India.

(b) Karbi Anglong District

As it will be seen, this demand has absolutely no leg to stand. The Sundaram Committee (observed Para 60), "Nagaland's claim to more than half of the present Mikir Hills (Karbi Anglong) and a small part of Nowgong district, covering 2,368 sq miles is even more unreasonable". The claim to the areas which now correspond to Diphu Police Station "cannot be sustained merely on the ground of its inclusion in the administrative unit provisionally called Naga Hill district. This was part of the Cachari Kingdom before the advent of the British and had no Naga tribes living in it. It was always an area inhabited by Cacharis, Kukis and Mikirs" (Para 61).

And again, Alexander Mackenzie observed (1884);

(i) "The Mikir Hills extend from the Jamuna to the Dhansri and their greatest distance from the Kalang and Brahmaputra rivers is 10 miles. They are separated from the Naga range by low undulating hills and small valleys and their average height is not more than 500 feet ....The Mikir villages are never situated more than half a day's journey from the plains and extend as far as the Koliani in Morung. Beyond that points the hills are occupied by the Rengma Nagas".

(ii) As J.P. Mills in his book on the Rengma Nagas said, the connection between the Rengmas in this region and the Rengmas living in the Naga Hills was geographically and otherwise remote. He said, "About 100 years ago or more, a body of western Rengmas emigrated north-west to the Mikir Hills where they are still living.....These emigrants have abandoned many of their

tribal customs. As long ago as 1855, Major John Butler said of them, "At the present day the Rengma Nagas appear to be degenerating". Thus, when there is not even the ethnic affinity between a single Naga tribe living in different parts of the hilly region and animosity amongst the different sects of the Naga tribes a fact of history, the dmands for territory of other States simply because a few of their fellow-tribes live outside their State does not provide even the straw of the drowning man to survive with.

(iii) The Sundaram Committee says, "Even though in the last century the higher ranges of the Mikir Hills were occupied by Rengma migrants from the Naga Hills, the position has since been changed vastly. The 1961 Census gives these population figures:

Police Station	*Total Population*	*Mikirs*	*Nagas*
Bokajan PS	55,495	30,746	933
Diphu PS	32,456	16,023	45
Howraghat PS	3,72,898	3,44,887	4

Corresponding figures of the 1971 census are not very different. Thus, there is no case whatever for inclusion of any part of Karbi Anglong District in the Nagaland either on geographical or administrative considerations nor is there any such case on the ethnic ground as claimed by the Nagaland Government.

(c) The Adjoining Areas

As mentioned above, one of the main contentious issues is that the Nagas scattered in the adjoining areas of Assam, Arunachal Pradesh and Manipur should be brought under a single unified Administrative Unit. Nothing could be more undemocratic and absurd than such a demand. Article 14 of the Constitution of India guarantees equality before law and equal protection of law and Article 19 guarantees the right to reside anywhere in the country to every citizen of India. The Constitution guarantees linguistic, religious and cultural freedom wherever in the country they might reside. As has been shown above, the Nagas in the adjoining areas included in Assam form only microscopic minority. If the States or the districts were to be reorganised and each citizen compartmentalised by segregating its population on ethnic, linguistic or religious considerations without having any regard to the number, then, unity and solidarity of India shall stand jeopardised and such measures shall violate the very principle of Indian democracy and sanctity of the Constitution. It will be seen that the contention of the Zeme Naga leaders about existence of 52 Zeme Naga villages in the Haflong Sub-division was found to be baseless after due inquiry by the Deputy Commissioner, as will be seen from the relevant Para.

9. The Harsh Truth Revealed by the Committee Reports/ Records/ Ground Realities

(i) The Sundaram Committee has established that towards the end of 1898, a large area was transferred out from Naga Hills district to Sibsagar district. It says, "This area at present constitutes Sarupathar Thana (including

the Diphu, Nambor North, Nambor Southand Rengma reserved forest…and also the southern half of Doyang reserved forest….", Para 68)

(ii) Commenting on Nagaland's claim on Sarupathar thana, the Sundaram Committee held, "It is well-known that the Nagas built their villages on top of the hill ranges and did their jhum cultivation on the hill slopes. Historically, …the area formed part of the Cachari Kingdom till the middle of the 16th century, and later was under the dominion partly of the Ahom rulers and partly of the Cacharis….Covered by thick, impenetrable jungles, it was almost wholly devoid of population" (Para 69)

(iii) Record of the Administration Report of the Forest Administration in Assam for 1874-75: The then Government recorded the relevant para of the Forest Administration Report, 1874-75 thus,

"That portion of the Naga hills Agency in which the Nambor Forest is constituted was formally included in the Nowgong District and was transferred, for convenience of administration, to the Naga Hills agency, but the Government had not by any means abdicated by this transfer, the rights it formally possessed over the soil and its produce" (Para 71 of the Report).

The Report continues, "Thus by 1887, the whole of what is now Sarupathar Thana was made in to four reserved forests and maintained as such. The public in general and the Nagas on the neighbouring hills in particular had no specific rights in the area. Some parts of the Nambor forests were de-reserved from time to time and thrown open for cultivation and settlement of villages or utilised for railway purposes. West and north of the foot of the hills were never treated as being in any special sense a Naga Area" (Para 74).

***(iv) The Naga Baat/Path*:** It is a fact that in order to enable the Naga people to come down to the plains for trading purposes, the authorities had created certain paths known as Nagabaat. This by no means assigned any right over the lands to the users nor could they claim this as any act of their occupation of the lands adjacent to these baats. The Sundaram Committee cites an example of this benevolence granted to the Nagas vide Para 97 of its report. It says, "It is noteworthy that the revised notification mentions three Naga Paths within the Reserve and declares the public to have a right of way over them". None of these, at any rate, could have formed the boundary between the two districts." And, no doubts were raised by any one either during the detailed Survey of the boundary made in 1909-10, nor during the public inquiry that was conducted before the Reserves were created.

***(v) Reserved Forests as the Hub of Naga Terrorist Outfits: Assam's Hold and Control Thwarted*:** The Sundaram Committee had rightly observed thus, "Assam has complained that there have been large scale encroachments by Nagas in recent years on Rengma and Diphu Reserved Forests in this area. When hostile Nagas were active, these two reserves provided them with excellent hide outs and because of their activities, the Assam forest authorities could hardly maintain their lawful control over the forests. Even now they have no effective control over the greater part of Rengma reserved forest. In Diphu Reserved forest it is estimated that 21,000 acres out of a total area of 45,381 acres have been encroached upon in large patches, and much deforestation

has taken place. Removal of all these encroachments and restoration of full control over these two reserved forests would appear to be beyond the capacity of Assam Government (Para 76). This holds true even today and, if anything, with greater vehemence because of the Centre's inadequate understanding and attention and the callous and casual handling of the whole imbroglio of boundary disputes between Assam and Nagaland by the State Government of Assam.

10. Transfer of Dimapur to Nagaland is Unjustified

When the reformation of Naga Hills district was under consideration in 1898, the Chief Commissioner decided that although it would be "the base of supplies" (being the nearest railway station for going in to Nichuguard and Kohima), it was "not a sufficient reason for reserving under the Naga Hills an isolated spot within the jurisdiction of another district". So, the tract between Nichuguard at the foot of the hills and Dimapur was transferred to Sibsagar District. However, fifteen years later (i.e., 1913), the Deputy Commissioner of Naga Hills district thought that the transfer of Dimapur to the Naga Hills would facilitate better movement of goods. The local traders protested this proposal on grounds not only of inconvenience and higher costs of transporting goods but also that, "it would take out of the jurisdiction of the regular civil and criminal courts of Sibsagar district and place them at the mercy of the executive administration of Naga Hills district". But their feeble voice did not count and Dimapur which was the capital of the Cachari kings in the plains, far away from and inaccessible to Naga Hills, was included in the Naga Hills district purely on administrative exigency and without any legal and geographical basis as the then Chief Commissioner rightly held that that alone could not be a valid ground for transferring an area which belonged to another State.

The Sundaram Committee had also observed (Vide Para78), "Dimapur area was transferred to Naga Hills district from 1st December, 1913 for a very minor and unimportant administrative reason and not because the earlier transfer to Sibsagar district was improper or unfair to the Nagas. Assam could, with some justification, claim on historical grounds, the transfer of the ancient Cachari area of Dimapur to Sibsagar district".

11. Truth about Ladoigarh

According to E. A. Gait (Page 119, revised edn.), "Pratap Singh was a capable, energetic and ambitious Prince and though a great part of his 38 years of reign was distracted by wars with the Kacharis and the Muhammedans, he was still able to devote much attention to the internal organisation of his kingdom, the development of backward tracts and the construction of roads, embankments and tanks." There were several conspiracies during the first few years after his accession, which were repressed with the ferocious severity customary amongst the Ahoms. He even resorted to transfer of Ahom people from elsewhere to the frontiers from which raids or attack were feared. Gait says, "The want of an embankment as a line of defence having been experienced at the time of the Koch invasion under Sukladhvaj, the Ladaigarh was constructed with this object. Another embankment known as the Dopgarh was

thrown up as a means of protection against Naga raids. And no Naga was permitted to cross it". (Page 118-19). Thus, as already mentioned, that these *'Garhs'* were constructed with the sole object of protecting the land and the people from the raids of the hostile fronts which includes the Nagas enamours absolutely no doubts whatever and it is erroneous, if not preposterous, to suggest that these formed the boundaries between the Sibsagar/he Nagaon Districts *vis-à-vis* Naga Hills district. On the construction of roads and embankment, the Sundaram Committee further observes (Para 87): "These roads appear to have been constructed over or near the old embankment known variously as Ladoigarh or Deogarh or Naga Bund or Naga Ali." The epithet 'Naga' before the Ali or Bund must have been used to indicate either accessibility to Naga Hills or to indicate their object of construction to prevent the Naga raids that were common and frequent.

12. Major Incidents of Armed Clashes' between Assam and Nagaland Security Forces

The first heart rending attack by the Nagaland forces was made at Chungajan in 1979. In this brutal attack, 54 villagers were killed and 39 were injured. In addition, 467 huts were burnt down by the Naga miscreants. The second was the New Chunthia incident which took place in 1982. New Chunthia is a Border Outpost (BOP) in the Dessoi valley Reserved Forest area which the Sundaram Committee recommended should be transferred to Nagas. Geographically, it is close to Dessoi River. And the BOP is surrounded by the Nagas. The Forest Department, Government of Assam had set up a BOP there which was performing its duty of patrolling and preventing further encroachment on the reserved forests till 1981, when it was overran by the local Naga miscreants. When the Forest Department of Assam took steps to re-establish it in 1982, a large mob surrounded and besieged the outpost. This resulted in firing and in the process one person was killed. Since then, the Border Outpost was never established again. Then came the unfortunate armed clash of 1985 at Merapani wherein the Naga tribesmen came from the hills and overran the Merapani Police Station as also the BOP. In this incident, 41 people including 28 police men lost their lives. Then again in 1989, the Raja Pukhuri clash took place where about 25 innocent villagers were ruthlessly killed.

13. Views of the Shastri Commission on Merapani Armed Clash

The heart-throbbing bloody clash near a small township called Merapani between Assam and Nagaland took place in June, 1985 when the Nagaland armed police after making warlike preparations by digging bunkers, depositing arms and ammunitions inside the reserved forest areas attacked the Assam police forces and the villages, caused havoc by killing people, burning houses and terrorising the entire border areas. For several months after the carnage, the people inhabiting the border areas of Jorhat and Sibsagar district were overwhelmed with shock, horror and surprise and their sense of insecurity and helplessness gripped them so decisively that their loss of confidence in the Government machinery was absolute. When this writer as the Deputy Commissioner of Jorhat district visited the devastated areas in and around

Merapani, the horrified people cried inconsolably to tell their story of misery and insecurity; the only means left to them to take solace from and seek relief through their streams of tears. For as Voltaire said, "Tears are the silent language of grief". This massacre was so ghastly, rude and ruthless that it had surprised the Government of Assam, shocked the conscience of the people living around the border area and left them paralysed and helpless for years.

It is to go into this sad incident that the Government of India had appointed the Shastri Commission to go into the whole gamut of issues pertaining to boundary disputes between the States of Assam and Nagaland. The Shastri Commission had submitted a voluminous report to the Central Government and while the details of the recommendation are lacking the real fact, it is known that the Commission was convinced, by and large, about the genuineness of Assam's case and the want of justification for Nagaland's claim and action, and concluded that irrespective of the merits of the territorial claims of Nagaland, Assam has the unquestioned authority and right to be in full administrative control over the areas within its existing Constitutional boundaries. One fails to understand as to why the concerned Governments should continue to sit over the various Reports of the Committees without showing any semblance of political will and administrative action to implement such recommendations so painstakingly prepared at the public expense. The question that hovers over one's mind is: Should the political bosses be allowed to carry on such gimmicks of appointing Commissions and Committee with no intention of, much less political wisdom, for implementing them and burying them in bosom of invisible eternity?

14. Interim Agreements and Violation by Nagaland as the Barometer of the Naga Mindset

In spite of several agreements between the Nagaland and the Assam Governments to keep peace and maintain status quo as also appointment of Peace Committees for the purpose, there have been aggressive violations of these efforts by both Nagaland Government and the terrorist outfits. For example,

(a) In 1947, a Pact was signed between Sir Akbar Haidari and the Naga National Council (NNC) led by A. Z. Phizo. Though as per clause six of this Akbar Haidari Pact, the issue of the forest areas of the Sivsagar district which were once part of Naga Hills district being retransferred to Nagaland was sorted out, the Pact having not been ratified had lapsed because the Nagas themselves had resorted to violent armed activities in pursuance of their goal of independent Nagaland.

(b) In 1960, a Sixteen Points Agreement between the Foreign Secretary to the Government of India (GOI) and the Naga representatives led by Dr A. Z. Phizo was signed. Point No. 12 and 13 related to transfer of the Reserved Forests and of the contiguous areas inhabited by the Nagas to the Naga Hills District. The decisions arrived at were that before such transfer could be made, provisions of Articles 3 and 4 of the Constitution of India had to be gone through. Under Articles 3 and 4 the ultimate authority of such transfer of areas from one state to another vests in the Parliament and the Bill for transferring

areas from one state to another has to be introduced on the recommendation of the President and furthermore, the President has to obtain and consider the views of the Legislatures of the States concerned before allowing the Bill to be introduced in Parliament. Moreover, it was also made clear that according to the First Schedule of the Constitution, the territory of Nagaland would have to be clearly defined in the First Schedule of the Constitution. Furthermore, these matters could be implemented only after the new State of Nagaland would come into being (Which was yet to come), as otherwise it would amount to putting the cart before the horse because, the new state of Nagaland came into being only in 1963, that is three years later. These decisions could not be carried into effect as the Naga leaders precipitated their agitation for independent Nagaland and resorted to violent activities.

(c) As the Sundaram Committee had observed vide Para 124, "Assam's efforts to prevent and remove encroachments on their Reserved Forests with the help of armed police forces met with resistance and led to their confrontation with the armed police of Nagaland. In March 1972, this took a particularly violent turn in Geleki Reserve with the two forces firing at each other and causing casualties." This ghastly situation was brought to an end by four Interim Agreements signed between the two State Governments. Two of them were signed by the Chief Secretaries on 31st March, 1972 at Shillong, the third on 2nd may, 1972 at Kohima and the fourth on 23rd may, 1972 at Shillong. However, as usual, these interim agreements were observed more in violation than in compliance.

(d) These four Agreements between the two Governments more or less defined the Assam –Nagaland Boundary. "No other boundary agreements were considered necessary further south between the two States as "there was comparatively less trouble and tension in the Rengma, Nambor and Diphu Reserves." In fact, the approach of the Assam Government in this whole imbroglio has been one of conciliatory and understanding, reconciliation and settlement. For instance, "the Assam Government agreed to Nagaland's widening and realigning at its expense that part of the Amguri-Tuli road which lies within the reserve, since this was necessary for the development of Tuli Paper and Pulp project already under way" (Para 126).

Unfortunately, however, the Nagaland Government as well as the extremist outfits had taken such concessions as its weakness but more as their rights which they thought the Government of Assam had usurped. This attitude on the part of the Nagaland Government and the extremist outfits has aggravated the situation driving it to a point of no return.

15. Some Eye Witness Accounts

Mr D.P. Neog, the former Principal Chief Conservator of Forest gives a revealing account of what he had encountered during his tenure of service. He says in a Souvenir published by the Retired A.C.S. Officers' Forum thus;

(i) "The agitation for an independent Nagaland had started ... and the rebel Federal Government and Federal Army came into being under the leadership of A.Z. Phizo in 1956. There were severe bloodshed and rebellion. Nagaland Security Regulation, 1962 (Regulations 5 of 1962) was promulgated

to control the access of unauthorised persons into Nagaland. The writer took over charge of Sibsagar Forest Division in 1962 with his jurisdiction over all the Reserved Forests in the border …except part of Nambor and Rengma Reserved Forests. The government established check posts in entry points to Nagaland manned by Assam Police Battalions. Battalions from other States on deputation, *Nagaduvasis* (interpreters) and NAP personnel were posted to assist the Check Posts in detecting undesirable infiltrators. It was found that the Nagaland Armed Police (NAP)…started establishment of almost permanent Nagaland Police Outposts in the check gates who took over control of these gates as soon as the battalions shifted from one post to another."

(ii) "Taking advantage of the hostile situation, the Naga villagers living in Hilltop far away from the reserved forests came down and encroached the flat plains areas for wet cultivation. As they are not acquainted (with the wetland cultivation) …, they engaged tenants to do the wet cultivation by uprooting of the stumps of the trees. The tenants developed such areas in to permanent paddy fields within two-three years. The Nagas then raised the crop share and engaged them (the crop sharers) in developing newly cleared area". He also says that in the process, many heads had fallen in the wake of resistance.

(iii) The Naga encroachers and the Federal Army started depredation by demanding ransom, royalty, revenue etc. from the villagers in and around these border areas including the tea gardens.

(iv) About the regular illegal felling of trees by the Nagas, Mr Neog says "The writer remembers a case where two Naga log cutters were arrested while felling trees in the Tiru Hills Reserved Forest. These two offenders were convicted by the Sibsagar Court and served with two months' jail." A joint verification of the site of felling trees was suggested by the Nagaland side and when the writer together with the Range officer Mariani went to the site, the Range officer pointed out to the map to establish that the site was very much inside the Assam side of the boundary. The Nagas refused to recognise the maps and said that since they were not a party to making the map. "Assam Government may keep the map but the land claimed by them would remain with them".

(v) The Assam Rifles, CRPF took over some Check Posts and BOPs from the Assam Police. The Assam Rifles with their sector headquarter in Nagaland were more close to the Nagas and ignored the matter of expansion and establishment of new villages, Block HQ, Circle HQ and Sub division HQ etc. in the Reserved Forests. And while the forces allowed the Nagas to encroach upon new forest lands and establish new villages there in, "they prevented the people from Assam side to take up even repair to the existing dwelling structure…" The BOPs did not have the minimum amenities like drinking water, road communication, electricity as no infrastructure could be built up by the Assam Government. …….. Some of the BOPs on the southern side of the encroached RF were rather availing some facilities like water supply, electricity and road communication to Dimapur built up by Nagaland Government from Dimapur side, for which they permitted such activities for their convenience". This is an eye witness account given by a very leaned and efficient top ranking Forest official which constitutes just a tip-off the Iceberg, so to say.

(vi) When this writer was a Deputy Commissioner of the then Jorhat District of which Golaghat was a sub-division, he frequently visited the Reserved Forests of Nambor, Diphu, Renma also Tiru Hills reserved Forests. etc. to keep a watch on the encroachment on the Reserved Forests and to ensure peace and tranquility between the two sides. Sadly enough, it was my misfortune to witness wanton, indiscriminate felling of Sal, Teak and other valuable timbers with big heaps of timber logs deposited by the Nagaland authorities in several Depots Large number of workers, almost all of Bangladeshi origin who took their new generic name of Naga-mia were found operating in the forest areas, particularly in cutting trees and clearing the roots for converting the cleared forests in to agricultural fields. The author also helplessly witnessed new hamlets coming up in the cleared forests taking Naga name. Once I had narrowly escaped being captured by the Naga miscreants when I challenged their authority of felling such a huge number of timbers. Within minutes, at least 20/25 ferocious looking people gathered there and involved me in an altercation. Sensing trouble I immediately left the place, making some lame excuse, much to their fun and sense of authority over the forests. A second instance was when I attended one of the routine meetings with my counterparts of Mokokchung District. When we detected a huge number of timbers felled from the Assam side of the reserved Forest, the Deputy Commissioner of the District admitted and assured that no such things would be allowed to happen.

16. Intervention by the Supreme Court of India

The imbroglio of boundary disputes between Assam and Nagaland as also with Assam's two neighbouring States of Meghalaya and Arunachal Pradesh has been allowed to escalate ever since independence due mainly to lack of political will and wisdom on the part of the concerned Governments which include the Government of India. The Supreme Court of India has on several occasions intervened either at the instance of the government of Assam or of the Government of Nagaland or under Public Interest Litigation (PIL) petition. Thus an Original Suit was filed under Article 131 of the Constitution by the State of Assam against the Union of India in 1988 for identification/demarcation of the boundaries between the States of Assam, Nagaland and Arunachal Pradesh. Then on 13th September, 2004, the Supreme Court of India ordered for appointment of a Commission under Order XLVI of the Supreme Court Rules, 1966 read with Order XXVI of the Rules of the Code of Civil Procedure, 1908, after consultation with all the parties concerned. The States were asked by the Court "to co-operate with the Commission and render all possible assistance so that the Commission can function and smoothly discharge the duties assigned to it by this Court". However, despite these orders of the Court, the State of Nagaland did not file any affidavit or do anything in compliance with the order of the Supreme Court. A final opportunity was given on 11th September, 2006 by the Court to the Chief Secretary of Nagaland to comply with the above direction.

On 25th September, 2006, the Supreme Court appointed Justice Variava, the Former Judge of the Supreme Court, as the Chairperson of the Local Commission which in fact was ordered by the court to be appointed in its order

of September, 2004. Justice Varuava was to be assisted by Mr Kamal Naidu, the Retired Principal Chief Conservator of Forest, Andhra Pradesh and Mr S.P Goel, Additional Surveyor, General of India as Members of the Commission. The mandate of the Local Commission was to- "identify the boundaries between the States of Nagaland, Assam and Arunachal Pradesh". The Court also held, "We may, however, clarify that the Local Commission is not the Boundary Commission postulated by the Constitution of India and that all factual and legal objections are kept open for the parties to be urged and agitated after the receipt of the report from the Commission. None should be taken to have given up any right on agreeing to the appointment of this Local Commission. We hope that the Local Commission will be able to furnish the Report within a period of one year or such extended time as may be considered necessary by this Court. It would be open to the Commission to such directions from this Court as may be deemed necessary". On Justice Variava's having expressed his inability to continue as the Commissioner, Justice (Retired) Tarun Chatterji was appointed as the Commissioner on 20th January, 2010.

However, these legal and judicial endeavours have not produced any concrete results due mainly to default /non-co-operation on the part of Nagaland Government which itself is under tremendous pressure from the extremist elements not to yield to such measures that would despair their dream of creating a *Nagalim* or a greater Nagaland by absorbing large tracts of land form Assam, Manipur and Arunachal Pradesh.

Resolving the Dispute through Mediation: On 20th August, 2010, a Division Bench of the Supreme Court of India directed that the decades-old boundary dispute between the Governments of Assam and Nagaland be resolved through mediation and appointed two of the foremost experts in mediation in India, viz, Mr Sriram Panchoo, Senior Advocate of Madras High Court and Mr Niranjan Bhatt, Senior Advocate of the High Court of Gujarat, as the co-mediators.

The Union Home Ministry was also to be associated with the process of mediation. The Co-mediators were required to submit preliminary report after three sittings, if the disputes could be resolved through mediation. The mediation proceedings were to be independent of the proceedings of the Local Commission. It is not known whether the sittings of the co-mediators have taken place at all or if held, whether any report, preliminary or final, has at all been submitted to the Supreme Court as directed or expected by the highest court of the country. But what is true as of now is that the disputes are alive as vibrantly as ever. It should not be forgotten that where the Constitutional provisions, judicial pronouncements and law of the land have failed to get the better of the Naga mind-set of getting what they think is their right or due irrespective of the ground realities, it is extremely doubtful that mediation would succeed. I am not a fan of or an addict to pessimism but the realities always bite and to ignore this is to expose oneself to great despair.

17. Conclusion

The bottom-line of the unsolved boundary dispute between Assam and Nagaland can be ascribed to several factors beginning from the British Rule which, while creating the Naga Hills District in 1866, had understandably left

certain boundaries undefined or without being defined inaccurately due to inaccessibility of the road less, devoid of human habitation deep forests. Even when these boundaries were defined later, they were either vague or inaccurate, which left confusion in the minds of the Naga people about the actual area which they could feel their own. It was not unusual that frequent changes in and shifting of boundaries of the Hill District marked by transfer of large tracts into and out of Naga Hill District had created in the minds of the Naga people feelings of unfair deprivation and grievances that Assam took advantage of their socio-cultural non-enlightened background to deprive them of their land and forests. But all these factors stand dwarfed by the surging giant of their dream for a free, independent nation, or short of it, at least a Greater Nagalim as they call it, by slashing down large areas out of Assam/Arunachal Pradesh and Manipur, devoid though of reasons to stand the scrutiny of history, geography and law of the land. The harsh truth is that there never was or still is a united Naga nationalism and further, that a handful of them scattered here and there outside their State cannot be allowed to break a State and throw to the wind the principle of federal democracy and the sanctity of the principles enunciated by the Constitution of India. The fact is that expansionism has become their ethos, arms their tools and encroachment on the Reserved Forest of Assam their avowed policy.

So, to ignite the fire of armed struggle has now become a routine matter of the Naga Revolts. It is not that the Government of Assam does not know these happenings. But for some mysterious reasons, the Government has lost the political will and wisdom to solve this problem once and for all, by pressing the GOI which created the State of Nagaland and defined the boundaries between Assam and Nagaland in the light of the historical and geographical facts, the Survey Reports, the latest Notification of 1925 of the British fixing the boundaries finally, the provisions of Articles 3 and 4 of the Constitution of India read with the First Schedule thereof, and finally, the recommendation of the various Committees and Commissions appointed by them. Letting loose the NSCN to run a parallel Government and exposing the people of Assam living along the long borders or the nearby tea estates of Assam to extortion in the name of collection of tax, tolls, killing or kidnapping of innocent persons etc. not only stain the image of the greatest democracy of the world marching towards being enthroned as a Superpower in 2020 but also throw to the wind the provisions of the Constitution, in particular, Articles 3 and 4 of the Constitution of India read with the provisions of the First Schedule. The Government of Assam whose inalienable duty it is to protect the people of the state living within the Constitutional boundaries of Assam from the onslaught of the dreaded armed Nagas and look after their proper development and welfare, have failed to live up to their expectations. Nor has it displayed their political will, wisdom and their administrative fortitude to take up adequate development of the border areas though, as recorded in the Administration Report of the Union Home Ministry, 2011-12, sufficient funds have flown to Assam for border development and welfare programmes.

In order to pay adequate attention to security, peace and development of the people inhabiting the huge tracts of the borderland, the Government of Assam has to rise from their slumber and take urgent steps including bringing

the Central Government to its sharp attention to adopt a package of special and speedy development programme, solve the protracted problem not only of boundary imbroglio between the two neighbouring States but also their socio-economic backwardness, if only to grant a healthy and vibrant life to our great Indian democracy. It must be remembered that poverty is the breeding ground for revolt, disunity and disintegration. The mushroom growth of the terrorist outfits like ULFA, NDFB etc. is explained by the feelings of neglect of the people of the North East by the Central Government. In fairness, to the Naga brothers whose socio-economic intercourse with the Assamese people has been traditionally and ideally cordial, the root of their grievances must be addressed urgently and effectively and the feelings of their genuine grievances removed with a humane approach. Let it not be forgotten that the entire North East is today burning because of the feelings which are only genuine that the Government of India has all throughout the post-independence history been pursuing a policy of neglect and exploitation of the North East by squandering the exuberant natural resources of the region. The socio-economic backwardness of the resource-rich, exquisite region has today ignited the flames of revolt in all the States of the North East. Worse, the Government of Assam has failed to convince the Central Government that the Nagaland Government must be compelled to abide by law of the land and inalienably abandon its claim which neither law nor history nor the ground realities support them. What is of utmost need to realise at the moment is that peace, progress and welfare of the people of India, irrespective of which part of India they belong to, is the only issue that matters, because, north or south, east or west, the great Indian democracy is the best.

References

- *A History of Assam* by E.A. Gait.
- *The Nagas in the Nineteenth Century* by Verrier Elwin.
- *Nagaland Nightmare* by P.D. Stracy.
- *Ahom Tribal Relations* by Dr. Lakshmi Devi.
- *The Comprehensive History of Assam* Vol. II by H. K. Barpujari.
- *Assam in the Days of the Company* by H.K. Barpujari.
- Report of the Province of Assam by A.J. Moffat Mills.
- The Assam Land and Revenue Regulations, 1886.
- *Constitutional Law of India* by Durga Das Basu.
- Administration Report of the Ministry of Home Affairs, 2011-12.
- Report of the Sundaram Committee, 1971.
- Souvenir of The Retired ACS Officers' Forum, 2001-02.
- Report of the Shastri Commission.
- Wikipedia.

4

Devolution of Power to the Panchayats and its Progress and Problems in Assam

Pranab Kumar Bora IAS (Retd.)

For a country of the size of India where majority of its people live in the villages, the need for a participative, decentralised planning in a democratic setup for meaningful rural development was keenly felt by many. Drawing on the tradition of the village level Gram Sabha which reaches back to ancient times and no doubt influenced by the concept of local self-government as it evolved through colonial times, a well-structured Panchayati Raj system well-tuned to cope with the necessities of modern times was therefore considered essential. Yet it took a considerable time to make its way to the Constitution as distinct Articles specifying composition, structure and other functional parameters. The provisions were enshrined in the Constitution by the 73rd Amendment Act, 1992 which came into force on 24th April, 1993.

A look back to the stages leading up to the Constitutional Amendment of 1992 will give an idea not only of the ideological commitment but also of contrary forces which created the gap between expectation and fulfillment. And in any case for a better appreciation of the progress of decentralisation and devolution of power in Assam this has to be considered in the larger national context of the basic issue of the role and functioning of the Panchayati Raj system which is common to all states.

It is worth remembering that even after Gandhiji's call of Gram Swaraj through revival of the Panchayats and rebuilding the village as self-reliant entities, the Panchayat did not initially find a place in the draft Indian Constitution. At the strong intervention of some Gandhians the final draft however included Panchayats as a Directive Principle of State Policy vide Article 40. It is not a mandatory prescription but it lays down that the state shall take step to organise village Panchayats and endow them with such powers and authority as may be necessary to enable them to function as units of self-government.

The first important national initiative at economic development and social welfare in rural areas with community participation came through the Community Development Programme of 1952. This was closely followed by the setting up of National Extension Service which was designed to strengthen the functioning of the Community Development Programmes. Blocks were set up in the states which were to be the hub of activities for socio-economic transformation of rural India. In spite of this positive step and some good works by the Blocks, the objective of self-reliance and community participation could not be achieved.

The Study team headed by Balvantrai Mehta on Community Projects and National Extension Service set up by the National Development Council in 1957 strongly observed that without people's participation and involvement in planning meaningful rural development objectives cannot be achieved and it is of great importance therefore to set up elected local bodies for devolution of power. The Committee made several important recommendations including setting up of a three tiers structure from village to the district bodies having organic linkage with each other and highlighted the need to make genuine transfer of power, responsibility and resources to them.

Following acceptance of Balvantrai Committee's report by National Development Council, a three tiers system for local government had been adopted through legislation in twelve states and one Union Territory. Four states and two Union Territories had a two tiers system. There were not only structural variations in the Panchayati bodies set up by the states, the functioning was also uneven. Most of them however suffered from lack of resources.

The first flush of enthusiasm and initiative gradually lost their edge and the system languished for a long period. Then in 1977, Asoka Mehta Committee was appointed to inquire into the functioning of the Panchayati Raj system. The Committee made several important observations analysing the reasons for the moribund condition of the Panchayats.

It will be interesting to note that several observations then made, are still very relevant even after the 73rd Amendment and highlights the constraints plaguing the Panchayats. The Committee observed that there was a lack of clarity about the concept of the Panchayati Raj itself—some treating it as an administrative agency, some as an extension of democracy at the grassroots level and still others as a charter of rural local government. The functioning of these bodies with weak resource base had become discouraging as there was lack of political will to foster these institutions. The tendency to take up development works directly bypassing the Panchayati Raj institutions further weakened the system. The domination of the PRIs (Panchayati Raj Institutions) by economically or socially privileged sections of society marginalised the weaker sections. Political factionalism and interference, corruption, inefficiency, scant regard for procedures, parochial loyalties and motivated actions—all these seriously limited the utility of Panchayati Raj for the average villager.

The G.V.K.Rao Committee set up by the Planning Commission in 1985 noted the lukewarm attitude of the states to the process of democratic decentralisation. In most states, the PRIs had been allowed to languish without powers and resources. The Committee wanted significant decentralisation at

the district level as they felt that Zila Parishad should become the principal body for management of all developed programmes that could be handled at that level. They further recommended that some of the planning functions at the state level could be transferred to the district level for effective decentralised district planning.

The L. M. Singvi Committee set up by Govt. of India in 1986 strongly underlined the concept of village Panchayats as units of self-government and held it central to the vision of the Panchayati Raj. The Committee recommended, among others, that local government should be constitutionally recognised, protected and preserved by the inclusion of a new chapter in the Constitution. Local self-government and more particularly Panchayati Raj institutions should be constitutionally proclaimed as the three tiers of government. Elections to the Panchayati bodies will have to be held promptly at the end of the specific term. No Panchayati Raj institutions should be allowed to remain superceded for more than six or seven months. The Committee emphasised the need for enabling these bodies financially in order that they can function effectively. The Committee also expressed the view that adequate training, research and public education inputs should be provided to strengthen the PRIs and the performance capabilities of the elected representatives.

All these efforts, the recommendations of various committees led up to the Constitution (73rd Amendment) Act, 1992 which came into force with effect from 24th April, 1993. We will do well to note the salient of this Constitutional amendment which provide a three tiers system of Panchayati Raj for all states having a population of over Rs twenty lakhs, to hold election for the PRIs regularly every five years, to provide reservation of seats for all Scheduled Caste, Scheduled Tribes and Women (not less than one third of the total seats) and to appoint State Finance Commissions to make recommendations regarding financial powers of the Panchayats. As per the Constitutional provision the Legislature of a state may, by law, endow the Panchayats with such powers and authority as may be necessary to enable them to function as institutions of self-government and such law may contain provisions for the devolution of powers and responsibilities upon Panchayats at the appropriate level, subject to such conditions as may be specified therein, with respect to (a) the preparation of plans for economic development and social justice; (b) the implementation of such schemes as may be entrusted to them including those in relation to the matters listed in the Eleventh Schedule (Article 243G). Part IX of the Constitution inserted vide the 73rd Constitutional Amendment contains all the Articles dealing with the Panchayats.

Following the 73rd Constitutional Amendment Act the states amended their own Panchayati Acts conforming to the provisions of the Constitutional Amendment. The Assam Panchayati Raj Act, 1994 was passed for this purpose. Earlier to this, Assam had the Assam Panchayat Act, 1959 which was followed by a number of amendments and also repeals finally culminating in the Act of 1994. At one stage earlier, Assam had a two tiers structure—one at the sub-divisional level (*Mahkuma Parishad*) and the other at the Gaon Panchayat level.

Though the Legislative measures were taken by all states, the one important and indeed vital matter where they lagged behind is the meaningful transfer of

the 29 subjects listed under the Eleventh Schedule to the Panchayats. The matters listed in the Schedule are in the domain of different departments and the concerned activities are implemented by the line departments. In order to avoid overlapping of function, responsibility, operational areas among government agencies and the three levels of Panchayati Raj institutions, an activity mapping with clear demarcation is essential. Many states have completed activity mapping but these have not been operationalised fully.

Govt. of Assam prepared an activity mapping document in relations to 23 subjects listed in the Eleventh Schedule vide Notification no. PDA 336/2001/ Pt-III/32 dated 25th June, 2007. In the exercise the functions and functionaries that are to be devolved to each tier of Panchayats are clearly defined. However, no fund has been quantified and the important task of earmarking the fund as per requirement of each activity has been left to the concerned line departments whose response mostly is anything but encouraging. Following this, government orders were issued for devolution in respect of seven of these subjects. However little has been achieved at the ground level. Even in respect of departments where this exercise was carried out, the activity mapping has largely remained on paper as they have not issued orders operationalising it. Similarly, placement of functionaries in terms of activity mapping at different levels has also remained mostly on paper. Devolution of fund as against transferred subjects as per activity mapping has nothing significant to show apart from fund passed on to them out of Central and State Finance Commission recommended fund. The Gaon Panchayats get fund under the Integrated Child Development Scheme (ICDS) and Total Sanitation Campaign (TSC). It may be interesting to note that these two schemes are part of three subjects listed in the Eleventh Schedule viz. Family Welfare, Women and Child Development and Social Welfare and fund for these two schemes come to the Gaon Panchayats direct from Government of India. PRIs at all levels also receive fund from Central Government channelised through the Backward Regions Grant Fund (BRGF) while fund under Mahatma Gandhi National Rural Employment Guarantee Scheme (MGNREGA) is received by Gaon Panchayats alone.

The 73rd Amendment Act makes it mandatory for the states to constitute State Finance Commission as soon as may be within one year from the commencement of the Constitution (Amendment) Act of 1992 and thereafter at the expiry of every fifth year (Article 243 I) to recommend to the State Government, among other things, the grant in aid to the Panchayats from the consolidated Fund of the State. Again, in terms of Article 280(3)(bb) of the Constitution the National Finance Commission is required to make recommendations regarding measures needed to augment the Consolidated Fund of a state to supplement resources of the Panchayats in the State on the basis of the recommendations made by the State Finance Commission. Since State government will look forward to substantial recommendation from National Finance Commission for the development of PRIs it is necessary to ensure that the views and recommendations of the State Finance Commission (SFC) are made available to the National Finance Commission for their consideration. It is therefore of utmost importance that SFCs are constituted well ahead of the

National Finance Commission and the period covered by the SFC is made synchronous with the period covered by the National Finance Commission. The Fourth State Finance Commission recommended such timely and synchronous constitution. The Third State Finance Commission also made similar recommendation.

The Fourth State Finance Commission was constituted on 23rd April, 2010 to make recommendations covering the period from 2011-12 to 2015-16. The Commission submitted the Preliminary report covering the period 2011-12 in March, 2011 and the final report covering the entire period in February, 2012. The Fifth State Finance Commission has been constituted by government in March, 2013 covering the period from 2015-16 to 2019-20. The Fourteenth National Finance Commission will also cover the same period from 2015-16 to 2019-20. The synchronisation of the period about which both the National Finance Commission and the State Finance Commissions had made emphatic recommendations will now be achieved even though there is some overlapping of the period with the Fourth State Finance Commission which had already covered 2015-16. But the synchronisation is important and once achieved can be repeated in the Constitution of successive SFCS.

Article 243M of the Constitution excludes the Sixth Schedule areas of Assam comprising the two Autonomous Hill districts and the Bodoland Territorial District areas from the operation of the Part IX of the Constitution. The recommendations of the SFC therefore do not normally extend to these excluded areas beyond the 2407 number of PRIs in the General areas of which ZPs are 20 in number, APs 185 and GPs 2202. Nothing however prevents the State government to give some grants to these areas as well to maintain some parity with other areas. The Thirteenth Finance Commission has made a recommendation for such a grant to these areas.

The main sources of the revenue of the PRIs are (I) Internal revenue mobilisation from tax and non-tax sources statutorily allocated to them, (II) resource transfer from the State under the award of State Finance Commission, (III) grant-in-aid from government of India under the award of the National Finance Commission and (IV) grant-in-aid from government of India for implementation of poverty alleviation programmes including State's share thereof. PRIs do agency functions to implement various rural developmental programmes under Centrally Sponsored Schemes funded mainly through DRDAs.

One perennial problem of the PRIs is not having enough funds to meet their administrative and functional cost. Apart from some core functions the Panchayats are also involved in a number of Centrally Sponsored Schemes. Some of these are as follows: *Swarnajayanti Gram Swarozgar Yojana* (SGSY)—a self-employment programme combining the objectives of earlier programmes like IRDP, TRYSEM, DWCRA, SITRA, MWS and GKY which are no longer in operation now; Sampoorna Gramin Rozgar Yojana (SGRY)—a wage employment programme combining objectives of earlier programmes like EAS and JGSY and Indira Awas Yojana (IAY)—a rural housing programme. PRIs also do agency functions to a number of other schemes. While the PRIs receive substantial funds from Central Ministries to implement these programmes their access to

discretionary funds to meet their own cost is meagre. This leaves hardly any scope for improving the quality of their traditional services.

The Assam Pannchayat Act, 1994 has made provisions for tax and non-tax revenue of the PRIs. Apart from the fact that the tax base is not large there is also a limitation as to how much can be collected from the rural poor. In any case, these sources are not properly tapped by the PRIs. There is also a reluctance to resort to additional resource mobilisation as such measures are likely to be unpopular. The Assam Panchayat (Financial) Rules, 2002 which deal with rules, procedure, budget, accounts, audit, also fixed ceilings in respect of rates of various taxes, duties, fees falling within the jurisdiction of PRIs. Apart from restricting the scope of revenue raising initiative it is also an encroachment into the financial autonomy of the PRIs. The Assam Panchayat has provision for imposition of levies for which the PRIs are required to frame bye-laws indicating the rates of taxes to be collected by them. The bye laws are yet to be framed.

All these lead to the inescapable conclusion that the PRIs, if they aspire to the status of a decentralised, self-governing institutions, must have adequate financial resources at their command. One legitimate expectation is to get grant from the State government. But for a problem-ridden backward state like Assam there will obviously be limitation as to the amount that can be spared after meeting the obligatory nature of their expenditures. The State Finance Commissions are in fact asked by the State government that while making their recommendations due regard be given to the resources of the State government and demands thereon, in particular, on account of expenditure on maintenance of law and order, civil administration, debt servicing and other committed expenditure. The other legitimate expectation is for grant from the National Finance Commission. The Report of the State Finance Commission is therefore of great importance both for consideration of the State government and the National Finance Commission. But for computing the non-plan revenue gap as well as other work requirements on the basis of which the entitlement of the PRIs are mainly worked out, it is necessary that reliable data is made available to the Commission. Here the infirmity of the data base of the PRIs created formidable problems to the successive State Finance Commissions. The Eleventh Finance Commissions had earmarked fund for build up of data base but the improvement had not been significant.

PRIs will need considerable infrastructural back up as also skilled manpower not only for attending to their core functions efficiently but also for implementing schemes of socio-economic development including activities under the subjects listed in the Eleventh Schedule. Staff requirement will obviously be much beyond what is prescribed in the Assam Panchayat Act, 1994. The Fourth State Finance Commission had been asked by government to recommend staffing pattern for the PRIs and LLBs and the Commission had accordingly submitted their recommendations.

Accounts and audit are two areas which need focussed attention. Successive SFCs have underlined the importance of this. The department has taken some measures in this regard. The release of grant to the PRIs from the State government should be prompt and regular. No scheme should be allowed to languish for delayed release of fund.

The 73rd Amendment Act has brought the PRIs to the centre stage for purpose of building it up as self-governing institutions but in actual practice they are largely dependent on DRDA. The Third State Finance Commission had recommended merger of the DRDA with Zilla Parishad and the Blocks with Anchalik Parishads. The merger has not been effected till now.

Assam Panchayati Raj Act, 1994 made provisions for holding regular election of members to the PRIs in line with the 73rd Amendment Act which conceived the three tier of government as a decentralised entity and not as a bureaucratic set up. But having made the legislative arrangement elections to the Panchayats were put off a number of times since 1997. Finally, the elections were held in two phases towards the end of 2001 and became a regular feature by and large thereafter.

Prior to the holding of the elections to the Panchayats in 2001 the State Government introduced a new programme (RPRS) described as a people centered development process and a forum for redressal of public grievances at their door steps through people's participation. Elaborate procedure was worked out for holding the meetings at every Gaon Panchayat on fixed dates. A Nodal team consisting of all the Block/Village officials of all the Line departments including the Sub Inspector of Police was to conduct the Gaon Sabhas. The Nodal officer heading the Nodal team had been assigned specific duties. The Gaon Sabha meetings had agenda like lectures on awareness of new developmental schemes, selection of beneficiaries, review of self help groups, and receipt of grievance petitions and discussion on problems and distribution of individual and community benefits. There was an elaborate reporting system. Deputy Commissioners were fully involved and when the programme was launched it received lot of public response. In the absence of elected representatives, a kind of revitalisation programme for the Panchayats was organised involving the State bureaucracy. In spite of some good work the enthusiasm for the programme gradually lost its edge and when the programme was persisted with even after the Panchayat bodies were elected, public interest dipped even lower. A democratic, participative system cannot be sustained by bureaucratic props alone.

An analysis of the post 73rd Amendment scenario reveals that decentralisation and devolution of power, function and resources which several well acclaimed Committees and successive Plan documents have been advocating, have not yet materialised. The PRIs have largely remained implementing bodies performing some specific jobs assigned to them rather than becoming vibrant self governing Institutions. The Zilla Parishad remains dependent on DRDA, the Anchalik Panchayat on the BDO and Gaon Panchayat on the Secretary who is a government servant.

There are several reasons for this, the most important being the lack of genuine political motivation to share power with a newly emerging centre of power. There is also a perception that the PRIs are ill-equipped to deal with the complexities of development programmes. They are poorly staffed, lack professional competence and generally not enlightened enough. It is also alleged that there is corruption.

It is the responsibility of the State government to provide the PRIs with adequate manpower and financial resources to enable them to function efficiently. There has to be well, drawn training programme for the functionaries and it is also necessary to expose the elected representatives of the PRIs to the developmental schemes, the responsibilities and accountability attendant to these. Corruption is a general pervasive issue and the PRIs cannot be singled out as the preserve of this social menace. It has to be tackled firmly but to desist from allocating fund, function and physical resources to these bodies created with Constitutional sanction will be a defeatist and retrograde step.

Panchayats are involved with a large number of Schemes but the people at the grassroots level are not likely to be impressed by the high talks about their utility unless they see these in actual operation and the benefits accruing to the community. A transparent, impartial functioning promotes confidence so essential in a democratic set up. But oligarchic forces often tend to undermine people's confidence. Unlike many states, caste is not a dominating factor in Assam as is the domination of well to do section. This section does not necessarily come from the land owning class which in any case is not large in number in Assam but the newly emerging rich, contractors, power brokers/ middlemen having nexus with political groups. Domination, interference of vested interest, politicians, unenlightened bureaucracy will have a deleterious effect on the functioning of PRIs and no amount of talk about decentralised self-governance with devolution of resources will help in the healthy growth of this social institution.

These are not problems specific to Assam alone but common to most states and many have already risen to the occasion to achieve better devolution and competent functioning. But overall, the progress has been slow. Noticing the recalcitrance of several states to share their fiscal powers with the PRIs and ULBs (Urban Local Bodies) despite the 73rd and 74th amendments, the National Commission for Review of the Constitution has proposed that the Constitution be amended and the subjects listed in the Eleventh and Twelfth Schedules be mandatorily assigned to rural and urban local bodies respectively so that these subjects could statutorily form a distinct fiscal domain of the local bodies, rural as well as urban.

The Thirteenth Finance Commission has not gone as far as that but has recommended grant to the states having a basic component and a performance based component. While the general basic grant will be available to the states without any conditionality the general performance grant will be available only if states comply to as many as nine conditions designed to induce the states to improve the decentralisation system. These grants pertain to the recommendations of the Commission on Local bodies.

In the march towards democratic decentralisation Assam has traversed the same path as other states and have encountered as many problems, mostly administrative and quite a few attitudinal. The progress is slow and sometimes faltering but the travel is in the right direction.

5

Updating of Land Records and Post Resettlement Scenario in Guwahati

Dangshi Burman, ACS (Retd.)

There has been a lot of criticism on the Land Revenue administration of the State both in public platform as well as in the press and to remove the abuses, the government enacted a number of land reform laws to tide over the arising situation since independence. But these land reform measures have also failed to yield desired results as expected by the Government. The reasons are many and to remove these drawbacks some positive steps shall have to be taken at the district level of the Land Revenue administration as a routine work. One of such most important work is the up-dating of Land records.

It is a common phenomenon that like a currency note land has also a tendency to move from one person to another. This tendency necessitated up-dating of land records at regular intervals. Although it has been argued that the Assam Land and Revenue Regulation enacted by the British rulers as back as in 1886 ought to be modified now to meet the changing needs of the Society, yet this can serve as a useful treatise even for another century to come if its provisions are properly applied by the concerned authorities at required levels.

Section 50 of the Regulation says that every person obtaining possession over a plot of land either by inheritance or through sale or mortgage must apply to the Deputy Commissioner for mutation of his name within six months from the date of obtaining such possession.

But at the same time, under note (2) of the same section, there is a mention that the Deputy Commissioner should also get information from the Sub-Registrar's office regarding all deeds affecting rights in land which are produced before him for registration. If necessary, he is to depute a clerk to extract the required information from the Sub-Registrar's office once in a week. It is further said that the Sub-Registrar is to submit a monthly statement regarding transfer of land to the Deputy Commissioner with the following information:

1. Name of the Sub-Registry office,
2. Name and address of the transferor,
3. Name and address of the transferee,
4. Schedule of the land,
5. Specification of share-transferred,
6. Date and description of deed, and
7. Remarks.

Thus, this has provided responsibility of *suo-moto* granting of mutation by the Deputy Commissioner (in practice by the Circle Officer) in the greater interest of updating the land records in the state.

Then coming to the provision contained under Section 53(A) of the Regulation we find that if the Deputy Commissioner gets an information that a person has succeeded over a plot of land accompanied by possession, he may take steps to grant him mutation over that plot of land without petition from the party in interest. In this respect note (2) under Section 50 of the Regulation has clearly mentioned regarding instrument for collecting such information. This is really a novel provision contrary to the customary practice that it is the duty of the transferee to apply for mutation and pursue the same in the office of the concerned circle officer for orders. Application of these provisions will, thus, open a new dimension in the process of updating the land records.

Further, considering the importance of updating the land records, Section 203 of the Assam Land Records Manual says that from 1st October to 15th June every year the circle officer is to make tours at least 125 days and take 25 days night-halt within his circle. But in view of the area of the revenue circles becoming compact due to creation of as many as 154 Nos. of revenue circles in the State as on today, there is no necessity of making 25 days' night-halt to be made by the Circle Officer within the area of his jurisdiction. Earlier, the power of perfect partition was vested in the Deputy Commissioner which has now been delegated to the circle officers to enable them to bifurcate the joint-pattas speedily. But the situation has not been remarkably improved as there are joint-*pattas* still exists in the revenue circles.

Under Section 4 of the Assam Alienation of Land (Regulation) Act 1980, it is provided that if it comes to the notice of the District Revenue Authority that a foreign national has purchased *patta* land in the State this should be cancelled and the land should vested upon the Deputy Commissioner who will put some local land-less people in the land. But no such thing has so far been detected since 1980 which shows that neither any foreign national has purchased *patta* land in the State nor this has been managed to be escaped with the help of concerned authority of the Revenue Department.

During his field tour, the circle officer is to chalk out programme for field mutation. Section 211 of the Manual says that after due notice given by him, he is to pass undisputed mutation noted by the Lot Mandal is Column 8 of the *citha*. Generally, he should pass such mutation by campaigning in the Local Panchayat Office. The disputed cases should be disposed of by taking office mutation. The provision of updating of land records locally is now known as Rajah Adalat, which is also not regularly held by the circle officers.

Another situation has handicapped the process of updating of land records in the State. The terminal year of the *pattas* issued in the year 1965 in many district of the State has already been expired in the year 1995. The Revenue Department of the Government off and on issued notification for extension of the validity of the said *pattas*; but this has not at all helped in updating the land records of the concerned districts. The collected report reveals that there is no vandyak maps in most of the Revenue Circles of Darrang district. The land revenue administration in many villages of Sipajhar Revenue Circle is going-on without authenticated maps.

The Assam Land and Revenue Regulation, 1886 provides that after expiry of the terminal year of the *patta*, a resettlement operation in the district is to be made for updating the land records and pattas are to be issued and distributed person-wise among the land-holders. The Government of Assam in the Revenue Department issued a notification vide No. RSR.645/86/Pt/9 dated 06-07-1988 to start a resettlement operation in the city of Guwahati which was concluded on 05-01-2010 after long 22 years of working and thereafter the *pattas* were issued to the land holders for a period of 20 years. For this purpose, the Government appointed one Settlement Officer, one Senior Assistant Settlement Officer and three Assistance Settlement Officers apart from a huge L.R. Staff, chainmen and other Grade IV staff.

The very surprising thing done in the last resettlement operation of Guwahati is that instead of giving individual *pattas* to each member of a joint-*patta* the old records were simply copied and joint-*pattas* were issued by Settlement Officer at the closure of the resettlement operation. For example, the Khiraj periodic *patta* No. 248 in Noonmati was jointly issued among 345 co-pattadars, another Khiraj Periodic *Patta* No. 1465 was issued in Borsojai jointly among 24 co-*pattadas*, so also Khihaj Periodic *Patta* No. 300 was issued jointly among 20 co-*Pattadars* in No. 1 Hengrabari. Sources revel that out of the total numbers of *pattas* issued and distributed, about 50 per cent were such joint-*pattas* and thus updating of land records were totally ignored. It seems that in most of the cases the records of the old *Jamabandi* were simply copied and included in new records of rights prepared during the resettlement operation of Guwahati, like putting of old wine in a new bottle. This way khiraj periodic joint-*patta* Nos. 710 of No. 2 Japorigoge in Beltola Mouza was issued among 14 persons over an area of land measuring 5.27 Ares (1 *kata* 19 *lechas*). This land actually belongs to one Mr Pradip Kalita, Advocate and no other persons shown as co-*pattadars* has their share over the said land. Similarly, in Column 9 of the new *chitha*, the names of existing tenants have not been recorded where there is recorded tenant. This has opened a free-gate to sell the tenanted lands by the land-lords due to this serious lapse committee in the preparation of new land records during the last resettlement operation of Guwahati, wherein rights and privileges guaranteed to the recorded tenants under the law are found to be omitted which is not extinguished even if the land becomes Sarkari.

Then another illegal thing which was done by the Settlement Officer was that the original piece of such a joint-*patta* was given to one of the co-*pattadars* and the rest were given it's photostat copies. Such a provision is no-where

provided in the Land Laws of Assam and no court will accept a photostat copy of such a joint-patta as valid if its original is not produced in connection with a matter relating to such a Court. The next astonishing fact is that a batch of ACS Officers headed by a Settlement Officer do not know whether ex-President of India F.A. Ahmed is dead or alive. Because, in the last re-settlement operation of Guwhati a joint Khiraj Periodic *Patta* No. 758 in Dakhingaon was issued between Fakhruddin Ali Ahmed and Shyamanta Kashyap, son of P.K. Mahanta, Ex-Chief Minister of Assam. ppp

But strangely enough, no co-*pattadar* of such a joint-*patta* objected against this kind of serious and illegal action of the Settlement Officer. As a result, as many as 20,352 Nos. of mutation petitions and 8,568 Nos. of partition petitions as on 30-06-2013 have been filed by the suffering *pattadars* during the period from 08-04-2010 to 30-06-2013 before the Circle Officer, Dispur Revenue Circle. The numbers of such petitions are increasing day by day and this has now created a horrible situation in the Dispur Revenue Circle. This is treated to be the abnormal situation in the history of Land Revenue Administration in Assam. Report reveals that the total number of mutation cases registered in the remaining Circle Offices of the plains districts of the state during this period of time is must less than the number of mutation and partition cases registered alone in Dispur Circle Office, and there-by the Circle Office has now turned out to be the valley of sufferings of the concerned pattadars of Guwahati. This alarming situation is going to occupy a place in Gunniess Book of Records regarding harassment caused to the people.

Section 63 of the Assam Land and Revenue Regulation, 1886 says " Land-revenue payable in respect of any estate shall be due jointly and severally from all persons who had been in possession of the estate or any part of it during any portion of the agricultural year in respect of which that revenue is payable". So for the fault of one, even if the other co-*pattadars* pay their land revenue for their share of land, the joint-*patta* may be put to sell as defaulting estate. Hence, the partition of a joint-*patta* plays a vital role in the matter of updating of land records and to enable the revenue department to materialised the scheme for issuing *Patta* Passbook to the individual pattadars as planned for doing the same.

Annual *Patta* Land is another trouble creating issue in the Land Revenue administration of the State and more particularly in the city of Guwahati. In all the land policies adopted by the Government since independence, it was specially mentioned for conversion of Annual *Patta* Land into periodic. It was decided that there should be no Annual *Patta* Land in the town.

In Greater Guwahati there are about 30 per cent Annual *Patta* Land of which about 25 per cent are transferred in violation of the provision of Assam land and Revenue Regulation 1886 which are liable to be canceled and made be land Sarkari as per Section 1 (2) (C) of the Settlement rules of the Assam Land and Revenue Regulation, 1886.

As per Land Laws, a district is broadly divided into Cadastral and non-Cadastral areas. The Cadastral areas are those areas which are surveyed and dag-wise cadastral map of a village is prepared. But where lands are neither

regularly used nor under permanent habitation by the people, these areas are generally not put under regular survey for preparation of cadastral maps. In non-cadastral areas, there is only temporarily prepared maps on tracing papers by the *Mandals*, having no legal authentication. These areas are commonly known as N.C. villages (Non- Cadastral villages).

But, there are revenue village areas like Bharalumukh N.C., Kalitakuchi N.C., Borsojai N.C., Sarusojai N.C., Betkuchi N.C., Maligaon N.C., Jorsimualu N.C. etc. within Greater Guwahati where Cadastral Survey has not yet been done to prepare vandyak maps and legally prepared permanent land records till date, although these areas were included within Greater Guwahati, vide Government Memo No. RSR. 21/59/126 dated 1st October 1966.

Apart from the resolutions adopted in the earlier land policies, the clause 12.1 of the Government Land Policy of 1989 says that cadastral survey of non-cadastral areas found fit for cadastral survey should be taken up for the purpose for preparation of land records expeditiously. But the revenue department has not cared to materialised this suggestion even within the Greater Guwahati areas as stated herein above. This so happens as because there is no planning and action plan of the Revenue Department of the Government, which is functioning still in a traditional way. Hence, computerisation of land records was shown to be the only achievement of the Revenue department during last two years by the Publicity Department of the Government. This will also be of no use if land records of the state are not made uptodate. The purpose of computerisation will be fulfilled and the *Pattadars* will be really benefitted provided the L.R. staff and the circle officers sincerely perform their mandatory duty of keeping the land records uptodate and at the same time the administrative machinery of the revenue department is geared up to fulfill people's expectation.

6

People's Police or Policing the People?

(Reflections on the Police Act 1861, and the Assam Police Act 2007)

Harekrishna Deka, IPS (Retd.)

Till recently, the Police Act, 1861, provided the legal framework for the police all over India. A few states including Assam have adopted new laws recently but the old 1861 Act is still in force in most of the states of the country. The 1861 Act has mentioned only one primary task for police in its preamble and that is the 'prevention and detection' of crime. The framing of various sections, however, makes it clear that maintenance of law and order was also its one of the primary tasks, and in fact during the freedom movement, the police forces of British India were extensively used as a coercive law and order force. Here I presume that keeping peace comes within the ambit of law and order. The Section 13 of the Act speaks about deployment of additional force for keeping peace and the Section 14 allows even individuals and commercial concerns to requisition police for this purpose. The Section 15 which envisages use of police in disturbed and dangerous districts gives a law and order function to police. Thus according to this act, the main role of police is to combat crime and keep peace and this is abundantly clear from the text of this Act.

One has to remember that the Police Act was enacted by the Crown Raj in order not only to regulate an agency of the colonial government but also to keep a subject nation in subjugation. The provisions to regulate assembly of persons, quartering of additional forces in disturbed and dangerous districts and imposition of collective fines on inhabitants of a disturbed area all bear the stamp of this intention. The then central authority of the colonial government enforced this law uniformly throughout the country though the country even then was divided into several provinces. When the country became independent and policing became the responsibility of the states of the Indian Union, all states retained this law with minor changes without any fundamental change in the nature of policing. These minor changes were made only to reflect the

changed character of the new state governments. As a result, the police acquired in their practices during the colonial time could not change. When we talk of police role within the north-east perspective we have to bear in mind that they are also the inheritors of this sub-culture and are not different in attitude, bearing and perceptions from the police forces of other Indian states. After independence, police control just got transferred from a colonial administration to a politically directed administration where a representative form of government came under a party system and where in a twisted synecdoche the ruling party's interest became synonymous with the state's interest.

By specifying prevention and detection of crime as the police task, the Act gives police the responsibility of keeping a neighbourhood safe from criminal activities. The penal code and the criminal procedure code are the sources of their empowerment in this regard. But curiously, in this perception of security, the people have not been envisaged as a factor and there is no attempt in the Act to define a relationship between a people that forms a socio-economic community and the police that is tasked to secure an area inhabited by such a community. The word 'community' does not appear anywhere in the act nor the people. It may be that the colonialists deliberately avoided the use of these terms. There are mentions of 'person', 'inhabitants' and 'assembly', with negative connotations, that is, these words appear in the context of potential violence and civic offences. The absence of the words 'community' and 'people' has made these terms overtaken by amnesia. The framers of the Act did not make any attempt to make the police community-conscious and therefore people's security is not a term that guides their actions. The psychological reflexes of police do not respond to this notion. There is another Act enacted by the democratic government of India i.e., the 'National Security Act' that speaks about 'security of state' but the state is apparently not coterminous with the people here either.

It is aimed at containing the activities of potential trouble-mongers who may undermine the existing order of the state. Under this later Act, the police are required to ensure security of the state but they are not required to be conscious of the people's security at the same time. The state is a structure of governance which in turn is a seat of power and the power is wielded by some of the people on all others. The police force has all along been used as a tool in the hands of these powerful 'some'.

The higher formations of police that is the gazetted officers have been formed into different services after the country's independence. Interestingly, the word service was not used by the colonial government even for the higher formations. The Indian Police Service (IPS) was non-existent and there was only the Imperial Police (IP). It was no problem for the then government to call the highest bureaucratic service the ICS but they were weary of calling the IP a service. It was as if they wanted by all means to avoid a relationship between the police and the community.

The Police Act 1861, gave a lot of emphasis on calling police a force and the term 'police force' appears in the act again and again but not the word service. The term police force occurs in the act no less than 10 times right from

Section 1 to Section 17 and the Section 2 clearly says that the police is constituted as a force, the exact words being 'the entire police-establishment under a state government shall, for the purpose of this act, be deemed to be one police force' etc. A force is an organised body of people and to that extent there is justification in calling police a force. But the word has other connotations which not only includes power and exerted strength but also in some context coercion or compulsion, especially with the use or threat of violence (ref: Oxford English Reference Dictionary). Hence, when the police was called a force, its negative connotations should have been tempered by calling it a service and its relationship with the community should have been established in a positive context, which is people's security. But this was neither desired by the colonial government nor was felt necessary by a democratic government after the country's independence. The force remained under the control of an impersonal administration and no attempt was made to give it a human face. The force all along has been used by the administration to police the people and not allowed to act as the people's police. It was thought politically expedient to maintain an invisible dividing line between the police of the state and its people. Although in the Act itself the word 'force' was used to imply that it was an organised body brought under a discipline for the purpose of preventing and detecting crime and also to prevent disturbance, the absence of any reference to the people and its subsequent use in a coercive manner programmed the force to deal with only the negative social situations. Moreover, the police were called an 'efficient instrument' (preamble) and not a human agency and thus human concerns were not incorporated in the psycho-frame of the Indian police. The Indian police acquired a bad practice called 'third degree', an inhuman practice of torturing suspects to elicit information and despite conscientious efforts by many senior police officers this practice refuses to die. I feel that two of the reasons for the persistence of this practice are (1) the dehumanisation of the force in its constitutional make-up springing from the provisions of the Police Act 1861 itself, and (2) the political culture that made it an instrument of coercive use.

Security has a larger dimension than just to prevent and detect crime. It has a qualitative aspect. Those who are given security have to feel that they are being protected and are not exposed to danger. If the 'instrument' constituted for the purpose of providing security fails to generate this psychological sense of security, there is a big lacuna in its constitution. Today, people's security is not in the vocabulary of police sub-culture—an inheritance of the colonial use of the force. When I say this I do not mean the individual police person. I am speaking of the collective behaviour of a force always required to deal with the negative aspect of social behaviour and compelled to remain beholden to power-wielding political masters. Police sub-culture is not wedded to the society's value-based culture. In dealing with a stressful social situation they are programmed to look for potential trouble-mongers and their mind reacts accordingly. Many of the mishaps caused in dealing with public disturbance are not deliberate acts of police mischief, but are the fallout of the dehumanisation of the force in the framework of the law regulating them. Outside

the uniform, a policeman may not be different in attitude from a common citizen but once he is in the uniform and becomes an element of a force he acts within the dehumanised sub-culture acquired by the force.

It is not that there was never an intellectual effort to give police in India a new culture and a new spirit that fits the democratic values of the nation. The National Police Commission constituted in 1977 under the chairmanship of Dharmavira framed a model police bill for consideration of the government and expressly incorporated community-consciousness in the preamble of the proposed bill. It said, 'the police has a paramount obligation and duty to function according to the requirements of the constitution, law and the democratic aspirations of the people.' The bill also required police 'to be professional and service-oriented and free from extraneous influences and yet accountable to the people'. There was a clear attempt to incorporate the ingredients missing in the existing laws governing police functions. Unfortunately, the political mindset that has been ruling the country has so far failed to transcend the political sub-culture it imbibed post-independence to serve narrow political ends and has allowed the proposed bill to go to the oblivion.

As we come to the North-east scenario, we do not see any difference in the upbringing of police here since their sub-culture is a copy of the pan-Indian police sub-culture. Since they have been dealing with a complicated public order scenario for many decades, the absence of an equation between them and the people has been having a telling effect on their performance. When they fight insurgency they of course presume that they are fighting it on behalf of the people. But the people are not feeling so. The people feel that the fight is between the government forces and the insurgents and they are the victims of crossfire. For want of trust and consultation between the police and the community, the people instead of accepting police as a people's force treat them in the same footing as the insurgents—disturbers of peace and tranquility. This is an ironical situation. The people often suffer a sense of insecurity because of the violent activities of the insurgents, and yet they do not feel secure enough in presence of the police since they tend to perceive a culture of violence in police actions too. In a pamphlet captioned 'Police Act 1861: why we need to replace it' issued by the Commonwealth Human Rights Initiative, New Delhi, it has rightly been pointed out that 'policing in India has been by and large, a one-sided affair with communities having little or no say in policing plans and strategies that affect them the most.' The pamphlet has pointed out that in South Africa the Constitution itself makes it the '*Political Responsibility of Each Province to Promote Good Relations between the Police and the Community*.' This promotes joint identification of problems and ensures joint responses to problem-solving. Ashutosh Varshney in his book '*Ethnic Conflict and Civic Life*' has explained how civil society can play a major role in promoting ethnic peace. This applies also to all similar situations of human conflict. The police can succeed in providing security to the people only with the people's cooperation and not by distrusting them, nor remaining oblivious of them. The formulaic response of the police forces to the insurgency situation in the

North-east has missed this ingredient and as a result instead of endeavouring to promote people's security, they are only fighting insurgency on behalf of a state apparatus.

The British officials themselves had found the police in British India to be corrupt. Remarks like 'unscrupulous in the exercise of their authority' and 'very general reputation for corruption and oppression' emanated from some of them only, but they did little to reform the police in India. In Assam, the late Anundoram Dhekial Phukan, a leading light of the Assamese society of the nineteenth century, found police so corrupt and inefficient that in his submission to A.J. Moffatt Mills, officiating judge, Sudder Court, Mymensing, he complained;

"We beg to submit that the police system of the country is wholly inefficient to preserve the lives and property of the people. The *darogas* in the interior, to whose hands the Government has entrusted the duties of the police, fulfill their trust, with but few exeptions, without any justice either to themselves or to the people for whose protection they are entertained. That sordid practice which prevails among the ministerial officers of the courts prevails equally among the *darogas*."

Moffatt Mills in his report to Cecil Beadon, the then Secretary to the Government of Bengal, of course, disagreed with the remarks of Dhekial Phukan, as above. Despite Moffat Mills' refutation, one can feel the popular perception of the time regarding the police system introduced by the British administration in Assam in those early days by reading Dhekial Phukan's report (Assam was then administratively a part of Bengal). On the other hand, Moffat Mills' own remark reflected a typical attitude of a British official.

After the Independence, the political class assuming the mantle of the rulers of this country found it convenient to retain the same mould to suit their political ends. Only recently, at the intervention of the Supreme Court, which gave some binding directives to the central and state governments on hearing a petition of Prakash Singh and his associate, the Government of India appointed a committee to draft a Model Police Act under the chairmanship of the noted lawyer, Soli Sorabjee, and circulated the draft Model Police Act to the state governments in 2006 for adopting a new state police law modelled on the draft act. A few states do have adopted a new Act but after much dilution of the Model Act. For example, a new Police Act has replaced the Police Act of 1861 in Assam in 2007. In order to deprive the police of functional autonomy and retain a stranglehold over it, the directive of the Supreme Court to fix the tenure of the key police functionaries, particularly the police chief and the district police heads, to a minimum of two years has been ignored in this Act. The state, under political consideration, fixed the tenure of these key posts to one year with the rider that in 'public interest' the DGP and Superintendents of Police could be shifted at any time. In the prevailing political culture of this country, 'public interest' has become the other name of the politicians' interests. Moreover, though the draft Model Act made provisions for community liaison groups for each police station with participatory interest of the real stakeholders i.e. the people taken into consideration, the new Assam Police Act simply found it not worthwhile.

At this point, we may refer to the nine point principles pronounced by Robert Peel for that country's police in the second decade of the nineteenth century. Let us repeat the principles here.

1. The basic mission for which the police exist is to prevent crime and disorder.
2. The ability of police to perform their duties is dependent upon public approval of police action.
3. Police must secure the willing cooperation of the public in voluntary observance of the law to be able to secure and maintain the respect of the public.
4. The degree of cooperation that can be secured diminishes proportionately to the necessity of the use of the physical force.
5. Police seek and preserve public favour not by catering to public opinion but by constantly demonstrating absolute impartial service to the law.
6. Police use physical force to the extent necessary to secure observance of the law or to restore order only when the exercise of persuasion, advice and warning is found to be insufficient.
7. Police, at all times, should maintain a relationship with the public that gives reality to the historic tradition that the police are the public and the public are the police; the police being only members of the public who are paid to give full-time attention to duties which are incumbent on every citizen in the interest of community welfare and existence.
8. Police should always direct their actions strictly towards their functions and never appear to usurp the powers of the judiciary.
9. The test of police efficiency is the absence of crime and order, not the visible evidence of police action in dealing with it.

These principles were enunciated by Robert Peel for British Police in the second decade of the nineteenth century i.e. much before the colonial Police Act, 1861 was enacted by the British Raj for the police administration in India. The colonial administration had deliberately ignored these principles while enacting the Indian police act as they wanted an agency to suppress democratic aspirations of their Indian subjects. Today in Assam's new police act also, some of these principles get ignored as these are found to be politically inconvenient.

Speaking about democratic policing, an American scholar Jerome H. Skolnick remarked,

"Democratic police forces are not supposed to be insular, self-contained, or cut-off from the communities from which their power derives." (On Democratic Policing, Police Foundation, August 1999).

The new twenty first century Assam Police Act fails short of a democratic police philosophy as it keeps the force under political shackles and also fails to create a workable police-public institutional interface. Most unfortunately, the need for community policing fails to receive due attention of the policy-makers though some of its aspects find mention in a diffused way in the Act. There is a Village Defense Organisation in Assam with volunteers drawn from the villagers, mainly to assist police in rural policing by way of mounting night

vigilance and conducting night patrols in their own villages, but they do not represent the rural community as such and do not articulate the community's opinions on issues of social interest involving security of the society as a whole. There is only a cosmetic effort to create social consciousness amongst police personnel by way of incorporating a section in the Assam Police Act 2007 in a perfunctory manner but there has been no effort to make some much-needed structural changes in the force or to prepare its human resources providing for a training methodology where there will be no mismatch between professional needs and the social value-system, without which not much change can be brought about in the police sub-culture inherited from the colonial past. The new Assam Police Act fails to address these requirements. One structural change needed is either to do away with the post of constables as they are used like waste-products although they form the bulk of the force or to assign some productive functions to them after raising their quality and attitude through an appropriate training programme. Moreover, the Act speaks of police accountability but without allowing functional autonomy. Thus, many provisions of the Model Police Act 2006, intended to radically change police philosophy were side-tracked or diluted in this state statute.

Having mentioned of police philosophy above, I will like to say that a police philosophy should have the following elements:

1. **Professionalism**. It should get reflected in a police person's attitude to work, in his/her conduct in public, his sense of purpose, his/her integrity and honesty, his/her regard to a standard of performance. He/she should be sensitive to the cultural values of the people and responsive to the community in providing legitimate services. He/she must be effective in fighting crime to earn respect and feel proud of his/her work.

2. **Accountability**. To whom are police accountable? All members of a police force are accountable to the state through the disciplinary and command structure of the force but within the framework of the rule of law and not beyond that. Besides, though the police have been called a force, there has to be a clear understanding that police provide a service to the community and that they are responsible for securing human life and property, that they are the representatives of the people and therefore are accountable to the people. As Robert Peel said, "police are people and people are police."

3. **Respect for Human Rights**. It is a disquieting fact that 60 per cent of complaints against police received by the NHRC are of human rights abuses. The police in the lower rank are not even aware of the existence of the 'Protection of Human Rights Act 1993.' Many of them routinely abuse human rights thinking that the uniform gives them immunity.

4. **Operational Responsibility**. In a political system, police cannot have operational independence free from the control of the political executive. But they have operational responsibilities. To fulfill their operational responsibilities, they should function in a system where they are free from all extraneous influences in their professional roles.

5. **Impartiality**. It is not just that police themselves feel that they are impartial but they must be seen to be impartial in discharge of their duties.

Police philosophy based on the above elements should be enunciated clearly as a statement of principles in the working manuals of the police force. In Assam, though a new act is in force for a few years now, the old manuals are still in use despite the legal requirement that new rules/manuals under the current law should have been framed and enforced. Assam Police has a new law but no rules drawn from the provisions of this law. It does not have a clearly enunciated philosophy.

Coming to any thought of police reform, the first question to answer is where does it start? I have no doubt that the Police station should be the focal point of police reforms because that is the first contact point between the police and the people. If there is a trust deficit in public for police, it starts here. Certain lack/deficiencies have to be addressed at this point.

Some of these deficiencies are:

1. A small staff has to look after a very large area. (Police population ratio in India is 129 to 1 lakh population)

2. Police is too preoccupied with law and order duties to the neglect of investigation of crime. Often, preoccupation with law and order is taken as a pretext for neglecting crime.

3. In the political environment prevailing in the country, political acceptability has become the criterion for posting an officer at a police station rather than an officer's professional competence and actual performance.

4. There is no established system of compulsory refresher-type training. After the initial training, most police officers end their career without seeing a training institute except when they are required to attend the promotion cadre course, organised generally in a routine and perfunctory manner.

5. Recruitment procedures are not transparent and in most states recruitment is not done on merit but on political recommendations or by greasing of palms. For lack of transparency, corrupt practices in transfer and postings are rampant. Some posts are considered 'lucrative' and these posts carry a price. As a result, the quality of human resources suffers.

6. There is no satisfactory mechanism for police-public interface. As a result, neither the police understand the society's security requirement nor do the people understand police difficulties.

7. The Beat system has stopped functioning because a small police station staff has to perform too many other duties with inadequate manpower. Much of their time as well as their energy get spent on V.I.P. security duties. The Beat system is a very useful way of gaining local knowledge, understanding prevailing social climate, remaining visible, gaining familiarity with citizens, collecting criminal intelligence. Each police station should have a number of beats, properly notified, and sanction of manpower for a police station should take account of the requirement of the beat.

8. For prompt response, police need dependable communication and transport. In most police stations, they do with outdated communication equipments and transport. There is no established system of periodic review for updating these according to the changing requirement of time. Police is also slow in adopting new technology and adapting to it. In use of technology, the criminal world has been outpacing the police.

9. Although the bulk of the staff in a police station comprise constables, they hardly perform functionally useful duty as indicated above. The colonial government did not want to assign any important duty to the constables. The Police Commission of 1902 wanted that the 'duties of a police constable should be of mechanical character' and 'duties requiring discretion and judgement' should not be entrusted to them. There is no change of perception even now in this regard and therefore there is a huge waste of manpower resources.

10. Police in India is reactive—that is they are used to respond after an event takes place. The approach to crime has to change to a preventive-proactive mode.

11. Most police stations do not have a women cell staffed by women police officers. Women victims of incidents find it uncomfortable to open up before male police officers.

The new Assam Police Act has failed to address many of these requirements. The state needs to think of amending the Act to make it a proper framework for democratic policing.

Police reform should have a new emphasis on 'active participation of civil society' as was adopted in their declaration by the Commonwealth Heads of Governments in 2003 (see CSRI's 2005 report.) "Central to identifying problems and the solutions to local crime and disorder issues is effective community consultation… An organisation that truly reflects the needs of communities will inspire the trust and confidence and support of the people it serves.", as has aptly been said by Sir John Stevens, former Commissioner of the London Metropolitan Police. *

---

* An abridged version was published in "Human Security in North-East India: Issues and Policies" edited by Prof Akhil Ranjan Dutta (first edition 2009.) This article is a revised version of a paper read and discussed in a seminar on human security organised by the Political Science Department of Gauhati University in November 2006.

7

Need for Uniform Civil Code: An Analysis

Nagendra Chandra Dutta I.A.S (Retd.)

The Article 44 of Constitution of India stipulates that the State shall endeavour to secure for the citizens a uniform civil code throughout the territory of India. This article forms a part of Part IV of the Constitution that incorporates the 'Directive Principles of State Policy'. Article 37 of the Constitution enjoins that the provisions contained in this Part shall not be enforceable by any court, but the principles therein laid down are nevertheless fundamental in the governance of the country and it shall be the duty of the State to apply these principles in making laws. It is a well-known legal precept that the object of 'Directive Principles' is to embody the concept of a welfare State; however these 'Directive Principles' do not confer any enforceable rights and their alleged breach does not invalidate a law. These 'Principles' do not entitle a citizen to complain of its violation by any State so as to seek mandatory relief against the State. Similarly, if a legislative power does not exist in a particular legislature, then the legislature cannot seek to rely on a 'Directive Principle' for claiming that power. It can be stated without an iota of doubt that the 'Directive Principles' in regard to the 'Uniform Civil Code's is one of the most progressive mandates of the Indian Constitution.

Dr B. R. Ambedkar, the then Law Minister of India, speaking on the draft Constitution of India in the Constituent Assembly on November 23, 1948 had said, "We have in this country a uniform code of laws covering almost every aspect of human relationship. We have a uniform and complete criminal code throughout the country. We have the law of transfer of property which is operative throughout the country and I can cite innumerable enactments which prove that the country has practically a civil code, uniform in the content and applicable to the whole of the country. The only province the uniform civil law has not been able to invade so far is marriage and succession. It is this little

corner which we have not been able to invade so far and it is the intention of those who desire to have Article 35 (now Article 44) as part of the Constitution to bring about that change". K. M. Munshi, another member of the Drafting Committee added that there was no reason for any apprehension on the part of minor religious communities on the issue of uniform civil code. However, opponents of uniform civil code do not appear to be convinced and that too not without reason.

The object behind Article 44 is to effect an integration of India by bringing all communities on a common platform on matters which are at present governed by diverse personal laws but do not form essence of religion, i.e, divorce, maintenance for divorced wife. In these cases also the law-makers are under the obligation to strictly adhere to the provisions of Article 13(2) of the Constitution that prohibits the State from making any law which takes away or abridges the fundamental rights conferred by the Constitution. It is in this context that Justice Kuldip Singh held that a Common Civil Code did not violate the freedom of religion guaranteed by Articles 25, 26 and 27 of the Constitution. Despite these constitutional commitments, some sort of uniformity has been brought about through the Hindu Succession Act, 1956, the Hindu Marriage Act 1956, the Hindu Minorities and Guardianship Act 1956, streamlining numerous anachronisms besides bringing a uniformity in divergent sections of Hindu personal law.

The difficulties of bringing about a uniform civil code covering the Hindus and religious minorities have come to fore in a number of cases decided in the Apex court. The case of *Sarla Medgal* vs *Union of India* (1995) 3 S.C.C. - 615 is a clear example of such difficulties. The issues involved in three special petitions heard by Justice Kuldip Singh and Justice Sahai were whether a Hindu husband, having a wife married under the Hindu law could legally solemnise a second marriage after embracing Islam, whether the second marriage would be valid without dissolution of the first, whether the apostate husband would be liable to be punished under Section 494 of the Indian Penal Code. In this context, raising the question of Uniform Civil Code, Justice Kuldip Singh observed that absence of such a Code induced the Hindu husbands to convert to Islam and marry one or more wives under the Muhammedan law that permitted a Muslim to marry four wives at a time. The Court held that a marriage solemnised under the Hindu law could be dissolved only on the grounds specified under that Act, change of religion by a spouse did not invalidate the marriage. The apostate husband who marries for the second time during the lifetime of the first wife is liable to face criminal trial for contravention of Section 494 of the Indian Penal Code that prohibits taking second spouse during the lifetime of the first. In the same verdict, the Government of India through the Prime Minister of the country was requested to have a fresh look at Article 44 of the Constitution of India and endeavour to secure for the citizens a Uniform Civil Code. The Apex Court further directed the Government of India to file an affidavit indicating the steps taken in this country.

The Muslim Personal Law Board, comprising several legal luminaries is opposed to Uniform Civil Code while the BJP until recently voiced its strong

support in its favour. Senior Supreme Court advocate, Daniel Latif who strongly advocated for the right of a divorced Muslim woman for maintenance in *Md Ahmed Khan* vs. *Shah Bano Begum* case points out that the present anomalous status of the first wife married under the Hindu law, arising out of the husband's apostasy can be corrected by a suitable amendment of the Hindu Marriage Act, 1955, incorporating a provision ruling out dissolution of marriage upon embracing an entirely different religion. Mr Latif does not find it necessary to legislate a Uniform Civil Code, particularly, in view of the fact that the Muslim personal law is most progressive. However, there are other theoreticians like Asgar Ali Engineer who feels that all is not well with Muslim personal law as it is practised in India. Allahabad High Court has struck down triple '*Talaq*', pronounced without reasonable gap and deliberation, as violative of the Constitution and our laws. Even Bangladesh and Pakistan have declared the practice of triple '*Talaq*' to be illegal. Many other Islamic countries have done away with this practice though it is still prevalent in India. '*Talaq*' exposes a Muslim wife to extreme insecurity, despite '*Mehr*'– a settlement that is expected to take care of the ordinary requirements of the wife during her marriage. A Muslim husband is under obligation to maintain a divorced wife, but the responsibility is limited to the period of '*Iddat*' only, though she is unable to maintain herself. It was upheld by the Supreme Court that the right of maintenance available under Section 125 of the Criminal Procedure Code does not run counter to the personal law of the parties, governed by the Muhammadan law (*Md Ahmed Khan* vs *Shah Bano Begum*; AIR 1985, SC 945). The Supreme Court verdict extending the scope of this legal provision was followed by enactment of the Muslim Women's (Protection of Rights on Divorce) Act 1986. The rights of a Muslim divorced woman is now governed by this Act.

The issue of giving effect to the uniform civil code came up before the Apex Court in a broader perspective when it struck down as unconstitutional Section 118 of the Indian Succession Act, 1925. The judgment is a fall out of a writ petition filed by a Roman Catholic priest, John Vallamattom, challenging the constitutional validity of Section 118 of the Indian Succession Act on the ground of discrimination.

Section 118 says that a person having a nephew or niece or any near relative cannot bequeath his property for religious or charitable purposes unless the will is executed not less than 12 months before his death, or the will is deposited within six months from its execution to a place provided by law and it remains in such deposit till his death.

It was observed *inter alia* that this provision infringed the fundamental right of a Christian. Chief Justice V. N. Khare was constrained to observe that it was a matter of regret that Article 44 of the Constitution had not been given effect to. Emboldened by the pronouncement of the Supreme Court the BJP has called for a national debate on a uniform civil code. The party is of the opinion that the Law Commission should identify fair and equitable ingredients from the personal laws of the Hindus, Muslims, Christians and Parsis and formulate a common code. However, consensus required for such a sweeping legal undertaking is not perceptible. It is also a matter of concern for the

advocates of the uniform civil code that uniformity in most of other laws prevailing in the country is lacking. For instance, the Criminal Procedure Code and the Civil Procedure Code are not uniform in the country; because they have been amended and modified by various State Governments. In the regime of tax, the benefits enjoyed by the Hindu undivided families are not available to the same category of families of other communities. "A uniform fiscal code does not seem to have received adequate attention from the advocates of uniform civil code."A comparative study of the personal laws of the Hindus, Muslims and other minorities will reveal that the sheer diversity of these laws, coupled with the dogmatic zeal with which they are adhered to, cannot permit uniformity of any sort (A. Faizur Rahman: the Hindu; Aug 19, 2003).

One of the arguments against the uniform civil code is based on the concept of multi-culturalism as believed by some apologists. They believe that India is a country where multi-culturalism has taken a deep-root over the ages. They overlook the beauty and vibrancy of the confluence of diverse cultural streams. It is believed that each community has a different cultural character to be preserved to retain its distinct identity. The state is not expected to intrude into the cultural reams of the community. However, it is obvious that religion is not the only identity of a person. It is rightly argued by Mr Abhinav Prakash Singh that religiously defined personal laws cannot be argued on the basis of multi-culturalism and individuals cannot be forced into them in the name of their religious beliefs (blog, Feb 1, 2013). Though opposition for uniform civil code has been voiced by some theologians of Islamic law, dozens of Muslim countries and even non-Muslim country like Philippines have codified Muslim Law. Sweeping changes have been brought about in many Muslim States. Way back in 1926, Turkey abolished Islamic law introducing Swiss civil law and Italian Penal law. Egypt is another country that switched over to common enactments in preference to Shariah. Attempts at liberalisation in the realm of legal affairs has been gaining ground in many countries of the Middle East and elsewhere. Former Prime Minister of Pakistan Benazir Bhutto was a strong advocate for equality between sexes. Addressing a meeting of women law makers from thirty five countries, she observed, "Those Muslim countries that repress women do so not because of religion, but because of archaic traditions and ultra-orthodox groups who use ignorance to rule". Ms Bhutto's remark does have no relevance in Indian scenario. Nonetheless, her spirit of liberalisation seems to underscore the point that time has come to ring in the changes and to ensure equal legal opportunities to all women in the country, particularly, in secular matters like marriage, divorce and maintenance of a divorced woman unable to maintain herself.

Dr B. R. Ambedkar made the following remark in the Constituent Assembly in this context:

"I personally do not understand why religion should be given this vast, expansive jurisdiction, so to cover the whole of life and to prevent the legislature from encroaching upon the field. After all, what are we having this liberty for? We are having this liberty in order to reform our social system, which is so full of iniquities, discrimination and other things, which conflict with our fundamental right."

A Constitution Bench of the Apex Court speaking through Chief Justice Y.V. Chandrachud in *Mohd. Ahmed Khan* vs. *Shah Bano Begum,* AIR 1985 SC 945 held that, "It is also a matter of regret that Article 44 of our Constitution has remained a dead letter".

There is no evidence of any official activity for framing a common civil code for the country. It is the State which is charged with the duty of securing a uniform civil code for the citizens of the country and, unquestionably; it has the legislative competence to do so. Piecemeal attempts of courts to bridge that gap between personal laws cannot take the place of a common Civil Code.

8

Land and Ethnic Rivalry in Assam

D.K. Gangopadhyay, IAS (Retd.)

A series of ethnic clashes took place in many parts of Assam last year resulting in unfortunate loss of life and destruction of property. Administrative measures like curfew, flag march, shoot-at-sight, arrests of criminals had to be resorted to. Top Central and State Ministers and influential community leaders had to make repeated visit to the affected areas, and the government had to organise large scale relief and rehabilitation programmes to contain the situation. One, only hopes better sense will prevail and the concerned groups settle down peacefully reciprocating good neighbourly feelings, and eschew such violent methods in future.

Ethnic rivalry over land, as we have witnessed in Assam in the recent times, was indeed largely unknown in the past. *"In the historical literature of pre-British times, not a single reference to any ethnic rivalry or racial riot or hills-plains discord is found."* A blissful country with abundant natural resources, the North East India was very sparsely populated. Even as late as in 1874 when Assam was constituted a Chief Commissionership, population barely touched 40 lakhs. Vast tracts of fertile land remained follow, unoccupied and uncultured after the British annexation in 1826. *"Indian peasants are ignorant and wanting in energy and enterprise and slow to leave their homes"* (Census Report 1891).

Things were soon to change and change dramatically. Inclusion of Cachar and Sylhet two Bengali dominated Districts with sizeable Muslim population in the newly-formed Assam was an imprudent step with disastrous consequences. The brief regime of 'Eastern Bengal and Assam" (1905-1912), after the Partition of Bengal, made the Province Muslim majority abruptly.

Though Assam was restored to its earlier state, after annulling the Bengal Partition in 1912, the State was opened up. Census Report of India 1931 somewhat exasperately records: Where there is waste land thither flock the Mymensinghas. In fact, the way in which they have seized upon the vacant

areas in the Assam Valley seems almost uncanny. Without fuss, without tumult, without undue trouble to the district revenue swift a population which must amount to over half a million has transplanted itself from Bengal to the Assam Valley during the last twenty five years.

To be sure, there was a small Muslim population already in the Ahom Kingdom, settled in Sibsagar-Jorhat area, having migrated from upper India and truly assimilated in the Assamese society. Mr Inamul Majid ICS (1896-1984) from Jorhat was a distinguished gentleman, among several others known to me, from this stream. Similar assimilation is discernible in the case of traders from Rajasthan and Punjab, Bengali Hindus, tribal labourers of Orissa and Bihar, Nepalese, Sikhs, etc. who migrated to work and settle down in Assam in different periods.

The most significant and alarming immigration took place between 1912 until Independence, in the districts of Goalpara, Kamrup, Nowgong and Darang. Not all immigrants were Muslims though, as there were Hindus (e.g., *Namashudras*) as well; but they could be less than 10 per cent amongst immigrants from Bengal during the period. (I was SDO in Goalpara (1967-68) and Deputy Commissioner, Nowgong (1974-76), and was flabbergasted to notice

'Assamese' Muslim peasants conversing in Bengali with accent intact! Many such immigrant families would routinely apply to the Deputy Commissioner for grant of Passports for visit to Mymensing, Sylhet etc).

It must be observed much of the Khas (government) or 'forest land' encroached were lying fallow, close to the hills or rivers including 'Char' and consequently found unattractive and unoccupied to the indigenous people. Some such tracts had been converted to Professional Grazing Reserves (PGR) (for Nepalese Cattle farmers) or Village Grazing Reserves (VGR) for revenue augmentation. There were other ways by exploiting which the immigrants went about bringing land under them. One such method was by occupying the land deserted by the tribals after squatting for a year or two, as per their ancestral custom. The tribals would sometimes leave on entire village, out of habit or apprehension of approaching Immigrants, for new pastures. Or, would perhaps sell the land and other possessions and show up as 'landless' in a different District or as erosion affected cultivators. (I found a surprisingly large number of Bodos, apparently from Goalpara, encroaching forest reserves in Golaghat-Nagaland border when I was D.C. Sibsagar 1976-78). Quite apart from all these methods, there was legally speaking no restriction in purchasing any measure of land from settlement holders anywhere in Assam Valley districts.

What was the thinking of the then government to deal with such a huge immigration population looking for Cultivable land? District officials were already seized with the matter in a way. When under government of India Act 1935, Provincial Autonomy was granted and elected government took charge, matter started to become systematic. Four successive popular Ministries were installed between 137 and end of 1941.

1. First Coalition under Md. Saadullah (Premier) 1.4.1937 to 4.2.1938 (11 months).
2. Second Coalition under Md. Saadullah (Premier) 5.2.1938 to 18.9.1938 (seven months).

3. Congress Coalition under Gopinath Bordoloi (Premier) 19.9.1938 to 17.11.1939 (14 months).

4. Fourth Coalition under Md. Saadullah (Premier) 17.11.1939 to 12.12.1941 (25 months).

Governor's Rule continued between 25.12.1941 and 25.8.1942.

Then came the following three subsequent Ministries:

(5) League Ministry under Md. Saadullah (Premeir) 25.8.1942 to 22.3.1945 (31 months). (The longest among all Ministries).

- Coalition Ministry under Md. Saaduallh (Premier) 233.1945 to 11.2.1946 (11 months).
- Congress Ministry under Gopinath Bordoloi (Premier) 11.2.1946 to 14.8.1947 (18 months).

We are digressing a little to record here that no Ministry lasted long enough period (Congress had 33 MLAs and other parties had even less number of MLAs in the Legislative Assembly of 108) to concentrate and formulate Land Settlement policies.

After the resignation of the Fourth Coalition Ministry, the government of India took over Provincial Administration on 25th December, 1941, enabling the government to construct a much—delayed Land policy.

An extract is reproduced from the Memorandum of Assam's Wasteland and immigrant Policy prepared in 1942.

On 6th March 1942, the first of several subsequent Resolutions was passed to systematically deal with the issue of land settlement with special reference to the immigrant cultivators. In the Resolution of 1942, the efficacy of the "Line System" to protect and preserve land for indigenous tribals in submontane area, the progress of "Colonisation Areas" for settlement of immigrants and the so-called "Development Schemes" were reviewed.

In brief it was decided that:

"Line System" should continue to guide the D.Cs in protecting land for the tribals who *viewed without favour the close approach of Eastern Bengal immigrants to their villages.*

Land should be provided to the immigrants in the existing "Colonisation Areas" only in Nowgong, Darrang and opening up new ones in Kamrup District.

So-called "Development Schemes" that created erroneous impression should be dropped.

Categories of immigrants eligible for land settlement were detailed: those who migrated before 1st January 1938, Immigrants whose land was eroded, those who held annual patty, and those who faced eviction, having land too close to indigenous inhabitants etc.

Revenue Department issued a fresh Resolution on Land Settlement on 24th August 1943 stressing on "Grow More Food", increase of Land Revenue and favouring speedy allotment of land to the landless indigenous farmers.

The last two Land Settlement Resolutions were issued on 15th January 1945 and 13th July 1945, also during the Saadullah Ministry, in quick succession.

We would like to close the reiteration of government Land Policy resolution with a reference to the first Land Settlement Resolution dated 20 Feb, 1950,

Districts	1912 Total Population	1912 Muslims	1912 Others	1921 Total Population	1921 Muslims	1921 Others
Goalpara	600, 643	211,562	389,081	762,523	316,490	446,033
Kamrup	667,828	64,627	603,201	762,671	111,546	651,125
Darrang	877,314	20,305	357,009	477,935	36,535	441,400
Nowgong	303,596	15,689	287,707	397,921	70,582	327,339
Sibsagar	690,299	29,718	660,581	823,197	36,994	788,203
Lakhimpur	168,989	13,419	455,570	588,295	15,446	573,849
Total	**3,108,669**	**355,320**	**2,753,349**	**3,812,542**	**583, 393**	**1,226,919**

(Contd. Table)

Districts	1931 Total Population	1931 Muslims	1931 Others	1941 Total Population	1941 Muslims	1941 Others
Goalpara	882,748	387,709	495,039	1,014,285	468,925	545,561
Kamrup	926,746	240,422	736,324	1,264,200	367,322	896,678
Darrang	584,817	67,303	517,314	736,791	120,993	615,796
Nowgong	562,581	177,76	384,819	110,800	230,113	460,687
Sibsagar	933,326	63,907	889,419	1,074,741	51,769	1,023,972
Lakhimpur	721,582	25, 949	698,633	894, 842	84, 579	850, 263
Total	**4,661,800**	**913,252**	**3,721,540**	**3,693,659**	**2,303,902**	**4,391,750**

after Independence, which dismantled old Land Resolutions that catered to the requirements of East Bengal immigrants liberally, and decided that hence forward the government land would be considered only for the citizens of India, Hindu refugees and indigenous landless people.

Subsequent Land Settlement Resolutions/Policies issued in the years 1958, 1968, 1972 and 1989 were more or less on the same refrain, i.e., land for landless indigenous actual agriculturists, displaced persons and Muslim immigrants who came before 1st January 1938, cultivable and homestead land up to a certain limit, progressively brought down, owing to paucity of land and increased demand, screening of Applications at Sub-divisional Land Advisory Committees and innovation like issue of joint *Patta* in the name of spouse conferring title to both to avoid misuse, and so on.

Tribal Belts and Blocks

"Line System" was essentially left to the Deputy Commissioners' discretion empowering them to delimit certain areas as "closed" to the immigrants and non-tribals by means of imaginary lines so as to protect the tribal majority areas. Since this dispensation did not have any legal support, many immigrants continued to hold land by fair means or foul well within the demarcated lines. In any case they could lawfully purchase land even within the lines from indigenous landholders, whether tribal or non-tribal, who would sell the land for profit or otherwise, and get the purchase deed registered without prior permission from District authorities. In other words, the "Line System" had several loopholes.

As far back as 1936, the Government formed a Committee with Mr Hockenhull as Chairman to enquire into the working of the "Line System". The Committee recommended ejectment of unauthorised occupants from the areas within the "Line System" and enlargement of such protected areas for the tribal community. A decision was taken in 1939 after deliberating all issues that the whole *mauza* or compact parts of the *mauza* predominantly inhabited by the tribals and other backward classes should be constituted as protected areas.

Finally in the 1945 January Land Settlement Resolution a Para read as follows was incorporated to seal the issue:

13. *"Special provision will be made for protection of the tribal classes by constituting a tribal belt in the sub-montane tract where they predominate."*

The 1945 July Land Resolution further elaborated that all villages where tribal population exceeded 50 per cent over total population be marked for constitution of Tribal Belts or Blocks. A separate Chapter X was then added to the Assam Land and Revenue Regulation 1886 in the year 1947, to give the new concept a legal standing.

Between 1947 and 1951 as many as 31 protected Belts and Blocks were constituted converting larger delimited areas within the lines as 'Belts' and smaller areas as 'Blocks' in Goalpara, Kamrup, Darrang and Nowgong Districts. A total of some 47 Tribal Belts and Blocks have so far been notified ensuring protection of tribal interests, prohibition of land sale/transfer to non-tribals, eviction of unauthorised occupants, non-registration of sale/purchase deeds to non-tribals etc. A specially empowered Addl. D.C. has been posted in the

District to exercise responsibilities under Chapter X of the Assam Land and Revenue Regulation. One significant provision has been a complete ban on the exercise of jurisdiction by any Civil Court on any matter under Chapter X.

The decade 1941-1951 was marked by Administration's pre-occupation with war-time emergency, disturbed law and order arising outpeak phase of freedom struggle and revolutionary activities, partition, refugee relief and rehabilitation, economic dislocation and social tensions, etc. This fateful decade, conclusion is inescapable, also brought the best out of the government so far as addressing the intractable problems of land settlement with special reference to the migrants and protection of interests of indigenous people including tribals.

Such murderous ethnic clashes as happened in widespread parts of Assam in 2012, exactly a hundred years after Assam was 'opened up', must make us sit back and ponder where we have gone wrong, despite having a wonderful body of Land laws and Regulation and Rules in place.

Certain steps recommend themselves:

(1) Now that we have more than adequate number of Districts (27), Subdivisions (58) and Revenue Circles (150), the officers must be more conversant with ground realities, watchful about irregularities like encroachment over Revenue and Forest land and ensure corruption-free disciplined enforcement of all laws relating to Land/Forests.

(2) Greater vigilance over strangers/infiltrators/fresh immigrants, their activities/movements by Police. Harbouring of stranger/unauthorised foreigners/infiltrators must be firmly dealt with.

(3) BSF and Para-military forces must exercise more effective check at land and water borders.

(4) Curb the activities of anti-State, anti-Indian, communal elements, agent provocateurs who are disturbing /have the potential to disturb public peace, foment communal disaffection to destabilise the country.

(5) In a democratic, secular State all political leaders have a decisive role to play in promoting communal and social harmony, abjuring vote-bank politics, and rely on discussion and concensus, rather than on firearms, to iron out differences.

Epilogue

Even at the risk of sounding a discordant note I must assert that the British failed in Assam. I wish to record my total disappointment with the British Government's Land Settlement policies in Assam specially since 1912. Popular elected Government's sympathy towards one community or the other was obvious and explainable—they had vested interests to muse the particulars sections of the electorate, but they came rather late towards the close of a long British innings. The damage was done already between 1912 and 1937 by a series of wholly pernicious and highly unfair policy decisions. Successive Census Reports from 1911 onwards had highlighted the grave menace of influx from Eastern Bengal Districts. *"By 1921 the first army corps of the invaders had conquered Goalpara. The second army corps which followed them in the years 1921-31 has consolidated their position in that district and has also*

completed the conquest of Nowgong." Prospect of the State being overrun sooner than later by the unprecedented influx was well documented. Yet the Government of the day did nothing to restrict, discourage or stop the inflow of outsiders. If the government had the ingenuity of innovating the "Line System" to protect and secure a disadvantaged section's interests, what stopped them to take the next logical step of extending the same concept all through the Assam—Bengal border? If the "Line System" could be defended on administrative and moral grounds, border sealing would not have been found unjustified or discriminatory. The Assam government could have taken up this all important issue with the government of Bengal through the government of India, and seal the border/introduce a sort of Inner Line Permit or impose a tough condition like 10 years continuous stay before being considered as domiciled, to be eligible for land allotment for farming. The tragedy is that the Administration was well aware of the disease, having analysed the symptoms meticulously as only the British are capable of, but utterly failed to persuade themselves to apply the right medicine. "Line System" admirably served to save a small part of the body, leaving the major portion dangerously exposed, as it were, to a crippling disease. About the rationale of "Colonisation Areas" or "Development Schemes", the less said the better. They together constituted open invitation to the land—hungry immigrants to come and colonise!

The British government's. Land Policy measures clearly and unabashedly encouraged the immigrants, on the basis of misconceived notion of (a) shortage of agricultural labour, (b) self-imposed obligation of so-called 'Grow More Food' and (c) land revenue augmentation. The State might have reaped some short-term gains but all these counted for nothing in the long run.

The State of Assam, after the Independence, started with a severe handicap of an unrealistic, lopsided population burden. Even without any unauthorised influx from Eastern Pakistan the normal population growth would have caused a startling demographic shift, which process has now been hastened due a combination of factors far beyond the control of the government.

Acknowledgement:

1. Government of India Census Reports,
2. Publications/Reports/ Memorandum of Revenue Department, Assam,
3. Assam Land and Revenue Regulation 1886 (as amended),
4. Political History of Assam Ed. Dr H.K. Barpujari,
5. Social History of Assam by Dr M.L. Bose,
6. Revenue Administration in Assam Ed. D.K. Gangopadhyay.

9

Ethics and Values in Governance

Jatin Hazarika, IAS (Retd.)

In ancient time when the concept of State first appeared, 'state' and 'good governance' were synonymous. Political thinkers like Hobbes, Locke, Rousseau, Pain, Stuart Mill, even Karl Marx and Mahatma Gandhi held that all the men in society conceded coercive power to state only in the hope for realising good governance and the final judgement in this regard was left to the citizens themselves. In India, the concept of good governance came from the thinking that common good takes precedence over a private good pointing towards the full development of the potentials of individual as well as of the entire community. This concept had manifested in a lucid manner in *Mahabharata* where Rishi Utthya told king Mandhata. "All pervading one has instituted *Dharma* for the common good of all beings". (*Mahabharata, Shanti Parva*). In the classical usage of the term common good, the state has no other purpose than to serve the common good. Thus, the king became an embodiment of the common good for his people. When king's divine right to rule was subsumed by a state the government became an instrument to achieve ends related to promote general human well-being viz., peace, order, prosperity, justice and human dignity. (Bruce Douglas, Political Theory Volume 8).

In the great Indian epic *Mahabharata* Bhishma who was earlier known as Debabrata was described as a person who had mastered the art of governance says, "The foundation for good governance is righteousness in public affairs. The king, his son, his relatives, his ministers and other state employees who have taken the oath of their offices to uphold *Dharma* and to take care of public needs, must not act unjustly or unethically because if they do so, they will not only destroy the moral basis of governance but will also turn the state into hell" (*Mahabharata, Shanti Parva*).

Kautily's *Artha Shastra* defines good and ethical governance as *Raj Dharma*. It says *Praja Sukhe Sukham Rajya Prajanamcha Hitam Priyam. Natama Priyam Hitam Rajamcha, Prajanama Cha Hitam Priyam* (in the

happiness of the citizens rests king's happiness, in his welfare he should not consider as good that pleases him but treat beneficial to him what pleases the citizens at large). Here the word king implies the men in charge of governance. In Indian vernacular we call ethical governance as *Raj Dharma*.

Before we discuss about Ethics and Values in Governance let us go to the dictionary meaning of these two words. The word 'ethics' is concerned with human character and conduct. It implies professional standard of conduct. Similarly the word "value" signifies intrinsic worth or goodness –recognition of such worth which renders anything useful or estimable. It also implies efficacy and excellence. Over the centuries, philosophers have debated the relative merit of ways of looking at, and measuring ethics and values which are moral behaviour. Various sets of virtue and human goals have been advanced as the best ways to understand, and to implement achievement of what is good. Ethical pluralists, in more modern times have argued that single set of laws of ethics cannot define the means of good ends or explain man's obligations. A variety of tests, they say, must be employed to ascertain when choices and decisions serve morally justifiable purposes. Elaboration of no one virtue such as honesty, justice, selflessness, or courage will provide the satisfactory measure. Good behaviour emerges from applying them all. It would probably be relevant to mention that the ultimate ethical postulate in human being is not that man is good, but that he is capable of doing good, and not that he is wise, but that he is capable of using wisdom. Certainly, the pluralistic approach has the appeal of common sense and would seem most applicable to performance in the public service. But again applying any test to goodness of behaviour of administrators poses some very complex and agonising problems that transcend those common to other human inter-relationships. We cannot ignore some of these major issues when we discuss about ethics and values in administration.

Problems of ethical conduct arise for the administrator by virtue of the power and influence he commands and the commitment he undertakes of devoted and disinterested service to the public. In a democratic country like India, authority is derived from the consent of the governed. Public administration, therefore, must serve the public in a manner that strengthens the integrity and process of a democratic society. The fundamental principle has at least three implications for performance in a government position, specially as we move up the hierarchy to those greater responsibility. It means (one) all people must be served equally and impartially (two) this must be achieved with full respect for and reliance on representative institutions and (three) internal administration in public agencies must be consistent with these modes of behaviour.

All will agree that one of the most difficult concept to define is 'public interest'; but without getting lost in the finer points as to whether there is a single or whether there are multiple 'public' to be served, we can safely assert that the civil servants and political executives should above all, think in terms of the total welfare, the over-all good, the long range effect and eschew the temptation to please just the individual or group pressing its case before him. Prof Paul Appleby, an outstanding scholar in the discipline of Public

Administration; who in fifties was commissioned by Pandit Nehru to look into the Indian Administrative system put it well in his famous book, "*Morality and Administration in Democratic Government*", that nearly in all administrative decisions, the sense of virtuous performance is to be pursued by attempting to inject some increased allowance for the more public interest and some increased concern for those citizens not immediately present or heard. The responsibilities of civil servants to the public, to the law and to their political bosses are tied together by the common bond of democratic consent –which leads us to the second implication that may be perceived in trying to understand the democratic base for public service ideals. One of the most difficult principles for the average civil servant to appreciate and honour is his complete dependence on the will of the people. Having once joined the civil service, he is quite understandably inclined to resent any intrusion upon his time and his authority that appear to sway him from pursing his mission as he understands it. It becomes difficult for him to reconcile – how any legislator or any citizen could possibly have an interest in what he does. He very often forgets that, in exercising those discretions that are left to him he is obliged in his deliberations to listen to, to consider carefully and to weigh the view points of others as to the meaning, intent and the spirit of the law he administers.

One of the tests of the civil servants dedication is his earnestness in recognising the importance of letting the people decide for themselves what policies and objectives the public administration shall have. He must have an abiding faith in democratic process in making certain that it is not just his personal view but that of the people as expressed in law and declared policy to which he gives effect. Where he has latitude to make choices, he must continually apply the rule –is this action consistent with all the objectives and requirements that impinge on it? Democratic government can succeed only provided its agents which include civil servant display a healthy respect for, and intelligent understanding of democratic environment. Finally, we must also consider the character of a public agency's internal administration. A cardinal tenet of our democratic faith is respect for human personality, for individual dignity and worth. The success and coincidentally the moral behaviour of an administrative undertaking depends ultimately upon the capacity, the integrity and the motivation of its workers.

An organisation is effective in almost direct proportion to the degree to which its employees have pride in its work; identify personally with its goals and sense a genuine, open opportunity to participate to their fuller capacity in attaining its mission. Ethical necessities in their broadest sense require that the administrators commit themselves; to quote another scholar Prof Hurst A. Anderson (Ethical values in Administration) "to a philosophy of personal and group living which allows everyone to live, work, and contribute to the general good." We must also remember that in all governments, totalitarian or democratic, laws and rules are set for governing in the individual's conduct in his relation to others and to a society as a whole. But the methods by which these controls are arrived at, and the protection which a citizen enjoys against arbitrary action affecting his person and his possessions, comprise the major

area of distinction between totalitarian and democratic government. In democracy, "means" are as important as "ends", in other governmental system they are not.

When we examine the role of administration on the basis of above parameters, we could define the primary responsibility of the administrator as enforcing order in public affairs as to reduce arbitrariness and subjectivity as far as possible. This of course does not mean that he acts or should act mechanically like a robot. Even then, he cannot move very far from the constraints imposed by his position in the administrative hierarchical apparatus as well as rules governing the matter under consideration. In fine, the aim of public administration is to supply services to people according to their needs and treat all such customers of services equally. This objective compels the administrators to maintain a role of strict impartiality based on principle of equality of individual citizens *vis-à-vis* their government. But this imperative has frequently been mistaken to mean that civil servants should also be neutral with no views or commitment relating to the policy he wants to implement. There is clear difference being neutral and being impartial. Civil servants must fully grasp the spirit and purpose of a government policy or in short its orientation. This does not mean commitment or political bias, but it is also not neutrality in cold, aloof, untouched robot like sense of the term. It is definitely imperative that public servants must not become political partisans or engage in political activities. Fortunately for us the ideal of a welfare state is not in our country a controversial political issue it is the goal laid down in our Constitution itself and we are all committed to reach this goal. To achieve this goal, far from being a neutralist, the public servant should be one rich in human sympathy and with a fully awakened social conscience. To his work he must bring not only competence, but faith and fervour and mind receptive as well as constructive, able to see, beyond the immediate difficulties, the opportunities that lie ahead. This does not mean that the civil servant should degenerate into a 'yes-man' but it also does not mean that he should on no account be a 'no-man' the man who can only see snags and pitfalls and whose instinctive reaction to external stimulus is one of obstruction. This type of man is a danger to society, particularly at a time of growth and development.

In a developing country, the state has become the instrument of economic development and social change and its goal is to raise the level of living of all sections of people. When the state is required to perform this type of developmental functions, the scope of public administration has also been widely enlarged with the object of accelerating economic growth with particular emphasis on removal of poverty. In a vast and poor country like India, the copy book concept of Economic Growth does never operate, because the resources of the society are not equally distributed. In agrarian economy land is the prime social resource, but this prime resource is not equitably distributed among the people who depend on agriculture for their livelihood. In a situation of unequal distribution of resources, hence of income as well as economic power, the choice of products and techniques of production tends to be dictated by the wants of the few; rather than the needs of many. Growth of a kind may take

place under these circumstances and may even be quantitatively impressive, but the natural productivity of the system is to direct resources towards the growth to meet wants of a very few 'haves' who happen to own and control the resources of the society at the cost of the needy 'have-nots' who are vast in number. This type of economic growth has hardly any impact in the general economy in real sense and on the other hand it creates unemployment and underemployment instead of removing the same, thereby widening the gap between the rich and poor, substantially.

Moreover, such type of growth is not spatial and confined to particular region/s or area/s only. Ironically, in a situation like this, the wealthy often benefit more than the poor from public social services. As more than one third of our population is below poverty line, first priority before the administration is poverty alleviation. Therefore, not to speak of administration, entire process of development must be reoriented to the needs of the poor and this constitutes the basis of all administration ethics and values for the present.

In view of this type of economic situation, the enlarged function and primary responsibility of the administration today includes new activities like rural development, public distribution, different employment schemes, family planning etc. and the intensity and coverage of these functions have also enormously expanded. The task of administration today is to attain maximum efficiency, efficacy and economy in the administrative functions with the object of development administration being the primary concern. Thus there is qualitative change in the concept of public administration today. It is increasingly felt that development administration requires a positive attitude, managerial competence and capacity to work with people and these traits combine to form the concept of responsiveness in the administration. Owing to this changed role of public servants, their primary responsibility is to function as the catalyst, but the general grievance is that, there is often lack of trust and understanding between the catalyst and the people, whom the catalyst is expected to serve. This type of lacuna creates implementation gaps in programmes launched for the benefit of the poor.

The only way to bridge this gap is to motivate the officials in charges of implementing the programmes so that they could discharge their duties with high level of dedication, spirit of service, integrity and involvement. An administrator must be able to understand the human social facts for what they are, unfettered by his own emotions or prejudices. He must be capable of appreciating and interpreting the wide spectrum of economic, political, social and several other parameters involved in his day to day functioning. If we can reorient the personnel incharge of administration with this motivation, the administration is bound to be responsive to people's aspiration. Administration must also be capable of identifying the basic features of economic growth and initiate short-term as well as long-term measures for their development. If this can be done properly, many of the difficulties faced by people could be removed easily. This will be the real transformation of the concept of ethics and values in administration to actual action.

It has been already mentioned earlier that, in a developing poor country like India, development has become the greatest challenge before the policy makers, planners, political scientists, economists, the administrators and the general public. But what does development imply in a country like ours? Basically, it implies two fundamental propositions-- it is concerned with alleviating poverty, ignorance and disease — thus it is related to social, political, economic and cultural factors. It also implies that the concept of development applies to everyone and not just to a small privileged class or elites in the society — that is reduction of economic and social disparities between the haves and have-nots. To achieve this type of development as mentioned above our entire administrative system needs re-orientation to face this challenge effectively and adequately. Those who are responsible for administration of the society must look beyond the traditional confines of a stereotype system and instead become change oriented catalyst. This goal suggests that the development is a national process of comprehensively changing a whole society directing it towards growth with equity, redistribution of social benefits and community mobilisation. This is no doubt a gigantic task. To tackle such gigantic task within a limited time frame all administrative ethics and values must centre round this objective.

I strongly feel that, redressal of public grievances, particularly grievances of the poorer people is a pre-condition to achieving development, and this is also an important field for acid test of ethics and values cherished by administrators.

A clean, effective and efficient administration is essential in our county both at the Centre as well as in all States irrespective of the political philosophy of the government in power. The objectives of adequate and sustained growth based on social justice, accompanied with the uplift of those below the poverty line places a very heavy responsibility on all who are in the helms of affairs whether at the Centre or in the States or in the districts. Public administration as a professional activity is concerned with a multitude of processes and practices and they are as widespread and diverse as are the goals and purposes of government and its various agencies. Moreover, the perspectives of administration are changing very fast and so are the expectations of people. In discharging the responsibility as the instrument of economic development and social change and achieving the goal of raising the level of living of all sections of people — with particular emphasis on the vulnerable sections who are at the bottom of the economic and social strata, it is necessary that people at large are fully involved in the state's efforts to implement the development programmes. Since democracy has been defined as "Government of the people, by the people, for the people" — one of the main obligations of the democratic government is to secure a "Government for the people."

This basic concept can be translated into action by a democratic government only by adopting specific measures to secure all round contentment and satisfaction with the policies of government and the methodology of implementing such policies. Therefore, the removal of prevailing or lingering sense of injustice springing from an administrative act is the *sine qua non* of a

popular and ethical administration. A popular administration must also be capable of generating people's enthusiasm for constructive purposes by attending to their genuine grievance promptly and effectively.

The unprecedented increase in the volume of functions of the state following the acceptance of the welfare state ideal and consequent growth in its structures, power and discretion rendered all traditionally available means of control over its operations and personnel; ineffective. As "power corrupts and absolute power corrupts absolutely" and as "where there is discretion there is room for arbitrariness" it becomes a compelling necessary to search for an effective means of exercising control over the vast power and discretion enjoyed by the state functionaries. The gradual culmination of the ideal of welfare state into reality of what ultimately came to be known as the administrative state, soon led to the realisation of its possible danger for enjoyment of fundamental democratic rights by citizens. In view of this change in political and social perspectives, there is a great concern today with the capability of the government to deal with the grievances of those who have suffered injustice or believe they have suffered from the officials who govern. The right to complain, the right to be heard, and the right to have remedial action, if one has suffered harm from the government functionaries, are human right. Legally rather philosophically citizens' rights are protected by the constitution, charters and other laws of the country – but in practice the remedies prescribed in the statues are not easy to obtain for a common man for obvious reasons. We have no doubt different judicial and administrative forum like *Lokayukta*, for redress of citizens' grievance but these institutions have hardly any impact of the redressal of the genuine grievances of a common man. To him there is none to look after his woes and worries, difficulties and problems which appear to be very small to others but are question of life and death to him. There is none to protect his legitimate claim of getting Rs. 1000/- from MNREG scheme without spending Rs. 500/- as the cut. This small man makes the bulk of the society, but has been rendered helpless and is incapable of asserting himself.

To redress him grievance or provide remedies to him, he has to depend and rely mostly upon the bureaucracy, which itself according to public rhetoric not a fit instrument for successful working of democracy and socio-economic transformation. Here again, the administration needs to be restructured and re-oriented to respond to the popular will by having systems of easily accessible quick response to public grievances, within a fixed time frame. The need of a suitable system is of topmost priority at the cutting edge points in the grass-roots level, where general public have frequent contacts for their day to day living. While redress of individual grievances should continue to receive attention, more stress needs to be laid on identifying the systematic deficiencies which are causing the grievances. These deficiencies could be clumsy organisational structure, dilatory and cumbersome procedure, wrong attitude etc. After identification, quick steps should be taken to remove the deficiencies. The procedure should be so streamlined that even when a citizen does come to government, his work is simplified and there is proper monitoring of the delay, if any, in the disposal of such work.

Before I conclude, I would like to reiterate that broad ethical drives combined with the stimulus of tackling society's major problems suggest a pattern of administrative behaviour that can treat each member of the administrative machinery as if he is himself is a worth-while human being bent upon doing his utmost, to help get the job done. This is what we may term as "work-centred motivation". Motivation to perform and morale, with its concomitant should be the basic driving force of the administrative service. We all know that morale is the capacity of a group of people to pull together persistently and consistently in pursuit of a common purpose, i.e., the possession of a feeling of being accepted and belonging to a group through adherence to common goals and confidence in the desirability of those goals. The importance of these factors to the effectiveness or productivity of any enterprise can hardly be overestimated. Just as public administration is essential to the collective operations of an advanced society, so the elements of morale and work-centred-motivation is vital to modern administration. For a civil servant what can be more satisfying than to be engaged in work in which every capacity or talent one may have is needed, every lesson one may have learnt is used, every value one cares about, is furthered. But we must remember that public administrator is functioning in an environment where lofty purposes evoke compulsion for idealism, power caters to the ambitious, control of wealth attracts the venal, and fallibility serves the inclination of every citizen who imagining the emotion of ruling without its commitments can indulge his boundless will to criticise their functioning.

It may be reiterated that we have three basic values of our constitution viz. Democracy, Secularism and socialism. Unfortunately in today's context, all three are seriously threatened. Democracy does envisage change, but change in a peaceful and constitutional manner. It is inconsistent with violence which distorts democratic process such as rigging and booth capturing, not to speak of secessionist movement with terrorism as the vehicle. Again Secularism which assures equal treatment to all citizens irrespective of their religious affiliation is threatened by fundamentalism preached by some sections of people.

Socialist values of development envisaged balanced development of various regions of the country and various sections of its population, which would reduce disparities of wealth and income among them – but in actual field we have seen aggravation of existing imbalances in the society instead of reducing it and that has in turn given rise to the ugly phenomenon known as concentration of wealth and income causing not only social discontentment but also generating economic power that distorts the democratic process contradicting our constitutional obligation of preventing concentration of wealth and means of production to the common detriment.

Prof Paul H. Appleby, held that government action reflects a basic moral tone. To him basic moral character of government action manifests itself when, action conforms to the process and symbol designed for general protection of freedom. It leaves open the way for modification and reversal by public determination. It is taken within the hierarchy of control in which responsibility for the action is readily identifiable. It galvanised leadership to the concrete

structuring of response to the properly felt needs. It has nothing to do with the private needs of the leaders.

Appleby further holds that moral ethos begins in individual self-discipline of a public servant. It is not enough for democratic morality at a particular point of time or for a particular case. It must be in his psyche and he must have a mind set. Group character is equally important which means devoted guardianship of the democratic morality in continuity. Public servants work in a group with a certain hierarchy. Ethics and group behaviour can be developed and sustained with appropriate values and character inculcated by the leadership at each level of public governance.

Dynamics of governance call for educating the public servant in updating his skill and knowledge to cope with the changing need of time, rising expectation of people. It also calls for constant upgraduation of skill of a public servant to meet the demand of time for which he should be more professional. That will improve the delivery system both in regulatory and developmental administration. Therefore, at certain states of career, training of the public servant is absolutely necessary to improve his capability. Deficiency in knowledge and skill make the public governance weak and less effective. In course of time, new ideas emerge to meet new challenges in public administration. Countries in the globe introduce novel practices to cope with changing situation in the realm of governance. Public servants, who join different branches of administration and undergo initial training at the time of entry into service, will find themselves out of date unless they re-induct new skill for capacity building and ethical standard of governance will go down the line.

Lastly we must recognise that at macro-level, for ethical good governance system, we cannot loose sight of an important relationship between Rule of Law, Good Governance and Sustainable Development. Deficiency in the rule of law encourages indiscipline in the Society, breeds high rates of corruption with devastating consequences on the confidence of law abiding citizens, making the administrative system itself irrelevant.

10

Indices of Police Performance and Assam

S.P. Kar IPS (Retd.)

The police in India have a distinct mandate for performing certain duties that include, among other things, the maintenance of law and order, giving the citizens a sense of security and bringing to book persons who commit criminal offences against individuals and the society at large. Though policing had been a historical process for hundreds of years, there was no codification of a law for the purpose at any point of time during the ancient and middle ages. It was all but whims of the rulers that determined how crimes, or alleged crimes, were to be punished and with what severity. The medieval ways of dealing with alleged crimes were too horrific and repulsive to deserve a full narrative here. The conventional regulatory system operated those days by the police (in whatever name they were called) was essentially to strike hard on the opponent, or the suspected opponents, of the regime in power. It was less for justice to the victims. A lot of sadism was involved in the then prevailing practices. In this connection, one can recall the martyrdom of the legendary lady, Sati Joymati, who gave up her life after days of inhuman torture by king's men (read police) sometime during the rule of a despotic king in upper Assam.

Policing in India did not have a clear aim and methodology till the British government in India came up with the enactment of the Police Act 1861. It is about 150 years now since the said Act had come into being and its countrywide operation in both pre-and post-Independence periods gave us a unique opportunity to build up our own doctrine of policing based on the experiences gathered during these long years. Thus, in recent times, people have mentally shaped up a long range of expectations from the institution of police. Needless to mention here that the increasing democratisation of the Indian society and the growth of concern for preservation of human rights during the last four decades have greatly contributed to the concept of a people-friendly police in

the country. How much of it has so far been achieved is a matter of factual analysis.

Mr Robert Peel, a former Home Secretary of England who later became Prime Minister, had laid down a number of principles, known as Peel's principles, for the police in the UK and the rest of the British Empire. The said principles, noted below, are as much valid now as they were then.

(a) The police must be stable, efficient and militarily organised under government control.

(b) The absence of crime will best prove the efficiency of the police.

(c) Crime news must be widely distributed.

(d) Territorial distribution of the force by hours and shifts must be accomplished.

(e) No quality is more indispensable to an officer than a perfect command of temper; a quiet determined manner has more effect than violent action.

(f) Good appearance commands respect.

(g) Proper training of personnel lies at the root of police efficiency.

(h) Public safety requires that every policeman must be given a number.

(i) The Police headquarters should be centrally located and easily accessible to all people.

(j) Policemen should be appointed on probation basis.

(k) Police records are necessary for the correct distribution of police strength.

(l) The best way to select men is 'to size them up' and find out what their neighbours say about them.

Unfortunately, policing in India does not follow the valuable maxims laid down by Peel though we had historically inherited British legacy in many other fields. In fact, expectations of the modern society from the police are much more than even the above. It, among other things, wants police participation in all community-based activities, including the sharing of its weal and woe. In this connection, it is pertinent to admit that corruption and political interference in the process of recruitment of police personnel are having their toll on the quality of the police force everywhere. Besides, low educational qualification which, by today's standard, is almost at the margin of illiteracy at the level of constable (class 8th or matric passed) is also a reason for inefficiency and bad image of the police at large.

A Presidential Commission on the Police in the US had said as follows in 1967:

"The quality of police service will not significantly improve until higher educational requirements are established for its personnel. The complexity of police task is as great as that of any profession. The performance of this task requires more than physical process and common sense. Personnel who in various unpredictable situations are required to make difficult judgements should possess a sound knowledge of society and human behaviour. This can be achieved through advanced education."

The Police Act 1861 was an all-India Act, applicable to the whole of the then British India. It is said, and perhaps a great deal true, that the British

colonial administration had ironically used the Indian police, largely consisting of Indians (except the top brass of the Force), to commit unwarranted atrocities on Indians for the purpose of perpetuating their rule in the country. Meanwhile, the Constitution of India that came into force in 1950 provided that the police would be a State subject under the Seventh Schedule to be controlled by the State government concerned. This virtually made the 1861 Act irrelevant and anachronistic. The legacy of the British rulers, however, continued for years on end even in independent India and the people in general kept bearing the brunt of their police being highly arbitrary in actions and insensitive to the people's needs. They continued to be the rulers' police and, as a former IPS officer, Ved Marwa, had said, 'ruler-friendly'. The system having become totally outmoded by modern standards reached its *nadir* during the state of internal emergency (1975-77) declared and put into effect by the then prime minister, Indira Gandhi. The 'emergency' saw the extremes of unlawful arrests and detentions, custodial violence and a lot many other activities of the police not permitted by law.

These aberrations in the police working, however, came about not entirely because there was lack of moral fibre only among policemen. In a democratic system like ours, there are many institutional checks and balances that should have taken care of the ongoing flippancy at that time. Even those institutions, both formal and informal, that ought to have curbed or taken a stand against the excesses of the so-called state of emergency the judiciary, the civil service, the civil society, the intellectuals among others are supposed to be the standard-bears of a civilized nation looked the other way when the police, as an agency of the government, had gone totally berserk. However, it is permissible to say that those bodies an essential part of the system may have been too terrorized to raise a voice.

The result was a total collapse of the rule of law during the time. As a matter of fact, the Shah Commission formed to probe the excesses of the Emergency indicted the whole lot of governmental machineries at the Centre and the States for countless number of illegalities against citizens. They used the police as a tool to perpetrate innumerable outrages over the common people and even on the opposition leaders to throttle the voice of sanity. Towering personalities, like Loknayak Jai Prakash Narain, Morarji Desai, Jyotirmoy Basu, Atal Behari Vajpayee, L.K. Advani, Maharani Gayatri Devi and scores of other national leaders received extremely bad treatment in the hands of the police and other state agencies during the Emergency.

In this process, the worst of the cut came when a Supreme Court bench presided over by the then chief justice of India, A.N. Ray, decided that the state had power of life and death over its people during an 'emergency' and that the citizen had no redress against such a situation. Thus, there was no reason to blame the police alone for the wrongs that they committed during the time.

In the post-emergency period, the then Janata government at the Centre appointed in 1978 a National Police Commission (chaired by former Governor of West Bengal, Dharam Vira, a retired member of the then ICS), which, after

due deliberations, came up with the proposal for a number of fundamental reforms in the police system. This was basically aimed at introducing 'accountability' of the police to law for their actions. Later, the Supreme Court of India in *Prakash Singh and Others* vs. *the Union of India* [Writ petition (civil) 310 of 1996] laid down that each of the States in the country should enact a Police Act of its own incorporating the provisions recommended by the National Police Commission in their model draft.[1] Accordingly, the Government of Assam enacted the Assam Police Act 2007, though many of the States are yet to do so.

However, the essential functions and responsibilities of the police under the above Act have a lot of similarities with those in the 1861 Act and thus there has barely been any break from the old system of policing. Police inefficiency and arbitrariness continue to be on the headlines, more or less as before. It is therefore time now to make an assessment of the police performances in the State of Assam with the help of a set of given 'indices' or indicators.[2]

State of Law and Order and A Sense of Security

This is one of the best indicators by which to decide how successful are the police in the State in one of their most essential functions. The best person to evaluate the state of law and order or whether there is a sense of security in a given area is the ordinary man or woman in a village or a town. He is not exactly aware of the actual number of incidents happening all over or of their complexities, but he still knows for certain how safe or unsafe he is from an armed militant, if there is any, or a robber or an extortionist going round to attack him. Similarly, a girl feels insecure on the roadside from possible eve-teasers or rapists when there is a real danger of such a thing happening. The above personal safety ranking is based on 'measures of internal stability, crime levels and law enforcement effectiveness'. Negative feelings of the people are an indicator of policing being not up to the mark. The people's confidence, or the lack of it, about the security environment in their respective localities is an important factor here. In Assam, there has perceptively been a good deal of improvement in the last couple of years in so far as armed militancy is concerned. However, on the crime front, the picture is dismal.

The citizens know that their life and property are under threat. Rampant violence on the streets, attack on women and children, kidnapping, molestation, rape, snatching, extortion, robberies, house-breaking in broad-day light, trafficking in drugs, arms and the girl child, among other things, are now taken by citizens in their stride. On the other hand, the law-breakers of all varieties do all these apparently with a sense of full impunity and enjoy an unbarred freedom from the law's supposedly long hand. On the militancy front, persons directly charged with mass killings, serial blasts, etc. in the recent past are seen rubbing shoulders with the powers that be, throwing the sanctity of the law to the winds. They even openly carry weapons – precisely the same set of weapons they had used earlier to commit murders and other types of bedlam – to silence any ripple of protest against their illegal activities. This naturally sets an example for ordinary criminals to follow.

People thus suffer, both individually and collectively, from a sense of injustice and a real-time state of insecurity but have no remedy. A state of

affairs like the above does not behove well for the State, though the police cannot perhaps be held entirely responsible for it. However, people perceive the situation as a failure on the part of the police. The political executive being the controlling authority of the police, the latter are obliged to look the other way in many cases, knowing fully well that things were wrong. The only recompense in the torrid picture is that the media, particularly the electronic media, has been bringing the whole gamut of things to the public view and discourse, though not with much success in remedying the same. The worst part of the scenario is that the political executive who wield the real power do not show any intention to cry a halt to this state of affairs. Very often reasons are given to justify inaction.

Number of Crimes

The statistics of crimes taking place in an area are an index of the state of policing in it. The following crime figures speak for the present situation:

All India	2007—57, 33,407	(IPC + Spl. and Local laws)
	2010— 67, 50,748	do
	2011— 62, 52,729	do
Assam	2007— 48,967	(IPC only)
	2010— 63,493	do
	2011— 66,714	do

Source: [Crime India 2011, NCRB]

Moreover, there has been a major spurt of crimes against women in Assam in recent years. According to the NCRB report of 2012, the State, of late, has recorded a simultaneous increase in the number of serious crimes against women, like kidnapping, rape, murder, dowry death, domestic violence, trafficking, outrage of modesty, witch-hunting, etc. This owes to a plethora of failures on the part of the police and administration as well as sociological degeneration of the society.[3]

The picture of a phenomenal rise in the number of total crimes in the State of Assam in a matter of three years is of concern. It would therefore stand to reason to conclude that the inverse is true of the quality of policing. Moreover, to keep the figures low, police stations tend to be reluctant to register FIRs – a proven fact that implies that the actual number of crimes is higher than the official figures. The crime rate (which means the number of crimes taking place per (1, 00,000 people) for the entire country rose from 504.5 in 2007 to 516.7 in 2011. This is indicative of a general trend towards increasing criminalisation of the populace across the country. The fact of the matter is, there are many more crimes happening than what is recorded and shown. Better policing can reverse the trend to a reasonable extent. It means not only better detection of crimes and prosecution of criminals, but also putting in place effective methods for their prevention.

In 2009 in Assam, the total number of criminal cases, including those pending since the preceding years, stood at 1,16,292 for offences under Indian Penal Code (IPC) and 7, 133 for offences under Special and Local Laws (SLL).

The charge-sheeting rate was 56.6 per cent and 66.2 per cent respectively. [Crime India 2011, NCRB]

This, in effect, means that numerous cases which ended in closure because of what in police parlance is known as 'lack of evidence' would never see the light of justice. Injustice is thus perpetrated thanks to police inefficiency.

The above data reflect the failure of our criminal justice system to cope with the deteriorating internal security scenario that involves crimes, insurgency[4], left-wing terror, etc. affecting the lives of citizens. The remedy lies in effecting a proportionate increase in the number of police officers and better training for them for the situation that is becoming increasingly complex by the day. Simultaneously, it calls for the strengthening of the judiciary, both in numbers and in quality, particularly at the lower level. Delivery of justice is closely related to the quality of the police (at their cutting edge level) and the lower judiciary, so much so that once either or both the institutions fail, the higher bodies of the government and the higher judiciary cannot reverse their failure at a later stage.

Arrest Rates

The police are supposed to investigate objectively criminal incidents reported to the police stations and arrest the accused when evidence collected is found 'adequate'. Arrest is a means by which to ensure that a law-breaker or offender does not evade or flee from the process of law. Though 'arrest' takes away the constitutional liberty of a person for the time being, it is allowed in the legal systems of all established democracies of the world because the offender cannot, in the interest of justice, be permitted to continue enjoying his freedom and even escape the process of law at the cost of a fellow citizen. This, therefore, ordains that when a functionary of the State, here the police, is authorised to arrest a person, his act of curbing the physical liberty of a person should be well-reasoned and based on legal parameters. Unjustified arrest by itself causes injustice that arrest aims at preventing. Arbitrary arrests are a crime by themselves. However, in reality, it is found that the police make random arrests of people much larger in number than even accused of. This signifies that proper application of mind is not done in this serious business.

Hundred per cent arrest will mean that all the wanted accused persons (against whom reasonable suspicion exists or evidence collected) have been arrested. When the actual number of arrests exceeds the wanted numbers, it is absolutely capricious and not lawful. Yet the practice of the police is such that they resort to such arrests, which means their policing is highly flawed. This also signifies violation by them of the fundamental right to life and liberty of the victims of such arrests (Article 21 of the Constitution). The rate of arrests in some of the States, including Assam, is shown below:

1. Meghalaya, Tripura, Manipur, Nagaland = up to 200 per cent.
2. Assam, Meghalaya, Mizoram = 200 per cent to 250 per cent.
3. Tamil Nadu, MP, Gujarat, Haryana, Himachal Pradesh = above 300 per cent.

Source: [NCRB]

It is highly obnoxious that States like Assam, Meghalaya, etc. have a rate of 200 per cent arrests. It is unthinkable that arrest rates could reach up to 300 per cent in many of the States. The net result is that the prisons remain packed with under-trials, a high percentage of them being innocents, mostly poor.

Disposal Rate

The police are supposed to dispose of all the cases received for investigation promptly. When they fail, it is negation of their responsibilities and denial of justice to the victims concerned. But for reasons partly beyond their control, they keep adding to the pendency of cases every year. *This puts justice seekers in waiting even as evidence evaporates with passage of every single day, month and year. Pendency of cases under investigation and trial keeps justice on hold, and leads to its eventual denial.* The following are the disposal rates in the North East:

Assam —— up to 50 per cent;
[At the end of 2009, pendency of cases in Assam was 67,540 under IPC and 5,887 cases under SLL)
Arunachal Pradesh —— 70 per cent —80 per cent
Meghalaya, Manipur —— up to 50 per cent
Nagaland —— 50 per cent— 60 per cent
Tripura, Mizoram— above 60 per cent

Source: [NCRB]

It is certainly a matter of regret that the police machinery in States like Assam, Meghalaya and Manipur have not been able to raise the rate of disposal of cases investigated by them beyond a lowly 50 per cent. Their citizens suffer injustice to that extent.

Conviction Rate

All India —41.1 per cent in 2011
It varies from state to state from year to year.
Assam: 20 per cent — 30 per cent [In 2011, it was 19.9 per cent]
Tripura, Maharashtra, Orissa, West Bengal, Bihar: up to 20 per cent
Karnataka, Andhra Pradesh, Haryana: 30 per cent — 40 per cent
Arunachal Pradesh, Meghalaya, Manipur, Kerala, J and K, UP, MP, Gujarat, Sikkim, Andamans: 40 per cent —— 60 per cent
Nagaland, Mizoram, Tamil Nadu, Rajasthan, Uttarakhand: above 60 per cent.

Source: [NCRB]

Convictions take place only on the cases charge-sheeted. Therefore, it is obvious that those cases which end up with 'closure reports' being filed by the police as 'true but having insufficient evidence' have no chance of a trial and conviction though being true even by police admission. The victims in such cases, which include murder, rape, dacoity, kidnapping and other heinous offences, go without justice and no one cares. If a case was true, why did the

police fail to gather sufficient evidence in it? This is, in simple terms, a failure of the police.

A low conviction rate is the result of tardy and inefficient investigation and prosecution. The state of affairs is such that investigating officers generally lack knowledge of law, procedures and, above all, the skill for investigation in a wide variety of crimes. They are also overburdened. At times, prosecution ends up in acquittal or discharge of the accused partly due to the lack of co-ordination between the investigating officer and the prosecuting officer. Supervisory officers of the police mostly fail to play a role in this regard.

Custodial Violence

Custodial violence and deaths are an unambiguous indicator of police failure and culpability. They are sure signs of the fact that the police have been using extra-legal methods to cover up their failures in investigation. It also shows that citizens are not safe in police hands. Except in a handful of cases in which persons in police custody may die due to medical reasons, custodial deaths always result from assault and torture in custody. There have been 84 deaths in police custody in Assam during the period 2001-10. The comparative figures of custodial death in the States of the North East for same period are: Meghalaya – 17; Arunachal Pradesh – 10; Manipur, Mizoram and Nagaland – two each; Tripura – eight;

The following were the figures of the recorded custodial deaths in the country in 2011:

Of people remanded by the courts - 29,

Of people not remanded by any court – 75,

Lack of proper supervision of the working of police stations by senior officers can be cited as a basic reason for custodial deaths. It would be appropriate to add a provision in the Cr.P.C. to also hold the district superintendent of police accountable for any custodial death in his jurisdiction *– a measure that can secure full accountability in this regard in so far as it is this official who can really keep custodial violence under full check in the present scheme of things in the police.*

Missing Persons

The police approach towards the reports of persons going missing is generally seen to be lukewarm and efforts to rescue them are but perfunctory, unless it concerns some high profile people in the society. As and when a child or a woman abruptly disappears without a trace, it is a matter of great concern for the family and the society at large, because, in such circumstances, he or she is very likely to have become a victim of some serious crime, such as organs trade, child prostitution, bonded labour, human trafficking, murder, etc. But the ground situation is such that the affected people are hardly able to draw the full attention of the police to missing persons.[5] Moreover, no proper procedure is followed by the police in conducting the enquiries in such cases.

All that the police do on receipt of a missing report is to record the gist of it in the General Diary of the Police Station and if anything, the officer-in-charge endorses it in a routine manner to a junior police officer, like an ASI or at

the most an SI of police, for enquiry. The enquiry officer takes his own time to find out the time, place and circumstances of the disappearance of the person or the child concerned and hardly makes an intelligent enquiry to ascertain the victim's whereabouts. There has so far been no established police format for enquiry in a missing case and as a result no record is found maintained of any diligent effort having been made after the receipt of the missing report. As the case becomes old, it is all but forgotten. It is only when a person connected with a so-called VIP goes missing that the top brass of the police get on the job and does all that is possible to find the missing person out. The Supreme Court took a serious view of the prevalent police non-chalance in the matter and has since ordered that a missing case be treated as one of kidnapping and investigated. The police are now obliged to maintain a case diary in a missing case and record the actions taken from time to time to solve it.

Year	*Children untraced from Assam*	
	Girl Child	*Male Child*
2001	269	NA
2002	313	241
2003	244	214
2004	231	224
2005	190	103
2006	285	293
2007	345	274
2008	432	300
2009	394	208
2010	NA	137

Source: [Assam Police]

Complaints against Police

Complaints against the police are a pointer to the quality of policing in a given jurisdiction.

All India – 2007 – 51,767
2011 – 61,765

In 2011, the number of complaints against every 100 policemen in the North-Eastern states was as follows:

Assam – 6
Tripura – 19
Arunachal Pradesh – 115
Mizoram – 4
Nagaland – 8
Manipur – 4
Meghalaya – 2

Complaints against police personnel are a sign of a number of issues; for example, the quality of policing, dissatisfaction of citizens with police corruption, inaction where immediate action is called for, misbehaviour with people going to the police for redress of some grievances or at a public or private place

without any provocation, arbitrariness, violation of human rights, insensitivity to human problems and the like. Of course, some complaints exhibit a sense of straightforward hostility of the complainant towards the police without any appreciation of their problems and limitations. A larger number of complaints against the police in a given state or district does not necessarily mean that the police have not been performing their duties properly. Such a thing could well follow from a pre-conceived attitude and a desire of the complainant to malign the police without sufficient reason. However, any complaint against the police has to be taken seriously and disposed of appropriately, with information about the action taken being given to the complainant. Absolute silence of the authorities to a complaint, however frivolous, causes misgivings. Response must emanate from the authorities and if necessary, be explained. It is relevant to say here that misgivings about the police fritter away co-operation of the people and make the former's task more difficult.

Conclusion

Given the above, it is necessary for the authorities to try to improve the situation. To be fair, we have to say that it is not entirely within the power of the police management to effect the required improvements unless the government extends full support to the department by augmenting its human resources and equipments, including arms, ammunition, vehicles, scientific gadgets, etc. It also requires the provision of heavy incentives to the members of the force by way of compensatory pay, allowances, better housing, health care, facilities for children's education, etc. for putting in not only the hard work but also the extra work necessary for the purpose.

All this requires heavy funding by way of annual investments in the subject of policing. The present system of treating expenditures on the police as non-plan expenditure is a big hurdle. The police budget should be brought under the heading of Plan expenditures. The following remark of Jawaharlal Nehru is apt to be quoted here:

"A strong Army and an efficient Police are likely to do more for India's self-esteem and independence than any result that could possibly emerge from 'planning'. The army and the police provide the background for development because they create the condition in which development is possible."

The police now require 'a perspective plan' for a period of at least ten years in each State for their institutional reconstruction commensurate with the developments taking place in various other spheres in the system. But, at the same time, full accountability must be established at all levels of the police hierarchy for the mandatory duties and responsibilities assigned to them. Any 'failure' or 'negligence' should have penal consequences. It is encouraging to note that the Criminal Law (Amendment) Act 2013 has made the refusal of an officer-in-charge of a police station to record an FIR under section 154 CrPC a punishable offence.

Training of officers and men of the police for necessary skill development has been neglected for far too long, leading to inevitable institutional decay in many States. The training institutions imparting training to various ranks of the police personnel have, in many cases, become repository of rejected officers

designated as trainers. While in the Army, the profile of a successful officer depends much on his successful stints in its training institutions, the practice is reverse in the police. This is a bad omen. Professional training upon which depend the quality of human resources of the police force should have the most brilliant of officers. This aspect should be particularly taken care of.

With astonishing developments taking place today in all fields of human activity, technological wonders taking over social and personal conduct of a whole generation of people and a sharp decline occurring in our value system, the subject of crime management has become tough and unpredictable. Law-breaking in all its subtlety has now turned into a profitable business. Criminals are openly challenging the authority of law. Mafias have become respectable in the society though it is the society which suffers from its activity. Such elements have come to control much of the economy of the country. In such circumstances, it is the police which are expected to take a good deal of guardianship for the society. Unfortunately, policemen are not unaffected by the overall deterioration of the sharply falling social and ethical values. Moreover, they are not looked after well and thus temptation to abuse their authority and power for personal aggrandisement is no less.

It has to be realised by all of us that the arm of law need be nurtured well in order to get it deliver. Health-care, housing, children's education, working hours, recreation, etc. are some of the aspects most neglected in respect of police personnel in the State of Assam and other north-eastern states. It is futile to expect that that they would be humane, caring and of high efficiency in their performances even while living in ghettos, doing unending working hours in most trying conditions and facing a state of general hostility of the people.

No one has cared to take into account the mortality rate of policemen at a relatively early age, the type of ailments they suffer from and the lukewarm medical care they receive. Do the people comprehend what happens to a traffic policeman who keeps standing on the road-crossing for hours on end under the tropical sun, inhaling continuously the exhausts of vehicles without a moment's break? He hardly has a relief because the manpower of the Force is too limited to allow it. An unofficial survey has shown that many of such policemen suffer acutely for waist pain and respiratory diseases even before retirement and certainly after retirement. A non-complaining policeman does not necessarily mean that all is well with him. Though some amount of improvement in the welfare of the police personnel has taken place in recent years, it still has a long way to go to achieve a reasonably good standard comparable to that of their counterparts even in the third world.

Notes

1. The Supreme Court's order for each of the States to enact a Police Act of its own followed from the fact that police matters are a state subject under the Seventh Schedule of the Constitution of India. The 1861 Act was invalidated on another additional ground that it had failed to ensure accountability of the police to law.

2. Even in Assam, there is some basic inertia in the government in taking the newly-enacted police law forward. It is yet to put in place a Manual – the Rules that

should govern the police working – even after five years of its enactment. As a result, the Assam police are still following the old Manual that was framed during the colonial rule under the 1861 Act. This is totally anomalous.

3. The Assam Police do not really have a clue to this situation and proposed to make a thorough study of the factors leading to the development. The State DGP told the press in July 2013 that a reputed research organisation would be commissioned for a study in the matter to identify the real causes for the rise in the crimes against women. [*The Telegraph*, July 18, 2013]

4. The activities of insurgents, Maoists and the like that involve murder, kidnapping, extortion, trafficking in arms, drugs, etc. are nothing but crimes in the eye of law. In that sense, they all are criminals.

5. The discovery in January 2007 of the serial killing of about 30 children, which took place over a period of a year or so at the house of a businessman at Noida (Delhi) and the ham-handed handling of the related kidnapping and murder cases by the police, including their unsympathetic response to the pleadings, from time to time, of the grief-stricken families of the missing children, have been extremely sickening. It was stunningly surprising that the macabre doings of the businessman and his domestic help remained under wraps over such a long time in a high-tech modern city. Obviously, there was not even a semblance of policing in the area. Skeletal remains of many of the murdered children were later recovered from the drains right in front of the slaughter house –the residence of the businessman.

11

Good Governance: Crisis and Challenges

Shyam Bhadra Medhi, IAS (Retd.)

Once I was invited to Kohima (Nagaland) to attend a National Seminar on "Institutional Barriers to Development" in North East India—organised by the Indian Association of Social Sciences Institutions, New Delhi in collaboration with the Nagaland University and Omeo Kumar Das Institute of Social Change, Assam.

I was the first speaker in an assembly of about sixty participants—coming from various parts of India. And I decided to speak on the topic with special reference to *Governance,* for various reasons. Good Governance is not an end in itself: It is a means to an end. The end is Sustainable Development. The question is what is development?

Development is a very complex word and the development process is also equally complex in any country at any point of time. If we look at the paradigm shift in the approach to development we find that in the 1960s it was maximisation of growth. In the 1970s, it was structuralism (rural institutions, ownership, tenure of land— not the market). And in 1980s, we find stress on neo-liberalism—i.e., neo-liberal market-dominated liberation (migration, export-promotion, industrialisation, public sector etc.). In the 1990s, there is again paradigm shift to Human Development — calling for understanding of the interaction of the market and institutional factors in poverty alleviation: The human development approach to development lays emphasis on social sector-—(health, education, housing etc.) in development and recognises that market cannot cater to social sector automatically. The state should therefore use its power to ensure the humanisation of social institutions--particularly the market.

Against this background, we may recall that as early as in 1986 the United Nations adopted the Declaration *of Rights to Development* as enshrined in International instruments. The aim is to have constant, sustainable and symbiotic

improvement of the well-being of the entire population and of all individuals on the basis of their active, free and meaningful participation in the development and in the fair distribution of benefits resulting there from. Development with equity and justice is crucial—as the *Right to Development* is an inalienable human right and equality of opportunity for development is a prerogative both of the regions as well as the individuals who make up the region. It is not yet properly realised by many that human person is the central subject of the development process and that development policy and the process should therefore make the human being the main participant and beneficiary of development.

Our GDP will rise many more times if we divorce our wife and use her as maid servant. But should we do this? Rise in GDP must lead to peace, happiness and good quality of life of all individuals. Economists like Colin Clark, Schumpeter, Amartya Sen and many others talked on development and today most of us are bound to accept the UNOs Millennium Development Goals by 2015 (declared in 2000) for all—with the highest emphasis on poverty alleviation, education and health. The emphasis is again on people's participation, and bottom-up approach, equity and access to justice to all. We have many Reports and recommendations on the development of North-East India (including Assam) by various Committes/Commissions. It is high time to implement at least some of the recommendations in the light of human development approach and to reflect these in our State Human development Index.

Institutions like Government, Private Corporate Sector, Civil Society (Including NGOs), Family, Customary laws etc. help development. And development also helps growing good institutions. There are many countries which are developing even without good institutions. On the contrary, we-have examples to show that good institutions are vital for equitable and sustainable development leading to good quality life. No doubt there are institutional barriers to development: for example customary laws in many tribal areas of NE India are discriminatory against women. And barriers may be natural or artificial. Natural barriers are due to geography, location, history, culture, tradition etc. and artificial barriers are created by persons—owing to obstinacy and inflexibility which are dangerous. To overcome these artificial barriers there is urgency for development of capacity for strategic thinking without forgetting valuable indigenous knowledge and traditions in the society.

Of all the institutions *Governance* is the most important for sustainable development in any society at any point of time. There are ample examples in history. It has been noted after various analysis that governance is more important than resources (natural or imported), and foreign aid. Governance is weaker in poorer and less developed countries. And because of poor governance for more money goes out from poor to rich countries (than the amount of foreign aid received)- due to flight of capital including money laundering and the total capital flight from poor countries amounts to about five per cent of Gross World Production. India's $ 64 billion dollars are lying idle in American treasury earning only 1.5 per cent interest-according to one estimate. Good governance is very vital also for policy performance.

In Hong Kong foreign aid did not help much as in Egypt and Tanzania. Japan has no natural resources but there is good governance. Nigeria has more than two million barrel of oil production but bad governance is reflected in high corruption and police misbehaviour. In the Netherlands–27 per cent people live below the sea level but it is the best country as per UN Human Development Report because of very high quality governance (reflected by elastic decentralisation and politics of accommodation, pragmatism and consensus). In Ghana institution of governance is affected by too much personalise: local government has no power. Life in villages is worse and women have no role. Singapore has the example of very good governance and it has the most respected bureaucracy and judiciary in Asia. Lee Kwan Yew started, "cultural engineering" (1959-1990) to make people skilled and bureaucracy helped effectively in this cultural change as they were responsive to people's needs and corruption stopped. In Singapore there is no natural resource and despite severe racial, religious and political turmoil good governance and discipline led the country to development (per capita income more than $ 30,000) with best programmes in housing, health, education, urban areas. In Jamaica there is democracy with two party systems—but there are criminal gangs: civil servants, police and judiciary lost public faith and we find the worse governance leading the country to a stagnant situation. In Mexico, we find the highest rate of export growth (being the 8th largest exporter in the world) but there is no good governance. There is no reform of civil service, judiciary and Law and benefits of Globalisation are not achieved. On the other hand Spain has a true civil service and there are good regulatory practices. Spain publishes Annual Progress Report on Governance. Good Governance is also reflected in willingness to reform in various critical areas.

Good Governance is the most important institution or factor for development in any country. Insurgency and demographic transformation problems of various areas can also be solved with good governance.

In fact good governance is needed not only for public sector but also for private sector and civil society (including the NGOs or EGOs). Today corporate good governance is a very important subject in all countries and various measures have been attempted for corporate good governance by national authorities. Abraham Lincoln, the American President stated as early as in 1860 the importance of role of government and sound government institutions to support changes and to implement policies.

Institutions local, national, international are ways of doing things. In any country we have various institutions; social, economic, political, spiritual etc. But of all the institutions governance is the most important for various reasons as noted in the history of almost all countries. According to dictionary meaning the word 'Governance' means government, control, direction, and behaviour. Of all the four wings of the government viz., legislature, judiciary, executive and the army, legislatures have a bigger role to play for good governance. The "Hand Book for Parliamentarians and Policies" (published in April, 2001 by the World Bank and IMF), which was based on discussions among 351 parliamentarians from 18 countries underlined several contributions legislatures

could make for development and poverty alleviations and it was noted that legislatures played a relatively minor role in development process in many countries espcially in African countries. The UNDP claimed in its Poverty Report 2000, "If responsive and accountable institutions of governance are often the missing links between anti-poverty efforts and poverty reduction ... stronger legislative institutions may contribute to its solution" by playing crucial role in budgetary process and implementation.

Judiciary helps good governance: In India the Supreme Court (SC) directed states to identify BPL families by January 2002. There was also direction from SC to Election Commission on certain matters. The State and the National Law Commission have a crucial role to play as India is losing about two per cent of economic growth per year in view of man-hours lost in litigation proceedings. It has been noted that the rule of law has been intentionally subordinated to institutional goals and political values even in USA. Sen, the Nobel Laureate, has rightly said that even market economy relies on good Laws/Acts and proper regulatory control. The media reported that in India there are 150 judges with kin in the same court as lawyers. The role of the *Lok Adalats* and the Legal Services Authorities are important for good governance. The reported nexus between magistrate and lawyer in Ahmedabad for issuing warrant against the President and Chief Justice of India is a matter of concern for good governance.

The role of Governor as the representative of the President and as head of the State polity is important and it is not clear what is the recommendation of the Constitution Review Panel in this regard. The institution of Governor can also help to achieve the findings of the BRIC report (of Goldman Sachs) published recently that around 2040 India will be the World's Third richest country in GDP terms after China and USA.

The country will develop if all states develop simultaneously. The Assam Human Development Report--2003 indicates that we have a long way to go to catch up with other parts of the country although during 1988-89 and 2002-03 the Centre released over Rs 44,000 crore for NE States. The Central Sector programmes and Centre-State ties are getting complicated. The CAG Reports give us confusing pictures and it appears state level reforms are poor in many NE States.

The executives; the civil servants affect good governance. Today we are talking of transparency, accountability, efficiency, responsiveness, fairness, participation, citizen friendliness, quality in government and electronic delivery of services etc. Many high-level commissions were set up for civil service or administrative reforms e.g., Morarji Desai, Sathanam, S. Nath etc. Commissions and Committees. And the latest is the P. C. Hota Committee. We are improving but we have many more miles to go. It was reported that our government employees work only 164 days out of 365 days whereas in Saudi Arabia employees get only two and half hour holiday on the demise of their monarch. We have many disturbing news: ULFA opposes FDI in Assam, Assam spending Rs. 30 lakh per day to control insurgency etc. The executives are to be more serious on issues like border management, project management-planning, implementation, monitoring, evaluation, corrective action etc. with a highly

professional approach to have good governance. The executives have all the powers to do or undo a thing. If they undo they are dangerous. Albert Einstein rightly said, "The World is dangerous place to live, not because of the dangerous people – but because of the people who do not do anything about it". The executives are to handle many critical areas—such as, formulation of plans, correct rapport with North-Eastern Council, MP and MLAs, Finance Ministry, Planning Commission and DONER at New Delhi, expenditure of fund from Budget (or outside the Budget as alleged in the media), time-bound fiscal reforms programmes, local area development fund, use of NGOs etc. Will some of the executives having a negative mind-set? See in history how individuals, companies and countries have risen from ashes?

Most of us have forgotten the famous lines of Gandhiji "Politics without principles, wealth without work, enjoyment without conscience, knowledge without character, business without morality, science without humanity and religion without sacrifice. "Many of the executives would benefit in their life if they remember the lines of Albert Einstein. "Only the insane can expect radically different outcomes by doing the same thing over and over again." Good governance requires good government and government depends both on state structures as well as political parties. No doubt there is urgent need to improve the way political parties work and of course we need a parliament that is proactive, not simply reactive and we need leaders made strong by vision, sustained by ethics, and revealed by political courage that looks beyond the coming or next election: but a heavy duty rests on the people who executes as they are like the cooks in a kitchen.

By government we mean the machinery and institutional arrangements of exercising the power authority and by governance we mean the process and the result of making decisions for the benefit of all. The term Governance indicates; values, ideologies and policies by which a society manages or executes its affairs through state, the private sector and civil society.

We have good governance when the governments, Private Sector, NGOs, and Cooperatives etc. serve the people by protecting and promoting their human rights. Good governance has been defined differently in terms of means, and in terms of goals which are often left to democratic choice and sometimes to predetermined goals. For good governance we talk about all types of reforms; political, judicial, administrative, institutions and human etc. And good governance at cutting-edge level is very important for us today.

Good governance is a dynamic concept changing with various factors and as such it needs remodelling from time to time. There is also relationship between good governance, political stability and cultural diversity. The talk of good governance started from ancient times from the days of Kautilya, the Moghuls and the British days till today. At all times, we notice that for good governance there should be rule of law, accountability, honesty, right judiciary, concern for human rights, equity and fair distribution of benefits, people's participation, responsiveness, sensitivity and a sharing and caring mind-set of the people who govern. Happiness for all— *Sarve Bhavantu Sukhinah* is Indians age-old philosophy for rulers and kings from ancient times — as reflected

in the *Mahabharata*, Manusmiriti and Arthasashtra etc. The aim of good governance is happiness and welfare of the citizens. And this aim is attempted in almost all countries of the world today.

We have challenges as good governance is in crisis for many areas. For this we need government to be reinvented and this would need ethical consistency and flexibility at various levels. However, change appears to be difficult as—Machiavelli stated; "there is nothing more difficult to take in hand, more perilous to conduct, more uncertain in its success than to take the lead, in the introduction of a new order of things". Can we not be optimistic and have a positive mind-set and a strong will.

Often we talk of God's governance. Scientists have concluded that behind apparent chaotic systems there is a majestic pattern of order, a majestic interrelationship of life. If we accept that there is a pattern, a Governance, an order and a direction in life—we may realise the coherency in the governance of God. Let us think about the meaning of the few lines of philosopher—poet Robert Browning in his poem "Paracelsus" as noted below—

> "Truth is within ourselves; it takes no rise,
> From outward things, whatever you may believe.
> There is an inmost centre in us all,
> Where truth abides in fullness; and around,
> Wall upon wall, the gross flesh hems it in,
> This perfect, clear conception which is truth."

12

Yes Minister

Hilary Pais IAS (Retd.)

As India is said to follow the Westminster type of government let us start by looking at how it runs in the United Kingdom. That also suits my title which has been lifted from the popular satirical sitcom of the eighties on the BBC.

The first-person to acknowledge the need for a defined regime governing the conduct of civil servants was the Irishman Edmund Burke the outstanding political philosopher and parliamentarian of 18th century. Burke laid down the fundamental requirements in a civil servant as;

- Integrity,
- Honesty, and
- Objectivity and Impartiality–including political impartiality.

Burke's fundamentals remain unaltered to this day. En route there have been changes on the periphery to keep up with the times. Notable among them are contribution of scholars T.H. Green and Haldane. The Northcote—Trevelyan recommendations in 1854, brought about a civil service appointed on merit through open competition. The prescriptions governing the interaction between civil servants and politicians in office have now been codified. The latest edition of the code that was published in June 2006 contains an item that is particularly relevant to our discussion. That is; if a civil servant believes that that he/she is being asked to behave in a way which conflicts with the code, he/she may now report the matter direct to the Civil Service Commissioners. It is now clearly specified that the code is part of the contractual relationship between the civil servant and his/her employer. Just as there is a quote for civil servants there is a code of conduct for ministers.

So far we have dealt with the civil service and politicians generally. In this paper we are interested in the relations between ministers and senior civil servants. That item found clear expression in the proceedings before a recent committee of the House of Lords that was going specifically into the subject. I quote from the proceedings.

"The civil service possesses a number of means by which it can help to ensure the constitutional propriety of government actions. Ministers cannot require civil servants to act in a manner which is illegal. Similarly, the Ministerial Code contains a requirement that ministers must not ask civil servants to act in any way which would conflict with the Civil Service Code or the requirements of the Constitutional Reform and Governance Act 2010. The Ministerial Code places a duty on ministers to give fair consideration and due weight to inform and impartial advice from civil servants, and civil servants in turn are under an obligation to provide ministers with impartial, honest and objective advice, including on matters of constitutional propriety.

Where a minister declines to follow civil service advice, and decides to proceed in an unconstitutional manner (which, under the UK's uncodified constitution, may not necessarily amount to an illegal manner), the position was set out by Lord Wilson of Dinton:

"If [civil servants] think the Minister is behaving in an unconstitutional manner, it is their job to make very clear what they believe the constitutional position is ... If ... they do not get an answer that they think is the proper answer or that is defensible, it is their job to go to the head of the civil service, who would take it up with the Prime Minister if necessary ... If a Minister, in the end, rejects the advice, and if the Prime Minister rejects the advice and insists on going ahead, then in grey areas it is the job of Ministers to decide where the line should be, and there is a limit to how far the civil service can enforce the constitution, except in the ultimate, nuclear deterrent of resigning. Therefore, under the current arrangement civil servants are ultimately unable to prevent ministers from breaching constitutional norms. Indeed, an attempt by civil servants to resist enacting a ministerial decision which they considered to be unconstitutional, but which was taken after following the correct process, would be a breach of the Civil Service Code."

Let us see how things are done in the United States. In fact, the United States does not have a problem between civil servants and ministers simply because in that country there are no senior civil servants and there are no ministers.

The American Constitution is based on clear separation of powers between the executive, the legislature and the judiciary. Persons who head departments in the federal government are appointees of the President. They are not civil servants and they cannot be members of the Congress. In the states, the heads of department are appointed by the Governor in a similar manner. Just as you do not have a civil service you do not have a police service. The Attorney General and his deputies are appointees of the president. In the states, the attorneys general are elected as are the chief secretaries in most of the states. The case of James Comey, who has been selected by President Obama to be Director of the FBI, will illustrate this. Comey has varied experience including federal attorney, and hedge fund manager. Currently, Comey teaches law at the Columbia Law school. He is not a policeman. George H. W. Bush who went on to become the 41st President of the United States was appointed by President Gerald Ford as director of the CIA between 1975 and 1977. Prior to his

appointment, he was chairman of the National Republican Committee. It will hurt some egos, but the US experience shows that for a large country, it is not imperative to have the kind of service like the Indian administrative and police. The President's appointees come and go with the President. Often they leave mid-term to do some other job. The American practice and experience is important but not of practical use to us on the present subject. The British system because of the supremacy of the Parliament is heavily weighted in favour of the minister. In reality however the situation in Britain is far different and that is not because of the civil service code or the ministerial code. It is because the process of arriving at policy decisions has become increasingly transparent. Any disagreement in principle between senior civil servants and ministers cannot be shielded from the public. If the minister is bent upon doing something that is improper, that soon becomes public knowledge and the minister would have to go.

Let us look at the position in India. There are long-standing and well-established civil service conduct rules which apply to senior civil servants. There is no code of conduct for ministers. Nevertheless civil servants and ministers in India have been working together for over sixty years and we have to assume that there is a practice in place that has not been codified. The absence of a formal system however makes evaluation difficult. We therefore have to take alternative routes. Indian conditions differ from that of Britain fundamentally because we have a written Constitution that was made by the people through their representatives. The Constitution prescribes in detail the manner in which government will be constituted. It also prescribes the powers and functions of the government. What can be seen very clearly is that the government is essentially a delivery system set up by the people through their Constitution to deliver a series of services that are essential to the well-being of the society. That includes maintaining law and order, maintaining the territorial integrity of the Republic and performing those other activities that advance the well-being of society. It is the people who pay the government to perform all these activities that they have prescribed by raising taxes and also through monies borrowed in peoples' name. In simple words, the so-called public debt of the Republic is the people's debt. Therefore, to judge whether the civil service and minister system is working efficiently or otherwise, we have to see if the objectives for which the people have created the government have been achieved optimally. We cannot measure functions like maintenance of law order and the function of maintaining the security of the country, objectively. But in today's conditions there are well-established ways through which we can evaluate whether the development and well-being of the people that they have financed and entrusted the executive to perform are working at full efficiency. Objectivity is ensured by having United Nations agencies to do the survey and evaluation.

The United Nations Development Programme uses a multi-dimensional poverty index developed by the Oxford University to measure the human development index. The UNDP study covering the period between 1999 and 2006 found that while India had made some progress in reducing poverty

during those years, the rate at which this was done—1.2 per cent per year, was one 3rd of the speed of its poorer neighbours Nepal—4.1 per cent and Bangladesh 3.2 per cent. Unfortunately, we do not have a comparison for the subsequent years because India failed to send the necessary data to the UNDP. The report clearly shows that in real terms, the resources earmarked for development programmes for the poor people in India are being taken away by those in the administration, both politicians and officials. As compared to Nepal and Bangladesh which are known to be corrupt, we are more corrupt. It also shows that the civil servant—politician relationship is working harmoniously for the betterment of both these categories at the cost of the public welfare.

People are not getting their worth. Politicians and civil servants are making more than they are worth.

I have been away from Assam for quite some time and in the absence of direct knowledge I will not make any comment. I spend quite some time in Bangalore and while I am not there I track important events on the net. Justice Venkatachala was the Lokayukta from 2002 to 2007. He came to the conclusion that Karnataka was the most corrupt state in India. He was succeeded by Justice Santosh Hegde. Close to the end of his tenure Hegde said that finding an honest officer in Karnataka was like finding a needle in a haystack. It is the same condition with the politicians.

People who had very little or nothing thirty years ago are today bursting with wealth. The sum of their earnings in their political office will only be a small fraction of their total possessions. On quite a few occasions the Lokayukta has raided senior officials and found them with property grossly disproportionate to their earnings. The list of properties displayed by the Lokayukta is amazing. Three houses, four building sites, three commercial properties, two agriculture farms, three SUVs is a sample list. Despite all this, the Lokayukta has not succeeded in prosecuting a single officer whose premises he had raided. In most cases government refuses to sanction prosecution. Civil servants and ministers extend perfect protection to each other. People spend a lot of money in sustaining the Lokayukta machinery. In return they get nothing. There is not a single senior civil servant in jail for corruption. In a sense the civil servant and the politician in India are in perfect sync. There are no complaints from either side. So we can say that whatever the system that governs the relations between the two, that system is working perfectly for both. Unfortunately, it is not working for the people. That is why you have a score of 1.2 while Nepal has 4.1 and Bangladesh scores 3.2. So, we can say that the relationship between the civil servant and the politician is working beautifully but it is not working for the people. That is not how it was meant to be.

Let us get back to the early days of independence when India's Constitution was being worked out. There was a lot of discussion in the Constituent Assembly and outside among politicians whether India should have All India Services namely the Indian Administrative Service and the Indian Police Service. The majority of politicians did not want the All India Services. They said the provincial service would suit them better. It was only Sardar

Vallabhbhai Patel who wanted the All India Services and saw to it that they were included in the Constitution. The Sardar had good reasons for doing so. The first was that he wanted the All India Services to be a prime instrument in holding the country together. Apart from Jammu and Kashmir there were problems in Travancore, Hyderabad and in Manipur. With the IAS and the IPS with roughly half the number of officers coming from the rest of India, the Sardar thought that he could hold the Union together. Important as this reason is, it is the second reason that is of interest to our subject.

The Sardar thought that the IAS and the IPS would hold the politicians in check. Do not be surprised by this statement. Within months of politicians coming to power in the provinces in 1937, congressmen complained to Mahatma Gandhi about corruption indulged in by their colleagues. There were complaints from the Punjab, The United Provinces and Bihar. Gandhi writes about this in the *Harijan*. He handed over those complaints to Sardar Patel. The Sardar thought that the IAS and the IPS officers would act as a check on political corruption. The Sardar was familiar with Edmund Burke's core values for civil servants and assumed that we would have them. Unfortunately, for the people of this country, that was not to be.

What could be the reason for this state of affairs? I remember what we were told at the National Academy of Administration. The minister is the boss the civil servant is the servant. It is your duty to advise the minister. If the minister accepts your advice and makes a decision accordingly, good for you. It is your duty to see that the decision is implemented. If the minister disregards your advice and takes a decision, it is your duty to accept that decision and implement it. You will see that there is a basic flaw here that assumes a master - servant or a superior - subordinate situation. That is more in line with the British system. In India, the minister and the civil servant are both public servants. The people are the Masters. The point that the minister represents the people is often overdone. If we analyse the election pattern of voting, you will find that under our system the winning candidate gets about thirty per cent of the total number of voters in his constituency. Very often it is much less. For the victor when he gets into office, his priority is to hold on to that number in his electorate and all his subsequent actions are tuned to achieving that objective. Except in rare cases, he or she would work primarily to consolidate his hold on his people. That means giving them the most benefits. That also means attempting to keep the rest sixty or seventy per cent away from the benefits that are due to them according to law. You see this happening throughout India all the time. The minister's followers and their *chamchas* or *chelas* get the plum while the rest get the leftovers. And it is here that the civil servant has to come in. It is the duty of the civil servant in accordance with law to see that all people in his jurisdiction get their due irrespective of their political affiliation. On the macro-level things are worse. During the last 20 years vast chunks of the nation's mineral resources and spectrum were given away to cronies at sub optimal values with senior civil servants assisting and conniving with politicians. Matters came to light not because of any civil service activity but because of the Comptroller and Auditor General's audit. A kind of a reluctant

investigation is going on only because the Supreme Court is monitoring some cases. With capital rushing in to fill the gap between the sub-optimal and the market, the pyrrhic jump in market capitalisation that followed was hailed as economic growth by successive governments. That growth has now evaporated and it is now back to basics.

So, we come to the question to which the National Academy of Administration did not provide an answer. What is the civil servant to do when the minister orders him to perform something that is illegal or is contrary to law? It is the duty of the civil servant in that situation to refuse to carry out the illegal orders of the minister. What if the minister goes ahead and issues the order? The civil servant cannot go public. I do not think that taking the matter to the Cabinet Secretary or to the Chief Secretary would help. That might work in England. India is a different kettle of fish. The only way open to the civil servant in such a case is to quit. However, bad or dishonest the government may be, a civil servant cannot be permitted go public with his views. He can do so freely after he quits. It would help if officers with ten years of service are able to collect a pension and leave. The next Pay Commission may consider making that recommendation. There are other factors that have a bearing on the subject but for want of space we cannot discuss in detail. The first is the pay of civil servants. Things have changed in India and today in the private sector persons of comparable talent and ability are paid many times the emoluments that are paid to civil servants. The reality is that it will not be possible for the government to do anything in this matter. The huge work force that is present in our governments and which is called grade four, makes it impossible to have any major upward revision of emoluments.

The country just cannot bear the financial burden. In that context I find the euphoria that surrounds new entrants to the administrative and other services a tragicomedy. The fact is that with the kind of pay that the government can afford, the honest officer lives and retires poor. New entrants to service must know this and they must be told about it very clearly at the Academy. Competing talent outside government commands a much higher price. Becoming corrupt does not solve the problem. Rather it creates one for everyone. Serving the community has become a myth.

Or else, our performance would not have been rated below that of Nepal and Bangladesh.

13

What Ails Delivery System in India

Barada Charan Sarma IAS (Retd.)

A sound delivery system, which denotes any means or process for conveying a product or service to a recipient, is the hallmark of good governance. All modern societies throughout the world, imbued with the ideals of democracy, human rights and dignity, strive to achieve all round uplift and welfare of the people through an efficient delivery system. India is wedded to the lofty ideals of equality, equal opportunity and socio-political justice. It aims to achieve the targets of inclusive growth, millennium development goals, creation of a sound base of human capital with knowledge-based education, and empowerment of people through various measures of social security, enhancement of productivity and poverty reduction. For achievement of all these laudable goals, the setting up of a sound system of delivery of products and services *is sine qua non.*

In the last sixty five years after independence, India has made significant progress in many ways. After facing a catastrophic famine just a few years before independence, India is now surplus in food production, thanks to our industrious farmers and the technology of Green Revolution. The total food grains production has now exceeded 259 million MT which has enabled India to be in a position to provide food security to the people so that no one remains hungry. While the population has tripled, food production has quadrupled. Milk production has- turned into a White Revolution and the Blue Revolution is not very far either. Democracy is firmly entrenched in its soil, with, of course, some avoidable infirmities. People have become, to a great extent, participatory in development work. Today, the country has a huge reservoir of technically qualified personnel. The rapid developments in medical care have attracted even foreign patients from many countries. In information technology, India is one of the world leaders. In social welfare and justice with equity rapid strides have been made.

Despite the above multi-dimensional progress, India is still spectacularly lagging behind in several spheres. The Green Revolution has been patchy. Agriculture is still remains largely a gamble in rain. In Assam particularly, the regular visitation by floods a number of times every year causes widespread destruction of crops, dwelling houses, food barns, domestic and wild animals and rail and road infrastructure, causing misery to many. More than 30 per cent of the population of the country still lives below the poverty line, as measured by the intake of calories and purchasing power parity method. If the multi-dimensional poverty index, developed in the UN Human Development Report is applied, many more will be included among the poor. Human Development reports of the United Nations indicate that India occupies a ranking of 136 in the list of nations towards the end.

If we aspire to be one of the leading nations of the world, it is incumbent on us to have good governance in the country. Without the identification of some normative principles, it is difficult to understand the concept of good governance. Prof Paul De Waart included the principles of democratic decision-making, adequate governance, transparency, accountability, sensible economic and social policy measures to combat corruption, effective rule of law, and creation of a market-friendly environment and respect for human rights. The United Nations Special Agency, OECD, in 2001 identified eight major characteristics, namely, being participatory, consensus oriented, accountable, transparent, responsive, effective and efficient, equitable, inclusive, conforming to the rule of law and minimisation of corruption. A sound delivery system is possible only in good governance; or, when, at least, some of the important characteristics mentioned above exist.

One of the conditions, which are inevitable, is a government that is corruption free or one in which corruption is controlled. It is to be noted that in the past, mighty empires like the Roman and the Ottoman collapsed for reasons, one of which was the weight of widespread corruption. It is saddening that India has emerged as one of the-most corrupt countries of the world. In the Corruption Perception Index released in 2012 by the Transparency International India ranked 94th, out of 176 countries. Corruption has eaten into almost every organ of our country; it is a serious threat to our democracy and, in fact, to the humanity. In a democracy it would be ideal if the citizens are enabled to access all the rights and facilities made available. Unfortunately, it is not so in India. As a result, only a privileged few enjoy the rights and perquisites depriving the teeming millions. The benefits of the various plans and schemes do not percolate down to the desired target population.

According to a report by a prestigious consulting firm in Hong Kong, Indian bureaucracy enjoys "terrific" powers and this could be one of the main reasons for the negative perception of the average Indian and the foreign investors about the bureaucrats. They are rarely held accountable for wrong decisions. Efficiency-wise, India, according to the report, fared worse than Singapore, Hong Kong, Thailand, South Korea, Japan, Malaysia, Taiwan, Vietnam, China, Philippines and Indonesia.

Exercise of considerable powers without accountability and transparency as well as wide spread corruption are mainly the reasons for the inefficient delivery system in government and its agencies, be it delivery of service or of product. The parastatal organisations and the corporate world, barring some exceptions, are no different either.

India is predominantly an agricultural country. Agriculture is the main-stay of about 70 per cent of India's population providing for 58 per cent of its employment. The need of the hour is to do scientific and intensive farming in agriculture and allied sectors to enhance their output growth. For that delivery of inputs, namely, quality seeds, fertilizer, credit, irrigation facility and provision of extension services, training and field level supervision by experts are essential. Unfortunately, delivery of products and services are not either sufficient or timely. Then again, the ubiquitous leakage of money and material, illegally benefitting the corrupt officials and middlemen contribute to the malaise of input supply. Sometimes the targetted farmers for the supply of inputs are not correctly enlisted. There was a report a few years ago that in a Block office, a farmer, unwilling to lift a quantity of fertilizer was forced to accept it so that the target fixed for the Block for fertilizer distribution could be met. The farmer dumped the contents of the packet in a river on his way back home. Such thoughtless product delivery is harmful in ways more than one.

Let us now look at our Public Distribution System of food grains. The system is a result of a very laudable scheme aimed at feeding the hungry by providing food grains at nominal prices. The procurement and delivery of products in the huge network of distribution spread over the country is the responsibility of an elephantine government organisation, called The Food Corporation of India. The Corporation is frequently in the news for wrong reasons. Large quantities of food grains are wasted in storage and distribution. Sometimes grains of sub-standard quality, unfit for human consumption, are supplied to fair price shops. The supply of food grains is erratic in quality, quantity and time. On the whole, the operations of the Corporation are marked more by inefficiency and corruption than by a sound delivery system.

It would not be out of place to describe the performance of the self-governing bodies like Municipalities and Panchayats. It is true that a number of them are doing exemplary work in their respective fields; but majority of these institutions are inefficient and corrupt. The residents of a municipality pay taxes for providing municipal services, namely, water supply, sanitation and hygiene, facility of good roads and street lighting. They elect people's representatives to these bodies in the hope that the elected persons would be able to understand the problems and aspirations of the locality and take measures so that the citizens would be able to enjoy the rights and amenities granted to them by the Constitution. The Supreme Court of India has also interpreted Article 21 of the Constitution in a liberal manner giving a wide sweep of the right to life. Now right to life does not connote mere animal existence or continued drudgery but includes, *inter alia*, better standard of living and hygienic condition in the habitat and the work place. In other words, every person is entitled to a quality of life consistent with human dignity and personality.

But have our municipalities delivered services efficiently and effectively and thus discharged their statutory duties and obligations? The answer is an emphatic no. In the capital city of Guwahati, which is the gateway to the North East, regular water supply is still a far cry; consequently, every household is compelled to have an improvised water supply of its own. The stinking heaps of garbage by the roadside in most of the areas would put any visitor from outside to shame. Sewerage system is a term not found in the dictionary of the municipality. The city floats on sewage water. It is perhaps divine mercy that an epidemic has not yet broken out in the city. On the whole, public welfare is not in the priority of things of the municipal body. Here is an instance of denial and, not delay in delivery of service.

In the sphere of Land and Land Revenue administration, the least said about service delivery, the better. Whether it is a matter of payment of land revenue, mutation of record of rights, demarcation of land boundary or issue of *patta*, there is inordinate delay. Service delivery takes place only when palms are greased at some levels. As a young SDO of Serampore in West Bengal, I had once a strange complaint from a retired officer. He wanted to pay land revenue to the *Mouzadar* (called *Tahsildar* there) but the latter refused to accept it unless bribed. The *Mouzadar* was trapped by the police while accepting a bribe of a ten rupees note on which I signed inconspicuously. He was, after court trial, convicted and sentenced to five years rigorous imprisonment. The receipt of revenue is hardly any service and even that was refused by a public servant to a senior citizen.

The Serampore incident is not the only one happening around us. In whichever direction we see, such instances are galore, whether it is health-care, police, power supply, education, PDS of food grains, and what not. Media is rife with many instances of refusal, by the police, of accepting FIRS filed by the victims of rape, sexual assault and intimidation. Sometimes the victims are assaulted, insulted and driven out of police station. Needless to say, there are statutory legal provisions and court judgements which cast obligation on the police to provide prompt service to the victims and take up speedy investigation in such cases. It is sad that even such service to the hapless victims are not delivered but denied. Then again, instances are not rare, in which dying patients are denied admission even in well known hospitals on some pretext or the other though the doctor concerned is legally bound to provide speedy medical service to the patient.

In the corporate world as well delayed delivery of products and services sometimes takes place. Some non-banking financial institutions and insurance companies are particularly known in this regard.

Last but not the least; we may now discuss the service of delivery of justice in the country. The first thing that needs to be generally realised is that the delivery of justice is not the responsibility of the judiciary alone; the legislature, and, mostly the executive with its wide spread network of authority are equally responsible for dispensation of justice to the people. The doctrine of obligation of administrative authorities has been evolved to ensure rule of law and to prevent failure of justice. Unfortunately, as in the judicial system, it

is the rich, powerful and influential people that mostly get justice from administration rather quickly; the average man, poor and backward, have to run from pillar to post to get justice even in simple matters of day to administration. Mention may be made of, as few examples, getting assistance in agriculture, electricity, water and telephone connection or reply to a petition or application. As for legislature, the orderly and timely transaction of business, demonstration of good conduct in the House and flawless enactment of laws will deliver legislative justice to the people. It is observed that for reasons of political interest of a ruling party, sometimes laws are passed which are not in consonance with the ideals of equality. The passing of the IMDT Act with peculiar provisions, which apply only in Assam, instead of the Foreigner's Act is a case in point. The Act was resented by the indigenous people and after prolonged litigation; it was struck down by the Supreme Court as being unconstitutional.

As regards delay in the service of dispensation of criminal and civil justice by courts, Justice (Retd.) V. R. Krishna Iyre once observed: "Man lives in short run, but litigation lives in the long run." He further lamented the delay in justice delivery by describing the situation as the "Himalayan arrears of court cases, The Ganga flow of perennial forensic process, lucratively long lawyerly submissions and judgements jejune, delayed or undelivered." Justice delayed is justice denied. The system of justice dispensation becomes a mockery if it is delayed and long drawn out meting out an unfair and unjust treatment to all concerned. If the criminals remain unpunished for long, more and more persons will be encouraged to take to crimes, thus making the law abiding persons helpless.

It is imperative that every effort is made to improve our delivery system at all levels and in all the organs of the State as well as in the private sector. For this a thorough analysis of the malaise is required to be made. As regards the executive and its agencies, several measures like accountability, transparency, regular inspection and monitoring, review of performance and penalty for non-performance are required to be enforced. *E*-governance and networking of departments, strict enforcement of discipline and incentives for good performance are some of the other measures which will improve work culture and consequently the delivery system. Corruption will have to be controlled by quickly punishing the guilty and giving publicity to such action. The unholy nexus of politician-bureaucrat-businessman will have to be snapped.

In the USA the Administrative Procedure Act describes the procedure to be followed by the administrative authorities in deciding specified matters. This enforces accountability. The enactment of the Assam Administrative Procedure Act has been a step in the right direction. But mere enactment of the Act will not be of much use unless effective steps are taken for its strict enforcement.

Training has an important role in improving administrative knowledge and efficiency. There should be regular and compulsory training, both in service and pre-service, of all officers and staff. Lack of knowledge and confidence of the employees are one of the important reasons for delay in delivery. This is

true of the personnel of both the government and the private sectors. An officer or an employee should be made answerable for delay in disposal of cases without any justifiable cause. Along with these, enforcement of discipline is a must as an indisciplined worker cannot be productive. Of course there remains the curse of corruption. Gandhiji said, rectify one angle of a square and the other angles will be automatically correct. If corruption is controlled, if not eliminated, administrative efficiency and public service will improve which will generate confidence of the people in administration. If the government has the will, corruption can be controlled by giving more teeth, including statutory powers, to the anti-corruption and vigilance organisations. But it has not happened. The recent observations of the Supreme Court about government interference in CBI investigation in coalgate scam are a shocking example of attempt at shielding the allegedly corrupt at high levels.

As regards delay in dispensation of court justice, the Prime minister in 2009 observed that India has to suffer the scourge of the world's largest backlog of cases and timelines which surprise globally and cause concern at home. Various measures suggested to liquidate arrears in cases have given marginal results only. In India the conviction rate of heinous crimes is barely six per cent which speaks volumes about quality of investigation and prosecution of cases and delivery of service. The unabated number of incidents of rape and other serious crimes against women in the country may be attributed to a considerable extent to poor conviction of the accused in cases tried.

While the steps necessary to weed out arrears in court cannot be discussed here in detail, a few practical suggestions may be considered. The procedural laws, namely, the Civil Procedure Code and the Criminal Procedure Code are "complicated and cumbersome" and thus they aggravate arrears, as stated by Justice (retd.) V. R. Krishna Iyer. He stated that there are three or four courts one above the other in the hierarchy which prolongs litigation. Such number of courts should be suitably reduced. There should be restrictions on grant of adjournments of cases. In this respect the role of the legal fraternity is very crucial. While it is true that a lawyer is required for many reasons to pray for adjournment of hearing, it should the endeavour of all advocates to ask for the minimum number of adjournments and they should come prepared to the court accordingly. Courts should be vigilant in this regard. The legal fraternity should be able to bear some accountability for speedy dispensation of justice. The Supreme Court in Salem Advocate Bar Association case quoted the Civil Procedure, Alternative Dispute Resolution and Mediation Rules, 2003 and Model Case Flow Management Rules for expedition in justice delivery and dispute resolution. Many cases can be disposed of by mutual consent. In a good number of cases court can avoid adjudicating the case by adjourning it to a later date and encourage parties to work out a settle on their own.

Access to justice will remain a far cry unless the judiciary is competent, accountable and independent and the legal profession acquires knowledge of law and sympathetic to the litigant. It is also necessary to ensure transparency and legitimacy of the procedure for appointment of judges.

In conclusion India has no alternative but to enhance the quality, efficiency and efficacy of the delivery system in all spheres if democracy has to survive. For this some bold and innovative reforms are needed. The seeds of ideas for such reform can be found in the strength and weakness of our existing systems. If this is done, the delivery system of the coming days is expected to be more open, effective, efficient and equitable ensuring thereby transition of our country to a progressive, egalitarian and a modern democracy.

14

The Menace of Corruption in Democratic India: Cause, Effect and Solution

V. Ramakrishan, I.A.S. (Retd.)

Corruption as described by Shumaker and Longsdorf is an act done with intent to give some advantage inconsistent with official duty and the rights of others. It includes bribery but is more comprehensive because an act may be corruptly done, though the advantage to be derived from it may be offered by another.

1. As per the law seeking to prevent corruption by public servants, the term refers to a wrongful design to acquire or cause some pecuniary or other advantage. Corruption may encompass a variety of wrongful acts, such as, among others, bribes, kickback, and abuse of public office. Section 123 of 'The Representation of the People Act' deals with corrupt practices which include (a) bribery (b) undue influence, (c) attempt to influence voting through religious and other extraneous appeals, (d) promotion of feelings of enmity or hatred among different classes of citizens on grounds of religion, race, caste, community or language (e) making of deliberate false statements regarding the personal character of any candidate, (f) incurring or authorising expenditure beyond the permissible limit etc. It is thus clear corruption is not only restricted to bribery by way of cash or other gifts. Importantly it includes, among other things, misuse of power.

2. Corruption can take myriad forms. For this article, we may classify corruption into two broad categories pertaining to:

(a) The interaction of ordinary citizen with the official machinery for meeting his needs. The citizen has to be in touch with the various public authorities in day to day life e.g. police, RTO, supply officials, Sub-registrar etc. The police play a crucial role in maintaining public order and in prevention and detection

of crimes. They have been vested by law with substantial powers in order to discharge their duties. In the context of their educational background, inadequate training and the vulnerability of the citizens who may be poor and not aware of their rights and duties, the scope of misuse of power is very high in this sector. In the case of the RTO, an RTO issues driving licenses, certificate of road worthiness of vehicles and so on. Quite often it is subjective and licenses and certificates can be obtained through illegal gratification even in undeserving cases. The Sub-registrar deals with registration of landed property, power of attorney etc., which are of high value. Some of them expect their palms to be greased. Otherwise they will follow dilatory tactics.

(b) High level corruption, where the powerful persons in authority misuse their position; this may take the form of looting of public exchequer e.g., (i) Diversion of development funds for private gains (ii) Sale of patronage such as grant of nation's resources (mines, spectrum, etc.) to a favoured few without following any fair and just principles (iii) Plain extortion as in the case of an entrepreneur who has incurred enormous expenditure on a project being refused necessary clearances to complete the project unless he meets the illegal demands of the authorities.

3. The reasons why corruption thrives in democratic India are many. However, we may pinpoint the unfettered discretion and lack of transparency on the part of some public servants in cases where they constitute the cutting edge for meeting the citizen's needs. To illustrate, an investigating officer of the police who may be of a very junior rank, can detain any person for a period of 24 hours under the law. This power is expected under law to be exercised in cases where the accused deserves such treatment. But in practice this is done to settle personal scores and quite often at the behest of the political executive and other extraneous agencies. In earlier times the power to appoint Officer-in-Charge of police stations vested with the Superintendents of Police who jealously preserved their authority. Today, in some states, this power has been taken over by the Home Minister or even the Chief Minister. There will obviously be a *quid pro quo*, between the O/C and the political executive. There was a time when the O/C was regarded very highly on account of his powers and generally by the way he exercised them. There is an apocryphal story. A very competent lawyer was appointed as a District Judge. Before long, he was elevated as a judge of the High Court. When the Presidential order was received by him, he sought the blessings of his old and simple mother. His mother said "Son, you are most deserving of such promotions and will rise higher and higher and one day may even become a Daroga (O/C of a Police station). This story, even if imaginary illustrates the enormous powers of the police force. These days, contrary to law, they have been usurped by others who should have no role. Again under the law the powers of an investigative officer can be exercised by superior police officers. For examples, an Inspector of Police may be the I/O and in important cases, his work can be supervised by the Deputy Inspector General. It's unfortunate that in some cases, the senior police officers are either unable or unwilling to effectively supervise their subordinates.

The same position holds good in many other departments of administration and supervision and inspection do not get the attention they

deserve. I remember when I joined service as an Assistant Commissioner in a district, the visit of the Commissioner of the Division was a major event. The entire district machinery would be on their toes as the Commissioner would require answers to his various queries at the time of his inspection. Within a couple of decades, this system fell into disuse for various reasons.

4. As regards high-level corruption, the cause for this, apart from greed, is the need for funds for fighting elections. In a vast country like ours, it costs a lot of resources to fight and win elections. We follow the "First past the post', system of elections, where a small number in a territorial constituency may sway the election results. This has led to undesirable practices such as appealing to religious, caste or sectarian interests. The law fixes a ceiling on the election expenses. It is widely acknowledged that this is grossly unrealistic as even after funding by the political parties, the individual candidate has to incur expenses far in excess of the statutory limit. This has led to subversion of the process through paid news, submission of grossly understated election expense returns and importantly generation of huge quantities of black money. In my view, this is the most important reason for perpetuating corrupt practices. It is well-known that when an MP or an MLA enters the Parliament or the State legislature, his first act is to file a false statement in his return of election expenses.

5. The effect of corruption is to corrode and seriously undermine respect and authority of the establishment. Corruption is considered to be one of the greatest impediments on the way towards progress for a developing country like India. The economic, social and cultural structure of our country is very strong; however, due to the menace of corruption, it has been adversely affected and has become defenseless against the forces of anti-social elements. The desperation of the ordinary citizen, when he finds that justice is denied to him can shake his faith in the entire system. In a society where there are wide disparities in income and wealth, there is simmering discontent among vast sections of the population. When, there is blatant injustice and lack of fair play, this grievance can be exploited by anti-social elements whose agenda is to overthrow the existing democratic structures. This is an extremely serious situation as the aggrieved citizens may unwittingly, join hands with anti-national elements. India is a country of great diversities. Instead of emphasising the core values which bind the country together, there are vested interests eager to deepen and spread the fault lines. While corruption may not be the only issue, it is however a significant factor as it accentuates the sense of injustice.

6. It is obvious that speedy and effective steps should be taken to curb corruption which not only undermines a country's progress but threatens to shake the foundation of our vibrant, even if at times anarchic democratic edifice.

7. The causes leading to corruption as outlined above themselves suggest the solution.

8. The limit for the election expenses laid down by the law should be made realistic and periodically revised. For this purpose, a committee consisting of retired SC judge and reputed administrator with domain expertise should be

constituted which would make binding recommendations for a five years period. Obviously this would be far higher than the existing limits. It may be argued that a country like India cannot afford such large expenditure. But the ground reality is that enormous expenditure is being incurred in this regard. It is entirely hypocritical to peg the limit at a low figure. We should realise that democracy does not come cheap. However, such realistic limits should be scrupulously adhered to and any infraction should invite automatic disqualification for contesting elections. At present the candidates have to file a return of election expenses. Surprisingly, it is sought to be contended that their responsibility ends with filing a return and the Election Commission cannot scrutinise the veracity of such returns. This is totally anomalous besides going against Court decisions, as this provision will then be purely cosmetic without any substance. The power of the Election Commission to scrutinise the correctness of the return should be placed beyond any doubt.

The political parties and their candidates should maintain accounts, which should be subject to audit by approved auditors. In order to ensure transparency, corporate and other entities should disclose in full their contributions to political parties and candidates in their published accounts.

9. For reducing, if not eliminating corruption among public servants while dealing with the citizenry, it is essential that the public servants should be made accountable. Some degree of discretion should be available to them as it is not possible to envisage every situation and to frame rules to meet the same. Otherwise the administration would be hide bound and would be entangled in its own red tape. It is important to ensure that discretion is not unfettered but are bound by guidelines. Unfettered discretion results in other unauthorised actors including the political executive to manipulate and to fire from the shoulders of the public servants to the detriment of public interest. Senior officers entrusted with the task of supervision should perform their jobs effectively.

10. Transparency in administrative actions is vitally important. The Right to Information Act has been a step in the right direction. It should be used in appropriate cases to ensure that administrative actions are carried out in accordance with the principles of fair play and not with a view to harassing individual officials. An important tool to ensure this is computerisation. When train reservations were done manually, there were allegations of the booking clerk taking money to give an out of turn reservation. Computerisation has substantially reduced this malady. There are a number of departments in administration interacting with citizens, such as land records, supplies, tax authorities and even police and many others where computerisation on a large scale will give the public access to information and act as a built in check against malpractices.

11. India is a democracy. It is not as if corruption is non-existent in other countries, such as the USA, UK and others. The major difference however is, when corruption is exposed in those countries, effective and stringent action is taken against the offenders, be he the President or a Cabinet Minister. There is a strong perception that in India despite legal provisions, investigation

against the high and mighty facing corruption charges is deliberately diluted and often a minor functionary is made the scapegoat. There is talk of the need to bring in new laws like the powerful Lokpal to curb corruption. We should however introspect as to whether the existing laws are properly enforced.

12. The recent controversy regarding the allegation of the improper allocation of coalmines has led to a debate on the autonomy of the Central Bureau of Investigation (CBI). Reference is being made to the Supreme Court decision in Vineet Narain's case for insulating the CBI and other police forces from executive interference. The CBI, no doubt deals with many high profile cases. However, in the context of criminal investigations, the number of cases before the CBI is only a fraction of the cases before the State police forces. The fact that the CBI shared its status report on Coalgate with the Minister has evoked a storm of protest and it is suggested that suitable laws should be framed to stop such interference. Even as per existing laws, the Investigating Officer can be supervised only by his police superiors and no other person can interfere with such investigations. The question of showing the case diary or the status report to others including those who may be involved in the offence just does not arise. If such deviations occur, it is not because the existing laws are insufficient but because they are not properly enforced.

13. It is proposed that the CBI and by extension the State Police forces should not be under the administrative control of the executive but should come under Lokpal/Lokayukta. In a Parliamentary democracy the executive is answerable and accountable to the Legislature. It works on a system of checks and balances. To state that the CBI and the State Police forces should come under the control of Lokpal/Lokayukta which is not answerable to any other authority will distort the entire democratic structure. There is no guarantee that the Lokpal/ Lokayukta will not be swayed when granted vast authority without responsibility. Power corrupts and absolute power corrupts absolutely. In the USA, the FBI under J. Edgar Hoover almost became a Super State. India cannot afford such experiments. In the UK (whose model we follow), the Home Secretary (corresponding to our Home Minister) is answerable to the House of Commons in respect of subjects within his jurisdiction. It has in no way diluted the independence or effectiveness of the police force in Britain. There are clear lines of demarcation between policy issues and operational matters. The Minister does not interfere in police investigations and the same is seen to be totally free and fair.

14. There is a view, fortunately a minority one, that in order to root out corruption and other inequities ailing India, we need an authoritarian rule. The concept of a benevolent dictator is a contradiction in terms as no dictator will remain benevolent for long. A country like India has many religions, languages and ethnic groups and most of them have legitimate grievances. Periodical free and fair elections and democratic structures provide a safety outlet for letting off steam. In its absence, India may face violent convulsions.

15. The effort should be to strengthen our democracy and to remove its distortions and not to think of superseding it altogether. This can be achieved by a citizenry which is aware and constructive. Today, we have the elite

classes which are well off and not bothered about the polity's imperfections. The majority who are economically backward are too busy trying to make both ends meet and have no time for active involvement in the political process except by way of casting their votes. In any advanced society, the middle classes form the backbone for ensuring justice and the country's progress. In India, however, large sections of the middle class, while vociferously condemning the existing order and the endemic corruption, are too cynical to make any positive contribution to bring about improvements. This has to change. Obviously, awareness comes through better literacy and when the citizens do not have to fear economic distress. The State has to address these issues. In the final analysis, it is not the law books which ensure the sustenance of democracy; it is essentially the awareness of the citizens. We should be proud of our liberty and democracy. It is aptly said, that "Liberty does not descend to the people. The people must raise themselves to liberty. It is a blessing, which has to be earned before it can be enjoyed."

Let us never forget this axiom.

15

Role of Agriculture in Development of Assam

Bhaskar Barua IAS (Retd.)

In the wake of the Alarm Bell sounded by FAO about an impending global food crisis similar to the one that engulfed major parts of the developing countries in the first decade of this century, followed by decelerating agricultural growth in India and fatigue in the Green Revolution belt, it is necessary that agriculture plays a more prominent and vibrant role, in Assam as well as in India. The challenges are many, like fragmented land holdings, ailing soil health, increased vulnerability of the crop, livestock and fisheries sectors due to flood, erosion and intermittent drought confronting agriculture in the state and also the likely problems posed by climate change related issues. Distortions in the agriculture produce market represent another set of emerging problems as production increases. The looming danger relates not only to food security but also concerns rural livelihoods and the rural economy in general. Agriculture has not only to prevent a crisis but it has to be an engine of growth. It can place Assam in the forefront of agricultural production, productivity and the agricultural economy in the North Eastern region. This has to be seen in the context of declaration of the Government of India about bringing about a Second Green Revolution in the eastern Indian States including Assam.

The Setting of Geographical and Climatic Profile, Population

(a) The state of Assam is situated in the northeastern part of India between latitudes 240 44' N to 27045' N and longitudes 89041' E to 960 02'E. Assam shares boundaries with six Indian states and two foreign countries (Bhutan and Bangladesh). The state is endowed with fertile land and water resources, with a total geographical area of 78,438 square km divided into three broad physiographic units namely, (1) Brahmaputra Valley (2) Barak Valley, and (3)

Hill Region. The mighty Brahmaputra and Barak rivers with their 121 tributaries and branches flow through the two valleys contributing to the fertility.

(b) The plains of Assam are composed of fertile alluvial soil, which is well-distributed throughout the Brahmaputra and Barak valley plains. The soil of the Brahmaputra valley is less acidic than that of Barak Valley and is classified into two types: new alluvium and old alluvium. Both these types of alluvium were deposited by the Brahmaputra, Barak and their tributaries. The new alluvial soils are found in the active flood plains, *char areas* and the middle parts of the both banks of the valley. The old alluvium is particularly found along the tributaries from the foothill region to the middle part of the valley. The old alluvium is more acidic than the new alluvium and contains phosphoric acid. Besides, peaty cr silt soils are found in the low-lying areas of the Brahmaputra valley and Barak plains.

(c) Based on soil characterisation rainfall, temperature and terrain, six main agro-climatic zones in Assam have been identified. These are: (1) Upper Brahmaputra Valley (*Tinsukia, Dibrugarh, Sibasagar, Jorhat and Golaghat districts*), (2) North Bank Zones (*Lakhimpur, Dhemaji, Sonitpur, Darrang and Udalguri districts*). (3) Central Brahmaputra Valley (*Nagaon and Morigaon districts*), (4) Lower Brahmaputra Valley (*Kamrup, Kamrup) (M), Barpeta, Bongaigaon, Nalbari, Goalpara, Dhubri, Chirang, Baksa and Kokrajhar districts*), (5) Hill Zone (*Karbi Anglong and Dima Hasao districts*), and (6) Barak Valley (*Cachar, Karimganj and Hailakandi districts*).

(d) ***Climate:*** The climate of Assam is generally characterised as humid sub-tropical with warm humid summers and cool dry winters. However, due to its unique geographical location coupled with varied physiography, the state has a wide array of climatic conditions. The rainfall in Assam is high but its distribution over time and space is not uniform. The maximum rainfall of 1434.1 mm on an average (63 per cent) occurs during the months of June to September. The pre-monsoon months, i.e., March to May, receive erratic and unpredictable rainfall of an average of 597.9. mm (27 per cent), and 10 per cent rainfall occurs during the post monsoon and winter months The mean annual maximum temperature varies from 23.60 C to 31.7 °C and minimum temperature varies from 70 to 25.2°C, though a higher range of temperatures has been recorded recently.

(e) On the basis of variations in temperature, rainfall and humidity, the climate of the area may be divided into four distinct seasons (from the agricultural point of view), namely pre-monsoon, monsoon, retreating monsoon and winter season.

(f) ***Pre-monsoon (March-May):*** It is the transition period between relatively dry winter and hot summer and is characterised by a rapid rise in temperature. The average maximum and minimum temperatures are 3232°C and 20°C respectively. The average rainfall is around 597.9 mm and average humidity is 67 per cent.

(g) ***Monsoon (June-Sept):*** This is a rainy season with rainfall of around 1434.1 mm. The maximum and minimum temperatures are 36°C and 23°C respectively. The average relative humidity is 82 per cent.

(h) ***Retreating Monsoon (Oct-Nov):*** With the advance of the season, the temperature falls and fog appears. The average maximum and minimum temperatures are 29°C and 16°C respectively. The average relative humidity is 80 per cent and rainfall is 178 mm.

(i) ***Winter (Dec-Feb):*** This season is characterised by cool weather and fog. The average maximum and minimum temperatures are 25°C and 7°C respectively. The average relative humidity is 63 per cent and rainfall is 45.8 mm.

(j) The total population of the state according to the findings of the 2011 census is about 3.12 crore (rounded off). The projected population in 2012-13 is 3.17 crore based on the prevailing rate of growth. The rural population out of this is about 2.68 crore, at nearly 86 per cent. The density of population is 397 per sq. km. There were 954 females to every 1000 males and the child sex ratio (under six) is 957. [*Source: Assam at a Glance; 2012, Directorate of Economics and Statistics, Assam*].

Cultivable and Cultivated Area

Of the geographical area of 78.44 lakh hectares (1.23 per cent urban and 98.77 per cent rural area), the Total Cultivable Area is 30.16 lakh hectares, after taking into account the areas under forest (18.53 lakh hectare, 24 per cent of geographical area), barren and uncultivable land (14.08 lakh hectares, 17 per cent), total area not available for cultivation (26.26 lakh hectares). The Net Area Sown is 28.11 lakh hectares (36 per cent) and the Gross Cropped Area is 41.60 lakh hectares.

The area cultivated once is 14.62 lakh hectares and the area cultivated twice or more is 13.49 lakh hectares. The Estimated area under *jhum* (shifting) cultivation is 8.05 lakh hectares (10.3 per cent). The area under horticultural crops is 6.08 lakh hectares (14.62 per cent of Gross Cropped Area). Chronically, flood prone area is 4.93 lakh hectares (17.5 per cent of Net Area Sown) [*Source: Agri-Horti Data of Assam, 2013; Unprinted, obtained from the Directorate of Agriculture, Assam*].

The number of operational holdings of all sizes- ranging from under half a hectare to Large- is 27.20 lakh (rounded off) [p 64 of Statistical Handbook of Assam 2012; at p 330 of the same publication it is stated as 27.50 lakh (according to Agricultural Census 2005-06)].

The average size of Operational Holdings in Assam is 1.11 hectare. This is lower than the All States average of 1.23 hectares. There has been a gradual decline in the size of operational holdings, from 1.47 hectares in 1970-71, to 1.17 hectares in 1995-96, to 1.15 hectares in 2000-01 and now even lower.

The number of Farm Families is 27.12 lakh (rounded off) Agricultural Census 2005-06: Statistical Hand Book, Assam, 2012.

There was increase in respect of the number of marginal and semi-medium holdings and a decrease in case of small and large holdings during 2000-01 as compared to 1995-96.

As Assam is an agrarian State, the economy of the State is based on agriculture. The majority of the population of the State, around 75 per cent,

depends directly or indirectly on agriculture and allied activities. Agriculture is at the core of the primary sector of the State's economy and it contributed 26.2 per cent to the Net State Domestic Product (NSDP) at current prices during 2008-09 (Advanced Estimate 2009-10, 26.1 per cent). The state comprising 25 plains districts and two hill districts is in the high potential zone for raising agricultural productivity. Out of the total geographical area of 78.44 lakh hectares, almost over one-third is under net cultivation covering an area of 28.10 lakh hectares [Assam at a Glance, 2012]. Most farmers carry out mixed farming, with field crops, horticulture, milch cattle and backyard poultry.

Some Issues

Crop Husbandry

(a) Agricultural activity in Assam is a combination of peasant and tenant farming with the bulk of the cultivable land belonging to small and marginal farmers (83.10 per cent). The State can be called marginally self-sufficient in rice production, although the recent statistics would indicate that rice production is more than adequate to feed the population of Assam. The state is deficit in pulses and oilseeds and many fruits despite the high horticultural potential. Cash crops like sugarcane (for production of Gur and chewing type) and jute are also important crops of the State.

The area, production and productivity of important field and horticultural crops may be seen in the table below:

Horticulture

(a) Horticulture comprising fruits, vegetables, flowers, spices, nut crops, tuber crops and medicinal and aromatic plants is a traditional component of Assam's household system and an integral part of its socio-economic culture. Such crops are cultivated in the homestead gardens locally known as '*Bari*' and they are set up primarily to meet the day to day requirement of the families, social functions, religious and social festivals. The *Bari* represents a unique feature of Assam agriculture which can provide a platform for integrated agricultural growth. The sub-tropical climate as well as virgin soils of Assam contributes to the vigorous growth of crops in the '*Bari*'. The major crops grown are; Banana, Assam Lemon, Jackfruit, Oranges and other citrus fruits, Pineapples, Papaya, Mango, Guava, Litchi and various vegetables, spices and tuber crops etc. The total area under horticultural crop is 5.98 lakh hectares which is about 15 per cent of the net cultivated area of the State. The production of horticultural crops is now under gradual transition from traditional to commercial and the new generation of farmers finds growing of such crops attractive owing to the fact that return per unit area and time is higher, given proper market support.

(b) In spite of the potential for horticultural growth, Assam is yet to be recognised as a horticulturally advanced state, pointing to the need for putting the production on a secure base for which commercialisation is stated to be the answer. Producers of horticultural crops, particularly seasonal fruits and vegetables always tend to be at a disadvantage *vis-à-vis* the market forces and this militates against stabilisation of the production base. There are frequent

Sl. No.		Crop	2006-07	2007-08	2008-09	2009-10	2010-11
1.	Autumn Rice	Area	3.79	3.54	3.51	3.46	3.13
		Production	3.36	3.48	3.74	3.35	3.56
		Productivity	899	999	1084	982	1155
2.	Winter Rice	Area	14.98	16.47	17.73	17.89	18.59
		Production	19.5	22.39	29.24	32.14	36.49
		Productivity	1321	1380	1674	1824	1993
3.	Summer Rice	Area	3.12	3.23	3.6	3.94	3.99
		Production	6.3	7.32	7.72	8.6	10.28
		Productivity	2017	2267	2142	2180	2577
4.	Total Rice	Area	21.9	23.24	24.84	25.3	25.71
		Production	29.16	33.19	40.7	44.08	50.33
		Productivity	1349	1428	1638	1765	1983
5.	Wheat	Area	0.6	0.56	0.5	0.6	0.45
		Production	0.67	0.71	0.65	0.65	0.56
		Productivity	1132	1263	1300	1087	1256
6.	Maize	Area	0.19	0.18	0.17	0.19	0.2
		Production	0.14	0.13	0.13	0.14	0.14
		Productivity	744	725	726	718	714

(Contd.)

(Contd. Table)

Sl. No.		Crop	2006-07	2007-08	2008-09	2009-10	2010-11
7.	Arahar	Area	0.07	0.06	0.05	0.06	0.07
		Production	0.05	0.04	0.04	0.04	0.05
		Productivity	714	718	710	712	714
8.	Blackgram	Area	0.37	0.38	0.4	0.43	0.49
		Production	0.19	0.2	0.23	0.25	0.27
		Productivity	514	531	580	566	558
9.	Greengram	Area	0.07	0.08	0.06	0.08	0.09
		Production	0.03	0.04	0.03	0.03	0.04
		Productivity	460	460	459	457	470
10.	Rape and Mustard	Area	2.38	2.35	2.26	2.49	2.44
		Production	1.16	1.23	1.25	1.31	1.43
		Productivity	514	523	551	529	585
11.	Jute	Area	0.58	0.6	0.6	0.65	0.62
		Production	1.01	1.18	1.17	1.28	1.13
		Productivity	1744	1976	1939	1967	1808

(Contd.)

(Contd. Table)

Sl. No.		Crop	2006-07	2007-08	2008-09	2009-10	2010-11
12.	Mesta	Area	0.05	0.05	0.05	0.05	0.05
		Production	0.05	0.05	0.05	0.04	0.05
		Productivity	913	922	913	916	940
13.	Sugarcane	Area	0.27	0.26	0.29	0.27	0.3
		Production	10.55	9.8	11	10.62	10.76
		Productivity	39634	38075	38387	39110	36196
14.	Banana	Area	0.43	0.44	0.46	0.45	0.48
		Production	5.99	6.07	6.29	6.22	6.54
		Productivity	13846	13790	13801	13823	13721
15.	Pineapple	Area	0.12	0.13	0.13	0.14	0.14
		Production	1.92	1.99	1.95	2.1	2.15
		Productivity	15458	15524	15369	15463	15337
16.	Orange	Area	0.08	0.07	0.1	0.13	0.15
		Production	0.88	0.79	1.08	1.36	1.56
		Productivity	10966	11092	11073	10586	10520
17.	Papaya	Area	0.07	0.06	0.06	0.08	0.07
		Production	1.05	0.93	0.92	1.22	1.38
		Productivity	15377	15207	15171	15252	18783

reports of growers, particularly of vegetables such as tomatoes throwing away produce they bring to the market in the absence of economic prices. The markets are small and fragmented and reportedly mostly dominated by middlemen. Measure for preservation of horticultural produce can give a big boost to production. This sector has now been recognised as a sunrise area based on two major aspects primarily, income potential and employment generation. The momentum of growth can be boosted, accelerating the steady growth in area, production and productivity in case of many horticultural crops, which are below expectation presently.

Livestock

The state of Assam is endowed with large and diverse livestock population comprising many important species of animals and birds. But the present rearing practices of these species result in very low productivity leading to low production and insufficient supply of livestock products to meet the growing demand.

The livestock sector in Assam is, by its very nature, highly employment intensive and is the major source of supplementary income for most rural households. Livestock production is by and large a small holder activity. More than three fourths of total livestock in the state of all species are owned by landless, marginal and small holders. Development of livestock is therefore, not merely a question of balancing the demand - supply of livestock products, but also the critical pathway to alleviate rural poverty and usher in prosperity.

There are practically no big players in the livestock sector of Assam. Almost 90 per cent rural households in Assam keep livestock of one species or other, consume part of the products and earn supplementary income. This sector forms the single major source of supplementary nutrition and income for rural households in Assam. Cattle holdings are often three to four animals with at least one milch animal among them. However, of late, small to medium size specialised dairy farms are coming up around major demand centres, but these are still very few. Goats too are held in a flock of three to four while pig holdings vary in size from two to six. Goat, Pig and Poultry are distributed fairly evenly in all the districts and are more livelihood intensive than cattle farming. Back-yard poultry accounts for over 90 per cent of the fowls and almost all the ducks in Assam are mostly desi birds. Backyard poultry units consist of six to 10 birds on an average, often a combination of fowls and ducks. Organised commercial poultry in the State is confined to broilers only. There are hardly any layer farms. Even the organised broiler farms are small in size, mostly with about 500 birds. There is no parental stock farm in Assam and even private hatcheries are importing hatching eggs from other states.

Productivity of all livestock and birds in Assam across all species is extremely low due to poor genetic quality. Services for livestock production and management in Assam come almost exclusively from the Animal Husbandry and Veterinary Department.

Markets for all livestock products are fragmented, unorganised and involve a chain of middlemen. There are no organised efforts to link production to markets. Even the milk cooperative societies set-up under Operation Flood have not yet taken off, unlike in many other states.

Research

(a) The basic objective of agricultural research ought to be to make available appropriate agricultural technologies for the farmers and all other players in the agricultural arena, be it in crop husbandry, horticulture, livestock or fisheries. The existing infrastructure for transfer of technology needs to be made more effective and responsive to meet farmers' needs. In order to achieve these goals, efforts need to be accelerated through promotion of a type of technology appropriate to resource status of farmers, technology to meet the needs likely to be brought about by climate change, optimum utilisation of inputs including greater reliance on bio-fertilisation and bio-pest control, biotechnology, genetic improvement of crops including hybrid technology, post harvest technology etc. R and D support from AAU, ICAR, etc., has to be garnered for development of flood tolerant, drought resistant rice varieties along with extended dormancy period of summer rice variety of the State. The research and extension linkages need to be strengthened to improve the effectiveness of research and extension system for food security particularly for pulses and oil seeds. Development of appropriate storage technologies and acid tolerant varieties of pulses will have to be developed. Since farmers carry on rain fed farming and the prospects of any sizeable area of the state coming under irrigation in the near future are not bright, production technologies must result in optimum productivity under rain fed conditions. Also to be borne in mind is the factor that due to rapid climate change, rainfall has become erratic and water availability may well go down.

(b) Since most of the farmers of the state are small and marginal farmers, the technology offered must be technically and economically viable for small and marginal farmers. In this regard the risk bearing capability of those farmers, in the context of their poor resource base including small land holdings need to be taken into consideration by all concerned including the scientists. AAU should conduct research to develop technology based on farmers' needs adopting a PRA approach. Agricultural research has to maximise efforts both on the front of technology appropriate to present conditions as well of any future scenario induced by climate change.

Credit

(a) The flow of credit to the farmers is an important factor in encouraging them to go in for intensive farming. Availability of agricultural credit in Assam per hectare is only 30 per cent of the national average. The per capita credit disbursement to farmers in Assam is very low, only Rs 9120 in comparison to National Level of Rs 15,380. According to RBI report, 22 districts of the State still remain under-banked. The average area covered by the bank branches operating in the State is as large as 60 square kilometers per branch. Thus, many rural areas remain deprived of banking services. The banking requirements of the rural people are being served by a network of *Gramin Vikash Banks* (GVB) in Assam with 401 reporting branch offices. The Assam Cooperative Apex Bank is the only State Co-operative Bank, which advances credit to the farmer for augmenting the agricultural production and productivity.

Credit Deposit Ratio (as on 30th September, 2012)

Overall CD Ratio	*46.60 per cent (against national norms of 60 per cent)*
Banks with CD Ratio less than 20 per cent	3
Banks with CD Ratio between 20 per cent to	5
Banks with CD Ratio between 30 per cent to	5
Banks with CD Ratio above 40 per cent	14
Non reporting Banks	11

(b) As of today the base level co-operative structure of the State, i.e., the system of Gaon *Panchayat Samabai Samitis* is exceedingly weak and most of these societies are not carrying out any major activities apart from distribution of PDS articles. If credit delivery has to be increased, there is an urgent need to revitalise these institutions and to strengthen them through fresh infusion of capital and proper training of their manpower resources to ensure that they become effective co-operative institutions.

Farm Mechanisation

(a) Farm Mechanisation is a critical input, which facilitates timely agricultural operation and that is a key to higher level of production. The present availability of Farm Power in the state is 1.02 HP per hectare (National Level: 1.71 HP per hectare in 2010-11) of which mechanical power is only 0.25 HP per hectare. The growth of mechanisation in Assam is slow. Low availability of Farm Power has become the constraint to double or multiple cropping.

(b) Mechanisation helps in timely land preparation, timely sowing and timely harvesting of crops. Use of improved implements for land preparation reduces cost and time. This is important in the Assam context, where productivity is affected by late sowing of cereals. In order to promote farm mechanisation there is need to popularise improved small tools, small mechanical implements and to develop low cost and fuel efficient farm machinery, as increasing dependence on fossil fuels is to be discouraged. Emphasis should be given on gender friendly farm equipment seeing that so many farming operations are carried out by women. Farm mechanisation should be of the basic type, suitable for small farms, of such design and technology as to allow farmers to maintain these themselves, and above all be affordable by the bulk of farmers without subsidisation, for use in different farm operations and requiring least support from the government.

Water

(a) Farming in Assam is mostly carried out as a rain fed activity utilising the monsoon rain during the main Sali rice crop and in respect of Ahu, the rice crop preceding Sali, it is a dry sowing operation. During the Rabi season, the rice crop is Boro which is based on residual water available in low lying areas. Irrigation water availability is largely dependent on the shallow tube wells, which are usually diesel operated.

(b) The per capita water availability is the highest in Brahmaputra Valley amounting to 18,147 cubic metre year. The state has the potential of 24.72

billion cubic metre of restockable ground water of which 21.01 billion cubic metre is not available for irrigation due to geographical restrictions.

(c) It is estimated that gross irrigation potential of the state is 27 lakh ha, out of which 17 lakh ha can be irrigated from surface water resources and 10 lakh ha from ground water resources.

(d) Unfortunately, during the last 60 years the situation on the ground is that farmers do not have any reliable water supply when required from any surface flow irrigation potential created. Farmers have not been facilitated with either technology or otherwise for utilising surface water resources in *Beels*, water tanks/ponds and emphasis has been on construction activities and water availability to farmers has been given practically no importance.

(e) Considering the success thus far exhibited by shallow tube-wells, which can be exploited within a reasonable time and are within the reach of farmers, such wells can be further popularised in the feasible areas by providing reliable electricity instead of relying on fossil fuels, dependence on which should be gradually reduced to avoid further environmental degradation.

Marketing

(a) Farmers, planners and economists alike have identified marketing of agricultural products as a major constraint in Assam's agriculture. Farmers of Assam are predominantly small and marginal. With expansion of irrigation, mechanisation, inputs supply and better extension, agriculture is slowly changing to a surplus state in many products. But market linkage of farmers is low due to farmers' inability to be competitive in respect of product, quality, volume and price.

(b) Agricultural market infrastructure and support services are not well developed in Assam. There are four categories of markets in Assam. Highest number (3424) of market in the category of weekly market followed by daily (481), bi-weekly (286), all of the traditional type, characterised by haphazard growth and without any discernible farmer friendly features, and regulated markets (22).

(c) A major thrust has to be on development of marketing infrastructure in the State to ensure that the genuine producer gets a remunerative price for his produce. There is a vast market for existing and potential horticultural crops of Assam. Besides, regional and national market, there also exists wide scope for exporting these commodities. In order to minimise distress sale of food grains and other crops by the farmers, a well-designed programme framework for Post Harvest Marketing Management need to be evolved and implemented in consultation with all stake holders including the Central Government, State Agencies etc. Measures should be taken to establish Market Yards, institutions known as "*Apni Mandi*" elsewhere, Transit Storages etc. in different locations in the State by involving the Market Committees under the State Marketing Board and other agencies including private players.

Institutional Structure

Agriculture: To achieve the expected growth rate in agriculture, it is necessary to build a vibrant and viable institutional structure from the top to

the grassroots. An institutional structure for the provision of institutional credit, inputs and appropriate mechanisation and organised marketing services is necessary to assist a large number of farmers.

Flood and Erosion

(a) Every year the floods leave a trail of destruction, washing away villages, submerging paddy fields, drowning livestock, besides causing loss of human life and property cost in several billions. Floods have pushed thousands of people to an uncertain future; they have shattered Assam's fragile economy as a whole.

(b) Usually, Assam experiences almost continuous rainfall during the monsoon season, which normally commence from the month of May and remains till mid-October. Apart from this, occurrence of floods, Assam has direct correlation with rainfall in the catchments areas of neighbouring states like Arunachal Pradesh, Meghalaya, Mizoram, Nagaland and the adjacent country Bhutan. Deforestation is also a major reason for the floods becoming an annual feature. Indiscriminate deforestation has led to massive amount of topsoil coming down from the higher elevations during the rains, the soil flowing into the rivers and raising the riverbeds of the Brahmaputra and its tributaries.

(c) Statistically 21 out of 27 districts of the state routinely suffer from floods. Districts like Dhemaji, North Lakhimpur, Goalpara, Dhubri and Barpeta remain flooded for nearly three months.

(d) In view of the above, while efforts to control floods go on, Assam agriculture has to be made a flood free activity. This can be achieved by growing rice varieties which require less water under technologies such as SRI in the post flood and pre flood seasons.

The Way Forward

There has been a rise in production of rice, as per information from the Agriculture Department, increasing to 50.33 Million Tones (MT) in 2011. As rice is the most important food crop for the state, this is welcome news. Looking at the three years' average of production, the picture is similar. In going forward, it is important to bear the following factors in mind.

Has the increase in the production of rice improved the lot of the farmers of Assam or the rural areas where they live and work? The predominant aspect of Assam agriculture is the monsoon-based rice production system, covering about 70 per cent of the net cropped area. In Assam, the emphasis has been on rice and have other agricultural products received the necessary attention? Has intensification of production and diversification which can resultant improvements in the lot of farmers come about? These are constrained because of a number of factors, to deal with which the measures necessary are, among others:

(i) Give adequate emphasis on enhancing the area, production and productivity other crops, particularly pulses and oilseeds, fruits and vegetables, fish and dairy and animal products all of which are so important for nutritional security, which is more significant than food security alone.

(ii) In order that the farmers have the necessary where withal to better their lot, more attention needs to be given on generation and transfer of

appropriate technology suited to a small farmer rain fed farming system, so that farmers are equipped with the most important instrument they need, namely, proper knowledge of technology suited to their farming;

(iii) Espouse the cause of farmers and encourage them to use such level of inputs as is appropriate to the low resource base of the farmers, emphasising techniques and indigenous solutions rather than give importance to increasing consumption of fossil fuel based inputs brought in over long supply lines from outside the state.

(iv) As the majority of farmers do not have the funding to go in for costly chemical-based agriculture, consider declaring parts of the most productive areas of the state as organic and provide assistance to farmers by way of bio-fertilisers, bio-pesticides and in marketing of produce;

(v) Provide appropriate market intelligence and market linkage, so that farmers can plan their production based on market demand and are enabled to market their produce, getting proper prices; while this is no doubt very much required for rice, it is considered essential for encouraging the production of horticultural crops, milk and animal products as the latter group of agricultural produce is more perishable.

(vi) Assam and the Northeast are known as bio-diversity hot spots; at the same time, the natural resources are degenerating at human hands. In view of this situation, the time has come to take up conservation agriculture in a big way, particularly in the hills of Assam and the northeastern region and halt environmental degradation, as agriculture cannot thrive where the ecology is destroyed.

(vii) In the context of the poor market for agricultural produce that exists today, government/cooperative agencies, which could have provided support to producers, have also been found wanting; the Food Corporation of India is understood to be reluctant to procure paddy on the ground of moisture content being high and no state agency has been able to step into the breach properly. Cooperatives societies and SHGs at the local level and an appropriate agency of the state government at the state level have to be boosted to provide this essential support.

(viii) Since less than 20 per cent of farm land can be irrigated in the dry season, a big boost to on-farm irrigation, farm ponds and farm water management is necessary, not only for the dry season but also for assuring a successful Sali crop; water conservation and use of less water consuming varieties and techniques such as SRI have to be adopted to deal with the increasing vagaries of the monsoon caused by climate change.

(ix) Bank credit required for undertaking modern agriculture is not widely and adequately available with the result that asset creation in agriculture is not taking place; credit is also very important for procurement, storage, processing of food sad other agricultural produce, for fisheries, dairy and livestock farming. Bank credit has to be stepped up by proper coordination between all agencies concerned

(x) Up-to-date land records are necessary for accessing term loans for machineries for agricultural operations, post harvest management, storage and

processing, dairy, pisiculture etc.; making available such updated land records should be taken up on a mission mode.

(xi) There is need for recognising the importance of ensuring proper quality of inputs made available to farmers and the functioning of the state laboratories for testing of pesticides and fertilizers needs to be brought up to par, in the absence of which the farmers face uncertainties about the quality of fertilizers and pesticides they use.

(xii) Likewise is the case of the seed testing laboratory, if such laboratories are not functioning properly, the quality of seeds would always be suspect;

(xiii) The Assam State Seed Certification Agency, the functioning of which is most important for ensuring the standards of the foundation and certified seeds produced locally, which are preferable being more suited to the environment, is learnt to be in a moribund state and consequently Assam has to rely on seeds from outside the state; This Agency needs to be revived and strengthened.

(xiv) Farm mechanisation is necessary for double cropping, diversification and appropriate inter-culture operations. But mechanisation has to be suitable for the vast majority of small and marginal farmers and the small size of holdings which predominate in Assam; since for the foreseeable future a lot of land preparation and other agricultural operations would continue to be based on human and animal power, research and development efforts are necessary to make the traditional hand tools more efficient and productive and to make them available to the farmers.

(xv) The farmers are very dependent on the timely, competent and efficient service delivery, be in the area of extension, quality inputs, market intelligence, and the machinery for these purposes needs to be strengthened along with system upgradation, as well as greater coordination between different agencies such as between extension and research, with irrigation, power, credit, banks, rural roads etc.

(xvi) The producers of agriculture commodities have to be organised into cooperative societies not only to facilitate better service channelisation and connection to the market chain but also to enhance their bargaining power *vis-a-vis* the market; direct linkage between farmers and consumers can be established for mutual benefit.

(xvii) Food processing, particularly of fruits and vegetables, can play a very big role in adding value to the produce of the farmers and help in increasing farm incomes. Such processing units should be disaggregated and well spread out so as to give benefits to a greater number of farmers. Well dispersed units would provide opportunities to producers to bring their produce for processing without going through middlemen.

(xviii) The data on land, including land for agricultural purposes, included here refers to the data as available. It is not clear how far changes in land use, i.e., land no longer used for agriculture, such as land eroded by rivers, fields covered by sand deposits the area of which in districts such as Dehmaji is not insubstantial, land taken up for setting up industries, for roads and land now parts of towns and Guwahati city have been properly recorded and data

corrected. On the other hand, it is not unlikely that some land under forest cover is now used for crops etc. It is suggested that land statistics should be continuously made up-to-date and diversion of agricultural land for other purposes be strictly monitored and diversion not be allowed except in special cases only and never for speculative purposes.

(xix) It has been observed that farmer-to-farmer (including fishers, lives stock and, milk producers) learning is a very successful method of increasing the knowledge base of farmers, as has been seen in the case of Integrated Pesticide Management. Large number of Farmer Field Schools should be set up as this system provides learning in the local context, is problem based and eases communication gaps between the experts and the lay villagers.

In the context of the need for food security, the measures taken and planned to be taken under the Food Security Ordinance, it is very necessary to consider and adopt the concept and practice of Food Sovereignty. Food Sovereignty is somewhat akin to *Gram Swaraj* advocated by Mahatma Gandhi, where the village acting in concert decides on the crops to be grown, the methods to be followed, and dealing with the produce. It could mean that farmers decide plan the agricultural production in the village, through a cooperative society/SHG decide on what is the surplus that can be sold after meeting the needs of every last member of the village and dispose of the produce to the best benefit of the village. In essence it means Local Production, Local Procurement, Local Storage and Local Distribution. This would be a most important step in the direction of empowering the rural areas and change the terms of trade in favour of the villages. It would also mean less wastage by minimising storage, transportation and distribution losses. Reduction in transport requirements would result in ecological benefits as so much less fossil fuel would require to be burnt with less pollution.

The above are some of the measures considered necessary for agriculture in Assam to play a greater role in the development of Assam. There could be many more steps which may be useful and these can be considered along with these.

16

Agriculture in Assam Perpetually Waitlisted

Mayur Bora

Metaphorically speaking, the state of agriculture in this land of the red river and blue hills often reminds me of a languorous locomotive engine chugging into a station with a never-ending array of compartments teeming with far greater number of people than it can safely accommodate. But those tenacious travellers hardly have any grouse for this overcrowding, despite being conscious of the fact that the moments they start working in the fields, problems on various fronts have become their inseparable companions. Some of them try to address those thorny issues while the majority reconcile to the harsh reality of being perennially bedeviled by one problem or the other. Apart from many other factors adversely affecting the agriculture sector of Assam, this streak of fatalism exhibited by many farmers has created avoidable roadblocks in their path of progress. If productivity is the soft underbelly of Indian agriculture, in the context of Assam, production also joins hands with productivity creating stiffer challenges for the farmers, agripreneurs, bankers, government officials and policy planners. On the top of that, rhetorical statements and symbolic assurances made by our politicians to capture the fancy of the farmer community end up complicating the issue and obfuscating the minds. As a result, more votes are possibly earned than crops are harvested.

Now let's do some plain speak. What ails the agriculture scenario of the state and how to overcome those difficulties with some workable and implementable plans should be the main thrust of our present approach. Like any other people, the people in Assam are unified by their innate desire to have healthy food in adequate quantity. The production of healthy food in sufficient quantity primarily depends on how well our agriculture system is functioning. In the absence of this, we have to depend on food supply from other states. For more than a century, many great scholars have emphasised

on the importance of agriculture in Indian economy. After independence and more specifically from the 2nd Five Year Plan, although the focus had shifted towards manufacturing and more recently to the services sector, the contribution of agriculture and allied activities is still quite substantial for our national income. In addition to its contribution, the number of people involved in this sector is very large. Even for a casual observer of our agriculture scene, the spectre of disguised unemployment is too palpable to miss.

In the context of Assam, aforesaid developments in the agrarian sector tend to get a sharper focus due to our clear backwardness in secondary and tertiary sector in comparison to other states of the mainland India. But we would deliberately avoid touching certain deeply intractable problems of the agriculture sector like fragmentation of land holdings, labour shortage etc. as they can't be effectively tackled in the near future. We would prefer concentrating on those issues which can be dealt with provided the state government, banks and Assam Agricultural University work in a coordinated manner taking the farmer community in confidence. It is well-known to all that an archaic farming system relentlessly followed in the name of tradition coupled with huge blockages in credit, non-credit and knowledge delivery channels from the state's (banks, government departments, Agricultural Universities) side magnifies the current discouraging picture prevailing in this realm.

In order to systematically address the problems plaguing the agriculture sector of Assam, we have to be ruthlessly honest. I am referring to that kind of honesty which will goad us to admit everything with unrestrained candour for the larger interest of our agriculture. Otherwise similar kind of results and recommendations would emerge as they did in the past. The repetitive sameness of the observations resulting from many seminal studies of our agricultural scene conducted by several redoubtable scholars highlights our mechanical approach and also our inability to admit the shortcomings wholeheartedly. Therefore, the problems of agriculture in Assam always tend to get painted with the same brush which ends up triggering disinterest among the conscious citizens of the society.

First and foremost, agriculture being a state subject, the role of the State Department of Agriculture is of paramount importance for proper development of this sector. If we go solely by the number of schemes and their beautiful names, the whole scene would appear to be extremely hunky-dory. But that is not the correct picture. You scratch the top surface of this ticklish issue; many unseen warts would pop up. The Agriculture and Agriculture Engineering Departments are supposed to function mainly for the benefit of farmers so that agricultural production of different crops and their productivity are either near or above the national average. But till now, we are nowhere near that picture and our agricultural growth rate is far from satisfactory. The non-credit or input delivery channel for the agriculturists is of critical importance for adoption of scientific methods of farming. Owing to various reasons, the functioning of this channel represented by Agriculture and Agriculture Engineering Departments tends to get contaminated with political interference by politicians of all hues. It becomes well nigh impossible for any upright

officer of these departments to consistently insulate their functioning from these kinds of pressures. Very often, majority of them succumb to these undesirable tactics which leads to intentional wrong selection of beneficiary under some government schemes depending on the political affiliation of the farmer. In simpler words, instead of selecting 'A' who is a genuine and progressive farmer under a particular project, 'B' gets selected for the benefits as he enjoys a cordial relation with the local politicians. The sacrifice of genuineness at the altar of political expediency creates a very unhealthy atmosphere where many farmers develop a lingering sense of cynicism about the real intent of the government. Some officers don't discharge their assigned duties properly until and unless their palms are greased, especially before giving any benefit to farmers. Due to these factors, the honest officers of the department get demoralised. Even then, their robust presence in the department is one of the important reasons for achieving the present level of success in the agriculture sector.

Secondly, the role of the banks in providing required impetus to agriculture by providing timely, hassle free and adequate quantity of credit to the needy farmers leaves much to be desired. Notwithstanding the rosy statistical picture about the growth of credit in agriculture being exhibited by some banks, the real ground level situation is quite grim. For majority of the farmers, credit has remained consistently elusive which has ultimately hampered his farm income. In any district of Assam, the number of farmers who have availed agricultural loans from banks represents a tiny section of the total number of farmers. Many farmers' frank feedback about their experiences in the banks is obviously not music to the ears of the bankers. In certain bank branches, farmers don't get a respectful treatment and they have been made to visit the branches for a simple thing on several occasions. One visit of a farmer from a village to a bank branch entails a huge economic cost in terms loss of man-hours at the crucial time of cultivation. Moreover, simplified and farmer, friendly approach suggested by Govt. of India and Reserve Bank of India while scrutinising the loan applications of farmers is often not adhered to by some banks whose sole concern is to control their Non-Performing Assets (NPAs). As a result, for many cultivators, bank's role is not entirely satisfactory. However, while being critical about the functioning of the banking system, one should not lose sight of the fact that Assam and for that matter, the whole of North-East, has the highest rate of defaults in the country. A sizable section of those defaulters is willful which deepens the anguish of the financial institutions. The bankers' concern is also genuine because if people don't repay their earlier loans, it would certainly hamper the flow of credit into the sector in future. We feel if banks provide timely short term agricultural credit by way of *Kisan Credit Card* (KCCs) in an atmosphere of mutual trust and respect, the repayment performance of the farmers is bound to go up. Once the repayment rate improves, it would undoubtedly lead do the decongestion of the credit delivery channel which has hitherto been extremely susceptible to get clogged for a wide variety of reasons.

Thirdly, the knowledge delivery channel for the farmers is mainly handled by State Department of Agriculture, Extension Wing of Agricultural University

and *Krishi Vikas Kendras* (KVKs). Till some time back, it was perceived that agricultural extension had failed to keep pace with the demands of the sector. But after establishment/strengthening of KVKs in almost all the districts of Assam by AAU, that need has been substantially, if not fully fulfilled. However, in the recent past, the number of serious research works having far-reaching impact in farmers' fields and discovery of new crop varieties which has a direct bearing on agricultural productivity is not very encouraging in the state. The Extension Specialists have been forced to popularise and propagate more or less the same old varieties for a considerable length of time. Since the onerous task of agricultural extension can't legitimately be handled by public sector alone, there is an emergent need for private sector to chip in their contribution in the concept of Private-Public-People Participation with a strong linkage with the market. Progressive farmers themselves can play the role of a change agent in their respective areas for adoption of advanced technology and better varieties. A successful farmer's word is more likely to be taken at the face value by the fellow farmers than that of a specialist as they would find it easy to relate.

Last but not the least, the importance of the attitude of the farmers can't be overemphasised if we sincerely wish to have a holistic development of the sector. In the earlier times, the importance of the mentality of the people for whom the development programmes had been initiated by the state was not accorded due importance by the academicians and scholars. Rather it was either summarily dismissed or disdainfully relegated to the periphery. But nowadays, any dispassionate observer of human behaviour frankly admits that human attitude plays a pivotal role in the success or failure of any government programme. For example, if the farmers of a particular village stubbornly refuse to accept a newer and more scientific method of cultivation for some undisclosed reasons, no amount of coaxing and pressure from the government or university's side is going to yield results. It would be no exaggeration to say that different attitudinal responses of the farming community can sway the pendulum of performance of any government agricultural scheme either towards great success or miserable defeat. A voluntary association of progressive farmers of that village can make some positive difference in this regard more than any outside agency. However, outside agencies can discreetly inculcate the idea among the more reasonable section of the farmers so that insularity of the community towards scientific practices resulting from superstitious beliefs can be gradually dismantled.

It may be pertinent to mention here that in the recent years, a powerful movement vociferously asking for farmers' rights has been gaining momentum in Assam. They have successfully flagged several important problems of the farmer community before the government and the civil society. But the rhetorical demands and the rebellious overtones of their efforts have pre-empted a healthy debate in the intellectual circle for coming to a conclusion about the actual plight of the farmers and its likely corrective action. The bound duties of the farmer which are equally important for the overall development of the sector are never stressed by the leaders of the agitation

which has ushered in an avoidable asymmetry into the whole sector. The role of civil society in guiding the agitation is deplorably weak leading to a situation where its leaders are perceived by many as the sole saviours of the farmers.

All said and done, if these four issues can be forcefully tackled by all concerned in an atmosphere of convergence and synergy, the agriculture in Assam would certainly leapfrog into the league of other developed states of the country. As mentioned earlier, we have not touched upon many issues bedeviling this sector due to their intrinsic characteristic of not being amenable to any change easily. Our efforts have been restricted to identifying a few important ills which can be firmly dealt with provided everyone involved in this sector consciously decides to do so. It is high time also for the civil society to pull up its socks and become little more proactive in the greater interest of not only the farmers but also for the all the people. We should recall and internalise the intrinsic meaning of what Nehru said – "Everything else can wait, but not agriculture." Once we can successfully overcome the gnawing elements of platitude that have diluted the significance of Nehru's statement and our agriculture gets upgraded from the current waitlisted position to a superior one, we all would benefit immensely.

17

Sankaradeva Saint Extraordinary

Lakshmi Nandan Bora

Shrimanta Sankaradeva, the great *Vaisnava* saint of Assam of the medieval period is known as *Mahapurusa*, the great soul because of his extraordinary qualities, the evidence of which still influences the minds of his innumerable devotees in the north-Indian region. Besides north-east India, his field of activity extended up to Kooch Bihar of West Bengal and a sizeable portion of present Bangladesh. His fame as a spiritual leader, scholar and writer was acclaimed throughout India. He was an erudite scholar, one of the finest writers in India, a great musician, a pioneer in the field of drama and dramatic performance and above all a great religious preacher and reformer. In the Assam of his time, which roughly included the present north-east India, he brought about renaissance not only in religion and literature, but also in dance, music, painting and audio-visual media. He placed the region of his activities on a sound spiritual and cultural footing. He is the innovative preacher of a refreshingly new religion that goes by the names of Neo-*Vaisnavism* of *Eka Sarana Harinam Dharma*, which benefitted the common people immensely as they had been the victims of religious exploitation and oppressive religious bureaucracy.

As the innovator of *Eka Sarana Harinam Dharma*, Sankaradeva became successful in transcending time and space. This religion is based on the essence of the *Bhagavata-purana*, the Geeta, the Narada Bhaktisutra and other related scriptures dwelling on monotheism. Its essential elements are devotional with two characteristics of Bhakti. They are self-surrender to God and enrichment of the self with ecstatic joy, peace and happiness through worshipping him. Faith in God is the main plank for getting salvation and liberation from the misery of life. This Neo-*Vaisnavism* of Sankardeva does not encourage dialectics. It was molded by him in such a way that it genuinely conformed to the spiritual and cultural need of the common masses irrespective of caste, creed, sex and status. Thus, he had been successful in bringing the people of diverse ethnic groups

into the fold of this fascinatingly fresh religion he preached. For achieving this end it was necessary for him to know the common people very intimately and toil hard. The artist in him made the arduous task pleasant.

Teachings of Sankardeva

Sankaradeva urged people to desist from inactivities and engage themselves in action or to work incessantly and dispassionately. Work with attachment or the desire for getting the result is to be curbed. This was the motto enunciated by Lord Krisna in the Geeta.

Eka Sarana Harinam Dharma is based on Bhakti i.e.. devotion, which has to be practiced through (i) *Sravana*—listening to the glory of God, (ii) *Kirtana*—chanting prayers, (iii) *Smarana*—remembering the activities of God, (iv) *Padasevana*—serving the feet of God, (v) *Archana*— worshipping the deity, (vi) *Vandana*—saluting and prostrating at the feet of God, (vii) *Sakhya*—developing a sense of friendship between the adorer and the adored and (viii) *Atma-nivedana*—complete self-surrender. Out of all these nine ways of practicing *Bhakti*, Sankaradeva recommended only *Sravana*, *Kirtana* and added Dasya. He himself expressed his rapport with God by describing him as the slave of *Kŕṣn̲a*. For cultivating devotional qualities, a devotee should adhere to nam (names of the supreme deity), *deva* (deity), *guru* (spitual guide) and *Bhakata* (devotee). Hence, by the guidance of the *guru* and association with the likeminded devotees, *Bhakti* can be successfully practiced, and thus attainment of salvation will be a certainty.

This form of Vaisnvism belongs to the Adaitya School, advocating monotheism. It was primarily derived from the philosophical aspects of the *Bhagawata-Purana* and the Geeta in which God has been regarded as transcendental, possessing both *nirguna* (attribute less) and *Saguna* (attributeful) aspects. So, the *Saguna* God in the form of Rama or Krsna is worshipped. In the Geeta Saguna God Krsna says: *Sarba dharman parityaya mamekam saranam braja* i.e., giving up all religions, take initiation in me. This *sloka* of the Geeta is the basis of *Vaisnvism*. So *vaisnvism* should postulate that worship must be confined to one God only. In his philosophical treatise, Sankaradeva says: Narayana is the supreme soul and the only Lord of the universe. Nothing exists without Him. He is the cause as well as effect of the creation.

The religion preached by Sankaradeva is unique in the sense that the worship of only the supreme being (Krishna or Rama) is permissible, and Bhakti can be attained through *Sarana*, *Kirtana* and *Dasyabhava* (attitude of a selfless and faithful slave towards his master). But other forms of Vaisnvism prevalent in India have deviated from true *Vaisnvism* to some extent. As for example, *Vaisnvism* of Chaitanya worships Radha and Krisna. The devotees of Namdeva's *Vaisnvism* and those of Ramananda's worship Rukmini-Krihsna and Sita-Rama respectively.

Sankaradeva's Social Contribution

Sankaradeva preached equality in the spiritual domain, keeping no bar between a *Brahmin* and a *Candala*.

For the liberal outlook of Sankaradeva most of the ethnic groups of his region came into his fold and became his ardent disciples. His religion acted as a powerful integrating force. His moral teachings had been immensely successfully in transforming the society to be honest, truthful, kind, patient and discriminate in enjoying worldly pleasures, non-violent and pure in heart.

His religion teaches the doctrine of *Karma* as described in the Geeta. So it teaches the positive outlook on life and discourages fatalistic attitudes.

In the *Dasama*, the tenth part of the *Bhagawata-purana* Sankaradeva writes—

Life cannot be one of inaction, it will either be good or bad action. People enjoy or suffer inevitably according to the consequence of their deeds.

Sankaradeva's greatness lies in his effective methods of popularising his religious teachings. In his time, knowledge of scriptures generally written in Sanskrit was confined to a fortunate few, mostly to the priest class. As professionals of religion; they applied the texts of the scriptures to serve their own purposes, and people in general groped in darkness as knowledge from the scriptures was denied to them. But Sankaradeva's approach was revolutionary. With the object of lifting the common people from the mire of ignorance, he undertook the scheme of translating the principal scriptures into Assamese. He himself translated a lot, and engaged others too. As a result the true spirit of religion and details of *Vaisnavism* percolated to the grassroots. This helped him immensely to preach his religion. Thus, he demolished the rigid bureaucracy in religion, and became the bone of contention for the priest class who suffered heavily in their profession of exploiting the simple and ignorant masses. In the process Sankaradeva came to be known as a great literature. He made enormous contributions in Assamese literature. He wrote six long narrative episodes and translated part I, II, X, XI and XII of the *Bhagawata-purana* and part VIII of the *Ramayana*. He authored four theological and cosmological works, of which Bhakti Ratnakar was in Sanskrit. The *Kirtana*, his best work and the *Gunamala* were penned by him for prayer. He wrote six plays called *Ankia Nats* and composed a number of lyrics as *bargits, Bits, bhatimas, totoyas* and *chapayas*. He was the author of 18 major works. Interestingly, about fifty per cent of his total literary output was contributed after he attained the age of 95. Perhaps such an instance is rare in world literature. He enriched Assamese literature in many an aspect and coined many a new word enhancing the power of expression of the Assamese language. He is regarded as the father of Assamese literature and held in high esteem as a builder of the nation too.

Sankaradeva was a born genius. He excelled all other *Vaisnavite* preachers of his time because none of them was as innovative as him and used all types audio-visual media which had been prevalent then Sankaradeva-composed a large number of verses and translated a number of works, which could be sung in a number of tunes like *dulari*, *lechari* etc. Thus, the *Bhagawata* or the *Kirtana* recital was never boring. He was the creator of some musical equipments and a good number of musical accompaniments to be used in songs, dances and prayer. He composed nearly 240 gits (lyrics) and borgits

(divine number) which can be sung with 37 *ragas* and five *talas* which are also his creations. He introduced a number of dances, known as *Sankari* or *Satriya* dances and was also the innovator of *Bhawana*, a kind of open air performance which enjoyed great popularity. In creating or evolving all those audio-visual arts which still constitute the core of Assamese culture, common ingredients of the folk cultures of various tribes were aptly co-ordinated on the slender skeleton of classical dance and music prevalent in his time. Thus, the culture created by Sankaradeva, now known as ankari culture is a composite form of the popular ingredients of the folk cultures of different ethnic groups and as such, it has been able to touch the hearts of everybody and has been working as a powerful tool for uniting the people of the region irrespective of castes, creeds and communities. Sankaradeva is relevant in our strife-ridden age also because cultivation and popularisation of *Sankari* culture may act as a unifying force.

Sankaradeva introduced *namghar* (congregational prayer hall) and *hati* (abode of devotees) on the pattern of the Buddhist monasteries. The *namghar* in different places acted as centers of learning and administering justice. So he had sowed the seed of present panchayati system of dispensing disputes.

Kalaguru Bishnu Prasad Rabha, one of the stalwarts of Assamese literature and culture summarises the contribution of Sankaradeva with these words—

He (Sankaradeva) gave us music, dance, musical instruments like madanga and mil, literature, nam, kirtan, namghar, borgit, hati, housing designs, bank, society, religion, ethnics, justice, law, moral upsurge, non-violence, sacrifice and enjoyment of life.

As a result, Sankaradeva's *Eka Sarana Harinam Dharma* reigns supreme in the hearts of the people of North-East India and will continue to influence all spheres of life in the region. He has been regarded as the greatest amongst the greats from his time to the present.

18

A Paradise on Earth – Majuli

Justice Mukunda Kam Sharma

Assam, the Gateway to the North East Region of the country possesses god-gifted natural beauty in abundance. The mighty river Brahmaputra which originates in the Manssarovar runs through China, where it is known as '*Jchungpo*' and then enters; India through the Arunachal Pradesh and Assam. It practically runs through the Iran of Assam dividing the state of Assam into two distinct parts, one known as the North Assam and the other as the South Assam. The river Brahmaputra is a Male River and also behaves like a ferocious and mighty person while in full flow. It is indeed the life line for the people of Assam but at the same time could be called as sorrow of Assam as the River Nile in Egypt, is called. In full flow it inundates villages and acres of cultivable lands, brings untold misery to the people who lose their home and hearth during the flood period. In the year 1950, there was a devastating earthquake in Assam, and the intense effect thereof brought up the river bed which resulted in consequential erosion of the banks of Brahmaputra thereby causing flood in the nearby places. Dibrugarh which was one of the vibrant and leading towns of Assam during the British period has suffered worst as half of the town has been eroded and is now within the river and in fact, the river Brahmaputra now flows at a height more than the level of the town and thereby, posing a threat to the entire town during the monsoon period.

So is the case with 'Majuli', which is perhaps the largest riverine island in the entire world. Majuli is situated in the lap of the Brahmaputra, about 15 miles from Jorhat town to the nearest Ghat in the river called Nemati Ghat from which a motorboat/ferry takes about one and half hours to reach Majuli. Surrounded by waters all around, `Majuli' is indeed a unique creation of the nature. It can also be called as the God's own country because of its unique location in the lap of the river and also because the entire riverine island is resonant with singing of devotional songs.

The name 'Majuli' probably originates from the combination of two words, 'Ma' meaning Lakshmi, the Goddess of prosperity and 'juli' meaning granary. A number of anecdotes are associated with Majuli. According to one of the legends, the ancient King Arimatta being repentant of killing his own father offered various precious ornaments like gold, diamond etc. to the river Brahmaputra with the purpose for atoning the sin that he had committed. But unfortunately even the river Brahmaputra refused to accept the offering of the valuables from Arimatta; rather the river itself broke into two parts leaving the offerings in the high land which is called 'Majuli'.

According to another anecdote, Saint *Parshuram* after assassinating his mother with the axe in his hand travelled the universe to wash away his sin and finally resorted to worshipping Lord Krishna for salvation when two streams fell down besides his knees and the middle part of the same came to be later on known as Majuli. One other story is that Lord Krishna while eloping with Rukmini from Kundilnagar to Dwarka stopped to take rest at Majuli. Rukmini was so fascinated and enchanted by the beauty of the place that she commented that the said place is the Dwarka itself of her imagination. Being fascinated by her comments Lord Krishna commented that Majuli would thereafter be known as Second Dwarka in future.

May be because of these traditions and heritages connected with it, the island became the nerve centre of the neo-*Vaishnavite* religion at a later point of time. In fact the original *vaishnavite* religion was practised even in Assam but the procedure for such worship prescribed was complicated and cumbersome. With the rise of Buddhism and the Islam, religion in some parts of the country, the Hindu religion had to face a very strong and steep opposition from other religions. The people practicing *vaishnava* culture and religion found it difficult to practice this cumbersome and complicated form of worship and became attracted towards simpler forms of worship as practised in the Islam and Buddhist religion. To overcome the adverse situation, some of the Hindu saints thought that the *vishnavite* religion should also be made simpler in form so that there is no difficulty for the disciples to practice the various forms of worship provided. This thought process originated in the Southern states of India. The seers who propounded the new ideas were Madhavacharya and Ramanand. This *vaishnavite* movement found favour with the people and slowly it travelled towards the northern direction. After crossing the Vindhya mountain, it engulfed Mathura, Vrindaban and went as far as Gujarat and then it started travelling towards east and then crossing Bengal it entered Assam.

It was in the sixteenth century that *Mahapurush* Shankara Deva along with his disciples namely, Madhav Deva, Damodar Deva and Hari Deva laid the foundation of neo-*vaishnavite* religion in Assam. Shankara Deva, who was not only a religious preacher but also was a social reformer founded the "*Eka Sarana Nama Dharma*". Same professed that Lord Vishnu is the main God and if he is worshipped, all other Gods and goddesses would receive the prayers as when water is poured into the roots of a tree all its branches get a share of it.

Shankara Deva went to Majuli and while staying there he met *Mahapurush* Madhav Deva who soon got attracted by the towering personality of

Shankaradeva and became his closest and strongest disciple. They together established Belagiri Satra in the 16th Century which incidentally came to be known as the first satra to be established in Majuli. Slowly many other satras came to be established in Majuli consequent upon which the place became the nerve centre of satra culture of Assam. With the establishment of all the satras around Majuli it emerged as the crowning glory of *Vishnavite* culture of Assam. It is said that Shankara Deva, Madhav Deva and Damodar Deva established 64 satras in Majuli during the 16th and 17th Centuries of which only 22 remain functional as of present with the rest having been eroded away by the river or had to be shifted to other places due to flood and erosion of the river island.

After the devastating earthquake of 1950 the river bed of the Brahmaputra had risen and consequently the River Brahmaputra changed its course which became the main cause for causing erosion both in Dibrugarh and also in Majuli. Although various steps are being taken at different levels and by different organisations to protect Majuli and stop erosion of its land, yet it seems to be an uphill task for the measures taken for its protection, appeared to have failed. Every year population residing in entire Majuli has been facing tremendous difficulties and untold miseries due to the flood caused by the river Brahmaputra and other rivers and soil erosion of the banks of the rivers. But fortunately for us and the population there during the autumn, winter and summer months the island turns into a paradise in earth with lush green grass and agricultural produces and various species of migratory birds coming from far and wide. Majuli is situated in a serene and subline environment. It is also home to the population drawn from different strata and groups of people consisting of different castes: Ahoms, Kacharis, Koch, Rajvanshis, Michings, Chuttias, Sonowals and Nepalese etc.

Establishment of various satras in Majuli has brought in a deep impact and transformation to the life of the people. About 70 per cent population of Majuli are literates. The satras are instrumental in contributing immensely to the development and progress of Sanskrit literature and Assamese literature.

Not only translated works but a number of original literary compositions and books also have been brought out by the satras enriching the Assamese and Sanskrit literature. But the principal and the main contribution of the satras is to the development of the cultural life of Assam.

As Majuli was the residence of multi-ethnic group of people including the tribals, so the religion propagated by Sri Shankara Deva had to cater to the need of these groups. It had to be so designed so as to attract one and all and also had to be so simple so as to enable all strata of people to comprehend and understand the teachings.

The main emphasis of this neo-*vaishnavite* religion and movement is unstinted and profound devotion (*Bhakti*) to God Vishnu and total surrender to him. Vishnu is generally worshipped in the form of Lord Krishna, who is a friend (Sakha Krishna). But for Shri Shankara Deva, the devotee worships the Divine as his servant (*Dasya Bhava*). Sri Shankara Deva took up a challenge to transform the multicultural society of Majuli and then in entire Assam and

for that he accepted seven broad principles of Shrimad Bhagavata, which are as follows:

1. That the Supreme Being Narayana or Hari is the main or the principal God. All other gods are born from him and therefore, praying at the root would amount to propitiating all.

2. That the Lord took different forms at different time like Rama, Krishna and when Krishna is worshipped all other Gods are worshipped. The seed of salvation lies in the devotion to Lord Krishna only.

3. Complete surrender to Lord Krishna is the most suitable form of devotion.

4. Bhagavata scripture which highlights the magnanimity of Lord Krishna itself represents Lord Krishna.

5. Forms of devotion to Lord Krishna are the nine forms of devotion of which listening (*Shravana*) and recitation (*Kirtana*) are the foremost amongst them.

6. Satsanga or assembly of the devotees where all together sing and listen to the spiritual teaching is the best way to show devotion (*Bhakti*). In doing so, the tie of brotherhood gets stronger and binds them into a strong relationship.

7. For fulfilment of devotion, there would always be need of a *guru* or preceptor who would be the best person to teach the devotees, the ways and means of showing devotion and also to make understand the meaning of devotion.

Based on these principles, *the Bhakti* cult soon spread far and wide and attracted people of different: regions and different sects. To spread the message, Sri Shankara Deva and others like Madhav Deva, Sri Damodar Dev, Sri Haridev, Sri Gopal Ata adopted different ways and means and forms. They created devotional literature both original and translation from Sanskrit, wrote dramas-based on religious themes, and also wrote devotional songs in the praise of the Lord. These have become the literary and cultural asset of our culture and ethos and enriched our treasure house.

The Sattra institution of Assam is unique in character and style. There are many religious sects in India propagating Hindu religion in different ways and thoughts. But no where would we find a religious establishment preaching religion and its teachings amongst the disciple and people through literary activities, performing arts, music and such other means.

Dr Shri Pitambar Deva Gowami, the present Satradhikar of the Auniati Satra has spoken in nutshell of main objective of the Satra institution in the following manner: "Objective of the Satra is to motivate the minds of the people to realise the existente of the Supreme power of the world through the spiritual performances and through the execution of *Sharana*, *Prayer*, *Nama Prasanga,* religious festivals and the recitation of rhymes and scriptures based on Lord Srikrishna." This passage indeed gives a deep insight of the activities carried out by the various *Satras* of Assam.

All the Sattras, besides carrying out various religious activities and festivals also propagate and perform various cultural activities which through

the years have become priceless asset of the Assamese Society. The dance forms practiced in the Satras are commonly known as Satriya form of dance and has now been given the recognition of being a proper classical dance of India by none other than the Sangeet Natak Academy. There are different types of such dance form such as *Natua, Apsora, Sutradhar, Ozhapali, Chali, Zhumura, Rash Nrittya, Gayon Bayan, Mati Akhora* and *Dashavatar* to name a few. The Satras have also developed a distinct form of music known as Borgeet and devotional songs (*Nama*). Besides other forms of songs like *Ankia* geet, *Raja ghoria* song, *Guruvandana*, *Gopal Vairaga* geet are also practised and they have achieved a unique place in Assamese society and culture. The Satras are famous for their performances of Bhaona in Assamese which has a drama form. Sri Shankaradeva introduced performance of Ankia naat in Brajavali language which received tremendous response from the rural audience. It also helped in preaching of the religion propounded which is neo-*vaishnava dharma*.

Thus the Satra institution of Assam has remarkably contributed to the religious and cultural advancement and development of Assam. Majuli being the nerve centre for carrying out these activities is visited by the literary and cultural critics to explore and assert in its richness.

There are also various other art forms generated as activities of the Satras. One of these is undoubtedly the mask making. It is actually a traditional art and is being used for various activities like performance of dance and drama. Satras particularly Auniati Satra is known for making fan from cane. Different types of cottage industries exist in Majuli which also has given it a unique distinction.

The nerve centre of all these literary, cultural and spiritual advancement therefore, has to be saved from erosion by the river Brahmaputra at all cost. If we lose even a part of it, we will lose our culture, ethos and heritage. We must generate a movement for saving it from erosion and build the place as an epic centre of our culture and heritage. All the stake holders must get together and chalk out their future course to give an impetus to this movement.

19

A Sojourn in Sylhet, Bangladesh

Jishnu Baruah, IAS

I am a passionate traveller with an equal passion for history. While I have visited countries as far as South Korea and Mexico, I have always found it truly enriching to explore places in our neighbourhood, in view of our shared history. In my two decades of serious travelling in and around India, I have visited Myanmar, Bhutan, Sri Lanka, Nepal and Bangladesh among foreign lands. A visit to China and Pakistan has, however, eluded me till date. I went to Wagah and felt like crossing over to Lahore, which is just 26 km away, but the geo-political realities on the Indo-Pakistan border have always been coldly discouraging to such ventures. On the other hand, I went to Bangladesh in 1998, a visit which I still recall with pleasure, having been a guest of our own Jaideep Mazumdar, the then Assistant High Commissioner of India at Chittagong. During that visit, I had plans to travel to Sylhet, which regrettably did not materialise. However, recently, I was able to drive down to Sylhet and Moulvi Bazaar in Bangladesh with my family in what turned out to be a visit filled with unforgettable memories.

Before I pen down my experiences, I must briefly spell out Sylhet's close historical link with Assam. In colonial times, for as many as 73 years till the partition of the country, Sylhet was a district in Assam, and it played an extremely influential role in the politics and administration of the province. Sylhet was the most populous district in Assam. In fact, it comprised nearly 29 per cent of composite Assam's population in 1941. However, recorded history reveals that the Surma Valley had an uneasy relationship with the Brahmaputra Valley. Politicians and intellectuals of the two valleys tried relentlessly for years together, at least till the late 1920s, to sever the unhappy administrative union of the two valleys. While Sylhetis attempted valiantly in the face of stiff Raj opposition to seek the district's merger to Bengal by raising protests time and again, in the Brahmaputra valley there was no less desire to get rid of the district for political, linguistic, ethnic and demographic reasons.

Nothing happened till 1947. At the time of partition, with the ever-widening communal divide, Hindus who were earlier clamouring for a reunion with Bengal now wanted to remain in Assam fearing that their district would be transferred to Pakistan. A section of Muslims under Jamiat Ulema also opposed the district's merger with Pakistan. Indeed, in July 1947, a referendum was held to decide whether Sylhet should form a part of Pakistan or remain in India. The referendum went in favour of Pakistan by a margin of around 55,000 votes, but Sylhet was partitioned with most of the district transferred to Pakistan except for a large part of Karimganj sub-division, comprising three and a half police station areas, which came to India. After the liberation of Bangladesh, the composite Sylhet district was reorganised in 1985 and four districts were created —Sylhet (originally the sadar subdivision), Moulvi Bazaar, Sunamganj and Habiganj. Having read about the administrative and political history of the district including the Sylhet district gazetteer of 1905, I was keen to visit Sylhet and get a sense of how people there perceive us and how the area had developed in the last two or three decades. In my younger days, I was fascinated by Nari Rustomji's entertaining account of his life in Sylhet and Moulvi Bazaar as a young civil servant in his memoirs 'Enchanted Frontiers' and I yearned to retrace his footsteps in that part of Bangladesh. I, therefore, undertook a three-day visit to Bangladesh from 25th December 2012 to 28th December 2012.

We travelled to Sylhet by the land route by crossing over to Bangladesh at Sutarkandi in Karimganj district. It had taken a long and arduous journey through Meghalaya and Cachar braving terrible roads and almost unending traffic jams, for us, a nine members team including a child aged two, to reach Silchar on the 24th of December 2012. After having collected our passports, on which visas were stamped by the Bangladesh visa office at Agartala, we set off for Sutarkandi on 25th December 2012. At Sutarkandi ICP, we had hoped that the stoppage for the immigration formalities would be brief. That was not to be, as annoyingly, it took us much more than an hour to complete our formalities. Be that as it may, we reached the zero point on foot and were warmly received by Bangladesh officials on crossing over. Kuldip Dey, a local Bangladeshi official of the State Bank of India, Sylhet was also there to receive us with the two SUVs we had hired. After a warm welcome at the border, we boarded our vehicles and sped off to Sylhet city, which is only 46 km away.

My first impression of Sylhet district was one of disbelief as there was hardly any change in the landscape from the Barak valley and its verdant greenery. I had to pinch myself to come to terms with the fact that I was in a foreign land. But wait a minute, there were differences! The roads were so much better than those in Cachar with no potholes whatsoever! The signboards were almost entirely in Bangla. Private cars were relatively few though there were several reconditioned Mitsubishis and Toyota SUVs on view. We were soon in Sylhet city and reached the iconic Keane Bridge over the Surma River, named after Sir Michael Keane, who was the Governor of Assam in the 1930s. The bridge was narrow with very heavy traffic of rickshaws, light commercial vehicles, pedestrians, hand carts and what have you. There is now another

bridge, a few kms away, over the Surma. Soon we were at the other end and caught sight of another famous landmark of Sylhet the Ali Amjad Clock Tower. We were given to understand that the clock had fallen into disrepair, and only some time back it was repaired and restored to its former glory. Close to the Clock Tower, lay the spanking new Sylhet VIP Circuit House where on our arrival, we were received by the Nazarat officer and were immediately ushered into our well-appointed and commodious rooms. The new circuit house in Sylhet, I learnt, was built to cope with the heavy VIP movement to Sylhet city, which is now an economic powerhouse with a large expat population.

After a quick lunch of spicy chicken curry, fish, dal, brinjal fry and rice, I sought an appointment with the Divisional Commissioner of Sylhet. I wanted his help to locate the Sanskrit College (formerly the Assam Government Sanskrit College) and also visit the famous Murari Chand College, which was the second Government College in pre-independence Assam. The Commissioner, Mr Ziaul Alam received me with great warmth. He, however, was not aware of the existence of the Sanskrit College. Dr A.C. Bhagabati in Guwahati had specifically tasked me to visit the institution where his father had once served as Principal for long years, and he himself had lived on its premises as a child. I, therefore, pressed the Commissioner to make a quick enquiry, which he very kindly proceeded to do so. The results were encouraging. The Sanskrit College was not only in existence but was also functioning. I thanked the Commissioner profusely and rushed to the College. Soon, we reached an Assam type building of modest size at Kedwapara. It required a further confirmation to ascertain that the building indeed was the Sanskrit College now renamed as the Srihatta Sanskrit College. A banner indicating 'Sri Sri Gita function' was hung on the walls. A large number of colourfully dressed children belonging to the Hindu community were busily pacing up and down the corridor. I asked one of the onlookers, who turned out to be the current Principal, about the College. Initially, Dr Dilip Kumar Das Choudhury, the Principal did not seem frightfully friendly and forthcoming. Instead, on learning that I had come from Assam, he bitterly complained that hotels in Guwahati did not give him accommodation upon seeing his Bangladesh passport. I chose not to entangle myself in any debate.

Choudhury later warmed up and showed us around his office. We got ourselves clicked with the temperamental Principal. I also got through to Dr Bhagabati on the mobile and described to him his childhood home as I saw it. The Principal also spoke to Dr Bhagabati and invited him to the college. Mission accomplished, we drove through the crowded bazaars of Sylhet—the famous Zinda Bazaar, the Bondor Bazaar and the Chowhatta Bazaar. Here and there were modern high rise buildings, though Kuldip told us that Sylhetis preferred living in spacious bungalows to living in the cramped confines of apartments. The tall high rise buildings had come up in the last two decades as a result of investments made by Sylheti expatriates, particularly from the United Kingdom.

At Zinda Bazaar, we visited the Blue Water Mall, which, I must say, was disappointing. The tiny shops in the mall seemed to have appropriated all the

famous brand names— Debenhams, Marks and Spencer and soforth, though the products that they were selling were of local or Chinese origin. But I managed to check out a bookshop where I bought a couple of books, one on the Bangladesh civil service and the other an account of the liberation movement. Books in English were remarkably few, and I didn't have to browse for long. We noticed the Ramkrishna Mission and Ashram while returning to the Circuit House and decided to have a quick look at the mission. The mission is well kept and has a good library. As we entered the mission, chanting and loud prayers from the neat and beautiful temple inside the premises could be heard. Swami Chandranathanandaji, the head of the mission, who is a Bangladeshi himself, was kind enough to meet us. Speaking excellent English, Swamiji gave us a little background on the Sylhet mission centre and the Ramkrishna mission centres all over the sub-continent. The mission has, since 1926, been engaged in myriad welfare activities in the Surma valley. It seemed that this Ramkrishna Mission centre at Meera Bazaar was also the social and religious hub for the Hindu community in Sylhet city. We thanked the Swamiji for his time and sought his blessings. Thereafter, we headed for the Circuit House. On returning to the Circuit House, we had our dinner, in which the menu was identical to the one at lunch—spicy chicken, fish *et al.* However, no complaints, the food was good.

The next day i.e., 26th December, after a light breakfast of delicious local parathas and eggs, we headed for Murari Chand College, a college founded in 1892 by Raja Girish Chandra Roy, a leading Zamindar of Sylhet in that era. Many well-known academicians from the Brahmaputra valley like Asraf Ali, Umakanta Goswami, Girindra Nath Borpujari, Aswini Kumar Barkataki were also teachers in MC College at some point during their careers. Talking of the Brahmaputra Valley's connection with the Sylhet in general, it must be mentioned that there were other well-known personalities such as Durgeswar Sarma, a civil servant and Chandrakanta Borpujari, an eminent teacher who had also served in Sylhet for a considerable period of their service life.

After a short journey, the sprawling 44 acre campus came into view. The boys' hostel, I noticed, was housed in a cluster of Assam type buildings. Our entry to the college was greeted by its impressive gateway where embossed on it were the words 'Murari Chand College established in 1892' in Bengali. There were Assam type buildings and concrete colonial style buildings which dotted the landscape. We walked up the staircase and were soon ushered into the office of the Principal, Dr Dhiresh Chandra Sarker. Dr Sarker was very hospitable and told us how old boys from all over the world keep coming to their *alma mater*. Even elderly men in their 80s, he said, would often become 'like children' when they see their old haunts. Prof Riyas and another senior Professor were called to meet us, and we had a pleasant conversation. I handed over some archival material of the college which I had in my possession along with token gifts of Japi, gamosa and a wooden rhino. The Principal, in turn, presented me a copy of the academic calendar of the college of 2009-2010, a directory of academic and non-academic staff members of the college published in 2006 and a copy of the college annual magazine—'Purbasa' of 2007.

A quick glance through the academic calendar revealed that in 2009-2010, the college had celebrated Saraswati puja as an official function along with Independence Day, Victory Day, Idd and Fresher's Day. Indeed, there is also a separate department of Sanskrit in the college with two faculty members. A closer look at the directory would indicate that as many as 30 members of the teaching faculty out of a total of 113 were from the minority Hindu community. The Principal and his two colleagues proudly showed us around their campus—the staff room, lecture gallery, the library etc. We took leave and bade goodbye to our new friends and hurried to Kuldip's bank i.e., the State Bank of India, Sylhet branch. We had to quickly convert our dollars into Bangladeshi *taka,* which we were unable to do so the previous day, a Friday and, therefore, a holiday in Bangladesh. At the bank, Kuldip's senior Manager, Mr Abu Taher Sarker ensured that all paperwork was done in virtually no time. We thanked Mr Sarker for his prompt assistance and returned to the Circuit House for lunch. As we entered the dining hall, the aroma of our special lunch wafted across. We were served mouth watering *hilsa, pabda* and the usual chicken curry. The lunch was devoured in silence and, indeed, with complete satisfaction. In the afternoon, after lunch, I called on the Superintendent of Police, Sylhet, in his office. He was friendly and helpful. The SP, Mr M. Sakhawat Hossain wanted to know whether we had any information on some of his illustrious predecessors who had served in Sylhet before partition. I assured him that I would try and send the material.

Our next destination was Dhakadakshin, the family home of Chaitanya Mahaprabhu, the famous Vaishnavite reformer, who was born in 1484 A.D. Dhakadakshin is situated some 16 kms away from Sylhet city and it takes barely 25 minutes to reach there. A huge reception committee comprising both Hindus and Muslims waited on us at the newly-constructed Krishna temple in Dhakadakshin. Cameras flashed all around, and somebody was videotaping our visit, much to our discomfort. The local press wanted to know how we had heard of Dhakadakshin. The temple is newly constructed, and nothing of the old structure remains. It appeared to be a matter of immense pride for the locals that a potential tourist destination was in their locality. The head of the temple committee, Shri Mishra proudly told us about the communal harmony at Dhakadakshin and how the local Muslims were equally enthusiastic in maintaining the temple. Indeed, many Muslims were urging us to visit another Hindu religious place in Dhakadakshin. Time being short, we politely declined. Touchingly, Mishra told us how blessed they all were by our visit. I mumbled something in embarrassment. Our new friends were particularly keen to get themselves snapped with us, and so were we. Photographs taken, we bade goodbye to our friends in Dhakadakshin.

We returned to Sylhet and the ladies insisted on making a few purchases. We were taken to Aarong, which is the Bangladeshi equivalent of Fab India. Aarong is a retail chain with outlets all over Bangladesh and specialises in marketing the handicrafts and products manufactured by rural women like jewellry, pottery, fabrics etc. Aarong outlet at Naya sarak, Sylhet is a must-see for visitors. The three storied building Aarong, which showcases the local

handicrafts at their best, is highly impressive. Well-lit and with products wonderfully displayed, it is often choc-a-bloc with shoppers, especially from the well-heeled and chic category. The ladies in our group including my mother, wife, and sister-in-law, did a quick survey of the place promising to themselves that the last day in Bangladesh would be reserved for some frenetic shopping there. As dusk had already set in, there was only time for a short business like visit to a crockery shop at Mahajanpati. Mahajanpati was originally a Hindu dominated market, but not anymore, though there are still a few shops owned by Hindu shopkeepers with surnames such as Banik, trading in brass and iron utensils. Kuldip told me that some of the traders are quite rich but are not wont to display their wealth. We entered Muhammad Shafique Stores with which Kuldip's bank had a corporate relationship. My better half, Rashmi bought one bone china crockery set for 1200 *taka*, but not before successfully bringing down the price by 200 *taka*. Shafique was persuaded to happily sell at a lower price for the *'Mehman'* (guest) from India. Shafique was conversing with Kuldip in the racy Sylheti dialect. I vaguely understood that easy going Sylhetis do not stand a chance in business against the more hardworking people from other parts of Bangladesh. Indeed, I noted that standard Bengali is mostly spoken in the city since increasing economic opportunities in this expanding city were bringing in migrants from all over Bangladesh. The use of standard Bengali is a necessity as the local Sylheti dialect is not quite intelligible to people from other parts of Bangladesh. On the Sylheti dialect, the Sylhet district gazetteer of 1905 had amusingly pointed out that *'the sibilant, as in the case of Assamese, is often replaced by h, and the Sylhetti speaks of haph when referring to a snake, and talks of hakal instead of sakal. But, like a veritable cockney, he is content with inserting h's when they are not wanted, but frequently omits them when they are. The elephant masquerades as ati, and hatgao, which really should be satgao, is loosely spoken of atgao. The h is also reduced almost to the vanishing point in ghar, bhari, or in verbs like kahilam....'*

We made a quick visit to the Dargah of Shah Hazrat Jalal, which was a picture of peace and tranquility. The main shrine is located on a broad platform and is approached by a flight of steps. The tomb where the devout offer prayers is covered with a rich brocade, and at night the space around it is illuminated with candles the atmosphere is quite entrancing. The entire complex is clean and well-maintained. While women are not allowed to enter the main tomb, they can come into the complex, which exudes peace and quiet. Our local guide, in fact, advised that the ladies in our group, who were still seated in the van, should also come into the premises. This, he said, would also enable them to soak in the magical atmosphere of the shrine. The ladies did just that and, it must be said, it was a rewarding experience for them. Close to the shrine is a deep pond full of large-sized fish, particularly the '*Gaja*' fish or catfish. We had a close look at the well fed and contented '*Gaja*', which is somewhat like the '*Shole*' (as in Bengali) fish. On seeing the fish, my brother-in-law Ankush, in excitement, uttered '*Hole*' (as in Assamese). There were audible whispers from the crowd of onlookers who quickly concluded that we

were conversing in the local Sylheti dialect! Nobody is obviously allowed to fish and nobody would fish in such a holy place. It is believed that Hazrat Shah Jalal was given a sample of earth by his uncle who instructed him to settle wherever he might find earth of the same character. He accompanied the invading Muslim army who had set off against the last Hindu king of Sylhet, Raja Gour Gobind, and was eventually responsible for spreading Islam in not only Sylhet, but also all over East Bengal. According to the Sylhet district gazetteer of 1905, Hazrat Shah Jalal crossed the Surma on a praying seat and *"proceeded to reduce Gaur Gobind by methods no ordinary man could be expected to resist. The Hindu Raja had built himself a magical seven-storied tower, to which he retreated on the approach of the invaders. Shah Jalal each day offered up a solemn prayer, at the conclusion of which one of the stories of the tower collapsed."* The gazetteer goes on to say that Gour Gobind surrendered after sometime. Hazrat Shah Jalal soon found a match for his uncle's earth sample and settled down in Sylhet to propagate Islam. Another dargah that we visited was that of Hazrat Shah Paran, the renowned Sufi saint. Though this dargah was not as grand in its architecture as that of Hazrat Shah Jalal, it was packed with the devout who had strong faith in its magical healing and curative powers for those suffering from diseases. We then retired to the Circuit House for the night.

We were to drive down to Moulvi Bazaar the next day primarily to see the tea country and spend the night at the Moulvi Bazaar Circuit House. We did have second thoughts on staying the night at Moulvi Bazaar as Sylhet city itself had plenty to offer and we were not yet done with Sylhet. But our booking in the Sylhet Circuit House could not be extended, and luckily so, for our Moulvi Bazaar trip was the highpoint of our visit to Bangladesh. Before proceeding to Moulvi Bazaar in the morning, we noticed that the Sylhet Circuit House was agog with activities, much more than in the previous two days. We soon learnt that a senior cabinet minister had come from Dhaka. Departmental officers, the Deputy Commissioner and the Commissioner of Police, Sylhet city were all there. A guard of honour by the Sylhet Metropolitan Police was given to the visiting dignitary, who took the salute along with DC Sylhet, the Commissioner of Police and a former minister, one Suranjit Sengupta from Habiganj. After the ceremonies had concluded, the Commissioner of Police, Mr Amulya Bhusan Barua came over to us and introduced himself. We were pleasantly surprised to find another Barua and that too as the local city Police chief in Sylhet. Barua is a Buddhist who hails from Chittagong and an exceptionally friendly and gregarious person. We got ourselves clicked with the Police Commissioner, who in the short interaction, invited us to his home in Chittagong and also presented to us king-sized lemons from his kitchen garden and dried fish from Chittagong. In turn, I presented to him the usual *Japi, gamosa* and wooden rhino. I silently cursed myself for lack of imagination in selecting the same gifts for everyone, but the brief meeting with Amulya Barua was a pleasant interlude.

We then proceeded to Kuldip Dey's flat to meet his family. His young wife and her elder sister welcomed us and plied us with giant sized *rosogolas*

and other sweets. It was difficult to do justice to sweets in such a quantity and that too after a heavy breakfast! Mr Asfaque, the landlord also came up to meet us. He is a retired Executive Engineer who had lived in Nagaon till 1949. Like a typical Sylheti known for generous hospitality, he invited us for dinner, which we had to politely decline since we were leaving for Moulvi Bazaar the same day. Kuldip's sister-in-law requested me to visit her school 'Basanta Memorial School' which was named after a senior Sylheti leader Basanta Kumar Das who had once been the Speaker of Assam Legislative Assembly and the last Home Minister of Assam before partition. Interestingly, Basanta Kumar Das had a successful political career in Pakistan and even rose to be the Central Education and Labour Minister in Feroze Khan Noon's cabinet in 1957. Basanta Kumar Das' two sons had, however, migrated to India after partition. One son, an advocate, in fact, settled down in Dibrugarh. The school's Principal, Ms Arpana Chanda introduced me to her colleagues and proudly mentioned that the school was inaugurated by Brigadier Amin.

On the 27th of December in the morning, we drove down to Moulvi Bazaar in a 13-seater Mitsubishi van in which all of us were comfortably seated. The journey to Moulvi Bazaar via Fenchuganj took us less than an hour. Enroute, the driver of the van, Jewel, pointed out to us one of the famous 'Haors' of Sylhet. 'Haors' are, for those who are unacquainted with the term, water bodies or swampy areas, which during the monsoons cover large areas with sheets of water. Sylhetis call such water bodies as '*Haor*' since they resemble the sea or '*Hagor*' (as in Assamese). '*Haors*' abound in fish but today like Assam, Bangladesh too imports fish from Andhra Pradesh despite its numerous rivers and large water bodies. Moulvi Bazaar town at first sight resembles Tezpur with its natural drainage. The town has undulating features with hillocks and low hills interspersed with flat plains. Not surprisingly, Moulvi Bazaar district, particularly the Srimangal area, is Bangladesh's main tea growing area. 95 out of 165 gardens in Bangladesh are in Moulvi Bazaar. The Circuit House, a multi-storied building, itself stood on a slope on a huge campus amidst a social forestry plantation. Prime Minister Sheikh Hasina had visited the town some time back and planted a tree in the Circuit House campus. The old Circuit House, a heritage building constructed in 1912, has been recently renovated. I was told that Pandit Jawaharlal Nehru had also stayed at the Moulvi Bazaar Circuit House during his Assam tour of November-December 1937.

The attendant in the Circuit House was not expecting us, and it seemed no room had been booked in my name. I told him that I was a Commissioner from Karimganj, to which he responded by putting me in touch with the Nazarat officer, a Civil Service probationer by the name of Maruf. Fortunately, Maruf was aware of our programme and everything was soon settled. Maruf himself came over to the Circuit House and saw to it that we were comfortable. Young and energetic, Maruf quizzed me on the administrative system in India. I, in turn, had many queries on the similarities and differences between the Indian and the Bangladeshi system. At my request, Maruf took me over to the Deputy Commissioner's bungalow across the road. The house was not yet occupied

by the new DC, Mr Kamrul Hasan who had joined the day before. The old bungalow in the campus was now the DC's camp office and a new double storied building has been constructed as residential quarters for the DC. I was interested in the old bungalow which was once occupied by Nari Rustomji and R B Vaghaiwalla of the ICS Assam cadre in the 1940s. The incumbency list in the Deputy Commissioner's chamber lists the names of both Rustomji and Vaghaiwalla. I volunteered to Maruf to prepare an error-free exhaustive incumbency list of officers who had served in the district before 1947 on the basis of Assam Government records. Maruf readily accepted my offer and took down my email address. On returning to the circuit house, I found that the Director, Duncan Brothers (Bangladesh), Mr Shah Alam along with the Manager of the Mazdehee garden, Mr Zakir Hossain were waiting to meet me. Back home, I had contacted my old college mate Kevyn David of Williamson Magor to help organise a visit to a garden in Bangladesh. Mr Alam and Mr Hossain had now come to take us to Mazdehee for a short tour.

It was a brief journey of 15 minutes by road from Moulvi Bazaar to Mazdehee garden. Mazdehee is an old garden having been established in 1890. The garden itself appeared no different from any good garden in the Brahmaputra Valley neat and well-maintained. Duncans surely have a wonderful property in Mazdehee! Shah Alam and Zakir Hossain took us- men and children for a tour around the garden while the ladies proceeded to the Burra Sahib's bungalow. Like a bunch of excited tourists, we then got ourselves photographed at various locales including the factory. Shah Alam explained to us the processes involved in making tea. He also told us that Bangladesh tea, like India's, is finding it difficult to attract young men to a career in tea. I mentioned to Shah Alam that I had accompanied Jaideep Mazumdar for dinner at a senior Tea Executive's bungalow in Chittagong in my previous visit to Bangladesh in 1998. Shah Alam remembered that it was in his bungalow that India's young Assistant High Commissioner had come along with another young person! We realised that we had met earlier, almost a decade and a half ago! Small world! We entered the Manager's bungalow, a typical tea property, with neatly manicured lawns, to a warm welcome from Shamoly Hossain, the gracious lady of the house. Tea was a lavish spread and a brilliant conversation ensued. Shah Alam is extremely knowledgeable about the history of Bangladesh and its earlier avatar East Pakistan. He was a student of Dacca University and later as a young tea executive during the Liberation war in 1971, had seen it all. All West Pakistani planters were briefly detained and later evacuated to Pakistan where they started a new life barring two managers who rejoined the industry in the newly-created Bangladesh and continued serving till retirement. I was told that Bangladesh had only 17 districts in 1985, which were reorganised, almost overnight, to 64 districts. Senior Dhaka-based officers were posted to the new districts and asked to be present there at their formal inauguration. Many of these officers were reluctant to go to their headquarters, which had virtually no infrastructure. All these facilities came up by and by. Good roads in the Sylhet division since the last one decade or so are a legacy of the contribution of a Cabinet Minister from Sylhet who ensured that sufficient

funds were made available for road construction and improvement. During all this fascinating conversation, the ladies were having a separate discussion, and a delightful one at that, about life and markets in India and Bangladesh. Zakir and Shamoly very generously volunteered to take us to the local Aarong outlet. We bade goodbye to Mr Shah Alam and thanked him profusely for his time.

I returned to the Circuit House and called on the Deputy Commissioner, Mr Kamrul Hasan, an officer of the Bangladesh Civil Service from the 1993 batch who was temporarily camping in the Circuit House. He was extremely warm and friendly. All the three Additional Deputy Commissioners posted in the district were also present when I called on the DC. There was considerable curiosity on both sides about each other's system of administration and governance. Bangladesh civil servants have a great regard for the Indian Administrative Service and the Civil Service in India, in general. They believe that the IAS is indeed the steel frame of India. I chose not to disabuse them of that notion! However, I did mention about the proactive role played by the Higher Judiciary and how as civil servants in India, we had to be on our toes when it came to matters relating to compliance of court's orders. The DC invited us to dinner where his entire team was present. We continued our conversation over dinner. After dinner, I got myself snapped with the Deputy Commissioner and his team in front of the old Circuit House. Sadly, the photograph, taken in pitch darkness did not come out too well.

The next day, i.e., the 28th of December, we once again had the Deputy Commissioner's company for breakfast or '*Nashta*' as it is called in Bangladesh. We were joined by our friend Zakir and another planter, Mr Sujit Saha and his family. Saha was a classmate of the DC's at the Mymenshing Agriculture University and a close friend of his. He had lived in Dhubri, Assam as a child for a few months when the Liberation war broke out. A fond farewell was given to us by our local friends. The DC touchingly sought my mother's blessings. We expressed our heartfelt thanks to our hosts and wished them Khuda Hafiz. Thereafter, we headed for Sylhet city enroute to Karimganj.

Since we still had a couple of hours on hand in Sylhet, the ladies were dropped off at Aarong for a round of frantic shopping and, I along with my mother took a tour around the city. We visited the Manipuri Rajbari where during the Burmese invasion Raja Gambhir Singh had lived. Very little of the palace remains, though there is a temple dedicated to Sri Sri Gouranga. Mr Ajit Sharma, the priest of the temple invited us to tea, but we were running out of time and had to decline. We paid a hurried visit to the Shahjalal University of Science and Technology, the pride of Sylhet and the first Science and Technology University of its kind established in Bangladesh. Unfortunately, time being short, it was just a brief tour around the campus. I was keen to make a quick visit to the Sylhet station club about which Nari Rustomji wrote in his 'Enchanted Frontiers'— *"The station club was next door to the District Magistrate's bungalow. It was mainly a club for tea planters, but a few of the elite of the district were also members. I was soon taken in hand and found it quite fun. The planters seemed to like me — I was something of a novelty,*

if nothing else and it flattered my vanity. But I fell into a trap of opining that my faculties were sharpened by Scotch and that the best time for penning judgements was after a carouse at the bar. This opinion was not, however, shared by the Higher Judiciary when my judgements came up on appeal. Even Mohammed Khurshid frowned. So I restricted my visits to the club to once a week and a couple of pegs." I was excited to visit the club, which is still located next to the Deputy Commissioner's bungalow. Disappointingly, the station club today bears little resemblance to the one patronised by young Rustomji in the early 1940s. The old Assam type building was demolished some years back, and a new building has come up in its place. The club members whom we met were, however, very warm and hospitable. While leaving the club, I had a peek at the large rambling bungalow of the Deputy Commissioner, where the legendary Mohammad Khurshid, ICS, had once lived. The bungalow with a sprawling campus looked certainly larger than the DC's bungalow at Silchar.

I also had a keen desire to see a Zamindar's mansion in Sylhet. We had a quick look at the regal and imposing Khazanchibari mansion, which somehow, appeared to be soulless with the original owners having departed after partition. The mansion now houses a school. Kuldip knew the old and reputed family of Das brothers whose Zamindari used to cover the Sylhet town and extended even up to Karimganj in India. Dr Banadip Lal Das, a direct descendant of the last Zamindar cordially invited us in. The main house was severely damaged in the great earthquake of 1897, and the old house was razed to the ground by the Pakistan army during the liberation war. Dr Das constructed a replica of the original in the 1980s. The house did not seem particularly large, but it had high ceilings and huge windows. Dr Das mentioned that when the Zamindari properties were being taken over by the Government of Pakistan in the late 1950s, they were assessed at Rs 85 lakh for payment of compensation. Out of that amount, only Rs 1.56 lakh had been received by the family till the disturbances in 1969, when all payments were stopped. Dr Das is a Government medical doctor who has been serving as the district civil surgeon in Munshiganj near Dhaka. While seeing us off at the gate, Dr Das, whose children were studying in India, mentioned about the difficulties in obtaining an Indian visa, which is usually a single entry visa for six months. *'It was much easier to obtain a UK visa than an Indian one'* were his parting words as we bade him goodbye. We rejoined the ladies at Aarong and had a quick meal at Fulkoli, a sweetmeat chain in Bangladesh. We thereafter said our big thank you to Kuldip Dey and his bank for all help extended to us.

The journey to Sutarkandi got over before we could realise, while the immigration and customs formalities got completed faster this time. We conveyed our heartfelt thanks and bade our goodbyes to our Bangladeshi friends. We then re-entered India to a tumultuous welcome by our Karimganj friends marking the end of a memorable visit to our neighbours.

20

Two Highly Educative Experiences in the Early Part of My Career

Nishinath Changkakoti IPS (Retd.)

My first posting as Superintendent of Police of a district was in 1962 in the then undivided Darrang district with head quarter at Tezpur. Towards the end of July of that year, I received a situation report to the effect that the labourers of a tea garden known as Bamujuli within the jurisdiction of Paneri Police station in the Mangaldoi sub-division had resorted to strike for fulfillment of some of their demands. I also learnt that the Sub Divisional Police Officer Mangoldoi had stationed a contingent of Police officers and men in the garden for maintenance of law and order. I decided to go to the garden myself on the following morning to take stock of the situation and to do whatever is possible within the limits of the law to restore normalcy.

Travelling in my departmental jeep, I arrived near the gate of the garden at about 10 AM on the following morning from Tezpur. Then I saw at some distance ahead along the garden road, a large group male and female labourers were sitting across the road making it impossible for any vehicle to move ahead. In those days, it was not the practice of Police officers to move around with pilot and escort vehicles I had not taken any armed Police personnel in my jeep. The Police party located by the Sub Divisional Police officer in the gardens was also not nearby and the party had not known about my arrival in the garden already. I realised that I would have to deal with the labourers on strike very carefully to prevent any deterioration in the situation needing the use of police.

I asked the driver to drive the jeep very slowly and the stop it as we reach near the crowd. It had started drizzling. On reaching near the crowd, as I emerged from the jeep someone from among the crowd of labourers on strike held an umbrella over my head to protect me from the rain. I was in Police uniform and the labourers had not known me before. I was therefore

overwhelmed by this most unexpected respectful gesture of the labourers towards me. I felt confident that it would be possible to resolve the problem peacefully.

I told them that I happened to be the Superintendent of Police of the district and if they repose their trust in my judgment, I would make an earnest effort to remove their genuine grievances. After some discussions among themselves they agreed to apprise me about their grievances against the management of the garden to enable me to try to remove the same in the interest of restoration of normalcy in the garden. They also accepted my suggestion that instead of discussing the matter on the road, we should sit in a suitable place for the same. There was a primary school nearby. They took me to the school, brought out to the front verandah a small table and a chair and requested me to take my seat. The labourers sat down in the courtyard in front of the verandah. Instead of sitting in the chair I sat on the table to make me fully visible by every one of the assembled labourers. As I was feeling thirsty I asked one of the female labourers sitting in the front row to get me a glass of water to drink. She ran to a nearby house and brought me a glass of water which I drank straightway. Meanwhile my driver on his own had left in the jeep to locate the police party and inform them about my arrival. At that time Sub Divisional Police officer, Mangoldoi and the Labour officer of the area were also with the Police party in a shed provided by the garden authority. All of them rushed to join me. I of course immediately directed the armed police party to go back to the shed as I did not require their help.

The spokesmen of the labourers narrated in detail the difficulties and humiliations experienced by them from the garden officials, particularly the Assistant Manager and the Medical officer of the garden. I then told them that if they agreed to withdraw the strike and restore normalcy in the garden immediately, I would straightway from the meeting place go and meet the Superintendent of the garden and persuade him to cause a high level enquiry into their specific complaints and take appropriate action on the basis of the findings within a period of seven days. I also promised to come to the garden on the seventh day to satisfy myself about their action taken. The labourers agreed. The Superintendent of the garden also though somewhat reluctantly promised to cause the enquiry and take appropriate action as desired by me. I returned to Tezpur in the evening with the happy feeling of success. On the sixth day I got the disturbing news that heavy flood in the Dhansiri river demarcating the boundary between the Tezpur sub-division and the Mangaldoi subdivision had eaten away about 700 feet of the embankment and the road on the eastern side linking the bridge over the river severing the road connection between the two sub-divisions. There was also no other road to go the garden from Tezpur. However Shri R. Jaitley Additional Secretary Assam Branch Tea Association Tezpur who was also scheduled to accompany me to the garden on the following day arranged the Monoplane of the nearby Pratapgarh Tea state to take us to the garden. So, I could keep my word to visit the garden on the seventh day. The labourers were already in the open field of the garden where we landed. Presently, the Superintendent of the garden

along with some other garden officials also arrived. Superintendent of the garden told me that he had found on enquiry, the Assistant Manager, medical officer and one Mohorrer guilty of dereliction of duty and misbehaviour towards the labourers and he had already transferred them to some other garden. I then thanked both the parties for exhibiting appropriate of justice and responsibility and thereby bringing back normal conditions to the garden within a short time. Thereafter, we returned to Tezpur by the same Monoplane.

From this pleasant experience, I learnt at a very early stage of my career as a Police officer that common people generally even if they had not studied in any school and college and cannot claim to have a bookish knowledge are simple at heart and are basically endowed with good qualities exhibiting proper absence of justice and empathy, all their grievances can be sorted out amicably without use of force.

I now intend to relate another experience which made me much wiser in the early part of my career. As it is well-known to most of our countrymen, in the month of April 1954 India and China had signed a historic treaty popularly known as '*Panchsheel*' (Five principles). In the most important clause of the treaty, both China and India had pledged to respect the territorial integrity of and refrain from committing any act of aggression against the other country. India, therefore, sincerely hoped that the differences between the two countries regarding the common border in some areas can be settled amicably. But this fond hope was soon belied.

From the month of May to September 1959 Chinese army penetrated into some areas of then North East Frontier Agency (now Arunachal Pradesh), Uttar Pradesh (now Uttarakhand) and Himachal Pradesh of our country. During the period Chinese army killed three jawans of Assam Rifles near LONGJU within NEFA. Much before this hostile act, Chinese government had constructed a road linking Siankiang province of China with western Tibet by illegally occupying some portion of Indian territory in the Aksai Chin area within Ladakh. On 21st October 1959 Chinese army launched a surprise attack on a contingent of Indian Policemen near Kongkala within Ladakh and killed all of them.

I have mentioned earlier in the article that I happened to be the Superintendent of Police of then undivided Darrang district with head quarter at Tezpur in the year 1962. That year on the 8th September Chinese Army besieged the Dhola outpost of Assam Rifles located within NEFA after crossing the Thang La on Indo-China border. Our Army failed to drive back the Chinese Army and had to retreat. On 20th October of the same year, the Chinese Forces through a series of well planned attacks occupied within a couple of hour's fight the Indian Army posts at Dhola bridge, Khimzemanne etc. The Indian Army unable to face the much larger Chinese Army contingent started retreat in fast from the front line leaving behind their arms, Accoutrements and other articles. Within around two days since this event, the famous Tawang town of NEFA fell into Chinese hands with hardly any resistance from the Indian side.

As the Superintendent of the undivided Darrang district adjacent to the Kameng division of the then NEFA (now Arunachal Pradesh), I was receiving

the sad and disturbing news in a piecemeal manner about the rout of the Indian army in different forward areas of NEFA and the rapid advance of the Chinese Army into the interior of our country. Within the limitations of available manpower and other resources all possible steps were taken up to gear up the district intelligence machinery and to prevent any sabotage and subversion by an enemy agent or their sympathisers and for maintenance of law and order in general throughout the district. As a result of such vigilance measures and cooperation of the people as possible no untoward incident occurred throughout the district. On 18th November 1962 as per orders of the Government of Assam, all persons of Chinese origin and some political leaders who were likely to help the Chinese authority were taken into custody throughout the district simultaneously at a very short notice and they transferred to places as fixed by the Government. It was learnt that this measure was adopted as a precautionary measure.

On 19th November 1962, I was informed by the Assistant Sub Inspector of Police in charge of Missamari outpost near Assam-NEFA border that a contingent of Chinese Army reached a place called RUPA within Kameng district of NEFA, which place was about 50 miles away from Tezpur town. On the same night late Fakhruddin Ali Ahmed, the then Finance Minister of Assam and late Kamakhya Prasad Tipathy, the then Labour Minister of Assam accompanied by Mr Rana K D N Singh then a very senior IAS officer of Assam cadre and Deputy Commissioner designate of undivided Darrang district arrived at Tezpur to take stock of the situation in consultation with the Corps Commander of the Indian Army stationed at Tezpur. On the following morning Dr P.K. Das IAS then under order of transfer from the post of Deputy Commissioner Tezpur left for Calcutta by a courier flight of the Indian Air Force, to leave behind his family there. It may be mentioned here that Indian Airlines had stopped its flights to and from Tezpur more than a fortnight ago, fearing that Tezpur might fall into the hands of the Chinese forces at any time. Dr P.K. Das therefore failed to return to Tezpur same day and formally hand over charge to his successor to his successor Rana K.D.N. Singh. It is very sad that for this act of indiscretion, Dr P.K. Das had to subsequently suffer dismissal from service.

Meanwhile on the forenoon of November 20, 1962 the two Assam Ministers visited the Army headquarter at Tezpur where they were told that it was no longer possible for the Army to block the advance of the Chinese forces on the North Bank of Brahmaputra and therefore it had been decided to shift the Corps head quarter of the Indian Army and the forces under it to the South Bank. The Ministers were also told that it was not beyond the capability of the Chinese forces to paradrop at Saloni airport at Tezpur and occupy even before the arrival of the Chinese infantry on foot. As regards what the civil administration and the common people at Tezpur should do in such an abnormal situation, the Ministers were told that it was for the Government of Assam to take appropriate action.

The grim situation report of the Army Headquarters at Tezpur and the speed at which the Chinese army were descending towards the Indian Plains,

compelled Assam Government on the advice of the two ministers camping at Tezpur to pass orders on the afternoon November 20, 1962 for shifting of the civil administration at Tezpur to the south bank of Brahmaputra on the same day and also to direct the Deputy Commissioner of Tezpur to arrange advance payment of three months' pay to all Assam government employees posted at Tezpur on the same day. It will not be out of place to record here that Pundit Jawaharlal Nehru, the then Prime Minister of India had over the Radio already conveyed to the people of Assam his sorrow in the following words, "My heart goes out to the people of Assam". I received orders from the Police head quarters at Shillong for shifting to Dergaon my entire staff including all the staff, Arms and ammunition and all other government articles. It was a herculean task to fully carry out the order at such a short notice, particularly when there was no bridge to cross the Brahmaputra river and one had to depend on the ferry plying between Silghat on the South Bank and Bhurbandha on the North Bank. But my Reserve officer was able and loyal. Under his leadership and competent guidance, the Reserve staff accomplished the challenging task without any loss of article.

We had provided help to State Bank authority at Tezpur also to shift the bank records, money etc. to the South Bank of Brahmaputra. However, the Bank authority took the decision of burning the bundles of notes amounting to a few lakhs of rupees and to throw some bundles of loose coins in the Padum Pukhuri which was not far from the bank premises. But as the bank staff were in a hurry to leave Tezpur, they did not wait till the notes got fully burnt. Similarly the loose coins were thrown on the edge of the lotus pond. Because of it, some partially burnt notes could be misappropriated by some dishonest people later on. Similarly some quantities of coins could also be retrieved and misappropriated by some dishonest people subsequently. But in view of the highly adverse circumstances when even the trained Indian army personnel were running away to save their lives, leaving behind usable war material, bank authority cannot obviously be blamed for not disposing the bank notes and the coins in an unusual manner.

Two actions of the district administration had become the subject matter of considerable criticism in the press and among the members of the public. First was the release of the prisoners from Tezpur jail and the other was the release of all inmates from the lunatic asylum at Tezpur after the Government of Assam had ordered shifting of the district administration to the south bank immediately. Though I was not consulted before taking these decisions by the new Deputy Commissioner, I still feel that these decisions taken on the consideration that these Indian citizens (inmates of the jail and lunatic asylum) should also be given a chance to escape from the clutches of the Chinese, cannot be judged as wrong. In order to deny the enemy of the use of petrol pumps at Tezpur after their impending entry into the Tezpur town, the Deputy Commissioner wanted to know whether I had explosives in the police reserve to destroy these pumps. As we had no explosives in stock I advised him to contact the Superintending Engineer PWD at Tezpur. Eventually those were not destroyed.

It was not unnatural on the people of Tezpur town who were already nervous about their fate because of the defeat of the Indian Army in NEFA (now Arunachal Pradesh) and rapid advance of the Chinese forces towards the plains of Assam, to become quite panic on coming to know about the decision to shift the Corps head quarter of the Army and the civil administration from Tezpur to the south bank. Most of the people of Tezpur town and its outskirts therefore became quite restive to cross over to some safe place in the south bank of Brahmaputra. To facilitate their crossing over as quickly as possible, the officer in charge of the private ferry of RSN and IGN company, at my personal request arranged plying of the ferry between Silghat and Bhurbandha ghat as frequently as possible not only on the day hours but also during the night of that fateful day (20th November, 1962). There were of course many brave persons at Tezpur town like Late Dulal Bhattachayya, the then chairman of Municipal Board and the members of the youth organisation of Tezpur who rendered very valuable services in restoring confidence and arousing patriotic feelings in the minds of the people of Tezpur. I provided the services of my limited number of Police vehicles to carry from the Tezpur police station to Silghat as many people as possible who had thronged the Police station for help. However obviously a large number of people had to walk the distance to catch the ferry.

Even after the government order was received, for shifting of the district administration to the south bank of Brahmaputra and the specific order of Police HQ at Shillong to shift the entire police administration to Dergaon and even after carrying out this order of police HQ as has been mentioned already in the article, a few of us continued to stay at Tezpur, albeit, strictly speaking against the order of the government and the police HQ. In addition to me those of us of the police department who stayed on were now late Debendra Nath Bora, the then DIG of Police, now late Bhabendra Nath Phukan, then Deputy Superintendent of Police, late J. K. Sinha then Assistant Superintendent of Police, both the Additional Superintendent police of my district, late Narendra Nath Hazarika, then OC of Tezpur police station, my reserve officer and a few more police personnel of the district. I am sorry that I cannot recall the names of all of them. Though I asked my driver Baharuddin to leave Tezpur and to go to his village, he refused and continued to do his duty with me. I cannot forget his loyalty and dutiful habit.

After Assam Government had passed the order about shifting of the Tezpur administration to the south bank, all the Telephone Exchange staff under the Government of India left for safer places because of which telephone connection with other places from Tezpur became unavailable from the evening of November 20, 1962. I located a temporary police wireless station at Silghat to maintain contact with Police HQ at Shillong as long as possible. But that also stopped functioning after nightfall.

Around dusk, the two Ministers of Assam left for Shillong via Tezpur Mangoldoi road. Thereafter while proceeding to the 5th Assam Police battalion HQ at Salonibari, I witnessed the sorry spectacle of a number of abandoned army vehicles burning on the roadside, small disorganised groups of Army

personnel trudging towards the Army HQ and many such groups of local people proceeding towards Silghat to cross over to South bank. Around Saloni airport, could be seen a number of in the in private vehicles left behind in a hurry by people who had left Tezpur and some other nearby tea gardens by Indian Airlines flight till this service to Tezpur was stopped in the first week of November. In the 5th Assam police battalion HQ at Salonibari, the job of shifting the men and material were yet to be completed because of shortage of vehicles. I somehow managed to provide a vehicle to expedite the task. After return from Salonibari I positioned myself mostly at Tezpur police station, helping people to go to Silghat to cross over to the south bank. By about midnight there was hardly any people coming to thana to seek such help. Then I accompanied by Mr Bhaben Phookan, the then Deputy SP and Mr J K Sinha, IPS, the then ASP came to the office cum residence of Mr A K Palit, IPS who was then the head of the Subsidiary Intelligence Bureau office at Tezpur to know whether SIB Tezpur had any further news about Chinese advance and activities. There I found both Shri Palit and Mr S K Lamba, IPS, the then Assistant Director SIB at Tezpur. There after taking a round in the town, when it appeared to be almost empty, we came to my residence to meet the DIG who had been accommodated in the guest room of my official residence because of inconvenience in the circuit house. We found him to be resting in his room. Without disturbing him, we also decided to take some rest. But sleep eluded me.

Amazing thoughts about the future of Tezpur and the plight of the common men, who had left their hearth and home in a hurry in search of safety, obsessed my mind. In view of government order for shifting of the civil administration to the south bank and the order from the Police HQ at Shillong for shifting of the police administration of Tezpur to Dergaon immediately we should have also strictly speaking left Tezpur for Dergaon. In the event of our falling into the hands of the Chinese our Government would perhaps blame us for not leaving Tezpuir as per government order. Still I was feeling reluctant to leave Tezpur. There was also no indication, such as firing to scare the people about arrival of the Chinese troops into the town.

I happened to read a little bit about the people's resistance built up by Marshall De Gaulle in France and Marshall Tito in then Yugoslavia when the Nazi Army of Hitler subjugated these two countries during the Second World War. But in our country which earned freedom through non-violent means under leadership of Mahatma Gandhi, there was no such prior thinking, not to speak of, preparation. Therefore not to speak of Police officers, even Army officers as far as I knew, had any training for such a role. On the other hand till Chinese aggression started India unduly seemed to have reposed too much faith in the pledge given by the Chinese in the historic treaty of 1954, to adhere to the principles of *Panchasheel* in letter and spirit. Further till then there was no civil defence organisation in the state of Assam and perhaps in other states also.

While grappling with such disturbing thoughts, dawn seemed to arrive very quickly. Presently the Deputy Commissioner of the district arrived at my

residence. D N Bora, IPS, DIG of Police had also become ready by then. All of us then proceeded to the Army HQ to see the state of affairs there and to get the latest news about Chinese movements; if possible. There quite unexpectedly and by chance we came to know from a radio news that the Chinese government had declared unilateral ceasefire from the midnight of November, 20, 1962. It meant that the Chinese army had stopped its advance towards Tezpur and any part of India from the previous midnight. Immediately the decision was taken to restore the civil administration at Tezpur. I had directed my officers and men with various articles of Police reserve to remain at Bhurbandha on the south bank of Brahmaputra until further instructions from me. Therefore within 21st November 1962 itself it was possible normalise the police administration at Tezpur.

The most important lesson which I learnt from this experience is that every country functions according to its national interest and therefore, no country however apparently friendly should be trusted one hundred per cent. Secondly, our Indian Army was not at all trained and equipped and not adequately manned for mountain ware fare. Thirdly, our people particularly those inhabiting the international border areas needed to be psychologically and tactically groomed to be able to react appropriately in the event of enemy intrusion into our country.

21

Assam, in Memory's Path: An Adorable Experience

M. Gopalakrishna IAS (Retd.)

I was pleasantly surprised one fine day to get a phone call and hear a familiar voice from Gauhati. Mr Rohini Baruah IAS (Retd.) greeted me and briefed me about Assam All India Services Pensioners Forum (AISPF) and the good work being done to look after the interests of Retired Officers of IAS, IPS and IFS from Assam Cadre. As the Forum is planning to bring out a Book which would be a compilation of recollections of Retired Civilians of Assam, I was requested to write an Article. I was delighted that Assam had remembered a person who had many years ago served in the Assam Cadre.

I was pleased as Punch to know about the Forum and the idea of bringing out a useful reference like book. The idea of a book is indeed testimony of the futuristic vision of the Forum. After all, AIS Officers are witness to major events and in a way, contribute to the making of history. Their writings and memories would be an authentic record of the times when they served the state as well as a guide and compass to set the direction for the future civil servants.

My first acquaintance about Assam was from my mother, who told me about the ancient and venerated Shakthi Peeth of Mr Kamakhya near Gauhati. I had occasion to read the book "The Blue Hill and the Red River" by Mr Hem Baruah but never did I imagine at that time that I would serve in Assam.

I joined the 1962 batch of the IAS, more than 50 years ago. I fondly recall from memory, the incidents and happenings in Assam which shaped my thinking, actions, career and life. Assam has thus been an integral part of my life and more particularly at an impressionable age and formative period of my career in the IAS and has moulded my outlook on life.

In December 1962, when the Chinese incursion into India took place in the then, North-Eastern Frontier Agency (NEFA), the batch of 1962 IAS officers

was undergoing training in the National Academy of Administration at Mussourie. The Academy authorities and Government felt that deputation of some IAS probationers to Gauhati would give them a preview and real-life experience of the aftermath of the Chinese incursion and the need for organizing Civil Resistance and Civil Defence measures. Along with four other IAS officers, I landed at Gauhati sometime in January 1963 just before the Republic Day Celebrations. We called on the Deputy Commissioner Mr P.H. Trivedi. Late Mr E.S. Parthasarathy, who was then the Asst. Commissioner in Gauhati received us and looked after us. He was a colourful, friendly, helpful person and a good conversationalist. Unfortunately, he died in a bomb blast in his office at Jorhat where he was the Commissioner. We lost a good officer and a gentleman.

Our first assignment at Gauhati was to attend a meeting of Civil Defence personnel which was addressed by a British expert, Major General Henderson Brooks about organization of Civil Defence Measures. We were also taken to Bomdila in Kameng Division of NEFA where we met the Dy. Commissioner, Mr Johri. It was our first exposure to Assam, NEFA and its international borders. We could understand the strategic importance of Assam and its role as a provider of logistic support and guardian of the supply route to the Himalayan Region of Arunachal Pradesh.

Six IAS Officers (i) Mr A. Bhattacharya, (ii) Mr C.D. Tripathi, (iii) Mr R.V. Pillai, (iv) Mr Temen Aonok, (v) Mr Terence Cajee and (vi) myself, were allotted to the Assam Cadre from the 1962 batch. I was posted as Assistant Commissioner at Gauhati and joined in June 1963. Mr E.S. Parthasarathy the Assistant Commissioner became my host and a good friend till he was posted to Kokrajhar as Sub-Divisional Officer.

After the usual run of formal calling on the Chief Secretary, Commissioner and other Senior Officers, my work as Asst. Commissioner commenced. As I had earlier undergone training and served in Andhra Pradesh civil service as a Direct Recruit Revenue Divisional Officer for a short time, I was well-acquainted with District Administration and Magisterial work. Luckily, I was provided Assistant Commissioner's Quarters near the District Library at Gauhati. The Deputy Commissioner's Office used to be busy from 10 am to 2 PM, after which there was hardly much work. I used to go home by 4 O' clock in the afternoon and spent a lot of time in the District library, learning Assamese and making friends. I was a constant visitor to the Gauhati University where I knew Professor Venkat Rao of the Political Science Department and through him made many friends in the university.

At Gauhati, I met several prominent citizens, educationists and officers and got acquainted with all varieties of restaurants. Mr Pratul Sarma EAC and Mr Taimur, Sadar S.D.O. were particularly helpful. My court clerk Mr Rehman was quite resourceful and organised my work nicely. My stay at Gauhati was like my probation period for understanding Assam's civil society. I participated in all functions at Gauhati particularly the Magh and Bohag Bihu and was well accepted as I started speaking in Assamese.

I recall a very interesting episode at Gauhati. Mr D. Sanjeevaiah, the then President of the Indian National Congress visited Gauhati in connection with

some political work. As I happened to know him from my college days, he wanted to meet me. I went to the circuit house to meet him when he said that he would like to spend the evening and night at my residence to discuss about Assam and would also like to meet local Andhras at Gauhati. As a bachelor, I was at my wits-end. Luckily, the Sadar S.D.O, Mr. Taimur came to my rescue along with his wife, Mrs Taimur who said that they would help me make arrangements for Tea party and dinner. Mrs Anwara Taimur later on, became the Chief Minister of Assam. The news that I was a friend of Mr Sanjeevaiah made me a VIP overnight for politicians in Assam. I was advised by the Deputy Commissioner to be on guard and ward off political pressures.

In June 1964, Mr K.S. Rao was posted as Asst. Commissioner at Gauhati. I took the role of a mentor and we used to spend a lot of time together. Mr Sridhar is a meticulous person with a flair for academic scholarship and a very upright and intelligent officer. Both of us once went to see the then D.C. Mr Phukan to seek advice on our training. He said that we should learn on our own and not expect any advice from him. Mr Phukan was a very fine gentleman, calm and collected and very patient.

As I was posted as S.D.O., Goalpara in 1964, I went to Shillong to call on the Chief Secretary, Mr A.N. Kidwai, I.C.S. He was aware that I had been in the Andhra Pradesh State Civil Service and had undergone one year training as Deputy Collector in Andhra Pradesh and one more year at National Academy of Administration, Mussourie. He suggested that with an overdose of training I should draft a Manual of Training for IAS Officers allocated to Assam State. I felt awkward that a trainee was asked to become a trainer. I did draft and submit the Manual which was approved. How good the training manual prepared by me is for others to judge.

I was posted as sub-divisional Officer (SDO) and sub-divisional Magistrate (SDM) at Goalpara in August 1964. It was an excellent posting and I was lucky to have very able E.A.Cs like Mr N.N. Baruah, Mr L.K. Baruah and Mr Gogoi. I learnt a lot from their interaction and advice. The DFO, Mr B. Datta, became my close friend. The Additional S.P. Mr Borgohain, the S.E, Mr Bhattacharya and the Executive Engineer, Mr B.C. Khataniar, who were my neighbours looked after me like my own folks at home and were very hospitable. There was a very informal atmosphere and officers would meet quite often and sort out issues. I then learnt that the informal Government often functions faster and more effectively than the formal Government.

When the Indo-Pak War broke out in 1965, there was a state of siege. I ordered the seizure of a Pakistani Steamer which was moving towards Gauhati. Incidentally, it was the only enemy property seized in Assam. In the wake of the war, a large number of East Pakistan Hazong refugees started streaming into Assam through the Garo hills. What started as a trickle soon became a torrent of refugees. Since it would be difficult to provide food and supplies in Garo Hills, it was decided that they should be accommodated in the Goalpara Sub-division. I had the rare experience of organising and running the largest Refugee and Rehabilitation camp in Assam for over one lakh persons at Matia. In this task, I received excellent support from the then Minister Mr Rupnath

Brahma, Mr B.S. Sarao, Secretary and Mr Ingty and other officers in organising construction of Bashas, supply of food and provision of health facilities. In a crisis, Government proves itself. I wish it does so even in normal times.

In 1966, the Mizo National Front (MNF), created a rebellion like situation in Mizo hills District by cutting off all the communications and bridges from Cachar District to Aijawl, the District Headquarters. My batch mate, Mr R.V. Pillai who was S.D.O. at Lunglei was kidnapped and taken by MNF to East Pakistan. At that time, the then IGP, Mr B. Baruah and the Chief Secretary, Mr A.N. Kidwai spoke to me saying that I was a tough guy and therefore was specially selected to go to Mizo Hills to assist in restoration of the District Administration. As a sop, they said that I was being promoted and would go as Additional Dy. Commissioner and Additional Dist. Magistrate. Soon thereafter, the Chief Minister, Mr B.P. Chaliha spoke to me on the phone and said that my services were essential in Mizo Hills and that both the C.S. and IGP felt confident that I would do well in the new post. He added that Government expected its officers to rise to the occasion in a crisis situation. I was overwhelmed by the confidence that the Chief Minister and senior officers had reposed in me. I accepted the offer to go to Mizo Hills. I received my orders through Police wireless and joined at Aijawl in April 1966.

The talk at that time among Civil Servants, in a lighter vein, was that I was a bachelor and therefore expendable cannon. It was indeed very true because four other IAS officers, all bachelors were posted as Assistant Commissioners to Mizo Hills to work at different places after briefing by me. They were Mr N. N. Mukherjee, Mr D.K. Gangopadhyay, Mr R. N. Muhuri, Mr M. P. Bezbaruah and Mr S.K. Agnihotri. As I had a good cook, they all stayed with me. We had a trying time organizing communications and supplies through protected Convoys, Air dropping of food supplies and restoring morale of the employees and reorganizing the administration to face the disturbed conditions.

The Army which had been called in was supplemented with paramilitary forces like CRPF and other State police battalions. Army-Civil liaison and setting up of Protected and Progressive Villages (PPVS) became an important task. Mr R. Natarajan joined as D.C. in place of Mr T.S. Gill. Mr B. Phukan was appointed as S.P. The Chief Minister and the I.G.P. both visited Aijawl and gave us a lot of moral support. It was a very difficult assignment, but with the support of all concerned, we were able to quickly restore law and order and also secure surrender of militants along with their Arms. Luckily, Mizoram is now a State which is progressive and does not have any major law and order or insurgency problems.

I remember a very interesting event when at Aijawl. My full name is M. Gopalakrishna Naidu. Mizos found it difficult to remember such a long name. They used to address me as Pu. Naidu. Mr Pakyntein who was posted as Commissioner for the Hills Division paid a visit to Aijawl by Helicopter. I received him and accompanied him to some places while he went on his own to some other places. Apparently, he had met some Mizos and enquired from them about my work in the District. On his return to Shillong, the Commissioner had apparently sent a confidential note to the Chief Secretary about the district

conditions. I received a call from the Chief Secretary, who in a very harsh and angry mood, said that my work in the District was not upto the mark and that I should immediately see him for which he had organized an helicopter to take me to Shillong.

I was unable to fathom the anger of Chief Secretary or make an assessment as to where I was amiss in my job. With some trepidation, I reached Shillong and putting on my best suit, entered the room of the Chief Secretary. He started laughing as soon as I entered the room. I thought that I had not properly buttoned up my Coat and looked askance. As soon as I came near his table, he asked me to sit down and said "Are you Mr Jekyl or Mr Hyde"? I was taken aback and thought that the Chief Secretary's behaviour was very strange and surmised that he must have gone off the rocker. He addressed me harshly as "Muddusetty Gopalakrishna Naidu (my full name)" and asked me to sit down. I was taken aback and perplexed. He said, "Tell me what should I do" and pulled out a note from his table drawer and asked me to read it. It was a note from the Hills Division Commissioner, Mr Pakyntein which said "Mizos feel that Mr Gopalakrishna is a very intelligent, sympathetic and good Officer whereas Naidu is a harsh administrator and a terror and people refer to him as Machine Gun Naidu. I suggest that Mr Gopalakrishna may be retained in the District and Mr Naidu may be immediately posted out of the District". The CS then burst out laughing and said;

"Your CS knows his officers but the pity is Commissioners do not know their officers. Anyway, Boy, since I cannot split you, I will retain both Gopal and Naidu in Mizo hills". He then said "Gopal, You have done a good job. The CM is also happy about your work". I felt greatly relieved.

The Deputy Commissioner Mr R. Natarajan went on leave for about two months when I was promoted as Deputy Commissioner so that the protocol equations with the army could be maintained. I fondly recall that SFHJ Manekshaw who was the then GOC of Eastern command stayed with me in the DCs bungalow. He was appreciative of the good work of the District administration.

I was subsequently transferred to Shillong and joined the Finance Department in the Secretariat. I worked in the Finance Department in 1967-68 where Mr Ganesh Phukan and Mr R.S. Paramashivan were Finance Commissioners. Subsequently, I was posted as Joint Secretary for all Departments under the Chief Secretary, where I had good exposure to Secretariat and Policy making functions. I was also taking down notes of the Cabinet meetings and putting up Draft Minutes to the Chief Secretary for approval. Assam Cabinet at that time was quite a high level and formidable team. It consisted of Mr B.P. Chaliha as CM, Mr F.A. Ahmed, (our President) as Finance Minister Mr Bhagawathi, Mr D.K. Baruah, Mr M.M. Chowdhary, Mr K.P. Tripathi, Mr A.H. Chowdhary, Mr B. Mukherjee, all stalwarts and leaders. The discussions in the Cabinet were a great learning experience for me.

I was posted as Deputy Commissioner of Sibsagar District at Jorhat in 1968. As the then Chief Minister, Mr B.P. Chaliha hailed from that District, my posting was considered something very special. I worked for over two years at Jorhat and had a most memorable and satisfying tenure, as each day was a

happy learning experience. I realised that if one stops learning, one stops growing. I found the people of the district, very friendly, likeable and highly cultured. I was also very popular and received many commendations from the government of Assam for the work done. I had the distinction of receiving the President of India, the Prime Minster of India, the Governor of Assam and Union Ministers while I was in the District. I used to frequently visit Majuli (World's largest river island) to understand the Satra culture of Assam. The second refinery agitation also took place during the period. Dr Bhupen Hazarika participated in the agitation and wanted to be arrested. I said that we would arrest him only if agreed to sing a song. He sang "*Luitor parore deka lora, moriboloi bhay nai*". We formally arrested him, thanked him for the song and released him to the applause of the crowd.

We had a long standing dispute with Nagaland regarding the border between Assam and Nagaland in the Kakodanga and Geleki Reserve Forest areas. Police forces were posted on both sides of the border to prevent encroachments and forcible harvesting of crops. Nagaland insisted on recognition of their tribal law and rights governing land while Assam argued for our constitutional Laws. It was a conflict between Tribal Law and Roman Law. The CM was very concerned about finding a solution to Nagaland insurgency and the border dispute as well. His first question when I used to meet him at the Kaziranga border of the district was "How is the Nagaland border"?

Nazira tea estate was acquired in an incredibly short time for setting up of Eastern Head Quarters of ONGC. I assisted the then Commissicner, Mr B.S. Sarao in preparing the background material and draft note for constitution of Kaziranga National Park. The Assam Agricultural University at Jorhat was set up and I played a part in popularizing multiple cropping and wheat cultivation in the district.

The Chief Minister, Mr B.P. Chaliha used to often visit the District. As I was a bachelor, he would occasionally tease me and say that I should get married quickly. DCs are expected to be elderly persons and not eligible bachelors. He would jocularly tell Mr Tilak Gogoi, an MLA and other political leaders to seriously search for a bride for the DC. The present Chief Minister of Assam, Mr Tarun Gogoi was an active student leader who organized Bihu Cultural Festivals at Jorhat. It is so heart-warming that Mr Tarun Gogoi makes it a point to call me whenever he is in Hyderabad which helps me to renew my ties with Assam. Mr B.K. Handique who was my neighbour at Jorhat and used to invite me for dinner. I was a welcome guest at Mr Mohini Phukan' house. Mr S.N. Phukan, Retired Judge of the Supreme Court was a real good friend and advisor. He was young but wise.

I thoroughly enjoyed my stay in the district for the variety of challenges and diverse nature of work. The hospitality of the Tea-Gardens and local people was beyond words. As we had excellent ADC's, like Mr J.N. Sarma and Mr J.M. Thangkiew who took care of Headquarters work. I was able to visit the sub-divisions, meet people and personally handle the Nagaland border issue. Mr Prabir Sengupta was the S.D.O. at Golaghat. Mr Gokul Khound who

was the District Public Relations officer was a real live wire and built up a good network and protected the developmental activities in the district. I visited Mokokchung in Nagaland and was in touch with the then DC Mr Deb. When Mr Deb fell ill seriously, I helped in his urgent evacuation by air to Kolkata for treatment. Nagaland Government gave me a commendation letter.

I recall an incident at Eastern Headquarters, ONGC at Nazira. There was an agitation for appointment of local persons and ONGC office was under seize by students who did not allow any ingress or egress of staff. The G.M. of ONGC had to attend his son's marriage at Delhi but was unable to do so due to the bandh. I went in my car ASJ-1 with the DC's name plate to ONGC. The student agitators allowed me to go inside the ONGC Eastern Headquarters for talks. I smuggled the G.M in my car and drove him to Jorhat which enabled him to board the plane to Delhi. It is all part of our work. All is well that ends well.

As Secretary in the Health and Family Planning Department we reorganised the Public Health Department in 1971-72 and gave a fillip to the construction of Gauhati Medical College. At the time of the Bangladesh operations in 1971-72 for Bangladesh, I was appointed as a Civil Administrator. I drafted the Secretariat Manual under the guidance of Mrs P.P. Trivedi, another accomplished officer and the most gracious host for all young officers.

After completion of my Inter-state deputation to Andhra Pradesh from 1972-76, I was posted between 1977-79 as Secretary Industries, Power and Minerals by which time the Assam Government had moved down to Gauhati from Shillong and housed in semi permanent accommodation at Dispur. Life at Dispur was somewhat cramped and confined. But officers and their families became not only neighbours but good friends. My wife always remembers the good friends and good times at Dispur. We could also see some good Hindi and Telugu Films.

The first Industrial Policy statement for Assam was approved by the Government. I assisted in setting up of the Bongaigaon Petroleum and Refinery Complex. As Chairman of Assam Gas Company we laid Gas Pipelines to Tea Gardens. The posting gave me a thorough understanding of the Industrial requirements and the need for entrepreneurially oriented Industrial Development Corporations in Assam. I was greatly assisted and guided by the then Chief Secretary, Mr Rana KDN Singh in my work.

In my Andhra Pradesh tenure, I was posted as Managing Director of Godavari Fertilizers, Secretary, Major Industries and Commissioner for Visakhapatnam Steel Plant as well as Special Chief Secretary before I moved to New Delhi. I found the subordinate staff in Andhra Pradesh very experienced and hardworking which made the task of superior officers quite easy. In contrast, in Assam, officers have to do homework, hard-work, smart-work, and build teamwork and network on their own. Assam has a truly officer-oriented system.

In 1982-83, Assam was placed under President's Rule due to the agitation of the All Assam Students Union on illegal migration and other issues. There was total non-cooperation from Civil Society and Government employees for the conduct of Elections which had to be done within the time limits set by the constitution. As I was on deputation to Andhra Pradesh Government, I was

recalled by the government of Assam to join as Home Commissioner in 1982. The Cabinet Secretary rang me up and advised me not to take my family but go alone as the law and order situation was very difficult.

It was a very difficult and strenuous assignment as there was practically no cooperation from Government employees and the public as well. The Governor was Mr G. Mehrotra while Mr R. V. Subrahmaniam, an Assam civilian and Mr Natarajan an IAS officer from Orissa cadre were Advisors to the Governor. I had a tough time in picking up the threads and building the morale of Government employees while making arrangements for conduct of the elections. Luckily, we received total support from the government of India and particularly, from the Police Officers namely Mr P.C. Das, Mr T. A. Subramaniam, Mr M.I.S. Iyer and Mr K.P.S. Gill who was a towering personality and an effective leader. Mr S.L. Khosla was the Chief Election Officer while Mr S.K. Agnihotri was the D.C. in Gauhati. We worked closely and coordinated effectively.

We had to organise and maintain the Food Supply Chain despite the resistance from government employees, and prepare for conduct of elections while maintaining law and order. We were faced with the problem of not getting services of Presiding Officers and Polling Officers for the election booths. We managed to get two Airbus loads of AIS officers under training in the National Academy of Administration at Mussourie. We also secured support of the Govt. of Bihar which deputed a large number of Block Development Officers along with vehicles to assist in the conduct of the elections. We had to press into service, people, vehicles, helicopters and elephants to move into remote and difficult areas to reach the election material and the personnel in time.

We had a lot of trouble and faced sporadic incidents all over Assam as people were opposed to the conduct of the elections. Law and Order situation became very difficult with frequent Road Roko, Bandhs, Gheraos and causing wanton breach of communications. The Officers in the District and sub-divisions rose to the occasion and proved that they can be relied upon to achieve the objectives set by the Government. A lot of innovative steps were taken with meticulous planning and the elections conducted successfully. One great regret, however, remains that despite all our efforts, we could not prevent the massacre at Nellie in Nowgong District. May be our intelligence failed us or our preventive measures proved inadequate.

After my permanent cadre change to Andhra Pradesh in 1984, I had many occasions to meet Officers of the Assam, Meghalaya cadre at Delhi where I was posted between 1990 and 1997. After my retirement, I was Chairman of Andhra Pradesh State Finance Corporation, which was turned around and is now considered as the most professional and best run State Finance Corporation in the country. SIDBI and the Govt. of Assam requested me to visit Assam Finance Corporation and assist them in revamping AFC. This gave me an opportunity to visit Gauhati and see the remarkable progress achieved by the state.

In my long service in Assam, I had privilege of knowing the President of India, Mr F. A. Ahmed and Chief Ministers like Mr B. P. Chaliha, Mr Barborah,

Mr S.C. Sinha, Mr M.M. Chowdhary, Mr Hiteshwar Saikia and Mr T. Gogoi. I also had the opportunity to know leaders of the opposition like Mr D.C. Baruah and Mr Pramod Gogoi. Working with the Ministers in Assam was a good and pleasant experience except for one or two black sheep among them. The Chief Secretaries like Mr A.N. Kidwai, Mr R.B. Vaghaiwala, Mr N.K. Rustumji, Mr S.K. Mallik, were ICS officers. Mr Paramashivam, Mr S.M.L. Bhatnagar, Mr Ramesh Chandra, Mr D. Das and Mrs Trivedi were outstanding Chief Secretaries and very considerate human beings. I had very good relationships with the Police Officers starting from Mr Imdad Ali, Mr B. Baruah, Mr I.P.M. Menon, Mr K.P.S. Gill etc. We had some outstanding IFS Officers like Mr Jacob who is remembered in Shillong by Jacob's Ladder, Mr Prabhakar Baruah, Mr B. Dutta, Mr B.P. Roy and several other Officers, too numerous to mention. There was a very rare comraderie and espirit de corps among the services. We also had excellent relationship with the Army and the Air Force Officers posted in Assam.

Many memories crowd my mind when I think of Assam. Its natural resources, its built heritage and more importantly, its intangible heritage, its people, their lives, their festivals their hopes and aspirations. To me, it is the friendships, love and support that I received in abundance from all those whom I got into contact in Assam which is an indelible part of my life.

I remember all the officers with whom I worked and learnt a lot. I also remember their commitment to work and their helpful attitude. I must mention a few among the many who made my life easy and taught me many good things. I fondly recall Mr A.K. Saikia, Mr H.N. Das, Mr B. Barua, Mr M.P. Bezbaruah, Mr Jotin Hazarika Mr Tapam Baruah, Mr Bhoumick, Mr Ajit Malla Barua and Mr Bireshwan Barua and all of them have left imprints in my mind and footprints of their work for Assam.

Assam's Problems

Having worked in Assam for over 12 years in different capacities and different regions of the State including the Hill Districts and later on, in Andhra Pradesh and Government of India, I understand the need to look at the problems of Assam from different angles and from a realistic and sympathetic perspective. Being part of the Himalayan Geology and situated in a valley, the state is prone to earth-quakes, floods and natural disasters. Environmental and ecological protection becomes an integral part of the Administration. Geography of the State makes it a narrow valley traversed by the mighty River Brahmaputra or the Lohit (The Red River) and blessed with good rainfall and fertile soil. Life in Assam revolves around the River, its course, its floods and its predominant rural cultural ethos with ethnic overtones. Brahmaputra is a unique river of India because it is the largest and only River named after a male. The difficult terrain and insularity of Assam, its hills and dales and its far flung Hill areas though quite a deterrent, attracts immigrants because of its fertile soil and natural resources. Such immigrations have defined the history of the state. But it has pronounced cultural and historical connections of *Vaishnava* religion and way of life of Eastern Bihar, Bengal and Orissa.

Its fertile soil, abundance of water and verdant growth has attracted invaders and immigrants from all directions through the centuries. Its demography has changed with rapid increase of population due to abundance of cultivable land, better security of livelihood and waves of immigration from other parts of the country due to land hunger; and massive illegal immigration from Bangladesh and Nepal. This has resulted in a change in the composition of the population disturbing the cultural, linguistic, religious and ethnic balance leaving a large and young population. This could prove to be a boon if the demographic dividend is reaped or become a bane if the people are not equipped with relevant skills and do not contribute to productivity, value addition and economic competitiveness. Heavy rainfall restricts working season in Assam and calls for appropriate technology and mechanisation to remain productive and competitive throughout the year.

The cultural diversity, linguistic and ethnic divisions of the population poses problems for administrators. Assam is a corridor State and the life-line of communications to Arunachal Pradesh, Meghalaya, Nagaland, Manipur and Mizoram and will become even more important as India looks towards the East for trade and commerce.

Assam is rich in natural resources, particularly Oil and Gas, Forests and Tea Gardens but has to import the bulk of its industrial and consumer goods and services from other parts of India. There is a shortage of skills which needs to be filled. Entrepreneurship has to be encouraged and employment generated. Value addition can come from Agro-industries and Small and Medium Enterprises. The above factors call for maintenance of Law and Order supply of essential commodities, provision of skill based education, health facilities and electricity in remote areas and Institutional capacity building to ensure employment to the growing population.

Administrators will have to work in a good Framework of Policy, Law, Regulation, Institutional Capacity building, Process and Practices with focus on provision of Opportunities. Ensuring security of livelihood assumes importance. It is here, that Civil Services must contribute their best effort by having Clarity of purpose, process, professionalism and provide a people-centric administration. Civil Servants must have clarity of Concept, Context, Content and Connectivity to goals and Communication skills. In addition, they need Clarity of Goal, Role, Responsibility, Resources, Route, Results, Recognition and Rewards.

Role of All India Services

In a diverse country with a federal set-up like India, the need for All India Services is well recognised. All India Service Officers serve both in the State and Centre and thereby bring to the Centre, local knowledge, experience and expertise to find solutions to the problems of the State and the Centre. They are expected to function with integrity, impartiality, neutrality, and accountability. Considered the steel-frame of the government they have been able to keep the country united and provided good administration and have been coping with crisis after crisis and meeting the rising expectations of the people.

The Services are now being called to provide not merely Law and Order but good Governance and better Governance. The call is to move from "*Raj*" to "*Swaraj*" to "*Suraj*". "People power must be in people's hands" is the new order of the day. It is said that good Governance comes only when people are good and ethics and values prevail. Therefore, Civil Servants must become role models for probity, good conduct and behaviour. Their slogan should be "simplify" administration and "exemplify" by personal conduct and actions. Civil Servants have to follow the six T's of time-tested Administrative values viz., Truth, Trust, Transparency, Tolerance, Tact and Technology.

The Civil Services constitute India's pool of administrative and managerial talent. But India now requires not merely talent, but ethical leadership. Only such civil servants can become prime movers of progress and drivers of development and engines of economic growth. Lord Nolan of UK while talking about Governance and Qualities of Public leaders and Public servants prescribed that they should be examples of "selflessness, honesty, accountability, integrity, leadership, objectivity and openness". May be, we need to consciously inculcate these qualities in the new entrants to Government service and the large number of serving officers.

Civil Services must continuously update themselves, upgrade their skills and professionalism and uphold values. They must follow good ethics, morals and values and continuously improve productivity and cost benefit ratios. Their skills lie in building camaraderie and *espirit de corps* and ensure good cooperation and co-ordination by personal example, team-building and leadership. They have to develop functional skills, interpersonal skills and integrative leadership.

Assam's All India Services Pensioner's Forum

The setting up of Assam All India Services Pensioner's Forum is a welcome and happy development. Senior Citizens have several problems as they transit from leading an active life to suddenly becoming idle without a purpose or hobby to fall back on. This can create feelings of neglect, loneliness and of being put on the shelf. Chronic and age-related health problems vary with the age of persons in their 60's, 70's and the 80's. Senior citizens clubs keep them active, enhance friendships and make them feel useful to society. The Forum can provide a meeting place where members can meet, exchange notes and help one another and solve common problems. These mostly relate to issues of adequate pension and health care, opportunities for service and to work in NGOs. Forum should also try to improve the functioning of the CGHS and take care of widows of Civil Servants and setting up or running of old age homes etc. They can also cultivate new hobbies and help government by providing their services for giving lectures, manning positions in Government companies or other organisations and become coaches or mentors to younger people in the government.

The breakdown of the joint family system, lack of an economic and social network, urbanisation and absence of children or spouse pose psychological and physical problems. The state must implement the National Policy for Senior Citizens sincerely and enable Senior Citizens to live a life of dignity.

Feminisation of ageing also has to be recognised and resultant issues solved. Ensuring an enabling and supportive environment for pensioners must be the concern of society.

Senior Citizens constitute a large talent pool. Given the increasing longevity, Government should consider raising the age of retirement and effectively utilising the services of retired officers, in various Governmental activities. Senior Citizens already constitute 11 per cent of the voters and this is likely to go up further. Politicians should note and cultivate senior citizens if they have to win elections in the future.

I do hope that Government of Assam will support the Forum and utilise its immense talents and experience and harness its wisdom to ensure good governance and accelerate economic and social development of Assam. The strength of a country or state is dependant on the strength of the human beings and their commitment to a larger cause. The Forum could become the prime mover for good governance which alone can confer prosperity unto posterity.

It has been one of my happiest experiences that long after I left Assam in 1983 and also retired from service, Assam Officers and Civilians visiting Hyderabad write to me for local assistance and also look me up when they visit Hyderabad. This reminds me of my halycon days in Assam and enables me to maintain contacts and know the latest developments in Assam. I may be physically away from Assam but Assam is always within me and my thoughts.

As President of All India Services Pensioner's Association of Andhra Pradesh, I deem it a privilege to be of service to Assam AISPF and similarly placed Organisations in other States. I wish the Assam AISPF all success in its pioneering efforts of maintaining and enthusing the "old boys" who have not forgotten the 'old days' and have admirably adjusted to the 'new days' and the "nowadays".

22

Centre-State Financial Relations in India

H.N. Das IAS (Retd.)

The Indian Polity is federal in structure but unitary in spirit. The architect of the Indian Constitution, Dr B.R. Ambedkar, described India's polity as a 'flexible federation.' The concept of federation in India has a native flavour also. We can trace it back to the kingdom of Vaishali in the 6th century B.C. Later the Mauryas, the Mughals and the British used this concept for administrative convenience while organising their respective empires.

The unitary features in the federal structure of India were introduced by certain provisions in the Constitution itself. Such provisions were warranted by the situation in the country at the time of partition. The overriding controlling powers over the States given to the Centre by various Articles of the Constitution are so strong that in certain circumstances the Centre can even take over the administration of a particular State under Article 356. Then there are certain unique institutions which reflect the unitary features of the Constitution. These include the Election Commission, the Union Public Service Commission, the Comptroller and Auditor General of India, the Finance Commissions, the Higher Judiciary, the all India Civil Services (Indian Administrative Service, Indian Police Service and Indian Forest Service) and the Central paramilitary forces including their deployment in the States (under the 42nd Constitutional amendment). Moreover, certain institutions have been set up for ensuring good governance such as the Planning Commission, the National Development Council, the National Integration Council, the Inter-State Council and others. These institutions also reflect the unitary features.

The distribution of legislative powers between the Union and the State legislatures is dealt with by Article 246 of the Constitution. This Article provides for political as well as fiscal federalism. Schedule VII, under this Article, contains Three Lists. The Union Parliament has full and exclusive powers to legislate in

respect of the items in List I (Union List) and also powers to legislate in respect of items in List III (Concurrent List). The State legislatures have exclusive powers to legislate in respect of items falling under List II (State List) and concurrent powers in respect of items falling under List III (Concurrent List). There are 97 items in the Union List, 67 in the State List and 47 in the Concurrent List. The executive powers distributed between the Union and the States include powers to levy duties and to raise revenues by taxes operating on mutually exclusive spheres.

The objective of providing adequate finances to the States, so that they may discharge the responsibilities entrusted to them, is achieved by a system of transfers of fiscal resources from the Union to the State Governments. By this system the Union Government shares its revenues with the State Governments. The objectives are to enforce national rules and standards and to remove vertical and horizontal imbalances. The vertical imbalances refer to imbalances between the Union and the States and the horizontal ones refer to imbalances among the States. The idea is to avoid uneven provisions of public services across different States, including allocations in respect of "merit goods" such as education and healthcare services. Similarly, successive FCs (Finance Commissions) grant debt relief so that the States are relieved of the burden of unsustainable debts. Unsustainable debts will arise "unless the growth of GDP is maintained at a level higher than the interest rate." FCs also provide for grants to cover any projected revenue deficits of States. This is called the "gapfilling" approach.

The FCs are appointed at intervals of five years. As many as 13 FCs have been appointed so far. Their recommendations have been accepted by the Union Parliament and implemented by the Union Government. The provisions relating to the FCs are contained in articles 280 and 281 of the Constitution. It is really fortunate that all the FCs have been free and fair and their recommendations have been almost universally accepted by the political establishments and civil society.

What the FCs have done is to make recommendations on the sharing of taxes which are levied by the Union Government. In addition, they have recommended grants-in-aid for specific purposes including those under article 275. The FCs have also recommended periodic debt relief and calamity relief to the States. It is significant that the immediate past four Commissions (FC-X to FC-XIII) have recommended fairly large transfers of Union resources to the Panchayati Raj Institutions (PRIs) and Urban Local Bodies (ULBs), which have become Constitutional entities after the 73rd and the 74th amendments of the Indian Constitution in 1992. The relevant Articles of the Constitution on tax sharing are Articles 268, 268A, 269, 270 and 271. PRIs and ULBs are covered by Article 243. In 2000 the 80th amendment of the Constitution relating to Goods and Services Tax enlarged the shareable pool.

The Thirteenth Finance Commission (FC-XIII) recommended that 32 per cent of the Union Government's net proceeds from the shareable central taxes shall be transferred to the States during the five years, 2010-15. This means a 1.5 percentile point increase from the recommendations of the Twelfth Finance

Commission (FC-XII) which was 30.5 per cent. The grants-in-aid recommended by FC-XIII is Rs 3.19 lakh crore during 2010-15. This includes Rs 24,068 crore for elementary education, Rs 27,945 crore for State Specific Projects, and Rs 15,000 crore for environment. The Commission has stressed on fiscal consolidation under the Fiscal Responsibility and Budget Management Act (FRBMA) and recommended some debt relief. As far as calamity relief is concerned the size of the State Disaster Response Funds (SDRF) have been worked out to be Rs 33,581 crore to be shared between Centre and State in respect of the general category states in the ratio of 75:25 and in respect of special category States in the ratio of 90:10. There will be an additional grant of Rs 525 crore for capacity building and an assistance of Rs 250 crore to be given to the National Disaster Response Force. The total amount of grant recommended for disaster relief, including capacity building, from the Central Government will be Rs 26,378 crore. For the PRIs and ULBs the amount recommended is Rs 87,519 crore. The grand total of transfers under the dispensation of FC-XIII has been estimated at Rs 17,06,676 crore during 2010-15. Out of this Assam is expected to get Rs 57,832.7 crore.

For Assam the percentage of devolution from the divisible pool of shareable Central taxes will be 3.628 from all other taxes and 3.685 from service tax. In FC-XII the percentage was 3.22. So there will be a slight increase in terms of percentages. In terms of quantum, however, there will be a much gain. Actually Assam's share has come down from 4.60 per cent of FC-I to 3.22 per cent of FC-XII. But worked out as a percentage of GSDP it has gone up by 2.63 percentile points from 5.16 of FC-XII to 7.79 of FC-XIII. Assam will get additional amounts under grants-in-aid, grants to PRIs and ULBs, debt relief and calamity relief. Announcing the acceptance of the recommendations of FC-XIII the Union Finance Minister Pranab Mukherjee had said in February, 2010 that "despite the fiscal stress being faced by the Centre the Government has accepted the major recommendations of the Finance Commission keeping in mind the larger interests of the federal polity". This is good.

The Planning Commission transfers huge amounts every year as assistance to the States taking cover of Article 282. In the case of the general category States such assistance is distributed as grants and loans in the ratio of 75:25 per cent. But in the case of the special category States the transfers are in the ratio of 90:10. Beside that Assam gets its share in the central sector and the centrally sponsored schemes. The Union Ministry for Development of North Eastern Region (DONER) and the North Eastern Council (NEC) also make allocations to the eight NER states including large grants from the non-lapsable grants. Out of non-lapsable grants Assam gets a share of 27 per cent.

One important point which needs to be mentioned is that the FCs in India meticulously work out the revenue and expenditure figures for the relevant five years period and project the gap as already stated. If any state is expected to have a deficit the same is filled up by a special grant. FC-XIII provided Rs 51,800 crore for eight States (not Assam) during 2010-15 as grants for this purpose.

This brief description of the Constitutional pattern of resource sharing between the Union and the States in India will show that there is a very close

and intimate relationship between the Union and the States established during the period of more than six decades after independence. There have been occasional protests and objections by some of the States regarding specific matters. But there has been a general acceptance and the States seem to be generally satisfied. This augurs well for the country.

A Critique of Centre-State Financial Relations in India

More than six decades of experimenting with federal finance has evolved a system of resource transfer and resource distribution, both vertical and horizontal, which has become fair and equitable to the extent possible. It is the thirteen Finance Commissions (FCs), headed by eminent personalities, which have advanced this process of evolution by their recommendations in keeping with the changing times. After the Thirteenth Finance Commission (FC-XIII) report has been implemented almost 40 per cent of the proceeds of Central shareable taxes now come to the States, Panchayati Raj Institutions (PRIs), Urban Local Bodies (ULBs) and a few other public entities as devolution and grants-in-aid. This is remarkable.

These financial arrangements have emerged out of the unique features of the Indian Constitution. Many scholars criticise the Indian federal structure because it is too much centralised. They feel that the sources of revenue allocated to the States are not only inadequate but also inequitable. However, the Constitution itself has provided the necessary safeguards through the system of revenue sharing. By this process the poorer States are being benefited. In a country where the difference between the rich and poor States, as measured by the per capita income, is as much as one is to four the present system of sharing of Central taxes is really an ameliorating factor.

Many advanced States feel that a premium has been placed on the inefficiency of backward States by giving them higher financial allocations which they are unable to transform into productive resources. The advanced States, therefore, feel that resources are being wasted on the poorer States. They particularly point out the cases of the *BIMARU* States of Bihar, Madhya Pradesh, Uttar Pradesh, Rajasthan and Orissa beside the eight small states of the North East Region (NER). But they do not realise that unless the people living in these States come up India as a whole cannot achieve progress. It is unfortunate that in some of these States corruption is rampant and inefficiency is wide spread. It is these issues which the Central Government and civil society must address instead of penalising the poor people of the States for the faults of their leaders. What is encouraging is the transformations being brought about by great Chief Ministers like Nitish Kumar in Bihar and Manik Sarkar in Tripura. We need many more of their ilk. It may be mentioned in passing that the divisible pool composed of the 32 per cent of shareable Central taxes is distributed among the States in accordance with a formula which gives weightage to population 25 per cent, area 10 per cent, fiscal capacity distance 47.5 per cent and fiscal discipline 17.5 per cent. This formula is advantageous to the poorer States. According to this formula Assam has a share of 3.628 per cent in the divisible pool.

In most federal polities the residual powers are with the States. In the United States of America (USA), for example, thirteen original States formed the Union and assigned certain specific powers to the Central government. They retained the residual powers with them. The other States joined later on the same conditions. In India, however, the residual powers have been assigned to the Centre by the Constitution itself. By entry No. 97 of List I under article 246 of the Indian Constitution "any other matters" have been entrusted to the Union. Many people find this to be odd. They feel that the residual powers should be with the States so that each State can develop in its own unique atmosphere of many different ethnic, religious, linguistic and cultural groups. I personally feel that there is no need to change the Constitution on this account and that these matters have been already looked after well by the various organisations and institutions created by the Centre and the States.

There is, however, a strong demand in some of the States for more autonomy. In the NER, for example, the militant outfits demand much more autonomy. They point to Jammu and Kashmir where there is a separate Constitution. My personal view is that while some more powers may be given to the States, as has been given to Nagaland, the separate Constitution for Jammu and Kashmir should be merged with the main Constitution after retaining the special features and without causing any hardship to any interest group. The financial requirements can be continued to be looked after by taking recourse to State Specific Grants of the FCs.

In the cases of PRIs and ULBs some funds were recommended by the Tenth Finance Commission (FC-X). The amount allocated to PRIs was Rs 4380.93 crore and to ULBs Rs 1000 crore during 1995-2000. FC-XI allocated an amount of Rs 8000 crore for PRIs and Rs 2000 crore for ULBs during 2000-2005. FC-XII allocated Rs 18000 crore for PRIs and Rs 4300 crore for ULBs during 2005-09. FC-XIII recommended Rs 87,519 crore for PRIs, ULBs and Special Areas during 2010-15. The break-up is Rs 63,050.5 crore for PRIs, Rs 23,111 crore for ULBs and Rs 1357.1 crore for Special Areas. These Special Areas have been defined as "areas covered by the Vth and VIth Schedules and the areas exempted from the perview of Part IX and IX A of the Constitution". In Assam the Special Areas will include Bodoland, Dima Hasao and Karbi Anglong Districts. From the total devolution of Rs 87,519 crore the share of States will be determined in accordance with a formula which gives 50 per cent weightage to population, 10 per cent to area and 15 per cent to index of devolution. The remaining 25 per cent, separately for PRIs and ULBs, will be on different weightage to other criteria. The actual amounts for the local bodies of Assam works out to be Rs 1577.4 crore for PRIs, Rs 253.6 crore for ULBs and Rs 61.8 crore for Special Areas during 2010-15.

The huge transfers to local bodies made by FC-XIII is really a good beginning because both PRIs and ULBs need funds for their running. Article 280(3) (bb) of the Indian Constitution enjoins the Central Finance Commissions to make recommendations regarding the "measures needed to augment the Consolidated Fund of a State to supplement the resources of the Panchayats in the State on the basis of the recommendations made by the Finance

Commission of the State". A similar provision has been enacted by article 280(3) (C) in respect of Municipalities. FC-XIII has recommended certain amendments to Article 280 so that it becomes more specific in regard to local finance. These should be adopted.

In Assam the Third Assam State Finance Commission (TASFC), which I chaired, had made several revolutionary recommendations including the most important one of transferring 25 per cent of the State Government's own revenues to PRIs and ULBs. For the four years ending on March 31, 2011 this amounted to Rs 4015 crore. The recommendations of TASFC were accepted by the State Government but allowed to lapse due to bureaucratic delay. This means that Assam will lose these amounts because the Central Finance Commissions will take such allocations into account while making their recommendations for transfers to the States. This is unfortunate.

One controversy which has surfaced in recent times is the ideal proportion of devolution and grants in the Finance Commission transfers. FC-XII preferred more grants. They transferred 18.9 per cent as grants. FC-XI had transferred only 13.5 per cent. FC-XIII has now transferred 15 per cent. I personally prefer more grants because such transfers are more specific and more focussed.

Huge amounts are transferred to the States every year by the Planning Commission in the shape of Central assistance to State Plans. The Planning Commission, however, is an entity set up by an executive order. There is no mention about it in the Indian Constitution. The time has come when the status of the Planning Commission should be formalised by giving it a place in the Indian Constitution.

In Assam the Annual Plan contains a Tribal Sub-Plan and a Scheduled Caste Component Plan. The amounts going to the Schedule VI areas of Dima Hasao, Karbi Anglong and Bodoland districts for Plan are shown separately. Moreover, substantial assistance is given to the States under the Central Sector and the Centrally Sponsored schemes and programmes. In the Union Budget for 2011-12, for example, the total Plan and non-Plan transfers to all States amount to Rs 2,01,733 crore. This includes Rs 13,731 crore for the local bodies.

Beside the Special Areas, mentioned earlier, there are certain new entities which have been set up in Assam. These are the 13 tribal and ethnic Councils set up to satisfy the political aspirations of different small groups. Very high financial allocations have been given to each of these entities in the State Budget. It will be necessary to integrate the fund requirements of these Councils by the next Finance Commission (FC-XIV). Actually, there are demands for more such ethnic Councils. The existing ones are demanding more powers, more finance and Schedule VI status. Some of the ethnic groups are demanding tribal status. In the case of the six main groups their demand for tribal status is under active consideration of Government. These matters require urgent consideration so that inter-ethnic disturbances or agitations against the State Government can be avoided. What is important is that these matters impact Indian federalism.

In the case of ULBs special attention will be necessary because of the rapid pace of urbanisation. Very soon 50 per cent of Indians will live in the

cities and towns. Both Mumbai and New Delhi have become very large metropolis. Along with the surrounding cities and towns each has become a huge urban conurbation. A large number of other cities will join the ranks of Mumbai and New Delhi very soon. FC-XIV will have to take account of their problems and make suitable allocations. The provisions regarding District Planning Committees and Metropolitan Planning Committees, enshrined in the Constitution, will have to be energised in order to accelerate the development process in these areas.

One of the terms of reference (ToR) of FC-XIII was to "review the present arrangements as regards financing of disaster management with reference to the National Calamity Contingency Fund and the Calamity Relief Fund and the Funds envisaged in the Disaster Management Act, 2005". Successive FCs had been entrusted with similar ToRs. Their recommendations have ensured that the States are reasonably provided with resources for disaster management. According to media reports Assam failed to utilise Rs 700 crore out of the money provided for this purpose during 2005-10. This is unfortunate. This should not be allowed to recur specially when thousands of victims in camps and make-shift homes suffer due to non-availability or inadequacy of succour.

One lesson that we learn from a study of Indian history is that whenever the Centre became weak India was divided. Therefore, the Central Government must remain strong. But the States will have to be given enough financial resources so that the people of India can progress in all fields. The local government institutions must also be given adequate financial support so that their services to the citizens improve. Beside that other political entities such as district councils, ethnic and tribal councils and state specific institutions must also be looked after properly. It is the duty of the Finance Commissions and the Planning Commission to ensure that these objectives are achieved.

23

Role of Foreign Direct Investment (FDI) in Retail Sector: A New Opportunity

A.K. Neog

Determinants of FDI in a Host Country/Economy: According to World Investment Report, 1998 the determinants of FDI in a host country can be classified under – (i) Policy Framework, (ii) Economic Determinants, and (iii) Business Facilitation.

Policy Framework: The components under this are—

- Economic, Political and Social Stability,
- Rules regarding entry, operations and exit of enterprise,
- Standards of treatment of foreign affiliates,
- Policies on functioning and structures of markets,

[Particularly policies on competition and merger and acquisition (M and A)]

- International agreements on FDI,
- Privatisation Policy,
- Trade Policy and its coherence with FDI policy, and
- Tax policy.

Economic Determinants: These determinants can be classified into (a) Market-seeking, (b) Resource/Asset seeking, and (c) Efficiency seeking.

Market seeking determinants are—

- Size of per capita income and market,
- Growth of Market,
- Access to regional and global markets,
- Country specific consumer preferences (structure of markets).

Resource/Asset seeking determinants are—

- Raw materials,
- Low-cost unskilled labour,

- Existence of skilled labour,
- Technological, innovatory and other created assets
- Physical infrastructure (e.g., power, tele-communication, roads, airports, seaports, river ports, etc.).

Efficiency–seeking determinants are—

- Low cost of resources and assets adjusted for productivity of labour resources.
- Other input costs e.g., transport and communication cost to/from and within host economy, and cost of other intermediate products.
- Membership of a Regional Integration Agreement (RTA) conducive to the establishment of regional corporate networks.

Business Facilitation Determinants: These are as placed under—

- Investment promotion and facilitation services,
- Incentives for Investment (investor-friendly)
- Low hassle costs (related to corruption, administrative efficiency, good governance, legal expenses, etc.).
- Social amenities (bilingual schools, quality of life, hospitality, etc.)
- After-investment services.

Investment Decisions on Rational Expectations of Return and Risk: Foreign firms like the domestic ones are governed by the motive of profit maximisation. While looking at the above determinants of FDI, the investors in the ultimate analysis tend to choose destination countries/economies by basing their decisions on rational expectations theorem of returns on investment and risk associated with the returns. They choose those countries/locations that give the highest expected returns for a given level of risk, or the lowest risk for a given set of expected returns. By plotting for different countries, the returns on Y-axis and risks (measured in terms of standard deviation of returns) on X-axis on a graph, they derive a curve called efficiency frontier. The countries (or places) which lie on or above the curve are perceived as profitable and are chosen, those below the curve are rejected.

Need for FDI: In the foregoing para, we have dealt with the demand side of foreign investors prior to their supply of FDI into the host country. In this section, we point out the factors that determine the need of or demand for FDI by a host country. In general, the following are the important factors that govern the need for FDI —

- Developing countries like India are capital-scarce and labour-surplus
- FDI is an important source of capital and can contribute to capital formation
- FDI provides access to inputs that are not available domestically
- FDI provides access to state-of-the-art technology
- FDI improves management system by providing world-class or global practices
- FDI can help in the improving competitiveness
- FDI can help in expanding and diversifying production and export capacities with economies of scale and comparative advantages
- FDI is an important engine of overall economic growth and development.

Necessary Conditions to Attract FDI: There is global competition among the countries to attract FDI. The conditions necessary to attract the same, in fact, are the determinants of FDI in the host country/economy dealt already. However, the followings can be considered as a set of necessary conditions :

- Open economy framework and outward looking,
- Market reform in the domestic economy,
- Sound economic fundamentals,
- Investor-friendliness of the political regimes and the civil society,
- Efficient and transparent regulatory system,
- Liberal economic environment,
- Good governance and responsive institutions,
- Improvement in infrastructure,
- Flexible labour market,
- Tax reform,
- State guarantee to global investors,
- Insurance at preferential rates to global investors,
- A package of incentives,
- Good law and order condition and speedy judicial system.

It may be noted that the above conditions are basically macro-level necessary conditions, which by themselves may not be sufficient. As for instance, in a federal democratic country like India besides the Central government laws, the states have also their own laws, rules and regulations. Hence, the necessary and sufficient conditions to attract global investments to the grassroots ultimately rest at the reforms at the state level.

Opening up of Indian Economy: India has opened up its economy in July, 1991 bringing reforms through liberalisation, privatisation and globalisation as the *Mantras*. These are, however, processes rather than one-shot events. Hence, they are continuous. Some of these reforms are yet to percolate to the state level in their entirety.

Inflow of FDI into India: According to data presented in Economic Survey 2007-08 published by the Ministry of Finance of the Government of India. The cumulative amount of FDI inflow (in terms of equity capital) from August, 1991upto March 2007 stood at Rs 2, 32,041 crore or US dollar ($) 54,628 million.

Year	*FDI Inflows*	
	Rs in Crore	*In million US $*
2009-10	1,23,378	25,888
2008-09	1,22,919	27,309
2007-08	98,664	24,579
From August 1991 Upto March 2007	2,32,041	54,628
Total upto March 2008 from August 1991	4,53,624	1,06,516
Total upto March 2010 form August 1991	5,77,108	1,32,428

On the other hand, according to Economic Survey 2009-10 and the DIPP inflows after that were as under:

FDI into India—An Appraisal: The top investing counties in India since 1991 are Mauritius, USA, Japan, Netherlands, UK, Germany, Singapore, France, South Korea and Switzerland. The top sectors attracting FDI are—services sector, housing and real estate, telecommunications, constructions, computer software and hardware, automobiles, power, chemicals (other than fertilizers), information and broadcasting, electrical equipment, hotel and tourism, trading, consultancy services, sea transport, petroleum and natural gas, and metallurgical industries. However, as per Economic Survey 2008-09, services accounted for 40 per cent, manufacturing 35 per cent, infrastructure 18 per cent and construction seven per cent.

Locational imbalance has been noticed in the flow of FDI into India. As for instance, during April 2000 to November 2007, FDI received has flown to already developed States which are infrastructuraly better developed or have sea ports. During this period, Maharashtra, Dadra and Nagar Haveli, Daman and Diu received 25.14 per cent of FDI; Delhi, Haryana and parts of U. received 22.68 per cent; Karnataka 7.03 per cent; Tamil Nadu and Pondicherry 6.69 per cent; Andhra Pradesh 4.12 per cent and Gujarat 2.84 per cent—these 11 States cornering 68.5 per cent of the FDI. Thus, FDI is biased towards developed States. This is going to aggravate the problem of regional imbalance, 'haves' having more and 'non-haves' not getting the due. Further, as has been noted by Megha Mukim *et al* in their study that large metro areas divert FDI projects away from neighbouring districts, thereby perpetuating or even widening the urban-rural divide.

FDI inflow to urban centers is like 'carrying coal to Newcastle'. This shows the urban-bias character of the FDI. Hence, FDI cannot be depended upon as a panacea for inclusive development of backward and rural areas.

Dismal Flow of FDI into North East India: The North-East India comprising eight States viz., Assam, Arunachal Pradesh, Manipur, Meghalaya, Mizoram, Nagaland, Tripura and Sikkim seems to have been left virtually untouched by FDI. This is supported by the following facts. As per data of the Department of Industrial Policy and Promotion (DIPP), during August 1991 to March 2005 the amount of FDI approved for the country as a whole was US $ 67,649.38 million. Of this, Assam accounted for US $ 0.57 million, Arunachal Pradesh US $ 3.57 million, Meghalaya US $ 13.66 million, Manipur US $ 0.89 million, Mizoram US $ 0.35 million, Nagaland US $ 1.03 million and Tripura US $0.74 million (for Sikkim data are not available or nil). FDI into Assam is one of the lowest in the country. The above data are on FDI approved and not real inflows. As per RBI data, FDI inflows to the country during January 2000 to December 2006 stood at US $ 32,152.09 million. Of this, inflows to the eight States of North East India stood at meager US $ 9.03 million i.e., 0.03 per cent.

Assam and the entire North-East seems to be suffering from some sort of Pygmalion effect like the fate of the flower girl Elizabeth Doolittle in G.B. Shaw's Pygmalion. Despite its natural beauty, hospitable climate, virgin resources, the launching of Look East Policy and bonanza of incentives offered

under North East Industrial and Investment Promotion Policy (NEIIP), 2007, the region is not able to attract suitors in the investment fair. The villain of the piece is the availability of power, which is the Achilles' heel, let alone good governance and militancy. Solution lies in tackling these factors.

New Windows of Opportunity: With the launching of the Look East Policy (LEP) in 1991, new development opportunities are emerging in the entire North-East India, especially in the export-import (EXIM) front. The States and the new generation must gear up to avail of this new opportunity. The government should set up a 'diplomatic township' under the Look East Policy. It will generate linkage effects. The process of implementation of the policy should be accelerated.

Opportunity for Inflow of Foreign Direct Investment (FDI) under Retail Sector: The North-East India is a capital scarce and labour surplus region. There is big potentiality for inflow of FDI. The Look East policy is envisaged to act as a catalyst. The region has several advantages like high degree of literacy English medium education system, generous hospitality of the people, unexploited resources, proximity/access to ASEAN markets, ease of doing business, etc. which can attract foreign investors. According to World Bank's report on "Doing Business in India 2009", among 17 places in India, Guwahati occupies eighth position in terms of "ease of doing business' taking only 38 days to start a business compared to 40 days in Bengaluru, only 600 days to enforce a contract against 1,420 days in Mumbai, 8.3 years to close business against 10.8 years in Kolkata and only 22 days to export against 28 days in Kochi or 26 days in Hyderabad. (*Source: Government of India, Economic Survey, 2009-10, page 29*). The bonanza of incentives offered under Government of India's North-East Industrial and Investment Promotion Policy (NEIIP), 2007 has made the region a kind of Special Economic Zone (SEZ). Thus Guwahati has more comparative advantages *vis-à-vis* other places of India to woo foreign investors.

The approval of FDI policy on retail in both the Houses of Parliament in the first week of December 2012 on 100 per cent FDI in single brand and 51 per cent in multi-brand retail has opened another new opportunity not only for the country at large but also for the North East India. It may be mentioned that the notification of the Central government to permit upto 51 per cent FDI in multi-brand retail was issued in September 2012. The Parliamentary approval has set the stage for global super markets to come to the country. FDI in multi-brand retails is envisaged to be beneficial for the economy as it would bring foreign investment, help set up modernised efficient supply chains, reduce wastage in perishable agricultural produce through investment in back-end infrastructure, bring gains to producers and consumers, vertically integrate wholesaling and retailing efficiencies i.e., efficiency gains, reduce inflation and increase employment in organised retails. This seems to be in line with Dixit-Norman model of trade which envisages that when there are monopolistic distortions in the domestic trade, opening up the economy for foreign trade expands the total market, increases competition and thus reduces monopolistic distortions, and reduces the price and inflation.

"Keep a shop and shop will keep you", so goes the proverb. But retails are much beyond. Retails trade sector is growing all over rural and urban areas with rising income and consumption of the people. According to data published by Technopak Advisors Pvt. Ltd (a consultancy organisation) in the Financial Express dated 11.12.2012, the share of the organised (medium and large) retail in total retail market in the country rose from four per cent in 2001 to seven per cent in 2011. Unorganised (Kirana) retail market (93 per cent) is still huge. There are different forms of retailers—street vendors, hawkers, independent small grocers and other retailers, medium size modern independent retail outlets, and corporatised retail giants. The class of stake holders in retail ranges from farmers, millers, community organisations, cooperatives, consumers, small and medium enterprises, industry associations to State government. This shows the range of opportunities for the North-East India in retailing. As the GSDP and consumption continue to grow, employment in the retail sector would grow. Retailing is not a zero-sum game. It is 'positive sum' and 'win-win'. There are conditions and safeguards to the domestic stakeholders under the upto 51 per cent FDI in multi-brand retail scheme like permitting the stores to be set up in cities with a population of one million, minimum 100 million dollar in FDI in multi-brand of which 50 per cent has to go for creation of infrastructure, and 30 per cent of the product sourcing has to be from small and medium enterprises, and the licence is to be given by the state government.

To facilitate the growth of the retail sector, the States, cities and municipalities must come up with simplified licensing and permission procedures. Town planning must take into account land use and creation of space for stores in the nooks and corners. Government should bring supportive reforms in labour policy, Agricultural Produce Marketing Committee (APMC) Act and internal trade. Promotional agencies should train up the unemployed youths for jobs in retail trade. The banks should come forward to support the retail trade and improve their credit deposit ratio.

References

Government of India, Office of the Economic Adviser: *Hand book of Industrial Policy and Statistics*, 2006-07.

Megha Mukim, *et al.* (June, 2010): *The Location Choices of Foreign Investors - A District-Level Analysis in India*, in the Financial Express, 16.7.2010.

A.K. Neog (October, 2009): *Electrification in North-East India-An Economic Evaluation*, in Journal of North-East India Council for Social Science Research, Vol. 33.2.

A.K. Neog (March, 2013): Prof N.C. Das Memorial Lecture on Economic Development of North East India – A Glimpse Deptt. of Commerce, Gauhati University.

24

Handicraft and Rural Economy of Assam

Paramesh Dutta I.AS (Retd.)

A society is a group of people who join together to share the same custom, laws etc. in other words, a society is identified from its culture, tradition and living custom. In fact every society is keen to uphold their tradition and custom in order to preserve their uniqueness in the larger social body. Again between the two, cultural tradition plays the most important role in defining unique entity. No society will like to loose their cultural tradition and in fact they try to popularise and propagate the particular tradition among their upcoming members in order to ensure the sustainability of the cultural traditions.

Among various parameters of the cultural tradition like music, dance, food, habit, the handicrafts play a definite role in defining the cultural tradition of a society. So much so that, sometime some handicrafts become the identification marks of a particular society, which makes every member of that society proud. They become emotionally so attached that they try to resist all outside onslaughts which may pose to be a threat to their handicraft.

It should be noted that development of these traditional handicrafts is an inalienable part of balanced economic development. Particularly, employment opportunity of this sector is enormous. It is low capital intensive and extremely suitable for improvement of rural economy. In fact, it plays the role of speedy overall economic development and supplements the income of the rural families.

The evolution process of human civilisation targets to achieve more, productivity with lesser human effort. Scientific and technological researchers are constantly working with this objective making the economic activities very competitive while at the same time demands for traditional handicrafts are getting faded. The situation has got more aggravated with the Indian economy marching towards globalisation. In fact, we have reached a state

where survival of the fittest is gradually becoming the rule. This has caused the toughest challenge to the traditional handicraft sector of the economy.

Among the major threats to the traditional handicrafts are:

(a) Competitive economy,

(b) Conceptual variation of design, shape, weight, colour etc.,

(c) Mechanisation of process for productivity.

All the above points clearly indicate the vulnerability of handicraft *vis a vis* machine products, synthetic material and use of technologically superior methods. Globalisation has became as the greatest threat to the very extistence of this traditional sector, particularly in Assam.

Handicraft is primarily an activity which flourished with the support of the kings during earlier periods. They promoted this as an art with the motive to demonstrate their cultural superiority. But the survival is possible only when the handicraft items become utility products along with the artistic quality. These handicraft products are useful in day to day life of the society and thereby it becomes an integral part of the cultural tradition of the society. At the same time the handicrafts which are artistic in nature are facing serious threats of extinction. Assamese population and for that matter, the Indian population in general cannot afford to spare money for such artifact products which do not meet any utility requirement.

Let me mention a case study in which I had the opportunity to involve myself during my service period. I joined as Project officer of Rural industries Project in 1975 under the Industries Department of Assam and posted at Gauripur, in the then Goalpara district, comprising Goalpara, Dhubri, Kokrajhar, Bongaigaon and Chirang districts of today. I have found different handicrafts of several micro-level societies in the district, for example Sitalpati of Dubapara, Goalpara, Solapith works of Gouripur and Golokganj, terracotta of village Asharikandi near Gauripur, Mulberry rearing and Dokhana weaving among Bodo community in Kokrajhar and Gossaigaon areas. Sitalpati and Dokhanas were utility products, Solapith was decorative art work and terracotta was a combination of both. Its dolls were artistic products whereas the urns, tumblers, receptacles etc. were the utility products. This terracotta handicraft flourished during the time of the *zamindars*, popularly known as Rajas of Gauripur due to their support. As soon as the *zamindaries* got abolished the artistic items of terracotta had also lost demand. Only the utility items survived until cheaper, durable, easy to handle products replaced them gradually. Thus, the entire terracotta handicraft which once was a pride identity of the pal community of Asharikandi started fading and lost sight.

I started analysing the matter in order to find some ways to restore the lost glory of this handicraft so that the people of the society not only can regain their pride but also can make good fortune out of that. The revival of the handicraft has the potentiality to bring change in the living standard of this society consisting of Pal community.

Considering all this factors in a systematic matter and after discussing with the artisans and experts, a few important actions had been formulated.

Initially to start with the designs, shapes, sizes of the terracotta handicraft items were modified and the traditional uniqueness had been tried to be more

prominently focussed. The vision was to take these items to the modern living rooms of megacities, metropolis and other urban centers of if possible interior walls of high ranking offices of corporate and Banks sector.

Secondly, prices were raised for the products because that was one of the factors which the well to the customers care for as the cost of the items bring glamour to the items and proportionately enhances the impression of better quality as well as the desire of possession. The artistic item may decorate the interior of executive chambers and high society drawing rooms once they are priced suitably.

Thirdly, regular display of modified/diversified products in state level and national level exhibitions is necessary for market exposure.

The artisans were organised in a co-operative society with Mr Dhiren Paul as secretary to carry out this revival battle of terracotta handicraft. In Asharikandi near Gauripur in Dhubri district. Today the handicraft items in truck loads are sent regularly for sale through exhibitions and retail outlets. The artisans are not only proud of their handicrafts but also they are earning their livelihood out of it.

The efforts were noticed by the All India Handicraft Board and they decided to establish a marketing extension center under the eastern zone at Gauripur and I served as a nodal officer in that office in 1976 in addition to my normal duties till departmental officers were posted. They extended help in participation of terracotta handicraft in various exhibitions in the country, which makes this item well-known all over the country.

The practice of saving the traditional crafts by spoon feeding in the form of restricting the entry of alternate products coming from outside by enacting laws or by providing subsidy to the local handicraft is not a sustainable solution in the long run. The local handicraft must be able to face the challenge and stand by firmly on its own if only to check adverse effect of globalisation.

I took the help of SWOT analysis to find out some concrete steps to revive the handicraft feet. SWOT, as everybody knows, is a primary requirement for analysing prospects or feasibility of a project. SWOT stands for S-Strength, W-Weakness, O-Opportunity, T for Threat. The strength of the terracotta handicraft was its unique artistic value, local availability of raw materials (sandy clay) and above all traditional skill prominently available among all men and women belonging to 'pal' community residing as a cluster in the village Asharikandi.

Weakness lies in the fact that the products are heavy, brittle, difficult to clean which make it unsuitable for rough use. The manufacturing process is a drudgery such that the young educated youth started disliking it. Moreover, the products are not available in market at ease. The low price of the item leads to the impression of inferiority in quality and the well to do families are not attracted to possess these items.

Opportunities are that the artistic handicraft items may occupy decent places in the modern living rooms. Further with slight variations in design, the items may also find utility as well.

Threat was primarily from the aluminum utensils which were, more durable, light and easily washable. Artistic handicraft products of other states have gradually enriched the value of decoration in the interior of living rooms.

To name a few handicrafts of Assam, which are traditionally cluster-based, are silk, Muga and apparels of Sualkuchi, Kamrup, the Bell metal works of Sarthebari, Barpeta, Brass metal wares of Hajo, Kamrup, Dokhna weaving, Kokrajhar, Laisemfi of Cachar, Sitalpati of Hailakandi, Karimganj, Woolen sawls of Karbi Anglong, clusters of Japies of Nalbari, Assamese ornaments of Nagaon and Jorhat and also potters are a few to name with. Time has come to keep them alive through actions like modification of designs, use of quality material application of cost cutting method of production. Basically they must be able to overcome the challenges that may come from any inferior or duplicate products in cheaper rate.

The recent days confrontation was witnessed among the Sualkuchi Silk products and the inferior silk products coming from outside the states mainly from Banaras. So much so that some people irrationally burnt Benarasi silk apparels to express their protest. Some people even demanded ban on entry of silk products from outside the state. These steps are short-sighted approach and always counter-productive in the long run. Moreover, there are categories of clients who may prefer cheap variety of Banarasi cloths to Sualkuchi products because of affordability. The market must be free and fair. All violent actions to protect interest of one product in the pretext of preservation of a handicraft do not hold water. Sale of diamonds are not declined in spite of the fact that a lot of duplicate products are available nearby. In fact on many occasions these replicas excel real diamonds in apparent shining and glaze. There are customers for cheaper variety of items, no matter they may be duplicate products because they are less expensive. People cannot be compelled to restrict their choice in a free market system. Some people may buy Banarasi silk products because of obvious reasons. They may not be either able to afford Sualkuchi Silk or may prefer Benarasi Silk as their customs. This problem has not occurred in case of Kanjivaram silk of South India. This needs a proper analytical study so that Sualkuchi Silk products are not only protected but can also enter into the wide open market all over the country or outside with its characteristic brand name. These products must be able to create a Brand like Kanjivaram or Benarashi. They should be sold as Sualkuchi Silk products as a Brand. Required modification of production process, cost control measures, diversification of design, aggressive marketing should ensure sustained growth of the industry. Experts must put their heads together and find out the line of actions in this direction.

Handicraft sector provides considerably supplementary income to a large section of rural population which contributes to a great extent to raise their family income and to uplift the living standard of people. If established in appropriate scale the handicraft industry can provide gainful employment as well. This sector has the potentiality of undying contributions immensely to the rural economy of Assam.

We must not take a myopic approach in assuring the market for out handicraft products. Government is contemplating of opening trade link to

South East Asia through its catchy phase of 'look east policy'. But are we ready for such a trade links with those countries? What is there to trade from our side? As on today we have painfully noticed that only successful trade in the route is smuggling of drugs. Commercial giants like China is in the east and such an open trade link may open flood gates to the Chinese products further jeopardising our handicraft products. We must be ready with our products in price, quality and design, etc., to cater to the need of South East Asian market. It can be emphatically said that out handicraft products once developed suitably are competent to create a prospective market. Their potentiality has to be explored and implemented. It is not that easy as anybody could say or imagine. Today China by dint of arduous hard work and dedicated aggressive marketing approach has grabbed the major share of world market for its products. In many cases they have replaced the traditional brands originally produced by world famous countries. This is equally true for all categories of handicrafts in Assam.

Assam is a landlocked state with relatively inferior level of infrastructure. Small customer population made this area unsuitable for industrial growth. Unlike manufacturing industries Tea and Oil industries do not possess the required avenues for development of ancillary and allied industries. The transportation to major trade centers of the country is another great huddle. In this situation the State must concentrate on handicraft and cottage sector in order to attain commercial sustenance in the rural area. The rural economy cannot flourish through cheap and politically motivated spoon feeding measures like distribution of seeds, yarns, subsidies etc. Rather people should be taught to be competitive and should be provided trainings on appropriate design, process to enable them to overcome challenges and earn though sincere and hard work.

The sustained growth of rural economy cannot be achieved without hard labour. Government should focus more on continuous research in handicraft sector in order to augment the market by way of diversification, quality control, effective measure in production and above all on productivity. Guidance and training together with support in input like credit facilities could bring the desired change in the handicraft sector to usher in a positive contribution into the rural economy.

25

Sir Edward Gait's—A History of Assam: A Critical Review

Lalit Kumar Barua IAS (Retd.)

Sri Edward Gait's—"A History of Assam" has for long remained a benchmark for the students of the history of Assam. It is more than a century now, since the book saw the light of the day. From the point of view of modern readers it has been seen and interpreted, first and foremost as a colonial text. But for the bulk of readers it is still a very useful book, a base on which alternative readings of the political and social history could be constructed.

There is no doubt however that Gait's book on Assam History was born out of a colonial project, displaying the same type of need, and approach that made a few anthropologists to collate information from field investigations and bring out important studies relating to the north-eastern region. Such studies of the tribes and of encounters with the people for expanding the imperial frontier formed the staple of much historical writing in the 19th century. The basic idea-behind these writings was that these studies facilitated an understanding, which is extremely relevant for establishing effective control.

Sir Edward did not exactly belong to this school of writers. He did write within the given parameters of a colonial discourse then.

It is not surprising that Sir Gait did not find it necessary for his purpose to delve deeper into Assam's ancient history.

Some of the Indian contemporaries did not consider it necessary either to work towards a more complete historiography of Assam. R.D. Banerjee writes two decades later:

"Assam is the only province of India, the history of architecture and sculpture of which is still practically unknown. While the history of Assam begins with the conquest of the lower part of the valley by the Ahoms in the fourteenth century, the history of architecture begins with the introduction of Bengali masons and architects in the Sixteenth".[1]

Modern historians have admitted that Assam's history has a fairly Well Charted Course'[2] and that there is considerable archival material for reconstructing Assam's ancient and medieval history. Edward Gait's limited perception of Assam's antiquity and historical linkages was the result of his failure to pursue this line of enquiry more vigorously on the basis of the epigraphic and iconographic material available at that point in time.

In the process it was perhaps easier to draw the conclusion that a colonial historian was not properly interested in Assam's ancient history. The surprising aspect of it is that even later Indian historians carried on this legacy to some extent by grossly understating the importance of Assam in Indian historiography.

Edward Gait seemed to elevate the Puranic myths and legends, thereby misconstruing some important aspect of the ancient religious culture of Assam. The assumption that *Tantric* cults originated in Assam was certainly not based on historical evidence. The worship of the female principle, for instance in the form of *Shakti* or the mother goddess is central to the religio-cultural tradition of Bengal.

Gait also failed to pursue historically the pivotal position of the ancient *Pragjyotishpura* as the seat of an older civilization. About ancient *Pragjyotishpura* Gait wrote:

The capital of *Narak* and his descendants was *Pragjyotishpur*, the modem Guwahati. Prag means former or Eastern, and Jyotisha, a star astrology, shining. Pragjyotishpur may therefore be taken to mean the city of Eastern Astrology. The name is interesting in connection with the reputatation which the country has always held as a land of magic incantation and with the view that it was in Assam that the *Tantrik* form of Hinduism originated'.[3]

Later learned opinion definitely questions Gait's historical understanding of both Pragjyotishpura and the ASURA line of descent in ancient Assam'.[4]

Edward Gait wrote in much earlier times and it was a different constituency he addressed. As Percival Spear has stressed later, one has to take note of the changes that came over in Indian historiography in the intervening years.

Spear whose book A History of India (Penguin, 1965) was written from a very different perspective observed:

"The changes in the Indian scene are too obvious to need emphasis. Only two generations ago British rule seemed to most Indians as well as British observers likely to extend to an indefinite future; now there is a teenage generation which knows nothing of it. Changes in the attitude of historians have occurred everywhere, changes in attitudes to the content of the subject as well as to particular countries, but in India there have been some special features'.[5]

Edward Gait belonged to what Spear has described as the official school of historians; this kind of approach was suitably adopted and developed by Indian historians like Dr Jadunath Sarkar or Dr S.K. Bhuyan. There came to the fore two schools of historians. A nationalist School of historians and a colonial school so stridently different from each other. Percival spear has made an observation about the difference:

"The early official historians were content with the glamour and drama of political history from Plessey to Mutiny, from Dupleix to the Sikhs. But when raj settled down glamour departed from politics, and they turned to the less glorious but more solid ground of administration. Not how India was conquered but how it was governed was the theme of this school of historians".[6]

Edward Gait belonged to the colonial school, and found his answers within the parameters of a colonial viewpoint. He did not glorify the empire but had his own ground rules firmly in place.

One has to take note of the fact that Colonial historian as well as the ethnographers of north eastern India Carrie to regard caste and ethnicity as a central social fact for the writing of social history. Sir Edward Gait adhered strictly to this colonial classification of Indian Society.

Gait did not take recourse to a grand manner; his methodology was typically balanced in the manner of a seasoned administrator. Thus his narrative of Assam's history during the period of the Ahom rule and of the later period retains the reader's unflagging interest. He has given a useful chronological outline, combining the political, military and economic features of the rule with a cursory representation of cultural aspects of life.

On the theme of the consolidation of British rule Edward Gait was on very solid ground. He had an understanding of the imperial logic that took recourse to territorial reorganisation from time to time and imposed strategic limits of frontiers and boundaries.

It is important to recall that Edward Gait's history saw the light of the day in the year 1905 when Lord Curzeon's writ had combined a part of the province of Bengal arbitrarily with Assam. The change took away from Assam the right to send their representative to a provincial legislature.

The significant contribution of Sir Edward Gait was his interest in historical research through the studies of inscriptions, coins, historical and semi-historical materials which culminated in his undertaking to write a full-fledged history of Assam.

The limitations inherent in such as undertaking were not only the result of a colonialist's approach but also of the prevailing state of Indian historiography. Since then Indian historians have covered lot of lost ground; the sociological and the Marxist approaches have also brought in fresh tools of analysis and evaluation.

H.K. Barpuzari's volumes on the British period in Assam have been a major addition to the available historical knowledge of the province. There is here a persistent effort at objectivity slowly closing the gap between reality and the representation of it in political history. There are now good specific studies of the events or of historical periods conducted through closer examination of facts with a non-partisan approach'.[7]

Here the approach of the Subaltern historians brings in a fresh insight and a challenge to the conventional historian.

The following observation in one of the Subaltern texts would apply not only to Gait's summary of the social and political events of the province of Assam in the nineteenth century but also to most social histories of the

region. Assam's ancient period still continues to be starved of a thorough archeological and historical research; some of the myths or speculative notions presented in Gait's account continue to be encouraged by many scholars.

David Arnold writes: "Conventional historian has been too busy searching for what was presumed to be the grand, overarching themes of modern Indian history to concern itself greatly with the attitudes and activities of the peasants who constituted the great majority of the population. Peasants appear as victims of history, not as its principals."[8]

There are other larger concerns of political, economic and social import which the historians have to address adequately in order to complete the process which Gait's history had set in motion.

References

1. R.S. Banerjee Archeological Survey of India Annual Report, Amalendu Guha, 9924-25.

2. Medieval and Early Colonial Assam: Centre for Social Studies: Calcutta, 1990, p. 33.

3. Sir Edward Gait—'A History of Assam', Fourth Reprint. Lawyer's Book Stall, 1990. p. 15.

4. A. L. Basham: The Wonder that was India Grove Press. New York, 1954, p. 236.

5. Percival Spear, 'A History of India', Vol. 2, Penguin, 1965, p. 11.

6. Percival Spear, 'A History of India', Vol. 2, Penguin, 1965, p. 12.

7. A good example could be found in Dr Maheswar Neog's Socio-Political Events in Assam Leading to The Militancy of the Mayamaria Vaisnavas published by Centre for studies in Social Science, Calcutta. 1982.

8. David Arnold: Rebellious Hillmen: The Gurdem-Rampa Risings: 18394924 in Subaltern Studies: Writings on South Asian History and Society. Edited Ranajit Guha, Oxford, 1982, pp. 88-89.

26

Rise and Decline of Insurgencies in Assam

R.N. Ravi IPS (Retd.)

The post-British history of Assam has been a saga of relentless unrest. The state has been a playground of centrifugal forces leading to its vivi-sections and reduced stature. All the hill-tribes, except Dimasas and Karbishave weaned themselves off and are managing their affairs in their respective homelands-Nagaland, Meghalaya, Mizoram and Arunachal Pradesh. The grossly diminished Assam is not at peace with itself. Except for the tribes of Arunachal Pradesh, all others wrought their separations from Assam through sustained struggles. Mizoram and Nagaland were born after much bloodshed. Although the dynamic of insurgencies waged by each hill-tribe bore its distinct signature, the broad contours-initial denial backed with brute repressions by Delhi and Shillong, the seat of power of undivided Assam, and eventual umbilical separation, are common to all. The legacy of violence as an indispensable midwife for a new birth continues haunting the leftover Assam.

Paradigm shifts in the locus of power in the post-British North-East India have been at the root of much of the initial unrest.

The British kept a disengaged grip over the hills of Assam and did not interfere with the traditional power structures of the tribes dwelling therein. Although initial encounters of the British with the hill-tribes were fraught and often bloody, soon they reached a political equilibrium and developed a *modus vivendi* of grudging mutual respect notwithstanding occasional skirmishes. Absence of economic opportunities in the hills kept the colonial rulers disinterested in the hill-tribes. Their core concern in the hills adjoining the resource rich Brahamputra valley was in peace with the 'marauding' tribes who occasionally attacked the tea-gardens, inflicted damages on garden properties and at times took away precious labourers as slaves. Not willing to brook any potential adverse impact on the tea industry, arguably the most

lucrative of all contemporary trades, the British undertook several punitive military expeditions euphemistically called 'military promenade' into the hills and brutally subdued the tribes into mutual peace. Beyond that they did not establish, much less embed a system of governance foreign to the hill tribes. The tribal elites soon began viewing the British intrusion into the hills as a benign presence.

India's national freedom movement though did not enter the hills of the North-East except to a very limited extent in the Khasi regions, Shillong being the capital of Assam, thanks to the British policy of keeping them insulated with various measures including the system of 'Inner Line' restricting entry of plains people to the hills, the British civil servants in the hills primed the hill-tribes with toxic interpretations of the potential post-British scenario. They preyed upon the innocent minds of the tribes with fictions like how in the event of departure of the British the cunning Indians would oppress them including stopping them from eating pork and beef.

Conditioned to the notions of their likely frightful existence in the post-British India, the tribal elites recoiled at the prospect of loss of their traditional hegemony in an independent India. Infrastructures of a republican democratic state wedded to the notion of power to the people came as a rude shock to the traditional tribal elites. They faced the existential threat of being replaced by a set of new elites to be thrown up by the newly-constituted democratic architecture of power matrix. Beginning with some tribes in the Naga Hill district they challenged the imposition of the new architecture of governance. They couched their resistance in the language of a struggle for the protection to their culture and identity and thus freedom from India. Insurgencies spread to other hills and eventually led to separation of the restive hills from Assam and birth of new states.

Post-British Brahamputra Valley witnessed a different sort of power shift. The British had established a functioning architecture of governance. The region was segmented into districts for administrative convenience. Like rest of the British-India the tentacles of the British administration were extended up to the villages. The land owning gentry was subject to taxation and the people at large were subject to the civil and criminal justice systems established by the British. Capitalist commerce essentially based on extractive economy flourished. The Assamese gentry, subject to the British control, enjoyed their privileged socio-economic status. Unprecedented magnitudes of influx of population were mostly labourers for tea gardens, wet-cultivations and for road and rail constructions. This population did not in any way pose any challenge to the privileged status of the Assamese elite.

Diffusion of power to the citizens under the republican Constitution of India suddenly made demography the centre of gravity of the political power. Universal adult suffrage made every citizen an equal shareholder in the state power. Suddenly, the huge number of immigrant labourers who till the other day were mere minions became a potential existential threat to the privileged class. Much to the consternation of the Assamese elite subsequent elections to the state and union legislatures began throwing new and assertive leaders

from that very class. Alien ideologies brazenly challenging the traditional power structure began gaining momentum. The extreme and the not-so-extreme left movements with their avowed goal to opened the entrenched socio-political power structure spilled over from the West Bengal to Assam. Unprecedented growth of the Left Parties in 1970s further ruffled the peace of the Assamese elite and made the immigrant Bengalis suspect in their eyes. The fact that a significant section of Bengali Muslims had favoured the Muslim League's endeavour to integrate Assam with the East Pakistan compounded Assamese suspicion of their bona fide. The Assamese elite faced an existential threat. The threat was soon articulated in terms of threat to the Assamese identity.

A mass mobilisation popularly known as the Assam Agitation (1979-85) against the outsiders (*bahiragata*) for preservation of the Assamese nationalism erupted. The Agitation soon turned violent. In a tactical shift the agitation's war cry was changed from the one against the 'outsiders' to against the 'foreigners' (*bideshis*). Bengalis bore the brunt of the agitation.

In absence of an astute leadership, the agitation became a victim of its organisational entropy. Its social base soon began shrinking. Its wider resonance faded within the first three years. In a prodigiously heterogeneous society like Assam, the agitation leadership failed to resolve the inner contradictions of the Assamese nationality construct. The contradictions became apparent and fissures turned into gaping fault lines. The Union government rather than behaving like a benevolent guardian used wiles to defeat the agitation. A team of the Union government officials under the stewardship of Rajiv Gandhi outsmarted the weird agitation leaders and convinced them of the futility of their enterprise. They clinched a face saving deal for them, popularly known as the Assam Accord. The accord was a fig leaf for the agitation leaders. It was designed to fail in its promises.

Extensive use of arms and explosives during the agitation laid the foundation of armed insurgencies in Assam. An ultra-radical nucleus from among those along the sidelines of the agitation formed the United Liberation Front of Asom, arguably the first armed insurgent organisation in the state, for liberation of Assam from India. Its leaders sought and got military and moral support from the Naga secessionist, National Socialist Council of Nagaland. The war between the ULFA and the state began.

Like the Assam agitation, the leadership of ULFA lacked vision. The ULFA's excessive indeed almost total reliance on gun in prosecuting its secessionist politics led to its precipitous decline. Its ideologues and polemicists utterly failed in providing the campaign with a coherent strategy and an inclusive narrative. Unable to retain and consolidate its social base and pitted against asymmetrically strong Indian military power the outfit soon got onto a self-defeating trajectory. Mired in splits and dissensions the ULFA has been reduced to a shell of an insurgent outfit with not many in Assam inclined to shed tears for their 'liberators'.

The issues of foreigners and their influx remain unresolved and festering.

Ironically, the Assam agitation conceived and launched to safeguard Assam and Assamese nationality unleashed the most insidious forces of

divisions. Even before the ink on the Assam Accord dried the Bodos rebelled against the alleged hegemony of the 'Assamese'. They mobilised their community into a belief that their culture, identity and interests would not be safe within Assam. The rhetoric and idioms of secession used by the ULFA were regurgitated. A section of Bodo youths launched an armed militia, Boro Security Force in October 1986.They unleashed wanton violence against the non-Bodos. Its leaders holding apron strings of the NSCN leaders sought to internationalise their campaign. They sought membership of the Unrepresented Nations and Peoples Organisation, an NGO with international pretensions based at Hague. The UNPO provides an international platform and solidarity to nationality movements across the world. But there was a hitch. The constitution of the UNPO does not permit membership to an entity that espouses violence as a political resource. The word Force in the name of the outfit betrayed its military disposition. For tactical reasons the leaders changed its name to the National Democratic Front of Boroland. Meanwhile, yet another Bodo militia, the Bodo Liberation Tigers emerged and to woo the common constituency got into competitive killings of the non-Bodos. Wanton violence against the Bengali Muslims and Adivasis were unleashed. A section of the Muslim youth went to Bangladesh and Pakistan, received training and logistic support and formed Muslim militia-Muslim United Liberation Tiger of Assam.

The BLT hatched a deal with the Union and the Assam state government in 2003. Under the deal euphemistically called the Bodo Accord, they extracted the Bodoland Territorial Council under the Sixth Schedule to the Constitution of India for the north bank lower Assam. Its leaders also received a large sum of slush money from the Union government. Much to the chagrin of those who contrived the feat of political engineering called the Sixth Schedule while framing the Constitution, an exercise in substantive devolution of political power to a territory within a state, the BLT extracted an iniquitous and undemocratic deal. The Sixth Schedule though is in the nature of a mini-state within a state with executive, legislative and judicial powers on the transferred domains, however, it did not discriminate among the citizens living in that territory. Although the Bodos constitute barely 33 per cent of population of the Bodoland Territorial Autonomous District, they, through an amendment to the Sixth Schedule got 75 per cent seats reserved for the Bodos. The Bodo Accord made the majority population in the BTAD aggrieved and resentful. The Koch Rajbongshis and the Adivasis who together constitute majority population refused to reconcile to their perpetual political subordination and second-class-citizen status.

The newly-constituted Council was handed over to the BLT leaders on a platter on December 7, 2003 without any election. They were allowed to entrench themselves and a formal election was held at their convenience only in 2005. The BLT leaders, being distrustful of the governments retained an undisclosed number of armed cadres as a thinly disguised militia to enforce their writs while letting others surrender before the authorities. With the active use of their militia and tacit help of the Union and the state governments the BLT leaders decimated any democratic dissent to them.

Ironically, the Accord did not placate even the Bodos. The NDFB continued with its wanton violence and the suppressed democratic voices in the community rankled over denial of space to them by the BLT leaders. Disenfranchised Adivasis and Koch Rajbongshis kept the pot boiling. Peace remains elusive.

The Royal Bhutan Government with logistic assistance from India conducted operation 'All Clear' in Bhutan in December 2003-January 2004 and cleared its territory of the insurgents from Assam who had been camping there since early 1990s. The NDFB suffered heavy losses. However, they demonstrated their lethal capacity by unleashing wanton violence in lower Assam beginning October 2, 2004. After killing over 45 innocent people in three days of bouts of violence it offered unilateral 'ceasefire' with a warning to the governments not to delay engaging it in talks. The state government with alacrity responded by suspending all operations against the outfit. However, there was a major hitch to the NDFB extracting any substantial political concession from the government. The Congress government in the state was being carried on the crutches of the BLT that had grabbed 12 seats in 2006 Assembly elections and the Congress was reduced to minority. The BLT that has been sharing the state power with the Congress since then did not brook emergence of a parallel political force among the Bodos. The intra Bodos rivalries for hegemony kept the peace talks with the NDFB standstill.

On October 30, 2008 the NDFB while talking peace with the governments unleashed an unprecedented string of terrorist attacks that catapulted Assam on the global terrorism map. In Guwahati and other places it killed over 100 innocent persons and maimed over 400. There was widespread outrage among the people who demanded the state to stop cohabiting with the 'terrorists' and unleash the weight of the laws on them. The governments ignored the popular sentiments and cries. The charade of peace talk with Bodo ultras continued while peace remains elusive in the BTAD.

The centrifugal forces unleashed in the aftermath of the Assam agitation touched other tribes also. Demonstrative appeasement by the state of those who picked up guns encouraged other tribes to follow suit. Sections of enterprising Dimasas and Karbis youths picked up guns, formed militias and launched indiscriminate violence against the hapless 'others'. Over 1000 persons, mostly workers of construction companies, were killed. The state, true to its wont, rewarded them with largesse in the guise of buying peace.

The non-state violence became a low-cost high-return enterprise in Assam. The message was picked up by others. Rumblings of insurgencies began among Adivasis, Rabhas and Mishings.

Instead of pursuing an inclusive politics, a survival imperative for a heterogeneous state like Assam, the state pampered the politics of ethno-exclusivism. For electoral gains the Congress governments created a large number of ethnicity based politico-administrative entities on the eves of elections. Every such entity made the 'others' resentful and encouraged them to pick up guns. A vicious circle of violence has been set in motion.

Today, 'insurgency' as a credible organised resistance to the Indian state does not exist in Assam. Ironically, the non-state violent groups are now

patronised by the state. They have become beside other things political assets for the ruling establishment to be used whenever covert force is needed to promote its political and commercial interests. They are used for rigging the elections.

The state government has developed huge vested interest in sustaining the perception of insurgency. Thanks to 'insurgency', Assam is a 'special category' state. 90 per cent of its plan expenditures come to it as the Central grant and 10 per cent as loan. Besides the non-plan security expenditures are fully reimbursed by the Centre under the Security Related Expenditures. The state has no incentive, thanks to 'insurgency', to work for generating revenue for governance or development. It insists on perpetuating the perception of insurgency in the state. An attempt by the Central intelligence agency to remove the infamous Armed Forces (Special Powers) Act from the state as the necessary condition for restoration of the rule of law and justice was fiercely and successfully resisted by the state government. The result is the eclipse of the rule of law and justice, a blighted and diminished citizenry. But then who cares for the ordinary citizens!

27

India's North East Experience

Udayan Misra

The different ethno-nationalist struggles that have been occurring in the northeastern region of India, commonly referred to under the umbrella connotation of "North-East", have raised certain pertinent issues about the entire process of nation-building and the parameters of the nation-state. One of the earliest challenges to the nation-building process in post-1947 India came from the Naga struggle in the first years after independence. The differences between the leadership of the Naga National Council and the Government of India occurred mainly over the interpretation of a particular clause of the Hydari Agreement of 1946, wherein it was stated that after a period of 10 years both sides would be able to have a relook on their agreement.[1] The Naga National Council, from an initial position of acceptance of the Hydari Agreement, moved away into a more intransigent position once Angami Zapo Phizo and his supporters gained control of the organisation. With it began one of the longest and most protracted of ethnic nationalist struggles in the Indian sub-continent. Although it is not the purpose of this article to go into the course and content of the Naga struggle, yet it must be said that much of the human tragedy that engulfed the then Naga Hills district of Assam could perhaps have been avoided had the Indian leadership and the government they headed in Delhi attempted to move out of the mono-cultural groove of nationalism which they tried to promote at the cost of the diversity of ethnic nationalism in the northeastern region of newly-independent India. Fresh from the freedom struggle, the Indian leadership was clearly not in a position to appreciate a very different perspective as far as autonomy and even independence was concerned. In this connection one must recall the debate amongst the political leadership of India in the 1930s and 1940s as to whether India should go for a strict federal dispensation or opt for a loosely federal but unitary structure of governance. The Partition and its aftermath gave a fillip to those forces which wanted a centralised form of government and this was supported by no less an authority on the Constitution than B.R.

Ambedkar during the Constituent Assembly debates. Finally, the country opted for a loose federal structure where all the effective control, both economic and political, lay with the Centre. Hence, it was not expected of such a government structure to respond sympathetically towards the Naga demand for autonomy verging on independence. Both the Centre and the State governments initially saw the Naga struggle as a law and order problem, as a militant movement inspired by foreign missionaries and aimed at destroying the territorial integrity of newly-independent India. The result was a human tragedy of massive proportions. Within a few years, one of the largest armies of the world was pitted against a very small nationality made up of a few lakhs of people. That the Naga National Council could put up such a resistance proved that given a determination and a goal, even a very small nationality can challenge a mighty power and force it to come to terms. This is exactly what happened in the course of the Naga struggle which, unfortunately, is today far removed from its earlier stated goal and has got mired in the quicksand of narrow tribalism resulting in fratricidal killings and turf wars.

I have begun this essay with the Naga struggle not only because it was one of the earliest challenges to the nation-building process but also because it threw up certain issues which are extremely important and fundamental when one tries to trace the growth of the nation-state in India and the challenges it has been facing. It is important to note that in the course of its engagement with the Naga struggle, the Indian nation-state also went through a learning experience even as it moved from a rigid position of viewing the movement as a separatist one fuelled by foreign agents to its acceptance of the political nature of the struggle. This is what one may refer to part of as India's Northeast experience, something which has eventually led to the expansion of the parameters of the Indian nation-state and the redefining of very markers of Indian nationalism itself. How has this been possible? As one moves from the first stages of the Indian nation-state's engagement with the Naga insurgency, when every attempt was made to arrive at a military solution to a gradual acceptance of the national content of the struggle, we notice a distinct change in positions. However, it took quite some time for the newly-independent nation-state to even partially appreciate the Naga point of view because in the immediate post-independence years it was immersed in the nationalistic feeling stirred up by the freedom struggle and was nourished in the idea of a very distinct nationalism centered around the concept of a Mother India. Little did this leadership realise that there were several small nationalities in the northeastern part of the country who had never participated in the freedom struggle against the British and whose perceptions about freedom could be very different.

It may be mentioned that during the controversy over Grouping as proposed by the Cabinet Mission, several small ethnic nationalities of undivided Assam had expressed their desire to be left out of either India or Pakistan. The strong fight against the Grouping Proposals led by the Assam Congress put a check on the centrifugal forces and helped those who were in favour of integrating the region with a newly-independent India. Nonetheless,

there were quite a few small ethnic communities/nationalities that nourished their own ideas of freedom and this was evident during the Independence Day celebrations in the northeastern region. For instance, while people in the Brahmaputra Valley were quite enthusiastic about the end of colonial rule, perceptions were somewhat different in the hill areas which had not been touched by the freedom struggle. Hence, in the Naga Hills, the Naga National Council observed Naga Independence Day on August 14, one day ahead of India's Independence Day. There was more to such developments than a mere expression of secessionist sentiment as was seen by most of those belonging to the national political establishment of the rest of the country. In fact, if one goes into the documents of the Naga struggle, there is enough evidence to suggest that it began as a struggle for maximum autonomy. The entire course of the Naga struggle might have been different had those who were then at the helm of affairs of the country tried to understand the different perceptions of freedom and self-rule which were shared by the small communities/ nationalities[2] of the northeastern region.

It took the Indian nation-state more than two decades to accept the political content of struggles like the one being waged by the Nagas. Finally, it was the Peace Mission led By Jayaprakash Narayan (with Bimala Prasad Chaliha and Rev. Michael Scott as members) which acknowledged that the Naga struggle had a strong national content and reflected the political and social aspirations of the Naga people. This was significantly the country's first such civil society intervention in an armed conflict between the Indian state and a small nationality. The Peace Mission's initiative was followed by a ceasefire and negotiations which ultimately led to the formation of the State of Nagaland in 1963. But what is significant about the creation of Nagaland is that for the first time in the history of post-independence India, it was incorporated in the Constitution that " land and its resources" would belong to the Naga people.[3] The new Article 371A stated that the Special Provision with respect to the State of Nagaland would read as follows: " Notwithstanding anything in this Constitution, (a) no Act of Parliament in respect of the (i) religious or social practices of the Nagas, (ii) Naga customary law and procedure, (iii) administration of civil and criminal justice involving decisions according to Naga customary law, (iv) ownership and transfer of land and its resources, shall apply to the State of Nagaland, unless the legislative Assembly of Nagaland by a resolution so decides." Though apparently, no major departure from the unitary spirit of the Constitution had been made while creating a separate culture-political space for a small nationality, yet an important new beginning had been made in the very acknowledgement by the Indian nation-state of the land rights and rights over natural resources of the Naga people and that no changes would be possible without the assent of the Nagaland Assembly. It is indeed significant that for the first time that the Constitution recognises the rights of a constituent state and its residents to wide-ranging social and economic rights and makes it binding that any changes that may take place will be dependent on the will of the elected legislature of the new state.

This is much in advance of the Sixth Schedule provisions of the Constitution which were eventually nullified to a great extent by the contrary pulls between the District Councils and the elected legislature. It may be recalled that during the Constituent Assembly debates, the members from then undivided Assam had put up a strong plea for the rights of the constituent states to at least a part of its natural resources. But, their plea for financial and political autonomy was voted out. It is interesting to note that almost thirty years after freedom from colonial rule, the parameters of the nation-state were expanded for the first time to accommodate the demands being raised by a small nationality. A struggle which was initially seen as a secessionist one aimed at breaking up the integrity of the Indian Republic was not only accepted as a national struggle of the Nagas but negotiations were carried out with the National Socialist Council of Nagaland (NSCN-IM) on foreign soil as demanded by the latter. That the Government of India opted for negotiations with an insurgent group on foreign soil was in itself a sign of the confidence and growing maturity of the Indian democratic process. Today, despite negotiations with the NSCN (I-M) stretched over a decade, a final solution of the Naga issue evades us. But, what is really important for Indian democracy is that it has been able to provide space even to organisations which have repeatedly asserted the cause of a separate homeland outside India. All this is evidently a part of the Indians state's "north-east experience". It is also a measure of the strength and resilience of the Indian democratic experiment, its many shortcomings notwithstanding, that one of the longest surviving insurgencies is finally seeking a solution within the parameters of the Indian Constitution. It is ironic that what began as a random violation of constitutional rights and privileges of the common citizen by the Indian State during the early phases of the Naga insurgency is being marked today by a search for a solution within the ambit of the Constitution. The same applies to the case of the Mizo insurgent movement under the leadership of Laldenga which ended with the Mizo Accord signalling the beginnings of constitutional representative democracy in the state of Mizoram.

When one comes to the Assam experience, the challenge to the Indian nation-state has been of a different nature. That Assam, with its centuries-old links with the rest of the Indian sub-continent and the main currents of Indic civilization, could spawn a militant separatist organisation in the form of the United Liberation Front of Assam is in itself a challenge of major proportions. One understands the Naga psyche of preserving what is termed as "the Naga way of life", especially when one takes in account the non-involvement of the Naga masses in the Indian freedom struggle.[5] But it is certainly of great relevance to try to find out as to why Assam[6] could produce such an armed organisation committed to the idea of a *Swadhin Asom,* especially when large masses of the Assamese people took active part in the different stages of the Gandhi and Congress-led freedom struggle. Large sections of the Assamese people actively participated in the different phases of the freedom movement and scores were shot dead and hundreds imprisoned especially during the Civil Disobedience Movement and the 1942 Quit India struggle. How is that

despite such participation in a national struggle, within barely three decades of independence there emerged an armed group with substantial support among the people (especially in the rural areas) which put forwards an agenda of a sovereign Asom? There are certainly strong historical as well as politico-economic factors behind this and it is beyond this short article to go into all that in detail. But it may be pointed out in brief that the overall attitude of the Centre towards the constituent states of the Indian Union has been responsible for the rise of such separatist feelings. Starting from the immediate pre-independence days when Assam had to put on a relentless and rather one-sided fight against the central Congress leadership against the Grouping proposals of the Cabinet Mission, the state has had to deal with issues like massive immigration and demographic change, lack of economic development, high rates of educated unemployed, and finally, the threat to the identity of the indigenous people as a result of large-scale illegal infiltration. In all these matters, the Centre has been adopting an attitude coloured by a mix of indifference and prejudice.

When it came to matters of economic development of the region in the post-independence years, the Central government adopted a policy tinted by security concerns. If we go back to the days of the Constituent Assembly when the members from Assam argued for the rights of the constituent states to their resources, we discover that those committed to a strong and centralised form of government in post-partition India saw such assertions as having separatist hues and anti-national. Gopinath Bardoloi's plea in the Constituent Assembly for a special status to Assam particularly in view of the highly extractive nature of the economy that prevailed during British colonial rule, fell on deaf years. Assam's fight for political and economic distribution of powers by the Centre was lost in the Constituent Assembly and would re-surface by the 1970s in the form of autonomy/separatist demands. When it came to the refugee issue in the immediate years after Partition, the Centre under the Nehru-Patel leadership tried to browbeat Assam and even threatened to strangle its economically if it did not fall in line with the Centre's wishes. Again when the people of the state, through a mass-based peaceful programme, demanded a refinery for the region, the Centre cited security reasons for not being able to accede to the popular demand.[7] Security considerations have always marked the Centre's approach towards the entire northeastern region and this has been a major spanner in the overall developmental process. Even in matters like the opening of the Stilwell Road as part of the much-touted Look East Policy, security considerations have prevailed and the road remains unbuilt. Thus, prejudices and a skewed mind-set have marked New Delhi's approach towards Assam. It was only a matter of time when the overall sense of neglect by the Centre was channelised into a massive populist agitation on the foreigners' issue which lasted for six years (1979-85) and ended in the Assam Accord which never really took off. And, with its failure the stage was finally set for emergence of armed insurgent politics in the state which has, till date, claimed tens of thousands of lives in both militant and state violence. Whatsoever be the course and content of the ULFA-led struggle, whatever

be the factionalism within the armed outfit, whatever be its isolation from the masses which have been disenchanted over its ideological bankruptcy and anti-people tactics, the ULFA-led insurgency has thrown up certain issues relating to the relationship between the Centre and the states which will have to be addressed by the Indian nation-state. The lack of distributive justice, the failure of the rule of law which is a most important perquisite of the democratic process and the propensity of treating the region as a periphery and a borderland where violence by the Indian State can be condoned,[8] have all come up as important issues not only for the people of the region but also for social analysts and political thinkers throughout the country. India's "north-east experience" has given a sharp focus to the debate centred around the nature and function of the Indian nation-state, with issues like the federal re-structuring of powers taking on a new edge. It would certainly be no exaggeration to conclude that the future of the Indian nation-state would depend a lot on how effectively it tackles the issues thrown up by the different ethno-nationalist movements of the northeastern region.

References

1. The Naga-Akbar Hydari Accord was arrived at after discussions between Naga tribes represented by the Naga National Council and the Governor of Assam which were held on 26, 27 and 28 June, 1947. Clause 9 of the Accord stated: "The Governor of Assam as the Agent of the Government of the Indian Union will have a special responsibility for a period of ten years to ensure the due observance of this agreement; at the end of this period the Naga National Council will be asked whether they require the above agreement to be extended for a further period or a new agreement, regarding the future of the Naga people arrived at".

2. I am using the terms "community" and "nationality" inter-changeably because in the course of the struggles, several communities were politicised and developed the requisites which determine a nationality.

3. Refer, The Constitution (Thirteenth Amendment) Act, 1962.

4. Some of the Naga tribes did put up resistance against British rule on different occasions and the final struggle took place in the siege of Kohima which lasted for eleven days and in which as many as thirteen Angami "village states" including that of Khonoma participated. Refer Udayon Misra, *The Periphery Strikes Back: Challenges to the Nation-State in Assam and Nagaland,* IIAS, Shimla, 2000, chapter entitled "The Naga Struggle", pp. 15-47.

5. Made up today primarily of the Brahmaputra and Barak Valleys and the hill district of Karbi Anglong.

6. Nehru in his letter to then Assam Governor Fazl Ali dated June 12, 1957, regarding the Centre's decision not to set up a refinery in Assam cited security reasons. Referring to objections raised by the army authorities, he wrote "... Our Defense Chiefs having examined these various schemes said definitely that they could not undertake to protect the refinery if situated in Assam ...Nor could we accept the proposal to have the refinery in Assam,

when military opinion was dead against it." *Bishnuram Medhi Papers*, Nehru Memorial Museum and Library, New Delhi.

7. This is evident in the Centre's reaction to popular demands for the repeal of the notorious Armed Forces (Special Powers) Act of 1958. The UPA government refused to repeal the Act despite the recommendation of the Jeevan Reddy Committee which itself was constituted by the Central Government. New Delhi has made it clear that since the army establishment was against any changes in the AFSPA, it was unwilling to consider even amending the Act, let alone repeal it. This shows that according to New Delhi, border regions would always be in need of special laws with special powers which would make a mockery of human rights.

28

Demographic Changes in Assam with Reference to Land Laws: An Overview

Nila Nath Barua IAS (Retd.)

India attained independence on 15th of August 1947. It was a day of rejoice for every Indian including the people of Assam irrespective of caste, creed or tribe. I still remember the days when every person felt proud of being a part of the great Indian community who rejoiced in achieving freedom from foreign domination over a period of years marked by untold miseries and sacrifices of the common masses. Assam had a special occasion to rejoice as the state was saved from being a part of East Pakistan by the diplomacy of Late Gopinath Bordoloi and other stalwarts like Late Bishnuram Medhi and late Mahendra Mohan Choudhuri with the blessings of the father of the nation Late Mahatma Gandhi. Every one of us dreamt of a bright future for the people of Assam. Much water has flown down the mighty Brahmaputra since then. Now I ponder over what we have achieved during the last six decades or so. Today Assam is in the midst of a storm that is sweeping from the north bank of Brahmaputra to the south. There are serious law and order situations in the BTAD areas in the north and in the Rabha Hajong areas in the south. The indigenous people of Assam who are living in the state of Assam from time immemorial are in a state of identity crisis. The illegal migrants from Bangladesh are trying to grab land in every nook and corner of the state. The persons who dreamt of a prosperous Assam on 15th August 1947 are now counting the days when the indigenous people will be reduced to a minority and will not be in a position to run the affairs of the government. Those persons who are still living to witness this turmoil now cry in despair, "Oh, Bordoloi, thou should be living at this hour. Please save us just as you saved us from grouping and inclusion in Pakistan at the time of partition." While the colonial British rulers in pre-independence days tacitly encouraged migration of agriculturists from East Bengal to Assam, in the post-independence period the undeclared policy of

Ostrich hand in sand approach to the issue of detection and deportation of illegal Bangladeshi infiltrators due to political expediency in Assam is the main reason for the present situation. Another reason is the dearth of local people who can do hard work as the local indigenous people are always satisfied with whatever they earned from their own land holdings. All these factors combined to bring about drastic changes in the demography of Assam. Now, let us go back to the period of the British rule in Assam.

Assam under the British Rule (1826-1947)

The annexation of territories to what is known as Assam Province before independence started in the year 1826 after the Yandaboo treaty between the British and the Burmese was signed. The first Anglo-Burmese war started in the year 1824 and the British occupied Guwahati after chasing the Burmese army. Meanwhile the Raja of Darrang (of Ahom kingdom) and some petty chieftains chose to surrender before the British in the year 1824. The process of annexation of territories to greater Assam province by the British administration started after the yandaboo treaty in the year 1826. If we go chronologically, the annexation process may be summarised as follows.

1. The undivided Goalpara district which came under the British rule after the transfer of the Deewani from the Mughal Emperor in the year 1765 forming a part of North Bengal was subsequently transferred to Assam Province in 1828. The decision to transfer the undivided Goalpara district to Assam Province was mainly due to the fact that the area was predominantly inhabited by the indigenous tribal people.

2. In the year 1828, the Kachari kingdom was annexed as per the Doctrine of Lapse after the king Govinda was killed.

3. In 1838, Upper Assam which was a British Protectorate under Purandhar Singha, the erstwhile Ahom ruler was formally annexed to the British Administration. In 1839, the Moran and the Motok territory in Upper Assam were formally annexed to Assam.

4. The above mentioned territories annexed so far to Assam Provice formed a part of Bengal Presidency. In the year 1874, the Assam region was separated from Bengal Presidency. Sylhet was ceded from Bengal and annexed to Assam province.

5. In the same year i.e., 1874 the hilly areas viz., Khasi, Jaintia, Naga, Garo and Lushai hills were included in Assam Province with the capital at Shillong.

In this way the process of forming a composite Assam was completed.

So far as demographic changes in population are concerned, it is confined mainly to the six erstwhile undivided districts viz., Sibsagar, Lakhimpur, Nowgong, Darrang, Kamrup and Goalpara in the Brahmaputra valley and Cachar including Karimganj districts in the Barak valley.

Immediately after gaining complete foothold in Assam, the British administration had given priority to expand tea cultivation with mercenary interests. In pursuance of this policy the British administration had enacted simple and liberal waste land rules in the year 1854. As a result, there was a great demand for land for tea cultivation. The Chinese labour recruited earlier for tea cultivation left Assam in the year 1843, and they were replaced by local

labour belonging to the Bodo-Kachari ethnic group. From the year 1859, the British tea planters recruited labourers known as Munda, Oran and Santhal from Jharkhand, Orissa Andhra Pradesh regions.

The recruitment process of these people continued till the early part of the 20th century. These people known as Adivasis formed a part of the local indigenous people in course of time. With the expansion of tea industry, new avenues were opened up for trade and commerce. The businessmen from as far as Rajasthan came to Assam to take part in marketing of tea and other ancillary industries. Gradually, the flourishing of trade and commerce attracted Punjabi carpenters, cobblers from Bihar and Uttar Pradesh and Nepali grazers and cultivators.

A major development that took place during the latter part of the 19th century was the construction of Railway lines in Assam. In 1896, the Comilla-Akhaura-Badarpur railway line was constructed during the period from 1896 to 1898. The company extended the railway line from Badarpur to Lumding. During the period from 1902 to 1903 the railway line was extended to Dibrugarh. Saikhowa, Tinsukia and Guwahati. In 1902, the East Bengal Railway completed construction of railway lines from Parbatipur to Dhubri via Lalmanirhat, Gitaldah and Golokganj. This facilitated easy movement of people from East Bengal to the Brahmaputra valley and also from Sylhet to Nowgong via Badarpur and Lumding. The persons who migrated from Sylhet settled down in Hojai, Lanka and Lumding areas of Nowgong district.

During the pre-British days the education system in Assam was very poor. With the establishment of the British administration, vast avenues for employment in government offices, railway and other commercial establishments opened up. But there was a great dearth of local people to man such establishments. The persons from Bengal took full advantage of the situation. There was a gradual migration of educated people from Bengal to Assam to hold the posts in the administrative establishments. Although the migration of people from other states to Assam started in the 19th century in a small scale, there was a large scale immigration of Muslim agriculturists from East Bengal to the Brahmaputra valley from the beginning of the twentieth century. The main attraction for migrating to Assam was the fertile land in the thinly populated areas of the Brahmaputra valley. It is relevant to discuss the land laws which actually facilitated their settlement in the soil of Assam.

The British administration in Assam adopted the policy of absolute ownership of lands by the state. After gaining a firm control over the administration in Assam, the British administration initiated the process of systematisation and enactment of land laws in the province. While initiating the process of formulation of land laws and settlement rules, primary attention was given to tea cultivation and increased food production by the colonial rulers with the sole aim to augment the revenue of the province.

During the period from 1826 to 1886, the British administration introduced various rights over land in a piecemeal way. It was in 1886 that the Assam Land and Revenue Regulation 1886 was passed by the Government. As per the provisions of the Act, the erstwhile zamindari estates of undivided Goalpara

district and Sylhet including Karimganj districts were included in the category of permanently settled estates. The Zamindars were the proprietors of the estates with heritable and transferable rights. All subjects occupying or settled in the permanently settled estates were the tenants of the Zamindars. All tenants in undivided Goalpara district were governed by the Goalpara Tenancy Act while the tenants in Sylhet including the Karimganj districts were governed by the Sylhet Tenancy Act.

In the other districts excluding the hill districts, the subjects enjoyed the rights of landholder including settlement holder on periodic lease from the government. In addition, there was another class viz., Propritors of Revenue free estates which include Lakhiraj estates and fee simple grants. The land holders and the Lakhirajdars have the heritable and transferable rights of use and occupancy. The unoccupied land i.e., the waste land is the property of the government. The sole authority of disposing of the waste land by lease, grant or otherwise rests with the government.

The indigenous people of Assam continued to enjoy their rights over land under the British rule. Though most of the areas were brought under Cadastral survey for preparation of record of rights, large fertile areas in char or island thrown up in a navigable river were not surveyed due to frequent changes in topography. As a result, these areas remained as isolated areas without any survey and settlement. Due to erosion and frequent floods the local indigenous people were totally disinterested in settling in the char areas. Majuli, the largest river island in the world in the erstwhile undivided Sibasagar district was the only exception with Satras, the religious hub of Vaishnavite culture situated therein.

With the beginning of the twentieth century, there was large scale migration of Muslim agriculturists from Mymensing and Rangpur districts of Bengal province to the Bramaputra valley of Assam. The fertile lands in char areas of undivided Goalpara, Kamrup, Darrang districts had an added attraction for the land hungry Muslim agriculturists. They used Brahmaputra river to cross over to Assam and to settle in the char areas which became a safe haven for all their activities. As Eastern Bengal and Assam were ruled by a Lt. Governor during the period from 1906 to 1912, there was no administrative barrier to check the free movement of people from Eastern Bengal to Assam. Moreover, the Zamindars of the permanently settled estates of undivided Goalpara district preferred to settle landless Muslim agriculturists from East Bengal as tenants in the interest of earning more revenue from the agricultural produce.

In the subsequent years even after separation of Assam from Bengal in 1912, the trend in the migration of people from Bengal to Assam remained the same. The colonial British rulers had given priority to increase in revenue without giving any importance to improve the general condition of the local indigenous people. As result the British administration provided settlement to the landless Muslim agriculturists from East Bengal in the vast wastelands of undivided Goalpara. Kamrup, Darrang and Nowgong districts. The colonial rulers paid no heed to the protests and resentment of the local indigenous people while giving settlement to the Bengali immigrants. With the connivance

of the British administration the immigrants encroached upon grazing reserves, wetlands and swamps owned and used by the local indigenous people. As there were no restrictions in alienation of land many persons migrating to Assam purchased land and permanently settled both in urban and rural areas. Gradually, the continued encroachments and squatting by the Bengali Muslim immigrants posed a serious threat to the law and order situation. Though the Director of Land Records Assam proposed a colonisation scheme in 1916 to regulate the settlement of the immigrants, it did not find favour with the administrative hierarchy. Finally at the district level the line system under the colonisation, scheme was introduced to regulate the settlement of the Muslim immigrants. With the introduction of the line system, distinct areas were earmarked for settlement of the immigrants so that they did not come into direct clash with the local indigenous people. For this purpose a colonisation officer of the rank of senior Sub Deputy Collector was appointed in Barpeta, Kamrup, Nowgong, Darrang and Lakhimpur. The line system restricted further squatting and encroachment of the immigrants to a great extent. However, the system became a bone of contention at the political level between the Congress party and the Muslim League in Assam. With the enactment of the government of India Act, 1935 a Legislative Assembly with 108 members was formed in Assam. The question of introducing the line system was raised in the Assembly in 1939, when the government was formed with Late Gopinath Bordoloi as Premier. The assembly resolution was for abolition of the system. The motion was defeated in the Assembly. However, the Congress ministry in Assam, in spite of having majority members opted to remain out of power at the call of the national leaders on political considerations. As a result, Late Sir Syed Saadullah of Muslim league occupied office intermittently from 1937 to 1946. The Saadullah ministry initiated a "Grow more Food Scheme" and encouraged settlement of Muslim agriculturists from Mymensing of Bengal in Nowgong and Darrang districts. With the patronage of the Saadullah ministry the Muslim immigrants encroached upon the forest lands, grazing reserves and even in the deep jungles. Though the large scale migration of Muslim agriculturists from Bengal to Assam had a direct impact on the socio-economic life of Assam, the matter was not taken up seriously at the national level in the name of Hindu-Muslim unity.

Regarding rapid immigration of people from East Bengal, C.S. Mullan, Superintendent of census operations, Assam 1931 observed in his census report, "Probably the most important event in the province during the last 25 years, likely to alter permanently the whole structure of the Assamese culture and civilisation has been the invasion of a vast horde of land hungry Bengali immigrants, mostly Muslims from the districts of East Bengal and in particular from Mymensingh." In this connection it is important to note that in the year 1928, the Bodo-Kachari tribes of Assam demanded protection of their land and forest rights before the Simon Commission. As per recommendations of the Simon Commission a committee headed by a civil servant was formed to make a detailed examination of the subject. But the case was not followed up in right earnest. It ended without any result.

Year	*Population (lakh)*		*Assam as percentage of all India*	*Estimated decadal migration as percentage to Assam's population*	*Practical decadal variation of*		*Density (person per sq. km.)*	*Density (person per sq. km.)*
	Assam	*India*			*Assam*	*India*	*Assam*	*India*
1901	33	2,383	1.4	9			42	77
1911	38	2,520	N A	(0.40)	+17.0	+5.8	49	82
1921	46	2,512	1.9	N A	+20.5	-0..3	59	81s
1931	56	2,789	N A	N A	+19.9	+11.0	71	90
1941	67	3,185	2.1	6	+20.0	+14.2	85	103
1951	80	3,610	2.2	(0.50)	+19.9	+13.3	102	117

To sum up the result of large scale immigration during the period from 1901 till independence of India, there was an abnormal rise of population, and the trend is shown below:

Assam in Post Independence Period from 1947

In1947, following a referendum and the partition of India almost all the areas of Sylhet barring the Karimganj sub-division became a part of East Pakistan. Karimganj was included as a sub-division of Cachar district in Assam. The referendum was held on 3rd July, 1947.

After India attained independence on 15th August, 1947 a new ministry was formed by the Congress party headed by Late Gopinath Bordoloi as Premier in Assam. It is important to note that the government formed by the new ministry adopted the Act viz., Assam Land and Revenue Regulation 1886 for the purpose of land revenue administration in Assam.

Immediately after assuming power the Congress ministry took up the cases of backward classes of the state who were too poor to withstand the challenges posed by the rich immigrant agriculturists who had migrated from Mymensingh district of East Bengal. The available government waste lands were fast dwindling due to encroachments by the immigrants coming from outside the state. For protection of the backward classes a new chapter X was added to Assam Land and Revenue Regulation 1886 by an amendment of the Act in 1947. The intention of the legislature at that time was to regulate alienation, settlement lease, contract and agreement for protection of backward classes notified by the government. A section 164B was subsequently added and it reads as follows:

" If any transfer of land is effected in contravention of this chapter, both the transferor and the transferee shall be punished with simple imprisonment for a term which may extend to six months or with fine which may extend to one thousand rupees or with both. The term backward classes includes (i) Plains Tribals, (ii) Hills Tribals, (iii) Tea Garden tribes, (iv) Santhals, (v) Scheduled castes, (vi), Nepali graziers, (vii) Koch Rajbongsis, and (viii) Jogi community. It is an irony that the provisions of this chapter were overlooked by the subsequent governments.

The Problem of Illegal Migration in Assam

After independence the legal provisions in respect of citizenship were enacted by the government of India as follows:

Those persons of undivided India who migrated to Assam or any other part of India before July 19 1948 were deemed to be Indian citizens. From July 19, 1948 to the enactment of Constitution of India on November 26, 1949 all migrants who had applied for citizenship after continuously staying in India for six months were granted Indian citizenship. For the rest the Parliament had enacted the Citizenship Act to deal with the cases for acquisition and termination of Indian citizenship.

In spite of the legal provisions the flow of migrants from East Pakistan to Assam continued unabated. In order to check this illegal migration the

Parliament enacted on 24th December 1949, The Immigrants (Expulsion from Assam), Act 1950. In the statement of objects and reasons it was mentioned amongst other things that the stay of illegal immigrants from East Pakistan is detrimental to the interests of the general public or any section thereof in India. The exodus of illegal immigrants from Assam after promulgation of the Act raised hue and cry in Pakistan. Late Liaquat Ali Khan, the then Prime Minister of Pakistan took up the matter with Pandit Jawaharlal Nehru, the then Prime Minister of India. The result was that Pandit Jawaharlal Nehru inked a pact with the Prime Minister of Pakistan to take back all the illegal Muslim immigrants and he ensured safe passage to them in returning to Assam. As a result the whole purpose of the Immigrants (Expulsion from Assam) Act 1950 was defeated. Assam is still facing the problem of cross border migration of illegal migrants from Bangladesh across the porous border between Assam and Bangladesh.

The Government of India introduced Passport regulations in October 1952 and the Citizenship Act 1955 was introduced in the year 1955. The Immigrants (Expulsion from Assam) Act 1951 was finally withdrawn.

After partition of India in 1947 Assam had to bear the brunt of settling large number of Hindu refugees on Assam soil. Again in 1965 there was a large scale exodus of non-Muslim refugees from East Pakistan due to communal riots in East Pakistan to Assam for the second time after partition of India in 1947. There were as many as eleven camps in Matia circle of Goalpara district. At that time I was posted as Special Officer in charge of relief and rehabilitation at Matia. The Government of Assam had agreed to settle only eleven hundred refugee families in Assam. The Government of India had asked the Government of Assam to send the remaining refugee families to Dandakaranya in Madhya Pradesh. For this purpose special trains were arranged from Guwahati. Subsequently, it was learnt that by the time the train reached Alipurduar all the bogies of the train were almost empty. Many of them were reported to have returned to Assam.

The 1961 census showed a 34.97 per cent increase in population against the national all India average of 21.64 per cent in the decade 1951-1961 According to the 1961 census not less than 7,50,000 Bangladeshi nationals from the erstwhile. East Pakistan infiltrated into Assam during the decade from 1951 to 1961. But according to the estimate placed by the Government of Assam the figure was mentioned as 3.50 lakhs only. However 10 Foreigners' tribunals were set up to hear the appeals preferred by the immigrants against their detection. In the years from 1967 to 1969 1.29 lakh infiltrators were deported from Assam.

The liberation struggle of the erstwhile East Pakistan led by late Shikh Mujibur Rahman culminated in the creation of Bangladesh in the year 1972. During the period from March 25 to December 12 in 1971 it was estimated that as many as 12 lakh people came over to Assam from East Pakistan and took shelter with their friends, relatives and acquaintances who had come earlier to Assam. Many of such persons did not return to Bangladesh. As per the Indira-Mujib pact the government of India issued a circular to the government

of Assam vide Memo No 11/160/72-TX dated September 30, 1972 The circular specifically mentioned that "Indira Gandhi, Prime Minister of India, had arrived at an understanding with the Prime Minister of Bangladesh Shaikh Mujibur Rahman to the effect that such of the persons as had come over to India before March, 25, 1971 shall not be deported. In the case of persons who had illegally entered India after March 25, 1971 the State Government should prepare a list and forward the same to the Branch Secretariat, External Affairs Ministry Government of India at Calcutta in duplicates which would submit a list to the Deputy High Commissioner, Bangladesh at Calcutta to liaise with him for their deportation." But unfortunately the circular was not given effect to by the Government of Assam. As a result the Government of Assam lost a golden opportunity to detect and deport illegal migrants, who had come over to Assam after March, 1971. Another consequence of the Indira-Mujib pact was that the Government of India regularised all the illegal migrants who had entered Assam before March 1971. This amounted to the proposition that the state of Assam was excluded from the provisions of Articles five and six of the Constitution of India. The problem of infiltration of illegal migrants to Assam from Bangladesh was virtually kept alive for all time to come.

Another important development in the land revenue administration was that The Assam (Temporarily Settled Areas) Tenancy Act was passed in 1971. The Act applies to agricultural tenants and their land lords in agricultural areas. The settlement operations under the Act continued till the early part of 80s. As no action was taken by the Government of Assam for deportation of illegal migrants from Bangladesh as per Government of India's instructions in 1971, there was no doubt that many illegal migrants who are mainly agriculturists must have acquired tenancy rights. In such cases their deportation in future will be difficult as their claims for being genuine Indian citizens are fortified with important land documents.

Assam Agitation on Foreigner's Issue

In 1978, Hiralal Patowari, a member of Parliament from Mangaldoi Lok Sabha constituency died and his death required by-election to the constituency. When the election process was set in motion, the observers noticed that there was an exponential growth in the number of registered voters, majority of who were suspected to be foreigners from Bangladesh. All Assam Students Union (here in after mentioned as AASU) took up the matter seriously and demanded postponement of elections till the names of foreigners are deleted from the voters' list. This was the beginning of six years long Assam Agitation. AASU and All Assam Gana Sangram Parishad spearheaded the agitation creating a new chapter in the history of India.

Though the Assam agitation was otherwise non-violent, there were sporadic incidents of violence when the Government tried to suppress the movement by imposing general elections against the demand of AASU and the indigenous people to initiate the process of detection and deletion of foreigners from the voters' list before holding any election. The Nellie massacre in Nowgong district in 1983 was the direct outcome of holding general election

in Assam with the voters list containing names of lakhs of illegal Bangladeshi nationals in the name of saving democracy.

Close on the heels of Assam agitation, a new organisation viz., United Liberation Front of Assam, otherwise known as ULFA was born on April 7, 1979 at Rang Ghar in Sibsagar, a historic Structure of Ahom kingdom. The organisation was subsequently declared unlawful by the Government. Military operations against it by the Indian Army began in 1990 and still continues till the present date. In the past two decades some 30000 people died in the clash between the rebels and the Government Security forces as reported in the Sentinel.

In 1983, an Act. viz., Illegal Migrants (Determination by Tribunal) was enacted by the Government of India when late Indira Gandhi was the Prime Minister. The Act describes the procedure to detect illegal migrants from Bangladesh and to expel them from Assam. The sole purpose of enacting this piece of legislation viz., IMDT Act 1983 was to provide special protection against undue harassment to the minorities that were affected by the Assam agitation. It was applicable only in the state of Assam. The Act made the detection and deportation of illegal migrants more complicated. Some of the provisions of the act are mentioned below:

1. When a person is detected to be a foreigner under Section 9 of the Foreigners Act 1946, the onus of proving that he is not a foreigner lies on him. But in case of IMDT Act 1983, the burden of proving the citizenship or otherwise lies on the complainant and the police.

2. Under the IMDT Act, 1983 a person will be eligible to complain if he or she resides within a radius of three kilometers of the place of residence of the suspected foreign national i.e., the Bngladeshi national who stays illegally in Assam. Moreover the complainant will have to pay a fee of Rs 10 for filing a complaint petition. A Bangladeshi national could prove his citizenship simply by producing a ration card. Moreover, even if a person is detected to be a foreigner, only tribunals can decide in the matter of deportation based on facts.

The Act has been alleged to be one of the main reasons of rapid rise of Muslim population and demographic change in Assam. The IMDT Act 1983 which was promulgated by the Indira Gandhi government in the name of pseudo-secularism actually helped the political leaders in reaping good harvests by showing them as the champions of the cause of religious minority at the time of election in India. The constitutional validity of the Act having been challenged by AASU, this ignominious Act was finally struck down by the Supreme Court as *ultra vires* of the Constitution of India in 2005 after more than two decades since its promulgation.

Assam Accord

The Assam Accord (1985) was a memorandum of understanding between the representatives of the Government of India and the leaders of the Assam Agitation on 15th August, 1985.The following decisions taken on the main issue amongst others were as follows:

5.1 For purposes of detection and deletion of foreigners, 1.1.1966 shall be the base data and year.

5.2 All persons who come to Assam prior to 1.1.1966, including those amongst them whose names appeared on the electoral rolls used in 1967 elections shall be regularised.

5.3 Foreigners who came to Assam after 1.1.1966 (inclusive) and upto 24th March, 1971 shall be detected in accordance with the provisions of the Foreigners Act, 1946 and the Foreigners (Tribunals) Order 1964.

5.4 Names of foreigners so detected will be deleted from the electoral rolls in force. Such persons will be required to register themselves before the Registration Officers of the respective districts in accordance with the provisions of the Registration of Foreigners Act, 1939 and the Registration of Foreigners Rules, 1939.

5.5 For this purpose, Government of India will undertake suitable strengthening of the government machinery.

5.6 On the expiry of a period of ten years following the date of detection, the names of all such persons which have been deleted from the electoral rolls shall be restored.

5.7 All persons who were expelled earlier, but have since re-entered illegally into Assam shall be expelled.

5.8 Foreigners who came to Assam on or after March 25, 1971 shall continue to be detected, deleted and practical steps shall be taken to expel such foreigners.

5.9 The Government will give due consideration to certain difficulties expressed by the AASU/AAGSP regarding the implementation of the Illegal Migrants (Determination by Tribunals) Act, 1983.

The Accord brought an end to the Assam Agitation and paved the way for the leaders of the agitation to form a political party and to form a government in the state of Assam soon after. Asom Gana Parishad, a regional political party born out of the womb of six years long Assam agitation formed a Government in Assam in 1985. But the regional political party could not prove equal to the trust reposed by the massive mandate of the indigenous people of Assam in the general election held in 1986. During their term of governance from 1986 to 1990 the Minsters and the legislators were divided into two distinct groups, one led by Mr Prafulla Kumar Mahanta, the then Chief Minister and the other by Late Bhrigu Kumar Phukon the then Home Minister. The top leaders of the regional party were engaged in squabble leading to trust deficit amongst themselves. They were not successful in taking a cohesive action to deal with the matters relating to the detection and deletion of the names of foreigners from the voters list as per Assam Accord. As a result, there was a vertical division of the party into two regional parties viz., AGP and NAGP in 1991 before the next general election. This helped the Indian National Congress Party to defeat both the regional parties and to stage a comeback to the administration in 1991. In 1996 both the regional parties again combined into one i.e., the original party viz., AGP. This time they were returned to power by majority votes as they were fighting the election in coalition with CPI and

other small regional parties in 1996. But the regional party could not initiate any concrete measures in detection and deportation of illegal Bangladeshi migrants as per Assam Accord. From 2001 the regional party was completely dislodged in Assam and they lost the successive election battles losing faith of the indigenous people.

Demographic Changes in Assam

As per census record, the decadal variation in Assam shows an increase at the rate of 35 per cent during 1951-61 and 1961-71and 53.2 per cent during 1971-91, 18.92 per cent during 1991-2001 and 16.93 per cent in 2001-2011.

As there were no census operations in Assam in the year 1980-81 due to Assam agitation the figure 53.2 per cent covers the period from 1971 to 1991. Thus, the average growth rate of population during this period may be assumed to be 26.6 per cent. The decadal variation in population of Assam was the highest during the period from 1951 to 1971. The high growth rate of population can never be the result of sudden high birth rate or abnormal fall in the death rate This clearly shows that large scale migration of people from the neighbouring country i.e., Bangladesh (erstwhile East Pakistan) took place during this period.

As per census of India record the following table shows the growth of population and the practical decadal variation in respect of Assam and India from 1961 to 2011.

Growth of Population and practical Decadal Variation Assam and India 1961-2011

Year	*Population (Lakh)*		*Assam as Percentage of All India*	*Practical decadal variation*		*Density (Person per sq. km.)*	*Density (Person per sq. km.)*
	Assam	*India*		*Assam*	*India*	*Assam*	*India*
1961	108	4,391	2.5	+35.0	+21.6	138	142
1971	146	5471	2.7	+35.0	+24.8	186	177
1981	199	6838	2.9	+36.1	+24.9	230	230
1991	224	8463	2.64	+53.2*	+23.5	286	267
2001	267	10287	2.59	+18.92	+21.15	340	325
2011	312	12102	2.58	+16.93	+17.64	397	382

*Rate of growth of population during 1971-91.

Note: As there was no census operations in 1981 due to Assam agitation, Assam's population figure for 1981is a projected one.

As per 2011 census record the Dhubri district bordering Bangladesh shows the highest growth rate of population at 24.40 p.c. followed by Morigaon at 23.39 p.c. and Goalpara at 22.74 p.c. Kokrajhar district shows the lowest growth rate. According to the 2011 census report the density of population per sq. kilometre in Assam has gone up from 340 in 2001 to 397 in 2011, the state area of 78,438 sq. kilometre remaining constant. The report further added that Kamrup (Metro) has the highest density of population of 2010 per sq. kilometre followed by Dhubri (1171) and Baksa (763). The density of population was found to be the lowest in KarbiAnglong district.

During the last three decades large scale migration of people from rural areas to urban areas took place in Assam. Increase in the size of urban population is a common phenomenon all over the country. In Assam rapid industrial and infrastructure development attracted large number of people from rural to urban areas in search of employment and better health and educational facilities. It also caused migration of people from outside the state to the urban and semi-urban areas to join the work force in the industrial and particularly in the infrastructure development. As per 2011 census report there were 214 towns and 26,395 villages in Assam.

Analysis of Population Growth

The population growth of Assam is found to be higher than the national average throughout the last century. In 1901, Assam's population was 33 lakhs and it increased to 80 lakhs in 1951. Again it increased to 312 lakhs in 2011. Apparently, the growth of population in Assam is found to be exponential. The natural growth rate in Assam marginally declined during the period from 1971 to 2011 as per estimation data of Sample Registration system. During the period the crude birth rate per thousand declined from 38.5 to 23.6 while the crude death rate per thousand declined from 17.8 to 8.4. As there is no deviation in the natural growth rate of population, the natural conclusion is that the exponential growth in population of Assam is due to large scale migration of people from outside the state.

If we observe the changing demography of different religious groups in Assam particularly during the period from 1971 to 2001, we find that the average growth of Muslim population was 38.7 during the period from 1971 to 1991 and 29.3 during the period from 1991 to 2001 while the growth of other religions was 21.8 and 13.9 corresponding to the same period respectively.

During the period from 1971 to 2001 the Bengali speaking population increased by eight per cent from 19.7 to 27.5 while the Assamese speaking population declined by nine per cent from 70.1 to 60.8.The Hindi and other language speaking population increased by one per cent only during the period. The Nepalese speaking population remained the same. It is important to mention here that the term "Assamese speaking population" includes Boro, Santali, Dimasa, Miri, Munda, Oriya, Khariya, Karbi, Rabha, Lalung, Deori, Mundari, Kurukh and Bhumij.

Conclusion

The state of Assam is facing both inter-state and intra state migration of people for the last fifty years. With the growing industrialisation and expansion of trade and commerce, it is quite natural to witness the migration of people from villages to towns within the state and also from other states to Assam. But the most disturbing fact is the large scale immigration of people mainly from the neighbouring country Bangladesh. Such immigration was very high during the period from 1947 to 1971 and it is still continuing though in a lesser scale. The high rate of growth of population due to immigration has adverse effects on the economy of Assam. The main ill effects are (i) low per capita income (ii) increase in the number of people below poverty line, (iii) shortage

of essential commodities due to increase in demand with consequent rise in prices, (iv) unemployment problem, (v) social problems like problems of education, health, housing, land, water supply etc., (vi) retarding growth in capital formation (vii) inequality in distribution of income and wealth and lastly (viii) security threat due to the presence of large number of illegal Bangladeshi nationals. It has caused irreparable loss to the economy of Assam.

Remedial Measures

The Government of Assam did yeoman's service by promulgating two important land laws viz., (i) The Assam Hill Land Ecological sites (Protection and Management) Act, 2006 and The Assam Land Grabbing (Prohibition) Act, 2010. While the first Act provides for preservation, protection, regulation and maintenance of hill land and other ecological sites of the state, the other Act intends to prevent certain lawless persons operating individually and in groups to grab by force or by deceitful means or otherwise lands belonging to the government, a public sector undertaking, a local authority, a religious and charitable institution or endowment or any other private persons or a site of historical monuments. These two Acts will prevent all people including Bangladeshis from occupying and settling in any land at their will provided the Government implements the provisions in right earnest without any extraneous considerations.

The updating of National Register of citizens must be completed without further delay. Till the updating process is completed, no Adhar cards should be issued in Assam. The issue of fresh Ration cards should be kept in abeyance.

After completion of the updating process, all citizens must be issued electronic identity cards. The production of identity cards should be made compulsory for securing employment, contract, mortgage, bank loan and all other essential services like ration cards, Adhar cards, Driving license and above all in the matter of settlement, sale and purchase of land.

Last but not the least, all persons irrespective of caste, creed and religion should rise to the occasion and take a challenge to help the government in detection and deportation of all foreigners including Bangladeshis who enter Assam without valid passport documents.

References

1. Arun Bhuyan (ed.), (2000). *Nationalist Upsurge in Assam*, sponsored by Government of Assam.

2. *Aspects of Land Policy in Assam: Continuity and Change* (2012), Vivekananda Kendra Institute of Culture, M.G. Road, Guwahati-1.

3. Assam2001-Census of India Website http://censusindia.gov.in/maps/State_Maps/StateMaps_links/assam01.html (accessed on 29.3.2013).

4. *Assam's Problem of Infiltration* www.nenanews.com/OT%20July%207-%20July/2021.../ohz.him.

5. Bhupen Kumar Nath, Dilip C. Nath and Late Biswanath Bhattacharya, 2012. *Undocumented Migration in the State of Assam in Northeast India Estimates Since 1971 to 2001. Asian Journal of Applied Sciences, 5: 164-173.*

6. DOI:10.3923/ajaps.2012.164.173, URL:http://scialert.net/abstract/?doi=ajaps.2012.164.173, Accessed on 27.3.2013.

7. B.N. Das (2012), *The Land Laws of Assam,* Assam Law House, Guwahati, 2nd Edition.

8. Census-2011-Assam - Assam Online Portal *http://online.assam.gov.in/web/population-census* (accessed on 30.3.2013).

9. Economic Survey, Assam 2011-12-directorate of economicshttp://*ecostatassam.nic.in/ads_economic%20survey.pdf* (accessed on 30.3.2013 7 Hilary Pais, Assam: Introduction, hilary pais.org/ (accessed on 29-03-2013).

10. J.N. Das (1985), *An Introduction to the Land-Laws of Assam*, Bookland, Panbazar, Guwahati, Sixth Edition.

11. Mirror of Assam Population. www.vedanti.com/Assam_Mirror/Population.him (Accessed on 29.3.2013).

12. Wikipedia, the free encyclopaedia, Colonial Assam, http://en.wikipedia.org/wiki/Colonial_Assam.

29

Demographic Threats to Assam

D.N. Bezbaruah

The biggest problem facing Assam and the north-eastern States of India today is large-scale illegal migration from Bangladesh. The problem is very serious today because at the present rate of influx, there is the very real danger of Assam being annexed to Bangladesh in just a couple of decades from now. And the irony of the situation is that the problem has stemmed from greed on both sides greed for cultivable land on one side and greed for votes on the other. And now there is the interesting poetic justice of the greed for power having infected the providers of easy illegal votes as well.

However, it would be wrong to conclude that this invasion from present Bangladesh and erstwhile East Pakistan is a recent phenomenon. This silent invasion had started much before Partition. In the 1931 census report of Assam, C.S. Mullan, Superintendent of Census Operations, had recorded the following observations:

"Probably the most important event in the province during the last twenty-five year an event, moreover, which seems likely to alter permanently the whole future of Assam and to destroy the whole structure of Assamese culture and civilisation has been the invasion of a vast horde of land-hungry Bengali immigrants, mostly Muslims, from the districts of Eastern Bengal and in particular from Mymensingh. Without fuss, without tumult a population which must amount to over half a million has transplanted itself from Bengal to the Assam Valley during the last twenty-five years........ the only thing I can compare it to is the mass movement of a large body of ants."

Mullan had said this when the population of Assam was only around 5,561,000. He had gone on to make the prediction that the time was not far off when the Assamese people would be confined to the district of Sibsagar alone. What adds poignancy to that prediction today is that this is not only beginning to happen, but that the prediction is likely to hold good for the new

district of Sivasagar which is about a third in size of the Sibsagar district of Mullan's time.

The influx of Muslim cultivators from East Bengal was encouraged by the Muslim League government of Mohammad Sadullah in Assam ostensibly for the Grow More Food Campaign. However, Viceroy Lord Wavell wrote in his *Memoirs* that Sadullah was much more interested in growing more Muslims.

After the partition of the sub-continent in 1947, a large number of Hindus crossed over from East Pakistan to the States of West Bengal, Assam and Tripura. Later on, when the Pakistani Army started persecuting Bengalis, a large number of Muslims too crossed the border into India. After the break-up of Pakistan and the liberation of Bangladesh in 1971 with the help of India, it was expected that the new regime would ensure communal harmony and tackle the social and economic problems of that country in a manner that would eliminate or at least reduce the factors contributing to migration. However, this did not happen, and both Hindus and Muslims continued to pour into India from Bangladesh in large numbers. This is best appreciated by taking a look at the increase in the population of Assam over the decades. The figures are in millions.

1901	*1911*	*1921*	*1931*	*1941*	*1951*	*1961*	*1971*	*1981**	*1991*	*2001*	*2011*
3.29	3.849	4.637	5.561	6.694	8.029	10.837	14.625	19.896	22.295	26.656	31.169

* Assam did not have a census operation in 1981. The figure for the year is a projection made by the Census of India on the basis of earlier figures.

It will be noticed that Assam's population doubled in the 40 years between, 1901 and 1941, and more than doubled in the 30 years between 1941 and 1971. And going by the projected population of 1981, it almost doubled in the 20 years between 1961 and 1981. In the 70 years between 1901 and 1971, Assam's population increased from 3.29 million to 14.6 million a 343.77 per cent increase over a period when the population of India had increased only about 150 per cent. Obviously, this did not happen because the people of Assam had become twice as fertile as their compatriots elsewhere. In fact, the general fertility rate for rural Assam for 1978 was 126.5 (all-India rural rate: 137.3) and the rate for urban Assam was 94.3 as against the national urban figure of 102. This abnormal increase in population happened largely due to migration from former East Bengal and East Pakistan and present Bangladesh.

Increases in Assam's population during recent decades are even more interesting in establishing the kind of accelerated growth that has taken place. Between 1951 and 1961, Assam's population increased by 34.98 per cent. During the next decade from 1961 to 1971 too Assam's population increased by 34.95 per cent. As such, the projected population for 1981, 19.896 million was fairly accurate, since it represented a decadal growth of 36.04 per cent. This was very close to the population growth over the two earlier decades of 34.98 and 34.95. Interestingly enough, the projection of Assam's population for 1981 done by the *Statesman's Year Book* published by Macmillan from

London put the figure at 19.902 million – a difference of only about 6,000 from the Census of India projection in a population of nearly 20 million. However, after the census of 1991, the projected population figure of Assam for 1981 was revised to 18.04 million (down by about 1.85 million). This gave a 'normal' decadal increase in population of just 23.35 per cent for Assam against the national decadal growth of 23.5 per cent for the same period.

If the population growth rate of Assam has been very alarming, there are two other aspects of this that are even more alarming. One is the growth rate of voters in the State and the other the rate of growth of the Muslim population almost entirely due to illegal immigration. Between 1957 and 1962 (just five years), the number of voters increased from 4.493 million to 4.943 million (10 per cent). In the next four years, the number of voters increased by 13 per cent to 5.585 million. By 1970, the number of voters stood at 5.702 million. However, within a year after that the number of voters rose by 10.42 per cent to stand at 6.296 million. The objective of the ruling political party of that period was to ensure an easy victory in the elections, even if it meant getting foreign voters to vote in Indian elections, in total violation of our constitutional provisions. The party succeeded eminently, though it did not stop to think of the consequences either for Assam, the North-east or the country as a whole.

The 2001 census put Assam's population at 26,655,528. Of this, 17,296,455 were recorded as Hindus and 8,240,611 as Muslims. What was indeed remarkable was that the Census of India gave the statistical break-up of the population on religious lines only on September 6, 2004—three years after the census. Something similar had happened after the 1991 census as well, with the office of the Registrar General of India parting with the religious break-up only two years after the event. When the census data are published, one expects them to be complete in all respects including the religious break-up. Why should there be an attempt to suppress the religious break-up for two or three years? After all, *The World Almanac and Book of Facts,* which is an annual publication, has the religion-wise break-up of the population of each country in the very first paragraph of the data on that country. It is only a government unduly sensitive to the abnormal demographic changes that it has brought upon the country that would attempt to conceal such facts from the nation. In any case, the Registrar General of India did divulge one important change in the demography of Assam soon after the 2001 census: that out of the 27 districts of Assam, six districts —— Barpeta, Dhubri, Goalpara, Nagaon, Karimganj and Hailakandi had a Muslim majority. The decadal increase of population between 2001 and 2011 was 16.93 per cent, even lower than the national average of 17.6 per cent. However, the decadal growth in the nine districts of Dhubri, Goalpara, Barpeta, Morigaon, Nagaon, Dhemaji, Cachar, Karimganj and Hailakandi was over 20 per cent. In these districts, the majority comprises illegal and legalised migrants from Bangladesh.

There would be nothing very remarkable about this in a secular republic, had this demographic change been due to a higher fertility rate among the Muslims of the State. But here we have a case of an orchestrated and engineered demographic change (with the help of foreign nationals) just to ensure electoral advantage to a political party. And this is an objective that gets very well with

the motivations of the Bangladeshi nationals who have infiltrated into different parts of India in such large numbers as to account for over 11,000,000 of them in our country with at least four million in Assam and four million more in West Bengal, with Bihar accounting for two million. There is no Indian State without a few thousand Bangladeshis. What is often overlooked by New Delhi is the fact that the migrants from Bangladesh are polygamous whereas the indigenous Muslims of Assam are monogamous. This vital factor, stoking very rapid and high population growth among Bangladeshi immigrants, is never mentioned by ministers and officials discussing demographic changes.

It is indeed regrettable that Government of India should have reacted the way it did to the Census of India's report on the religious demography of India published on September 4, 2004. The report revealed that the decadal growth of the Muslim population of India had increased to 36 per cent from the figure for the earlier decade of 34.5 per cent. It also revealed that the decadal growth rate of the Hindu population had come down from 25.1 per cent to 20.5 per cent. This revelation set the alarm bells ringing down the corridors of North Block, and soon the Census of India had 'adjusted' and 'unadjusted' figures of the decadal growth of population by deleting the population figures for both Assam and Jammu and Kashmir. It was as though deleting the populations of the two States on paper would have the effect of eliminating them altogether on the ground as well.

However, the strongest motivation for the large-scale Bangladeshi infiltration into Assam and the north-eastern States is what German intellectuals have called *lebensraum* or "living- space". The population of Bangladesh is over 161 million. With an area of 55,599 sq. miles, it has a population density of 2,895 per sq. mile. Thus a large-scale exodus *anywhere* is a sort of godsend for Bangladesh. Bangladesh is only too well aware of the illegal vote-bank created by the Congress in Assam, and has taken full advantage of the party's vulnerability in the matter of detection, disfranchisement and deportation of Bangladeshis. Perhaps the earliest proponent of the idea of *lebensraum* for Bangladesh was Mr Sadeq Khan who wrote the article, "The Question of *Lebensraum*" in the weekly newspaper *Holiday* in its issue of October 18, 1991. This is how he began: "The question of *lebensraum* or living space for the people of Bangladesh has not yet been raised as a moot issue. All projections, however, clearly indicate that by the next decade, that is to say by the first decade of the 21st century, Bangladesh will face a serious crisis of *lebensraum*. No possible performance of population planning, actual or hypothetical significantly alters that prediction." Having had his say on the crisis of living space that Bangladesh will face by the first decade of the 21st century, he goes on to argue in the next paragraph how the "colonial devastation of Bengal in the 18th and 19th centuries, left the region of Bangladesh bereft of the traditional strength of technology and productivity." And then come the two crucial paragraphs that leave no one in any doubt about what Bangladesh's intentions are. This is what they say:

"It is said that a borderless world has become the prime requisite for economic growth under the new world order. In fairness, if consumer benefit is considered to be better served by borderless competitive trade of commodities, why not borderless competitive trade of labour? There is no

reason why Bangladesh should not insist on a globalised manpower market as consumer markets of nation-states are being progressively globalised under the dictates of monetarists. There is no reason why regional and international cooperation could not be worked out to plan and execute population movements and settlements to avoid critical demographic pressures in pockets of high concentration. There is no reason why under-populated regions in the developed world cannot make room for planned colonies to relieve build-up of demographic disasters in countries like Bangladesh.

"We shall hope for the best in international cooperation. We shall hope for the best in accommodation from the developed world. In reality, nevertheless, Bangladesh may expect little external relief in the short run on the issue of *lebensraum*. It is also doubtful that Bangladesh may develop sufficient sustainable urbanisation or can engineer sufficient reclamation of habitable land from its offshore potential to settle its projected population growth in the next decade. A natural overflow of population pressure is therefore very much on the cards and will not be restrainable by barbed wire or border patrol measures. The natural trend of population overflow from Bangladesh is towards the sparsely populated lands of the South East in the Arakan side and of the North East in the Seven Sisters side of the Indian sub-continent."

Put in simple language, what Sadeq Khan is saying is: We do not have enough land. So we will take land from Myanmar and India's North-east. And we dare you to stop us either with barbed-wire fencing or the BSF.

It would, however, be a mistake to jump to the conclusion that Bangladesh's motives for the large-scale illegal infiltration of West Bengal, Assam and the North-east in general has nothing more to it than population pressure within that country and a search for living space. This thrust is not just economic. The encouragement of insurgent activity in India's North-east through the simple expedient of providing asylum and training facilities to Indian insurgent outfits and the facilitation of ISI and al Qaeda collaboration with such insurgent outfits, speak of more sinister expansionist ambitions in this region. There is a clear move to establish an Islamic country in India's North-east, and the project is moving forward relentlessly because of India's weak response to such situations that poses a threat to the country's security and integrity. What is much worse is that Bangladesh has its eager collaborators within the country even among former ministers, but the Government of India has been able to do precious little to tackle even the collaborators of Bangladesh in India. What the demographic change of the north-eastern region wrought by the ceaseless illegal infiltration from Bangladesh represents for India is a major security hazard. The ISI of Pakistan is so well entrenched in Bangladesh that it is now in a position to call the shots in the governance of a State like Assam all through the all-powerful pro-Bangladeshi lobby in Assam. What the Government of India seems to have completely overlooked is that when the north-eastern States of India are annexed by Bangladesh it will also have the extensive uranium deposits of Meghalaya and Mizoram. Is this a security hazard that the Government of

India can afford to take lightly, considering the ISI activities in the North-east carried on from Bangladesh?

The greatest encouragement to illegal immigration from Bangladesh came from the separate and discriminatory immigration law enacted solely for Assam in 1983 called the Illegal Migrants (Determination by Tribunals) Act or the IM (DT) Act for short. Its salient features were: (a) it represented the only known case of any civilized democratic republic having two immigration laws one for the entire country and the other for just one State; (b) it was the only immigration law that was kind to the illegal migrant, making it virtually impossible for the state authorities to deport him even if he was detected; (c) it was the only known immigration law that took away the onus of proving nationality from the illegal migrant and transferred it to individual citizens who had to make a complaint before a tribunal and also pay a fee for doing this patriotic and hazardous duty; and (d) this immigration law took away the responsibility of detecting and deporting foreign nationals from the Executive and vested it with quasi-judicial tribunals manned by retired and tired judges. And we can thank our lawmakers for this mindless sabotage of the immigration law of the country and the conscious effort to create another Kashmir or Cyprus in Assam, so that the State could be annexed by a country that India once created. Ironically, the worst enemies of Assam and the nation as a whole have been our own elected representatives. It is important to bear in mind that the IM (DT) Act was legislated behind the back of Assam in 1983 when the Congress had a steamroller majority in Parliament, and when Assam, having boycotted the general elections had only one representatives in the Lok Sabha. In 22 years, the IM (DT) Act did incalculable harm to the interests of Assam.

It is not just that Bangladesh was unaware of the IM (DT) Act. In fact, it is the pro-Bangladesh lobby in India that got our MPs to commit hara-kiri on our behalf. But that is not all there is to it. The security threat for India arising from the Bangladeshi resolve to annex the North-east of India is spine-chilling. The presence of Pakistan's ISI agents in Bangladesh is a well-known fact. They not only arranged the training of the ULFA top brass in Pakistan, but have also been training insurgents from the North-east in the training camps located in Bangladesh. But what is much worse is that the al Qaeda is also in Bangladesh now imparting training to insurgents from the North-east. The *Time* magazine article of the issue of October 21, 2002 is a terrifying pointer to this.

Where do we go from here? The answer can be quite laconic: to Bangladesh. After all, have not our elected representatives worked quite assiduously for just this kind of an end result? But what can be done even now to save Assam and the North-east from being ceded to Bangladesh?

Whatever measures we think of, it is clear that any hopes of pushing back millions of Bangladeshis from Assam and West Bengal across the border would be a Utopian dream. Economic pragmatism would suggest the acceptance of a chunk of the illegal immigrants already here. Having done this, it is imperative to bring in the following measures quite ruthlessly:

- Greater border control with barbed wire fencing wherever possible and a larger and better equipped border control force with shoot-at-sight instructions just as we have on the Indo-Pakistan border.
- Sharing of the Bangladeshi immigrants by all the States of India (especially the Congress-ruled States) since this is a national problem.
- Total economic boycott of all illegal migrants. This is an idea that is held to be Utopian, but in the context of Assam, this is desperately needed since much of the illegal immigration was made possible just because we created an economic vacuum. We need major surgery now, and no major surgery is possible without some loss of blood.
- The proposal to issue work permits to Bangladeshis should be held in abeyance for the next 20 years.
- Multi-purpose identity cards should be issued to all Indian citizens (especially along the border areas). However, it is quite possible that the illegal migrants will among the first to get such identity cards.
- A uniform civil code should be introduced for everyone living in India (not just Indian citizens). Polygamy as a means of increasing the immigrant population very fast is standard practice among Bangladeshi immigrants and should be banned in a secular democracy.
- It is important to help the youth of Assam to acquire manual skills so that they can do all skilled work.
- We need coercive diplomacy with Bangladesh. We have nothing to lose but our reputation for weakness in dealing with a country we created.

30

Unabated Foreigner's Influx: A Real Threat to Internal Security in Assam

R.C. Borpatragohain

Historical Background

Illegal migration from Bangladesh into Assam needs to be viewed against the backdrop of past history, present realities and future designs. Illegal migration from Bangladesh into Assam has been taking place from the dawn of contemporary history. However, after the British annexed Assam, large scale population movement from the south (Bengal, East Pakistan and now Bangladesh) has been an ongoing phenomenon for over a century.[1]

In 1905, when Lord Curzon partitioned erstwhile Bengal Presidency, Assam was a Chief-Commissioner's province. It was merged with the new Muslim majority province of East Bengal. This lead to tremendous popular resentment in the country and it ushered political awareness, ultimately culminating in India's independence.

In 1911, when the British Government annulled the partition of Bengal, Assam restored its status as a province and was now placed under a Lieutenant Governor. The fear of losing their identity and being swamped by Bengalis goes back to this merger and even earlier. This fear had been aroused both by the Bengali Hindus dominating the administration and the professions and the Bengali Muslims altering the demography of the province. The Bengali Muslims were hard working peasants who occupied vacant land and put virgin areas under cultivation. They made a significant contribution to the agricultural economy of Assam.[2]

The British while developing the tea industry in Assam, imported laboures from Bihar and other provinces to work in the tea gardens. The Assamese people, living mostly in upper Assam and cultivating one crop per year were

not interested in working as labourers nor in increasing or expanding land cultivation to meet the additional requirement of food for the large labourers population employed in the tea gardens. Therefore, the British encouraged Bengali Muslim peasants from East Bengal (present Bangladesh) to move into lower Assam for putting virgin land under cultivation. This set in motion a movement pattern which, despite changed conditions, has been continuing to this day.[3]

During Constitutional Reforms, the country started advancing towards democracy which is a game of numbers. When the demand for partition was raised, it was visualised that Pakistan would comprise Muslim majority provinces in the west and *Bang-e-Islam* comprising Bengal and Assam, in the east. The Cabinet Mission Plan placed Assam in Group – C with Bengal. Both the Congress High Command and the Muslim League accepted the grouping plan but Lokapriya Gopinath Bordoloi vehemently opposed it. He was supported by Mahatma Gandhi. The Grouping plan was foiled and Assam was saved from becoming a part of Pakistan.[4]

Partition brought about a sea change in the situation. An International border now separated Assam and East-Pakistan. Population movement from East-Pakistan now Bangladesh continued but it was initially mostly of Hindu refugees, fleeing for fear of religious persecution. Unlike the west, where refugee movement lasted for a few months only, in the case of the East, this spreads over several years and is still continuing. The movement of Hindu refugees into Assam got largely arrested due to anti-Bengali riots and as a result of violence in the wake of insurgency in the state. However, Hindu refugee movement from Bangladesh has continued to Tripura and West Bengal. Illegal migrants from Bangladesh into Assam are now almost exclusively Muslims.

Situational Aggravation

The illegal immigrants, ceaselessly flowing into the North East India from Bangladesh, posed a threat to the integrity and security of the region and also to India. The students and youths of Assam, Manipur, Tripura, Nagaland, Meghalaya, Mizoram and Arunachal Pradesh have been protesting against the influx of foreign nationals from Bangladesh, Nepal and Burma during the last few decades.

The fear psychosis of the small nationalities in these states stands to reason on the simple ground that they are being swamped by these aliens; their polity and culture are polluted and damaged, the extremely limited job opportunities and economic resources are taken away and the administration has been wrecked from within. The apprehension is not without evidence since the indigenous Tripuris, who were once the majorities in their homeland till 1942 are nearly wiped out by the aggressive aliens who are now the undisputed rulers in Tripura.

The most dangerous implication on the North-Easterners is that the unprecedented growth rate of influx of illegal immigrants if continues, all the tiny states of the North-East are likely to be converted into the homeland of

the aliens, thereby wiping out the indigenous populace and nationalities permanently from their homeland.

The problem is not only connected with the rehabilitation and naturalisation of few stray illegal immigrants in the country which is the current state of practice in international law; but also deeply connected with ceaseless influx of a colossal wave which can easily erase the indigenous populace permanently and which has already threatened and jeopardised the existence of the citizens.

The demographic invasion in Assam started at the dawn of the last century. As per the census reports, the then district of Goalpara was the first district of Assam which witnessed this scenario in the year 1900. The population increased to the tune of 65 per cent between 1901-1921, out of which 35 per cent constituted the migrants. The district of Kamrup, Mangaldoi and North-Lakhimpur witnessed the scenario accordingly.[5]

In 1931, Mr S.C. Mullan, an ICS officer holding the post of Census Superintendent of Assam made an advanced warning that in another thirty years of time only in the Sibsagar district Assamese would find themselves at home.

After India's obtaining independence, as per the Constitution of India, the citizens residing in India on 19th July, 1948 were considered to be the citizens of India. But due to the continuous influx of foreigners after 19th July, 1948 to Assam from East Pakistan, realising the socio-economic crisis among the tribal people of this region, an Act namely 'The Immigrants (Expulsion from Assam) Act, 1950' was passed. And accordingly lakhs of illegal Pakistani citizens were expelled from the soil of Assam. But due to the protest raised by the then Pakistani Government, a Treaty was signed between the then Pakistani Prime Minister Liyakat Ali and the then Prime Minister of India Jawaharlal Nehru on 6th April, 1950.[6]

Accordingly, the persons expelled from India came back to India but none of the infiltrators from Pakistan has gone back to Pakistan.

In 1962, during the Chinese invasion, due to advancement of Chinese troupes' up to Tezpur, the administrative system of that area came into a standstill. Taking advantage of this situation, some miscreants hoisted Pakistani flags at Panchali and Thelamara. Investigating this situation, the Chief of the then Central Investigative Agency, Bholanath Mallik prepared a plan to save Assam for Pakistani infiltration which was approved by the then Prime Minister Jawaharlal Nehru. The plan was known as PIP or Pakistani Infiltration Project. The project suggested that:

(a) Strong wall should be erected between North-East India and East-Pakistan (Bangladesh).

(b) Five hundred armed police out posts be set up by the side of the wall.

(c) Photo identity cards be issued to the residents who reside within five miles of the border.

(d) Pakistanis to be deported who infiltrated (during that time).

(e) The entire cost will be borne by the Central government to implement this project.[7]

To implement the project, the Prime Minister Nehru directed to the then Chief Minister of Assam (Late) Bimala Prasad Chaliha. But Mr Chaliha did not

implement this project, because of the intervention of Mainul Hoque Choudhury, who was a leader of Cachar having strong inclination towards Pakistan. Chaliha who was defeated in election at his own constituency at Amguri, later was elected from Badarpur constituency with the blessings of Mainul Haque Choudhury. So, Chaliha refrained from implementing this project.

For the increase of Pakistani infiltration, the Government authority set up 10 nos. of tribunals at Assam to expel infiltrators and the tribunals after investigation expelled 1, 92, 800 citizens of East Pakistan up to 1969. But due to the protest with the leadership of late Mainul Haque Choudhury, Lt. Debakanta Baruah, and Lt. Sarat Ch. Singh at Assam Legislative Assembly, the expulsions came into a halt. And thus ends the expulsion of illegal foreigners.[8]

Assam's specific figures of illegal migrants have been worked out from available statistics as follows:

(a) Recent increase of electors in the voters' list in Assam by the Election Commission shows more than 30 per cent increase in 17 Assembly constituencies and more that 20 per cent increase in 40 constituencies between 1944 and 1997. Whereas the All India average growth for a three years period intervening the two intensive revisions in 1994 and 1997 is seven per cent the growth in Assam for this period is 16.4 per cent.[9]

(b) Relative decadal percentage growth of population of Assam. All India and Bangladesh is as follows:

Year	*Assam*	*All India*	*Bangladesh*
1901-11	16.99	5.75	9.1
1911-21	20.48	-0.31	5.4
1921-31	19.91	11.00	7.06
1931-41	20.40	14.22	11.6
1941-51	34.98	21.51	0.1
1951-61	34.95	24.80	29.83
1971-81	23.8	24.66	31.83
1981-91	23.8	23.85	22.00

The foreigner's influx has considerably agitated the minds of the North-Easterners for decades together and has brought about social tensions. The students' movement (AASU) against foreign nationals assumed the character of an unprecedented mass upheaval, involving people from all walks of life including public servants etc. The foreigners' problem has sown the seed of hatred, mutual distress, social disorder, and even jeopardy to the security of the people and the integrity of the state.

Another important step in this regard is the government policy. In the past, the policy which clearly laid down the procedure for identification of the foreign nationals warranted that documents obtained by fraud or by suppression of material facts have no legal validity and must be disregarded. The immigrants were found owning and cultivating land within tribal reserves, where even Indians from plains are not allowed to own any plot of land—a mother's grave, a patch of land, a rent receipt, a school certificate is no evidence

of nationality. Nationality is based on more substantial and fundamental considerations and the mere fact that a person's name is rightly or wrongly, inscribed in the voters' list does not prove or confer Indian Nationality or citizenship.

During the election of the Assam State Assembly, which was held in February, 1983 amidst bloodbath where nearly four thousand lives were lost and several crores worth properties were lost. Instead of postponing the election by suitable amendments of the Constitution, the election ritual was completed on the alibi of constitutional obligation. Only two of the 10 per cent of the electorate, of which majority of them are foreign nationals, exercised the right to franchise and the entire foundation of democracy, as peoples government elected by people necessitated a critical scrutiny. The recommendation of the Election Commission for the maintenance of national or house register and issue of photo identity card to each elector in the N.E. was not implemented. The Election Commission justly concluded that the seeds of the basic problem of foreign nationals were sown decades ago and therefore, all the governments, whether at the centre or at the state, must share the responsibility for not holding the problems by it forelock and allowing the situation to drift. The Mehta Commission constituted by the Assembly invariably found fault with the government in its conduct of the election ritual and connected activities.

Role of Political Dictators

The political dictators of Assam are unable to find a satisfactory solution to the problem of illegal immigrants in Assam. The All Assam Students' Union (AASU) and the All Assam Gana Sangram Parishad (AAGSP) have also expressed their keenness to find such a solution.

The AASU, through their Memorandum dated 2nd February 1980 presented to the then Prime Minister Smt. Indira Gandhi, conveyed their profound sense of apprehension regarding the continuing influx of foreign national into Assam and the fear of consequential adverse effects upon the political, social, cultural and economic life of the state.

Being fully alive to the genuine apprehensions of the people of Assam, the then Prime Minister initiated the dialogue with the AASU/AAGSP. Subsequently, talks were held at the Prime Minister's and Home Minister's levels during the period 1980-83. Several rounds of informal talks were held during 1984. Formal discussions were resumed thereafter.[10]

The unabated influx is partly attributed to the underestimation of and indifference by the Central Government to the magnitude and design of the problem. A government notification ordered, "No person entering India from any place in that part of Pakistan which lies to the East of India shall be required to be in possession of a permit."[11]

The past administrative lapses are also brought to light. No inner line permit system setting any kind of regulatory procedure had been observed specially during the mass exodus on account of internal disturbances first in the East Pakistan and then in Bangladesh.[12]

The DIP's scheme for prevention of infiltration of Pakistani nationals into Assam included:

A— Evacuation of belt along Assam's border with East Pakistan.

B— Keeping of thumb and finger impressions and photographs of Pakistani infiltrants and inhibit movement into other areas.

C —Issue of Identity Cards to Indian nationals in Assam.[13]

As the scheme remained in cold freeze, the problem of influx aggravated to unmanageable and unimaginable proportions. The PIP (Preventions of Infiltration Programme) drafted by the Director of Intelligence Bureau, S.N. Mullick in 1965 pushed back nearly two lakhs infiltrators till 1967, but the scheme was winded up on the pressure of Moinul Haque Choudhury.[14]

The Union Government's policy towards healing the aggravation caused by the chronic problem of Assam was less than consistent. Assam Government was secretly instructed to confer Indian Citizenship u/s of 5(1) (a) of the Citizenship Act, 1955 to the migrants who served ties with Pakistan and have settled in service, trade or profession in India. The instructions were withdrawn in 1971 after the liberation of Bangladesh, with the intervention of the Indian Armed forces and the Mukti Bahini.

Government of India issued instructions to discriminate between security migrants and those who came without travel documents. The Union Home Ministry has also instructed repatriation of the Bengalis only of post March 1971 entrants. Till so far the Governmental policy towards the illegal immigrants' problems has been discriminatory, favouring certain ethnic or religious groups. The social impact is the division of the populace and the refugees along certain artificial lines. The result is simply tragic.

Assam Accord of 1985

The Assam Accord was signed in 1985. The Clause 5.1 provides for the detection and deletion of the names of the foreigners taking 01.01.1966 as the base date.

Clause 5.2 says that persons who came to Assam, prior to 01.01.1966 and those whose names appeared on the electoral rolls used in 1967 elections shall be regularised.

Clause 5.3 provides that the foreigners who came to Assam after 01.01.1966 and up to 24.03.1971 shall be detected in accordance with the provisions of the Foreigners Act, 1946, and the Foreigners (Tribunals) Order 1964.

Clause 5.8 provides that the foreigners who came to Assam on or after March 24, 1971 shall continue to be detected, deleted and expelled in accordance with law. It is also provided that immediate and practical steps shall be taken towards expulsion of such illegal immigrants.

Clause 5.9 provides that government would consider the difficulties regarding the implementation of the Illegal Migrants (Determination by Tribunals) Act, 1983. The government of India of that time and of today has realised the situation created by the illegality of the IM (DT) Act, which was absolutely discriminatory in nature.[15]

Clause 6 of the Assam Accord assures for constitutional safeguards of the Assamese people. It provides that constitutional, legislative and

administrative safeguards, as may be appropriate, shall be provided to protect, preserve and promote the cultural, social, linguistic identity and heritage of Assamese people but till today due to lack of sincere political will, both of the Union and the State Government, it is not materialising till today.

Clause 7 provides that the government takes the opportunity to renew their commitment for speedy all round economic development of Assam, so as to improve the standard of living of the people. Special emphasis will be placed on education and science and technology through establishment of national institutions, but is found to be only a theoretical consolation.

Laws to Curb the Menace

In 1947 there emerged two dominions out of the Sub-continent, India and Pakistan with an international border. For the first few years, unrestricted trans-border movement continued in this sector. Bengali Hindu refugees from East Pakistan fleeing from their homes poured across this border seeking asylum. Concurrently, Bengali Muslims too continued to come across the boarder for economic reasons. There was also some movement of Muslims from Assam into East-Pakistan.

The demands of the mass movement include detection and deportation of all foreign nationals, deletion of their names from the electoral rolls, updating the 1951 NRC, introduction of the identity cards in the region, maintenance of birth and death register at the village levels, constitutional safeguards for the people of the region, demarcation of the Indo-Bangladesh border with barbed wire fencing, requisition of additional border forces and withdrawal of the power of the state govts., to issue citizenship certificate.

The formula introduced by Mr Ravindra Verma which is mainly for negotiation between Central Government and Students' Union include, among others, detection of foreign nationals with the help of the Constitution of India, Foreigners' Act 1946, Citizenship Act, 1955 and the Passport Act, 1967, grant of citizenship to the illegal migrants who entered from 1961 to 1971 and who have obtained citizenship certificate from Assam Government and the deportation of the post 1971 migrants. In this respect, the Scheme of the Pakistani Infiltration Project (PIP) is more relevant.[16]

In a landmark judgment in 2005, the Supreme Court declared the Illegal Migrants (Determination by Tribunal) Act, 1983 as unconstitutional and termed the illegal migration of Bangladeshi to Assam as an act of external aggression and internal disturbances. The Court directed the Central Government to issue Multi Purpose National Identity Cards (MPNIC) to Indian citizens in Assam and the North-East which should be the basis for citizens to avail themselves of benefits such as ration cards, school admission and inclusion of names in the voters' list. The illegal migrants without the MPNIC would not be able to avail these benefits. The SC also directed to increase the number of Foreigners Tribunals and expedite construction of border fencing. The SC had directed the Union Government to file a status report in eight weeks on steps taken to identify the illegal migrant, number of Tribunals set up and number of cases disposed of.[17]

Border Fencing

A boarder fence may not be a full-proof method for preventing infiltration but there is no better way of doing so than to this. To be effective, border fencing has to be supplemented by vigorous patrolling and other appropriate measures. The motivating factors behind infiltration must be addressed. If this can be done successfully, then a permanent solution of the problem can be found.[18]

Additional BSF battalions should be provided in the East with each battalion having a frontage of 30 kilometers. It is understood that one reason for thin deployment of BSF in the East is the fact that 16 battalions are deployed on counter insurgency tasks. Such diversion of forces from border to other duties, when the battle against illegal migrants is on, cannot but have adverse effect. The shortage of BSF units must be made up on priority basis through new recruitments.[19]

All country boats plying on the river near the border must be registered with their registration number marked on them and registration papers available with the crew for verification, when required.

The present arrangement of guarding the riverine border with some speed boats and out dated country boats is not adequate. There is a need to have floating BOPs on medium watercraft with four to five speed boats attached to them. A proposal for nine medium crafts has been put up by DG BSF. This should be sanctioned soon.

Certain other measures are also required to be taken to deal with illegal migration. These are as follows:[20]

(a) Our nationals in the border districts and for that matter in the whole state should be provided multi-purpose photo identity card. This task should be completely on high priority.

(b) Effective arrangements must be made for registration of birth and deaths in the state.

(c) The 1951 National Register of Citizens should be updated. Computerisation will facilitate this process. A separate register for illegal migrants (Stateless citizens) should also be maintained.

(d) Chars in the Brahmaputra should be handed over to the Forest Department and notified as forest land. Trees which can withstand 1 to 3 feet of water during the flood season should be planted on them.

The various measures recommended to stop illegal migration are non-controversial. No political party or organisation within the country can legitimately protest and demand that these steps should not be taken. Through these measures, we can bring about a huge change in this situation and trans-border migration will become stopped. If we do not take effective measures to stop this movement and allow trans-border migration to continue unabated, then it may spell the doom of Assam and put our national security in grave jeopardy.

Indo–Bangla International Border

There is difficulty in making a realistic estimate of the number of illegal immigrants from Bangladesh entering into Assam as they enter surreptitiously

and are able to mingle easily with the local population due to ethnic and linguistic similarities. The demographic composition in the districts bordering Bangladesh has altered with the illegal immigration from Bangladesh. The districts of Assam and West-Bengal bordering Bangladesh have recorded growth of population higher than the national average. The States of Meghalaya, Mizoram and Tripura have also recorded high rates of population growth. Illegal immigrants from Bangladesh have also been using West-Bengal as a corridor to migrate to other parts of the country.[21]

The large scale influx of illegal Bangladeshi immigration has led to large tracts of sensitive international border occupied by foreigners. This has serious implications for internal security.

The types of illegal migrants are as follows:

(a) those who came with valid visa/documents and overstayed.

(b) those who came with forged visa/ documents; and

(c) those who entered surreptitiously.[22]

Whereas in the West, the trans-border movement of refugees from India to Pakistan and *vice-versa* was a deluge which lasted only for a few months. But, in the East the situation was very different. Hindu from East Pakistan (Bangladesh) kept coming across for many years and indeed they still continue to come. Muslims from Assam going into East Pakistan were relatively much less in numbers. The traditional influx of Bengali Muslims into Assam continued unabated. The large scale movement of Bengali population, both Hindus and Muslims into Assam, caused considerable resentment among the Assamese people and there were instances of anti-Bengali riots.[23]

Neither the BSF on the border nor the Border Organisation in the interior could prevent large scale illegal migration from Bangladesh. The border is very porous and the illegal migrants enjoyed political patronage. As per JIC paper No. 04/95 of 3rd June, 1995, 1.5 lakhs illegal migrants were pushed back but many managed to re-enter from different points on the border.

Border policing in both Punjab and Assam should prevent trans-border movement of smugglers, militants and infiltrators. In the case of Assam, infiltration has a much bigger and a more dangerous dimension. Despite this, the measures to counter trans-border movement in Assam appear to have been given a lower priority than in Punjab. This is evident from the following facts.

(a) The decision to fence the border was taken in 1985 and reflected in Assam Accord but the work on fencing started seven years later in 1992. 27 years have elapsed since the Accord was signed and fencing has not yet been completed. In Dhubri sector of Assam, the work is in progress, but in the Cachar sector, only a little over half has been completed. As against this, fencing in Punjab started in 1988 and was completed in three years by 1991.[24]

(b) The quality of fencing in Punjab is superior. It is two feet taller. Observation towers and lighting of the fence have been provided in Punjab, all along the border. In Assam observation towers have been constructed in Dhubri sector only and there is none in Cachar sector. There is no lighting of the fence anywhere in Assam.

(c) The density of troops guarding the fence is higher in Punjab. A BSF battalion in Punjab holds a frontage of approximately 30 kilometers. In Assam, BSF battalions in Dhubri sector are deployed over frontages of 70 kms and in Cachar sector over a frontage of 40 km.[25]

Border fencing in Assam must be completed forthwith on a war footing as was done in Punjab sector and there must be lighting arrangements for the fence. Observation towers must be provided in Cachar sector.

Impact or consequences of such foreigners influx in Assam are as follows:

(i) Illegal Arms trade,
(ii) Drug-Trafficking,
(iii) Smuggling, and
(iv) Insurgency.

As a result of population movement from Bangladesh, the specter looms large of the indigenous people of Assam being reduced to a minority in their home state. Their cultural survival will be in jeopardy, their political control will be weakened and their employment opportunities will be undermined.

The silent and invidious demographic invasion of Assam may result in the loss of the geostrategically vital districts of lower Assam. As the influx of these illegal migrants turning these districts into a Muslim majority region, it will then only be a matter of time when a demand for their merger with Bangladesh may be made. The rapid growth of international Islamic fundamentalism may provide for driving force for this demand. In this context, it is pertinent that Bangladesh has long discarded secularism and has chosen to become an Islamic state. Loss of lower Assam will severe the entire land mass of the North East, from the rest of India and the rich natural resources of the region will be a loss to the nation.[26]

Post IM (DT) Act, 1983 Era

IM (DT) Act was enacted at the height of the anti-foreigners movement in Assam. The large scale violence during the movement including the Nellie massacre had led to understandable apprehension among the minorities of harassment and victimisation. Be that as it may, the fact is that on the pleas of protecting genuine Indian citizens, the IM (DT) Act was formulated but in practice, it has been found to be primarily serving the interest of the illegal migrants.[27]

The IM (DT) Act, 1983 was enacted with two objectives, namely:

(i) to declare 25th day of March, 1971 as the cut of date for granting Indian citizenship to those illegal migrants who entered India prior to this cutoff date and for detection of those illegal migrants who entered India after this date;

(ii) to declare illegal migrants as Indian citizens who entered India prior to this cutoff date and for their protection, the process of adjudication by the IM (DT) Act was introduced. This tribunal was also empowered to declare an illegal migrant not to be an illegal migrant. After the amendment of the Citizenship Act, 1955 by introduction of Section 6A of the Act, for the pre-1971 illegal migrants who were classified into two groups, this Act became infractuous.

The enactment was, therefore, never intended for expulsion of the illegal migrants, but for granting Indian citizenships to those illegal migrants [28]

However, we are of the opinion that even after repeal of the IM (DT) Act, the vexed problem of illegal migrants in Assam could not be automatically solved. There are other legal impediments which obstruct the detection of illegal migrants. Those impediments need to be taken into consideration while reviewing the issue of detection and deportation of illegal migrants from Assam.

The legal impediments that will subsist, even after the repeal of the IM (DT) Act are[29]

(i) Provision of Section 3(1) (a) of the Citizenship Act, 1955 (Amended in 1986) which provides that "every person born in India on or after 26th day of Jan 1950, but before the commencement of the Citizenship (Amendment) Act, 1986, is a citizen of India."

(ii) Section 6 A of the Citizenship Act, 1955 provides to confer citizenship to persons covered by the Assam Accord. The legislative spirit of the Section 6 A of the Citizenship Act was to grant citizenship to those persons who are detected to be foreigners who came to Assam between 1st day of January 1966 and 24th day of March 1971 and it was never intended to confer Citizenship to those persons automatically. The spirit was that the process of detection shall be expedited; once they are detected, they shall register themselves in accordance with the rules made by the Central Government in this behalf u/s 18 of the Act.

It is very unfortunate that neither the Central Government nor the State Government took the initiative in this direction. No record showing the number of persons detected belonging to this period of time and as to how many of such persons have applied for registrations, how many of them have been conferred citizenships and how many of them have been debarred form voting by delisting their names from the electoral rolls for a period of 10 years, has been properly made public till today. This inaction on the part of the Government has aggravated the situation, making the problem of detection of illegal migrants more difficult.

Unless this measure is taken within a specific time frame, the repeal of the Act alone will not solve the problem.

Mandate of Supreme Court's Decision

There were several national and international cases relating to foreigners influx. Some of these are as follows:

In *Che Chang Ping vs US 1930 US 581*, the United State SC held:

"The power of exclusion of foreigners being an incident of sovereignty belonging to the government of the US as a part of those sovereign powers delegated by the Constitution, the right to its exercise at any time when in the judgement of the government the interests of the country require it, cannot be granted away or restrained on behalf of any one. The powers of government are delegated in trust to the US, and are incapable of transfer to any other parties. They cannot be abandoned or surrendered. Nor can their exercise be hampered, when needed for the public good, by any considerations of private interests. The exercise of these public trusts is not the subject of barter or contract." [30]

In *Fong Yue Ting vs US 149 US 698*, where the court ruled:

"The government of each state has always the right to compel foreigners who are found within its territory to go away by having them taken to the frontier. This right is based on the fact that, the foreigner not making part of the nation, his individual reception into the territory is matter of pure permission, of simple tolerance, and creates no obligation. The exercise of their right may be subjected, doubtless, to certain forms by the domestic laws of each country, but the right exists none the less, universally recognised and put in force." [31]

In *Nishimura Ekiu vs US 142 US 652*, it was adjudged that although Congress might, if it saw fit, authorise the courts to investigate and ascertain the facts upon which the alien's right to land was made by the statutes to depend, yet Congress might entrust the final determinations of those facts to an executive officer, and that, if it did so, his order was due process of law and no other tribunal, unless expressly authorised by law to do so, was at liberty to re-examine the evidence on which he acted or to controvert its sufficiency. Thus, according to US Supreme Court, the determination of right of an alien even by executive will be in compliance of due process of law.

In *Louis De Raedt vs Union of India*[32], the court held that the power of the government of India to expel foreigners is absolute and unlimited and there is no provision in the Constitution fettering its discretion and the executive government has unrestricted right to expel a foreigner. So far as right to be a heard is concerned, there cannot be any hard and fast rule about the manner in which a person concerned has to be given an opportunity to place his case.

In state of *Arunachal Pradesh vs Khudi Ram Chakma 1994 (Supp) SCC 615*,[33] it was held that the fundamental right of a foreigner is confined to Article 21 for life and liberty and does not include the right to reside and stay in this country, as mentioned in article 19(1) (e), which is applicable only to the citizens of the country.

Thus, the Bangladeshi nationals who have illegally crossed the border and have trespassed into Assam or are living in other parts of the country have no legal right of any kind to remain in India and they are liable to be deported.

In the historic case of *Sarbananda Sonowal vs Union of India,*[34] the court held that the provisions of the IM (DT) Act, 1983 and IM (DT) Rules, 1984 are *ultra vires* the Constitution of India and are therefore struck down. The IM (DT) Act, 1983 contravenes the provisions of the Constitution.

Referring to the Supreme Court's observations in the *Sarbananda Sonowal's* case equating the unabated cross-border infiltration from Bangladesh with external aggression, the High Court said that unless "prompt and useful" action was taken by the Central and the State Government what was in store for Assam" can well be imagined.[35]

The Gauhati High Court in another case in the judgment dated March 26, 2008, held "The establishment of Foreigner's Tribunals and their decisions, even after being upheld by this court, has not yielded the desired result. The illegal Bangladeshis could easily migrate to Assam without any valid documents

and stay here at par with Indian citizens with all the rights, including the right of franchise. Even after passing of the orders by the Tribunal and upholding of the same by the writ court, the authority is not in a position to deport the foreign nationals."

In the above case,[36] the petitioner Ananda Kundu of Hojai, Nogaon, after being declared to be a foreigner by a foreigner Tribunal and subsequently deported to Bangladesh, came back to Assam easily and even invoked the writ jurisdiction of the High Court.

Internal Security Threat

Security is considered by all modern states to be a prerequisite for development. Security from external aggression or threat or from internal disturbances have always been accorded utmost importance by policy-makers. However, security of the state at times completely sidelines security of the people.[37]

The primary obligation of the state is to protect the citizens from external aggression and the protection of the people from any external design involving massive alien influx which adversely affects the integrity of the nation and security of the citizens is the primary obligation and duty of the state from time immemorial. The government does not stand to reason, if by lapse of its omission of its primary and most elementary duty towards its citizens, throws open its territorial boundary to a flood of illegal immigrants for more than three decades, clandestinely arrange to naturalise them as citizens, confine them to a set of tiny hill states without dispersal to the length and breadth of the vast territory, leave the citizens to self-preservation against a determined horde of aliens and unleash state violence against any voice of protest from the small nationalities whose extinction is more or less a settled fact under the present condition. The Illegal Immigrant Act, 1983 was explicitly legalising the illegal aliens which infiltrated and settled in the North-East during the past three decades.

The war in its most generally understood sense is a contest between two or more states primarily through their armed forces, the ultimate purpose of each contestant or each contestant group being to vanquish the other or others and impose its own conditions of peace. With the passage of time, the nature of war itself has become more distinctly clarified as a formal status of armed hostility, in which the intention of the parties, the so-called *animus belligerendi* may be a decisive factor. The modern war may involve not merely the armed forces of belligerent states but their entire population.[38]

As mentioned earlier, the influx of Bangladeshi nationals who have illegally migrated into Assam pose a threat to the integrity and security of North-Eastern Region. Their presence has changed the demographic character of the region and the local people of Assam have been reduced to minority in certain districts. In such circumstances, if the Parliament had enacted a legislation exclusively for the state of Assam which was more stringent than the Foreigners Act, which is applicable to rest of India, and also in the state of Assam for identification of such persons who migrated from the territory of present Bangladesh between 1st January, 1966 to 24th March, 1971, such a legislation could not pass the test of Article 14, as the differentiation so made

would had not have the rational nexus with the avowed policy and objective of the Act.[39]

Remedies: International and National

International Remedies: Under International Law, the foreign nationals problem was a consideration outside the purview of the municipal law viz., obligation of the International community towards sharing the burden of foreign nationals stalking the Indian soil, and international obligation of India with respect to the ceaseless influx of foreign nationals from the neighbouring countries; and the state responsibility of the government of the countries of origin of the illegal immigrants.

The latest standpoint of India on International obligations in the present context has been clearly mooted in its initial Report submitted to the UN Human Rights Committee as reported on July 13, 1983. The Report states that in India, treaties are not self-executing. The provisions of the treaties do not form automatically part of the internal law. Implementing legislation is necessary to give effect to the provisions of the treaties.[40]

Under customary international laws, the protection extended to the stateless and the aliens are weak, as the assimilation of non-nationals are difficult. They are commonly denied access to voting and office holding, rights incidental to citizenship. Alien's property and wealth may be expropriated without adequate compensation and aliens may be prohibited from gainful employment. Till so far, two different standards for the protection of foreigner's influx have been evolved by the International law:

(1) the doctrine of 'national treatment' or 'equality of treatment', and

(2) 'minimum international standard for treatment of illegal immigrant.

The permanent court of International Justice expressly recognised the existence of a generally accepted International Law respecting the treatment of aliens and which is applicable to them despite municipal legislation.

National Remedies

The recommendations of Governor[41] in the report on the Illegal migration into Assam submitted to the President of India are:

1. Awareness should be promoted about illegal migration into Assam being not only a threat to the identity of the Assamese people but what is more, being a grave threat to our national security.

2. Border fencing in Assam should be completed on a war footing. Observation towers and lighting should be provided on the same scale as in Punjab.

3. BSF battalions deployed in Assam should not be given responsibility to hold unduly extended frontages.

4. Diversion of BSF battalions from the border in Assam for other tasks, when the battle against infiltrators is on, must be scrupulously avoided.

5. All country boats, plying in the river near the border should be registered and their registration numbers marked on them.

6. Medium crafts for floating BOPs with adequate speed boats for the riverine sector, should be made available as early as possible.

7. Multi-purpose photo identity cards should be provided to all our nationals. Districts bordering Bangladesh should be accorded higher priority.

8. Effective arrangements should be made for registration of births and deaths.

9. The National Register of Citizens should be updated and computerised. A separate register of stateless citizens should also be maintained.

10. Vacant Chars in the river should be handed over to the Forest Department and trees planted on them.

11. Socio-economic programmes designed to improve the lot of women should be given, priority due to its multiple beneficiary spin offs-improving the family's income, women education curbing population growth and educated women becoming a bulwark against the spread of Islamic fundamentalism.

12. Hindu illegal migrants who have infiltrated after 24th March 1971 should not be given refugee status. They should be treated as illegal migrants.

13. While maximum effort must be made to stem the ingrain of illegal migrants, those who have already infiltrated after 24th March 1971 to date, may be deported.

14. [The IM (DT) Act should be repealed and replaced by].[42] A new legislation which should provide for detection for illegal migrants in a just, fair and expeditious manner, with due judicial sanctity accorded to the process. Those identified as illegal migrants should not be allowed to stay in the country as stateless citizens with no voting right and no right to acquire immovable property.

15. Survey teams working under Magistrate on deputation from other states assisted by policemen of Border Organisation, should identify illegal migrants in a fixed time frame of short duration. Those identified as foreigners by these teams should be given the right of appeal to tribunals set-up under Foreigners Act.

However, after the repeal of the IM (DT) Act, 1983, the Governments at the Centre and the State are not following the mandate of the Supreme Court in *Sarbananda's case* in letter and spirit. The detention of illegal migrants in the light of the Foreigners' Act, 1946 is not satisfactory. The declared illegal immigrants by the Foreigners Tribunals, though very negligible, vanish due to insincerity on the part of the State Government. The detention camps, though declared by the State Government, are not created to keep the detected illegal migrants. Hence, it is the high time that the public awareness campaigns must be made in continuous manner to build a healthy public opinion towards compelling the Governments, both the Union and the State, to discharge their constitutional obligation.

References

1. Governor's Report on the Illegal Migration into Assam 1998, p. 296.
2. *Ibid.*, p. 297.
3. *Ibid.*

4. *Ibid.*

5. Article on the Constitutional safeguards of Indigenous people: A Burning Issue of Assam today by R. C. Borpatragohain, p. 1.

6. *Ibid.*

7. *Ibid.*, p. 2.

8. *Ibid.*, p. 3.

9. Supra note 1, p. 301.

10. Judgement of the Case *Sarbananda Sonowal vs Union of India (2005).*

11. Notification No. 10, 1948 New Delhi signed by D. Dantiyagi, Ministry of Relief and Rehabilitation.

12. Election Commission of India's report on Assam Elecions, 1983.

13. Some of the documents cited elsewhere are from Foreigner's Problem Published by AASU 1983, Guwahati supra note 5 pp.71-72.

14. T.S. Murty, 1983 Assam in difficult years, New Delhi, p. 288 supra note 5 p. 80.

15. Supra note 5, p. 516.

16. Supra note 5, p. 2.

17. Assam Tribune, Jan 18, 2009, p. 6.

18. Supra note 1, p. 305.

19. Supra note 1, p. 306.

20. *Ibid.*

21. Supra note 10, p. 3.

22. *Ibid.*

23. Supra note 1, p. 304.

24. Supra note 1, p. 305.

25. *Ibid*, p. 306.

26. Supra note 16, p. 10.

27. The IM(DT) Act, 1983—A Report to the Nation, Swaraj Mission, Guwahati, p. 82.

28. *Ibid.*, p. 1.

29. *Ibid.*, pp. 14, 15.

30. Supra note 10, p. 34.

31. *Ibid.*

32. 1991(3) SCC 554.

33. *Ibid.*

34. 200013/WP.

35. Assam Tribune, March 28, 2009.

36. *Ibid.*

37. Assam Tribune Feb 16, 2009, p. 6.

38. *In Introduction to International Law* by J. G. Starke (ch.18), it is said that?

39. Supra note 10, p. 31.

40. UN Human Rights Committee Report, para 23, CCPR/C-10/Add. 8, Geneva

41. Supra note 1, p. 319.

42. The Supreme Court of India in *Sarbananda Sonowal vs Union of India* (2005) declared the 'Illegal Migrants (Determination by Tribunal) Act, 1983' as unconstitutional.

31

Managing Assam's Tourism Development

M.P. Bezbaruah, IAS (Retd.)

Background

While discussing the role of tourism in economical development of Assam, some basic issues should be kept in mind. First, tourism is primarily a means to an end and not an end in itself. And that end is public welfare. That is why 'people' are so crucial to any discussion on tourism. Therefore, the role of tourism should be seen in the background of the overall socio-economic parameters of the place. Tourism should be an input integrated into the development planning of the place, integrated with the many sectors on which the success of tourism depends. It is often an important input in the development process of a place. At the same time, because of the multi-disciplinary nature of tourism, projecting it as the only panacea for the economic ills would be inaccurate.

It is also useful to view the situation in Assam in the context of the overall situation in the NE. The 'NE Region Vision 2020' of the Ministry of DONER and the NEC clearly points out that the economic picture is worrisome. The region, with 39 million people (at the time of the Report) 86 per cent of whom are in rural areas, has 97 per cent of the land under food grains cultivation. However, agricultural productivity is low and the region imports large quantities of foodgrains. At the time of independence the region had average SGDP four per cent above the national average GDP. After 50 years of development planning the average SGDP has fallen to 31 per cent below the national average. Other important indicators like MMR and IMR are shockingly above the national average. The process of catching up will require increasing the growth rate from the present rate of four per cent to about 16 per cent by the 13th Plan and will require capital investment of around Rs 13 lakh crore. It is a daunting task and need a growth strategy which is focussed and multi-pronged. The

Vision document and many other expert reports including the Assam Development Report of the Planning Commission argue for a strategy which takes into account the "comparative advantage" of the region. Assam and the region have immense tourism potential and therefore sustainable tourism should be at the core of the development agenda.

More important, the economic situation also indicates the type of tourism that should be promoted—tourism based on exploitation of the rural resources, tourism linked to the great craft and cultural traditions of the region, tourism that helps the large number of women who are engaged in the creation of beautiful handlooms. The region has 50 per cent of the looms of the country and 95 per cent of the weavers in NE are women. NE has a strong bamboo culture—lifestyle of people revolving around the masterly weaves in cane and bamboo. The vision document refers to a UNIDO report that exploitation of bamboo can give the region Rs 5000 crore in the next 10 years. Sample Surveys by the Ministry of Tourism in Kerala and Rajasthan have established that 90 to 95 per cent of the income of artisans came from tourism and the earnings went up many times during peak tourism seasons. UNWTO and EU surveys have shown that 30 per cent of the international tourists travel solely for cultural experiences. What a treasure house we have still unexploited!

The potential is known and there are many plans to exploit the acknowledged potential. Yet like the story in Alice in Wonderland we seem to be running faster to remain in the same place. Many questions arise. Is the approach to tourism development professional? Are the policy-makers convinced of the role that tourism can play in development and poverty eradication? Do they give tourism its due in the planning process or tourism is pursued as a stand alone activity?

Proper planning implies a proper management approach. If tourism is to be treated as a 'raw material' for development the approach would be basically three-fold. First, an accurate assessment of the resources. Second, creating organisational capacity to harness the resources. And third, finding the financial resources to develop tourism.

Government of India has called the region a 'paradise unexplored'. But planning must start with more concrete data and not on broad generalisation. It will be useful to have a benchmark survey of what we have, so that we can categorise them according to our perceived importance and availability of financial resources. The focus of tourism development in Assam generally has been on the tangible and physical heritage and resources, rarely going beyond that to the depth of invaluable intangible heritage of music, dance, cuisine, folklore, lifestyle—traditions that can provide the "unique experience" that the tourists look for.

Numbers certainly are not the most important factors in tourism development—but they are important. They help in policy formulations as indicators. The numbers for NE and Assam are dismal. NE received only 53 lakh domestic visitors (as distinct from arrivals) against the national total of 7402 lakh and 48000 foreign visitors against 178 lakh for the whole country. Assam's share of the total foreign tourist visits is only eight per cent.

Certainly, the statistics can have many loopholes. Assam must decide on the type of tourists it would like to attract and the rest of the policy will follow. But in any case if we have to progress from the dismal numbers we will need to do a lot on infrastructure development. For example, availability of accommodation in the region and in Assam according to the figures cited by the Ministry of Tourism is pathetic. There are only 1752 hotel rooms as against the all India figure of 1, 18,000 rooms in recognised hotels category. Assam has only five such recognised hotels with total of 151rooms. Most certainly there are many more hotels and rooms in the state but apparently they are not evaluated for recognition for star category by the government. There is therefore no quality audit of the most important requirement for tourist flow—decent accommodation.

Lot of improvements in tourism infrastructure is required. But tourism is primarily a private sector driven industry. It is necessary for the governments to come out with specific PPP initiatives. It is also necessary to devise suitable and pragmatic land policies. The NEIPP 2007 has outlined incentives for entrepreneurs. It is necessary to take stock – how investor friendly is its implementation? What progress it has made? The Assam Tourism Policy has mentioned some excellent initiatives like –reimbursement of value added tax, luxury tax, State Capital Investment Subsidy, etc. Are they operational?

There are many areas in which PPP can play a pivotal role. Good tourist transport is practically non-existent. The abundance of water bodies and rivers that we have can be harnessed to make water sports a major attraction. Amusement parks, similarly, have immense potential. Lot can be done imaginatively to exploit the grand beauty of the majestic Brahmaputra and to develop Guwahati—gateway to the NE, as the most beautiful city in the country. And with the growing interest in the NE and the likely flow of investment into the region, it will be good opportunity to position the region as an attractive MICE destination. With a little bit of imagination and with a bit of 'will' Assam and the NE can be transformed through development of sustainable tourism.

We should begin the journey at the end, i.e., implementation, and end with implementation alone.

A Global Overview

At the beginning of the twenty-first century tourism had established itself as the biggest industry in the world. The journey of tourism over the past 50 years is fascinating and is considered to be one of the most notable developments of our times. United Nations World Tourism Organisation (UNWTO) has reported that the inflation adjusted income from international travel has grown at a staggering average of 11 per cent a year since 1950. In 1950 when UNWTO first started keeping statistics of international tourist arrivals there were just 25 million international arrivals. It has grown to 808 million in 2005- the average annual growth has been more than 6.5 per cent for more than half a century. According to UNWTO the growth in receipts from tourism has been almost double of the growth in arrival. The growth rate is much higher than the growth of the world economy as a whole. Tourism now accounts for a quarter of all export in services—the share increases to

40 per cent if the air transport revenues are also included. Tourism is on course to achieve the projected 1.6 billion tourist arrivals by 2020 creating $2000 billion in tourism revenues—a staggering $500 million a day.

Yet, such phenomenal growth does not fully reflect the total economic impact and future potential of tourism. It is reported that only about seven per cent of the total population capable of travelling are actually travelling at present. The statistics also cannot capture the full range of tourism's contribution to employment, poverty alleviation and other economic activities. Tourism creates widespread "ripple effects" across various economic activities in the society-statistics cannot fully reflect all of them. For example, in India most of such activities were clubbed under "invisibles" in the budgetary classification. The World Travel and Tourism Council (WTTC) have estimated that there are about 30 activities at the core of the tourism business of which only three to four are generally accounted for. According to WTTC we see only the tip of an economic iceberg and the main tourism activities remain hidden.

Why Tourism

The contribution of tourism is so widely recognised that it is hardly necessary to elaborate on them. However, it is worthwhile to briefly recount some of them. In recent times the focus of tourism development has shifted to areas of sustainability and its role in poverty alleviation. The UN General Assembly adopted a resolution recognising his role and the recent meeting of G-7 countries reiterated their faith in tourism as a tool for economic development. UNWTO has been spearheading campaign to create awareness about the potential of tourism to contribute to the top UN Millennium Goal of eradicating poverty. UNWTO has listed some of the wider contributions of tourism as follows;

- Tourism has very high multiplier effect on other economic activities providing jobs and income. The supply chain sustaining tourism activities is long and diverse. Therefore income and employment creation is extensive.
- It is labour intensive. It can create supplementary income in the rural areas and is particularly suitable for employment of women.
- Infrastructure essential for tourism development like transport, communication, water supply and health services also benefits local communities.
- Properly managed, sustainable tourism helps to create awareness about natural and cultural and environmental preservation.

Agriculture	44.7
Manufacturing	12.6
Mining and quarrying	2.6
Railways	0.9
Other Transport	13.8
Tourism	47.5
Hotel and Restaurants	89.0

• It creates opportunities for small and micro enterprises and is an industry with very low start up costs and low entry barriers.

It is pertinent to mention an oft quoted sample survey of the Ministry of Tourism of India which showed that for every million rupees invested (at 1985-86 prices) employment creation in tourism sector was the highest.

Elements of a Pragmatic Strategy

If the role of tourism in the development planning is accepted, the next step is to integrate tourism planning into the planning process. The Assam Development Report (ADR) prepared for the Planning Commission of India by the eminent economist, Mr Kirit Parikh succinctly explains the requirement of such a strategy. It recommends that;

(1) The development strategy should be based on the specific advantage of the place in natural resources;

(2) The development process should be participatory—involving the community as well as the private sector;

(3) Core growth sectors should be identified and thrust should be given to such sectors;

(4) In the identification process, "priority should be given to those sectors, which have both comparative advantage and high linkages with other sectors"

(5) Government has an important role to play and good governance should be part of the overall strategy;

(6) Sound fiscal management is an integral part of the strategy.

Tourism fulfills these requirements. And appropriately, the Assam Development Report mentions tourism as one of the eight thrust areas for the new development planning strategy. Some broad structures of the possible strategy for tourism development are enumerated below.

Perception: It is essential to start with a correct perception about the role of tourism in economic development. The first task of the governments should be to create awareness about the place of tourism in general and of sustainable tourism in particular in the development process.

Priority: But such awareness creation efforts can start only when the governments themselves are convinced of tourism's importance and provide it due priority in the planning process. Tourism should be moved from periphery to the core of planning process.

The starting point-domestic tourism: Domestic tourism plays a very key role in Indian tourism. Internationally the ratio between foreign tourist and domestic tourist is about 1:7. In India the ratio is about 1:80. Assam has a very insignificant share of this huge number of tourists who contribute to employment and income generation in other states. Movement of domestic tourists will slowly improve the image of the place, and help in removing wrong perception about security and safety. The demand created by domestic tourist flows will lead to development of essential infrastructure. This process will then facilitate movement of foreign tourists who normally expect a higher standard of infrastructure.

Creating an experience—building infrastructure: The modern tourists are mostly looking for new experiences and that is the area in which NE has an advantage over others. To create a good experience for the tourists, infrastructure will have to be developed in—

- Accommodation,
- Roads and other communication,
- Way side facilities,
- Transport,
- Product development and destination management, and
- Information-guides etc.

In many of these areas, it is necessary to develop models of PPP and provide incentives to the private sector to invest effectively.

A Definite Policy: The first requirement is to move away from ad hoc measures in tourism to a definite plan of action and direction of future movement. A pragmatic tourism policy not couched in general terms but clearly charting a plan of action indicating the government's commitment to sustainable tourism is the first step of this journey. The policy should, among other things identify the place assigned to tourism in the broad development planning, the role of government and of the other key players, the organisational pattern to implement the policy and a system of monitoring and accountability. Luckily Assam has adopted a tourism policy which outlines governments thinking and commitment.

An Integrated Policy: Tourism policy would remain the wish list of the tourism department alone unless it reflects total government commitment. Tourism being a multi-dimensional activity, depends on the involvement of the other departments for its success. Two types of integration are necessary—

1. Vertical—among all the service providers within the tourism sector.
2. Horizontal—integration with all other sectors like roads, culture, forests etc who make the total tourism experience possible.

Quite often the integration within the department is fragmented, having too many channels of command, leading to overlapping of jurisdiction and inefficiency in performance. The first requirement of any professional management is putting in place an appropriate organization which can deliver the goals.

For achieving maximum coordination, institutional arrangements should be put in place–the ideal arrangement being an effective policy planning and implementation Board under the chairmanship of the Chief Minister.

Organisational Structure to Implement the Policy: Most well intentioned policies fail due to weakness in implementation. Weaknesses in implementation arise when the organisation in place is insufficient to achieve the desired objectives. To implement the tourism policy professionally Assam needs a tourism organisation which is professionally managed, capable of taking quick decisions and is accountable. In the pattern suggested by the landmark report of the Yunis Committee an Autonomous Tourism Development Board with private sector participation should be considered. It should have a high profile, ideally being chaired by the Chief Minister and should include representatives

of key departments of the government, so that interdepartmental coordination can be achieved quickly.

How to meet the resource gap? Infrastructure development would require a lot of attention if tourism has to grow at a fast rate and has to become competitive. In the context of very competing demands for the limited resources of the state, new initiatives on the tourism sector may suffer from financial constraints. For example, the Assam Development Report has assessed that to achieve a growth rate of six per cent in the economy the quantum of investment required in the Trade, Hotels and Restaurants sector would be around Rs 7984 crore. As such levels of investment are not available, the normal reaction would be to forget about the idea. However, pragmatic thinking may find possible solutions to the problems of resources. In this connection, a comprehensive approach involving the following guidelines are suggested—

1. *A benchmark survey of tourism assets*: The general approach to tourism planning has been ad hoc because there is no comprehensive assessment of the resources and the potential. Tourism planning should start with a benchmark survey in each district of the tourism potential of the area. The survey should identify and classify the tourism products according to their importance into three categories—local, regional and national and international.

2. *Prioritise—a selective approach*: Because of the compulsions of the democratic governance system, there is a tendency to take up too many schemes in a routine unimaginative manner to satisfy local aspirations. As a result the investments fail to have any visible effect and impact. Instead, the source of funding of tourism projects and the quantum should depend on the relative importance from the point of view of the tourists. The projects which satisfy primarily local demand should be included in the District Development Plans. The schemes of regional importance should be included in the state plan schemes and those which are of national and international importance should be taken up with the assistance of the national government and international agencies. A Master Plan for these schemes should be prepared and allocation of fund should be based on the integrated plan of development.

Naturally, a comprehensive strategy would also require that the governments allot more fund than they are doing at present for tourism development. A planned and integrated approach would mean that with the available resources more effective investments can be made.

3. *Tourism focus in other department's schemes:* A tourism product cannot be developed by the tourism department alone. There should be general government policy that in respect of the identified areas and schemes, the other departments like roads, forest and culture should give relative priority to tourism components in their schemes.

4. *Build partnership with the private sector:* Tourism is primarily a private sector driven industry. A dynamic private sector can reduce the pressure on the government by taking on a lot of activities for tourism development. The concept of partnership is much wider than the commonly used expression of private participation. It implies a system of formalised cooperation between the government and private sectors where the partners share responsibilities,

resources, risks and rewards. Unfortunately private initiatives in the tourism sector have been negligible. The nature of partnership varies from country to country. The nature of partnership also is not limited to any particular areas and would depend on the local requirements and initiatives of the planners. Some of the areas where such partnership can be very meaningful are:

(a) Financing of new infrastructure projects-hotels, transport;

(b) Evolving a modern, focussed, comprehensive and intensive marketing collaboration;

(c) Collaborating in human resource development;

(d) Sharing development, beautification and maintenance of various tourism products;

(e) Participating in the preservation of the heritage;

(f) Providing leadership in creating awareness about sustainable norms by adopting good practices in the industry.

Prepare an ecology map: To ensure that mismanaged tourism does not damage eco-system and environment, government has to play a resolute and definite role. Synergy can be achieved only when the approach is systematic and planned. For this purpose—(a) Assam should prepare an ecology map of the possible tourism destinations and zones. The zones should be graded according to the fragility of the eco-system. (b) The nature of tourism planning will depend on the degree of fragility of the eco-system. Areas which are very fragile may even be closed to mass tourism and developed only for special interest group tourism like adventure tourism. (c) In other words, tourism development in these identified areas should depend on two factors—carrying capacity studies and environmental impact assessment studies. Any product development in these areas should be preceded by a project appraisal which includes these studies.

Design architectural norms: Architecture is part of the cultural heritage of a place. Unimaginative construction may not only spoil the tradition of the place but can also adversely affect the ecology of the place. Architecture should suit the local conditions and should blend with the environment around. Construction practices without any concern for aesthetics have been the bane of most hilly areas which have beautiful designs coming down the centuries. It would be useful for Assam to develop an architectural code that embodies the heritage of the place, takes into account the ecological and aesthetic requirements and blends tradition with modern needs, based on local skills and are functionally efficient. Government should make such a code obligatory for any new construction.

Legal and institutional framework for sustainable tourism: Even though there are plenty of regulations for the preservation and control of the environment both at the state level and at the Centre, many of them have become quite obsolete and irrelevant. Many of them do not address the emerging problems of the present day nor do they offer modern solutions. In most case implementation is slack and often they are implemented in isolation, often too rigidly by the controlling department without proper appreciation of the spin off problems created for other sectors. Government should therefore

put in place a set of pragmatic legislations which are in tune with the general government policy, and which can be easily implemented. In particular the states and the center should—

(a) Make an inventory of all the existing legislations on environmental issues;

(b) Weed out the obsolete ones;

(c) Frame new legislations which cover areas hitherto uncovered and reflect regional variations and avoid stereotype rigidity in implementation;

(d) Ensure strict implementation;

(e) For most effective implementation, public support should be enlisted by setting up monitoring mechanism involving the public.

Participatory implementation is the only solution to the problem of environmental protection and departmental coordination is the basic requirement for its success. The WTO has drawn up extensive action agenda for sustainable tourism in the form of Code of Ethics. It will be useful for the governments of the NE to adopt the basic issues of the Code and give it wide publicity.

Creating institutions for people's participation: "A mistake made by the community is thousand times better than a solution imposed by an expert." (Mexican proverb). We have seen that intergenerational well-being of the people is a fundamental objective of sustainable development. The local community should therefore be actively involved in planning tourism and also in sharing the benefits of tourism. Agenda 21 had recommended formation of local Agenda 21 committees and in many parts of the world such local committees have been formed and local agenda have been drawn up. It would be ideal if such local agenda can be integrated into the Panchayati Raj system.

Even if such elaborate arrangements, though desirable, cannot be immediately put in place, government should ensure people's participation by forming local advisory committees for tourism wherever prominent tourism attractions exist and also having such committees at the state level. Such arrangements will give a sense of belonging to the people and will improve the efficiency of operations of projects and tourism products.

Planning Sustainable Tourism for The poor—The Triple Bottom Line: Sometimes pre-occupation with sustainability issues tend to take attention away from the problems of the poor affected by such concerns. It is important to keep in mind the crucial importance of providing economic alternatives to the poor while planning sustainability. The triple bottom line sums up the components of such an approach—

- Environmental—ecological harmony
- Social—equity, empowerment, capacity building

Sustainable tourism to be pro-poor should be properly guided with the participation of the beneficiaries. UNWTO has identified 12 criteria which should be kept in mind while planning pro poor sustainable tourism—

1. Economic viability,
2. Local prosperity,
3. Employment Quality,

4. Social Equity,
5. Visitor Fulfilment,
6. Local Control,
7. Community well-being,
8. Cultural Richness,
9. Physical Integrity,
10. Biological Diversity,
11. Resource Efficiency, and
12. Environmental Purity.

In planning sustainable tourism that benefits the poor it is necessary to look for solutions that are of relevance to local needs and problems. Innovations and out of the box solutions lead to more success. Innovations should be a continuous part of the planning process-in transforming the production and consumption patterns and technology, institutions and policies. It is not the responsibility of government agencies alone. Experience has shown that initiatives outside the government can lead to spectacular results. The "Barefoot College" is such an Indian example based on the belief that solutions to rural problems lie within the community. It uses traditional knowledge to achieve objectives that government methods cannot reach and 100,000 people in 110 villages have access to safe drinking water, education, health and employment on their own efforts.

Human Resource Development: Tourism is a service industry and therefore the quality of the service makes a substantial difference in the demand for the tourism product. Human resource development should therefore be an important part of the future strategy for tourism development in the region. It will also be in tune with the objective of employment generation through tourism.

Sustainable tourism in particular depends on awareness and understanding, both of the tourist as well as the host community. The tourist has to be educated on the cultural ethos and the ecological concerns of the community. The human resource development should encompass training of all people who come to contact with the tourist at the cutting edge level like the tour operators, the travel agents, the tour guides, the taxi drivers all ranges of tourism managers who can educate the tourist.

NE Tourism Master Plan

The Ministry of DONER has sponsored the preparation of a tourism Master Plan for the region and presumably government will pursue the implementation of this plan. It is therefore relevant to have a look at the basic approach adopted in the Master Plan. It identifies the major challenges as experienced by the tourists as follows.

- High travel cost,
- Lack of infrastructure support,
- Security concern,
- Lack of linkages between the tour operators of NE with the rest of India.

The Master Plan therefore identifies the major issues for action under four heads—

- Resource related
- Development related—accessibility, infrastructure, tourist amenities and information system
- Management related—safety, lack of quality tourism service providers, institutional and policy framework, absence of visitor management plan
- Environmental issues.

The Master Plan proposes to tackle these issues by taking action on infrastructure development, creating conducive environment and giving attention to issues of security, ensuring community involvement, creating capacity for all the stake-holders and initiating policies for incentives for the private sector.

The Assam Tourism Policy

It is heartening to note that the Tourism Policy which indicates government thinking on the future directions, reflect most of the concerns mentioned above. The vision and the objective state.

"The Tourism Vision of the State is to manage its comparative advantage in tourism resources and attractions in a sustainable, sustained and integrated manner to make Assam a major national and international tourism destination so that tourism enriches the quality of life and culture of the people and becomes an important catalyst for economic development in general and for poverty alleviation in particular."

The broad objectives of the Tourism Policy are:

- To make tourism an important tool for socio-economic development of the state and place the tourism sector on a high priority in the economic development of the State.
- To fully harness the tourism potential of the State in such a manner that tourism becomes environmentally sustainable, socio-culturally enriching and economically beneficial to the people in all parts of the state.
- To create awareness among the people about the importance of tourism and evolve suitable institutional arrangements for effective participation of the people in promoting tourism, sharing the benefits and in developing a tourism friendly environment.
- To improve the quality of the existing tourism products to meet the new and emerging demands of tourists and to enable them to have "unique experiences" that they look for.
- To promote adequate and comprehensive development of infrastructure of international standards.
- To devise pragmatic and long term Human Resource Development programmes to create capacity for the local people to take advantage of the opportunities offered by tourism development.
- The strategy proposed is a focussed, planned and prioritised development where domestic tourism plays, as it should, a leading role. It identifies wildlife tourism, river and adventure tourism, tea, golf and nostalgia tourism, cultural and heritage tourism, rural tourism, mice tourism as the key

components of development strategy and recommends suitable incentives to encourage the private sector.

A policy only indicates the government's thinking about the future road map. Its relevance depends on the way a policy is implemented. It appears that in the last four years the incentive schemes have not been formulated. Many other components of the policy also remain unfulfilled. Assam tourism should devote its entire attention to implementation of its avowed objectives. Therefore, the constant reminder could be the words of Albert Camus—"I will tell you a secret my friend. Don't wait for the Day of Judgment. It takes place everyday".

The article incorporates my earlier writings and presentations like:

1. Seminar on "Tourism as an Engine of Growth" by Assam Management Association at Guwahati 18.08.10.

2. Article 'Sustainable Tourism and Economic Development of the NE' in the book 'Challenges of Development in NE India' published on behalf of Indian Council of Social Science Research).

3. "NE Development Trends and Role of Tourism" lecture in Administrative Staff College of India.

32

Economic Development of Assam by Proper Utilisation of Oil and Gas Resources, Related Infrastructure, and Trained Manpower

J.M. Bujor Baruah

Background

The birth place of the Petroleum Industry of India is Assam. AR and T (Assam Railway and Trading Company) made the first discovery of an oil-field in Assam at Digboi in the foot-hills of the Naga-Patkoi range in the north-eastern part of the Upper Assam valley during the year 1889. The Digboi oil-field was discovered on the basis of drilling of a shallow well near a surface seepage of oil. The oil accumulations of the Digboi oil-field were in sandstone reservoirs of the Tipam formation of Miocene age. The oil accumulations in the field are in structural traps-anticlines developed on the supra thrust beds associated with the Naga thrust.

The extent of the field was determined by drilling a large number of follow-up wells by AOC (Assam Oil Company Limited), a subsidiary of AR and T Company, based on surface geological mapping. The field development activities got a definite thrust after the take-over of AOC by BOC (Burmah Oil Company Limited) of the UK in early 1920s.

The oil production rate from the Digboi oil-field was gradually built upto a level of about 0.25 mtpa. At the time of independence of India in 1947, Digboi was the only oil-field in India. The crude oil produced from the field was processed in the Digboi refinery built by AOC near the oil field.

Major Expansion of Oil and Gas Industry in Assam During 1950-1970

With the development of the techniques of carrying out surface geophysical surveys like seismic reflection surveys, the hydrocarbon industry

got a method of deciphering sub-surface geology prior to drilling even in concealed areas. Use of geophysical techniques led to the discovery of oil in the Alluvium covered Upper Assam valley, and independent India's first major oil discovery was made at Nahokatiya in the Oligocene formation in the year 1953. This major discovery was made by AOC. Nahorkatiya had a plateau production rate of about 2.25 million tonnes per annum, and helped to increase domestic crude oil production of Assam by about ten times. The field is still on production, but the level of production has come down after the onset of permanent decline in early 1980s. The current oil production of the field is from the successful Enhanced Oil Recovery projects implemented in the field over the years.

The major discovery of Nahorkatiya oil-field in 1953 and subsequent discovery of Moran oil-field in 1956 with a plateau production rate of about 0.75 mtpa led the Government of India to get into the oil business actively. Oil India Limited was formed in 1959 as a joint-venture between the Government of India and the Burmah Oil Company of U.K. for development and operation of Nahorkatiya and Moran oil-fields and for extending exploration activities to the adjoining areas of Upper Assam and Arunachal Pradesh.

Meanwhile, two oil refineries were set up to process the additional crude oil produced from the new oil-fields by a new company, Indian Refineries Limited – a Government of India company. One of the refineries was the Guwahati Refinery in Assam and the other was Barauni Refinery in Bihar. For transporting the crude oil from the Upper Assam oil fields, a trunk pipe-line connecting Duliajan, the field head quarters of Oil India Limited near Nahorkatiya in Upper Assam and Barauni in Bihar was built by the Burmah Oil Company of the UK. The pipe-line was handed over to Oil India Limited in 1962 for operation and maintenance.

Another company was formed by the Government of India, Indian Oil Company Limited in early 1960s in order to market the petroleum products produced in Guwahati and Barauni refineries.

In the meantime, Oil and Natural Commission (ONGC) was formed by carving out the Directorate of oil of the Geological Survry of India for carrying out petroleum exploration activities throught the country including Assam areas not allotted to Oil India Limited. ONGC discovered Rudrasagar, Lakwa, and Geleki oil fields in the western part of the Upper Assam valley in the 1960s.

In Nahorkatiya, Moran, and Rudrasagar fields, Barail sands of Oligocene age are the main oil reservoirs, while in Lakwa and Geleki fields, Tipam sands of Miocene age are the main oil reservoirs.

After these hectic activities of the 1960s, there was a period of consolidation. During this period, the down-stream oil companies (Indian Refineries Limited and Indian Oil Company Limited) were merged and Indian Oil Corporation Limited (IOC) was formed. At the same time, the ONGC oil-fields of Assam were developed.

For proper utilisation of Associated natural gas produced along with crude oil, a fertilizer plant was set up at Namrup, about 30-km south-west of Duliajan, by HFCL (Hindustan Fertilizer Corporation Limited), a Government

of India Company for production of Urea and Ammonia. The Namrup Fertilizer Complex has been re-named as BVFCL (Brahmaputra Valley Fertilizer Corporation Limited) after bifurcation of HFCL with effect from April, 2002.

Simultaneously, a gas-based Power Plant was built by the Assam State Electricity Board at Namrup. At present, the Namrup Thermal Power Plant has been transferred to the newly-formed APGCL (Assam Power Generation Company Limited).

Additionally, the Government of Assam formed a new company, Assam Petrochemicals Limited (APL) — for production of Methanol and Formaldehide at Namrup-based on natural gas. In order to transport natural gas from the oil fields of Nahorkatiya and Moran, a natural gas transportation company was also formed by the Government of Assam with Head Quarters at Duliajan and gas pipelines were laid connecting Duliajan-Namrup and Moran-Namrup.

Petroleum Value Chain

The composite petroleum business has four individual value chains as indicated below:

1. Up-stream value chain,
2. Down-stream value chain,
1. Natural gas value chain, and
2. Pero-Chemicals value chain.

The relationship amongst these value chains is explained in Figure below.

Up-stream Value Chain

The segments of the up-stream value chain are exploration, appraisal of a discovery, development of oil and gas fields, production of oil and gas, storage and transportation of crude oil, and distribution of natural gas.

Down-stream Value Chain

The typical down-stream value chain comprises refining of crude oil, primary distribution of petroleum products, storage in terminals, and marketing of petroleum products including pricing, distribution to bulk consumers and retailing.

Natural Gas Value Chain

Unlike crude oil, natural gas could be sold in the retail market directly. Natural gas is also extensively used for generation of electricity. Natural gas value chain comprises of transportation and marketing of gas, and generation/ sale of electricity. Besides these uses as energy, natural gas value chain includes the fractionation of natural gas into various components like methane, ethane, LPG, natural gas liquids, etc. Some of these fractions are valuable and preferred raw materials for the petrochemicals value chain.

Petro-chemicals Value Chain

Petro-chemicals value chain starts with processing of naphtha obtained as a crude oil refinery product and selected fractions of natural gas for the production of various value added chemicals. The major petrochemicals value

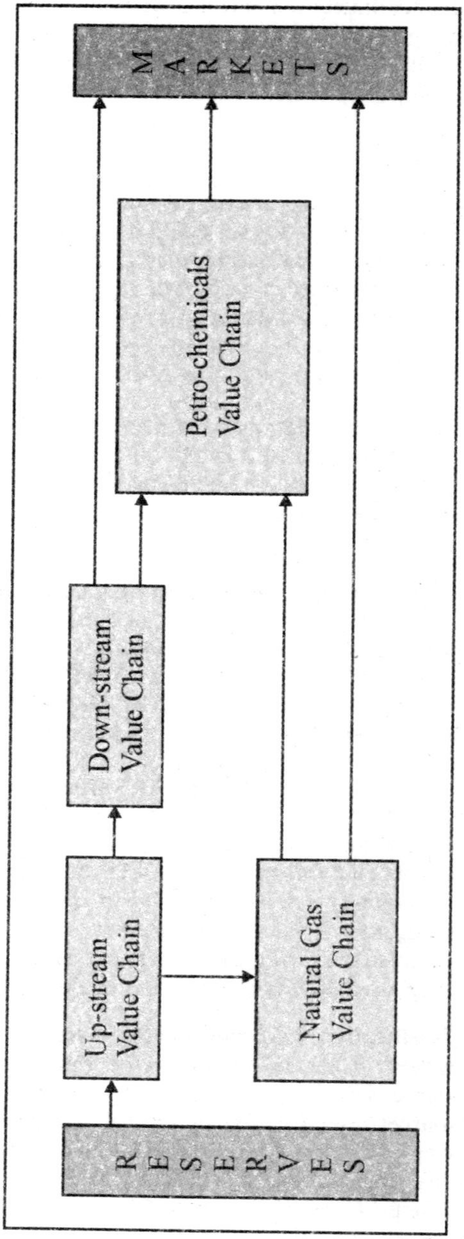

Value Chains in the Petroleum Business.

subchains relate to plastics, fabrics, and organic chemicals. Each of these subchains are long with several branches and will not be discussed here.

Special Features of Up-stream Petroleum Business

The up-stream business is highly risky. In addition to uncertainties with regard to underground reserves and production rates, E and P business is heavily dependent upon crude oil price, which fluctuates widely and does not follow typical market dynamics of demand–supply. Some of the factors contributing to price volatility of crude oil are areas of excess production being away from the areas of large consumption, excessive dependant on the OPEC (Organisation of Petroleum Exporting Countries) for supply, concentration of surplus availability in localised areas, wars/hostilities and other potential political changes/uncertainties in major oil producing areas like West Asia. The sharp increase in the demand for oil in the rapidly growing large economies of China and India has greatly reduced the surplus availability of crude oil. As a result, temporary shutdown of producing fields even outside the OPEC results in a near panic situation resulting in over-heating of the market.

However, increase in the availability of oil and gas from unconventional sources like shale oil, shale gas, and heavy oil is expected to significantly influence the petroleum industry in the foreseeable future. Increased availability of shale gas has already resulted in significant drop in the price of gas in the USA.

Asset values of an E and P company should ideally include all the assets that the company owns. Typically, these would include the producing fields, fields under development, and discoveries under appraisal, new discoveries, and exploration acreage. From the angle of risk and cash flow potential, the asset values may be classified as core values and upside potentials. The core values include producing fields and fields under development. Upside potential is far less certain and includes the contingent resources that may be currently un-economical or the discoveries whose commercial viability has not yet been determined. It is needless to state here that while determining the asset value of the company, the risk-weighted values are to be taken into account.

It is also to be noted that the E and P business is highly capital intensive and the time required for exploration, appraisal of a discovery, development of fields considered as commercial, and build-up of the surface facilities for production, processing, storage and transportation is usually very large. By the time production from the new areas becomes available, the older fields already on production from the basin could start decline.

Estimation and Classification of Oil and Gas Reserves

For any investment in the up-stream sector, proper understanding of under-ground resource is essential. The generally accepted classification of under-ground resources/reserves used by the oil and gas industry is outlined in the following paragraphs for an appreciation of the complexities.

The definitions adopted by SPE (Society of Petroleum Engineers), WPC (World Petroleum Congress), and AAPG (American Association of Petroleum Geologists) that are applicable to both discovered and un-discovered accumulations are outlined below:

• The quantities of petroleum estimated to be initially in-place in underground accumulations represent Total Petroleum Initially In-place. It contains both Discovered Petroleum Initially In-place and Un-discovered Petroleum Initially In-place.

• Undiscovered Petroleum Initially In-place consists of recoverable petroleum and un-recoverable petroleum. The recoverable part of the undiscovered petroleum initially in-place is known as Prospective Resources.

• Similarly, Discovered Petroleum Initially In-place consists of recoverable petroleum and the un-recoverable petroleum. The recoverable part of discovered petroleum in the known accumulations consists of produced petroleum, proved reserves, probable reserves, possible reserves and contingent resources.

Proved Reserves represents petroleum in known accumulations that are reasonably certain to be present and recoverable to a high degree of certainty and are recoverable under current economic conditions. Proved reserves may be developed or undeveloped.

Developed Proved Reserves may be producing or may be non-producing. Un-developed Proved Reserves should be such that the development plan is ready and is scheduled for implementation in the near future.

Probable Reserves and Possible Reserves include petroleum in known accumulation with variable degrees of geological uncertainty and may be recoverable under present or future economic conditions. However, there should be expectation that the accumulation would be appraised / developed within a reasonable time-frame.

Contingent Resources are potentially recoverable petroleum from known accumulations which are.

• Not likely to be developed within a reasonable time-frame as per current expectations.

• Directorate General of Hydrocarbons (DGH), who is the nodal agency of the Government of India, has notified these definitions for use in India in May, 2006 with the following modification:

• Discovered hydrocarbon which is considered as Contingent Resource in the SPE/WPC/AAPG classification is classified as Contingent Reserves under the DGH notification referred to above.

The reserves as classified above are related to the risk attached to the estimates. Proved Reserves represent the lowest risk, and Possible Reserves has the highest risk, with Probable Reserves occupying an intermediate position.

As per SPE/WPC definitions, if probabilistic method like Monte Carlo Simulation technique is used to estimate reserves,

• Highest risk, with Probable Reserves

• There should be at least 50 per cent probability that the quantities actually recovered will equal or exceed the sum of estimated Proved Reserves and Probable Reserves. (Proved plus Probable reserves together is referred to 2 P reserves) ; and

• There should be at least 10 per cent probability that the quantities actually recovered would equal or exceed the sum of estimated Proved Reserves,

Probable Reserves, and Possible Reserves (Proved plus Probable plus Possible reserves together is referred to as 3 P reserves).

The relation-ships between 1 P, 2P, and 3P Reserves are illustrated below considering actual oil and natural gas Reserves of Oil India Limited in Assam as on 01 April, 2011

	1P	*2P*	*3P*
Crude Oil (MMSKL)	42.83	91.16	136.19
Natural Gas (MMSKLOE)	33.88	55.47	78.44

The corresponding Proved Developed reserves oil and gas are 35.15 MMSKL and 33.88 MMSKLOE respectively.

Production Profile of an Oil Field

A typical production profile of an oil-field has three phases (see Figure) as follows :

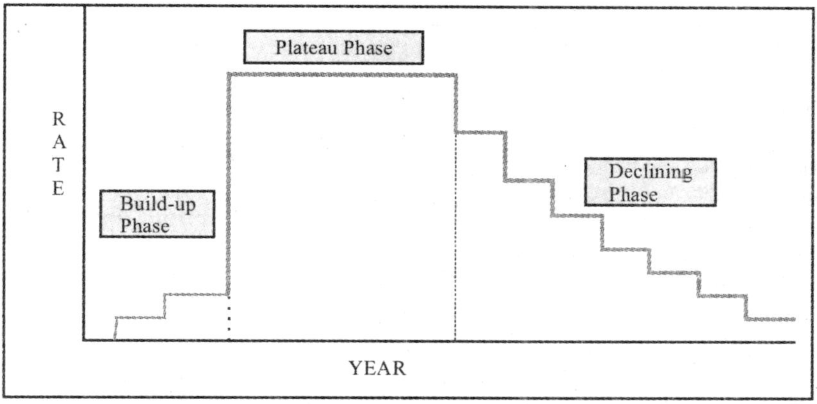

Typical Production Profile of an Oil Field.

About 50 per cent of the production takes place during the plateau production phase. The plateau production rate is about 1/11th to 1/15th of the reserves considered in the preparation of the production profile. This would translate to a plateau production period varying from 5.5 years to 7.5 years.

However, there could be significant variations depending upon various technical and economic factors. Some of the more important factors are—

- Cost of Development (Drilling Cost and Facilities Cost);
- Access to Market, and
- Political Risk Factors,

For example, in the cases of the North Sea fields, well productivity is high and the cost of development is also high. Usually, these fields have a short plateau and high peak production rate. Similarly, some of the on-land fields (e.g., of Russia) have evacuation constraints. The cost of development of some of these fields is also on the low side. Typically, such oil-fields have long plateau production period but low plateau production rate.

The plateau production phase of deep water off-shore fields usually have high production rate and short period. High investments required to develop these deep water off-shore fields demand that the returns are high in the initial period in order to improve project economics.

Plateau production rate as a per cent of initial recoverable reserves also vary on the following considerations:

(a) Oil-field *vis-a-vis* gas-field;
(b) Major fields *vis-a-vis* small / marginal fields;
(c) Onshore field vis-à-vis offshore field;
(d) Shallow water off-shore field vis-à-vis deep water offshore field.

Reserves to Production Ratio

Depletion rate of a field could also be worked out on the basis of R/P ratio. R/P ratio (Reserves to Production Ratio) of a field is the ratio of balance recoverable reserves at the end of the previous year (X – 1) and annual production of the current year (X).

In this connection, it is of interest to note that R/P ratio of oil fields having conventional crude oil varies widely from country to country from a low of around six in the case of the UK to a high of around 115 in the case of Kuwait.

R/P is the highest at the beginning of the plateau production phase. R/P ratio decreases fairly rapidly during the plateau production phase. During the subsequent declining phase of production, R/P ratio decreases slowly. R/P ratio is the lowest at the time of abandonment, when the rate of production is about 5-10 per cent of the plateau production rate.

Determination of production profile of a field is also dependent upon the Depletion Policy of a country, when such a policy exists.

Depletion policy of a country depends upon various parameters like self-sufficiency level in energy to sustain GDP growth, share of oil/gas revenue in GDP, sustainable level of development, etc. Considering various technical, economical, social, and political factors, the level of oil production from the countries with high R/P ratio could be increased by undertaking additional oil–field development activities in the already discovered oil- fields in the immediate context.

Indicative values of R/P ratios that may be considered for the first year of the plateau production phase of different types of fields are given in Table below:

Indicative Initial R/P Ratio of Different Types of Fields

Items	*Oil Fields*	*Gas Fields*
Major Fields		
Onshore	15	20
Offshore	11	15
Deep Offshore	7	11
Small/Marginal Fields	5	5

It must be clarified here that the above tabulation are meant primarily for showing the relative differences of R/P values of oil-fields of different types. Actual values could be different depending upon field specific techno-economic considerations.

Re-development/Uneven Plateau

In reality, it is often observed that the plateau production phase of a field has a number of peaks connected to different phases of Development and Re-development in the life of the field involving drilling of additional (in-fill) wells, adoption of secondary and/or tertiary recovery techniques, modification of artificial lift techniques, etc.

Important developments of oil-field drilling and production technology like drilling of horizontal wells, drilling of multi-lateral wells, field automation, etc., could help in extending the plateau production phase much beyond the original plan.

Declining Production Phase

Decline in the production rate of an oil-field may follow different patterns depending upon various reservoir rock and fluid parameters of the field. Prevailing reservoir drive has an important bearing on the decline trend as indicated below:

(a) A reservoir producing under depletion drive would follow a Hyperbolic Decline.

(b) A reservoir producing under an active natural water drive normally follows an exponential decline.

(c) A reservoir producing under pattern water flooding would tend to follow a Straight - line Decline.

Typical production profiles of oil-fields operating under different reservoir drives are indicated in Figure below.

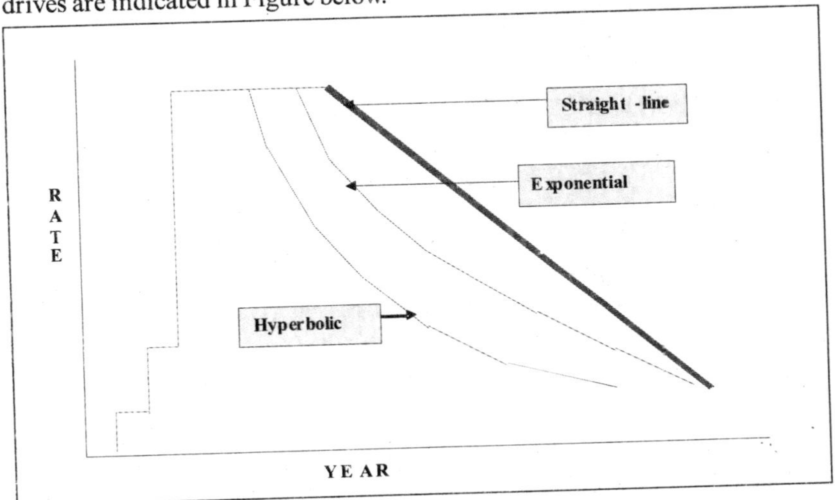

Different Types of Decline of Production in an Oil Field.

Extending the logic, a field producing under depletion drive and showing Hyperbolic Decline may show an Exponential Decline after start of water flooding to improve oil recovery.

The declining phase of an oil-field is normally long. In active water-drive reservoirs or in reservoirs under water-flooding, water production continues to rise as progressively larger parts of the oil reservoir are invaded by water. It is quite common to see oil-fields with over 95 per cent water cut yielding economic returns. Of late, fields are being developed with water cut reaching as high as 97.5 per cent. Exponential decline is the most common decline pattern in an ageing oil-field operating under the water drive / water flood.

Secondary Peaks in Production

As already mentioned, secondary peak in oil production rate is seen in fields where there is delay in implementation of IOR or EOR projects. Secondary peak in oil production rate of a field is also possible with adoption of new technology.

Improved reservoir characterisation and introduction of improved reservoir performance monitoring techniques like production logging, 4-D seismic, etc., could result in significant slowdown of the rate of decline and extension of the producing life of a field resulting in higher recovery of oil and gas.

New Discoveries in Assam After 1970

In the case of Upper Assam basin, the peak production rate of about 6.0 mtpa was achieved in the year 1989-90.

Several new discoveries have been made in the Upper Assam basin during 1970 and 2012. Majority of these discoveries are in the eastern part of the basin. The major new discoveries are as out-lined below:

- *1970-1979*: In Santi and Jaipur structures located to the east of Nahorkatiya oil-field in Barail sands of Oligocene age. In Kathalguri, Langkasi, Nagajan, and Jorajan area to the east of Sant-Jaipur. In Barail / Tipam sands of Oligocene and Miocene ages.
- *1980-1989:* In Shalmari area mid-way between Moran and Nahorkatiya and in Hapjan area north-east of zaloni area of Nahorkatiya oil-field in Barail sands of the Ologocene age.
- In Dikom structure north-west of Nahorkatiya in Lakadong + Therria sands of Eocene age and Langpar sands of Paleocene age.
- Dikom oil-field in Lakadong + Therria sands of Eocene age and Langpar sands of Paleocene age.
- In Makum and North Hapjan structures near Hapjan oil-field in Barail sands of Oligocene age.
- 2000-2012: In Chabua area near Tengakhat oil-field in Lakadong + Therria sands of Eocene age and in Langpar sands of Paleocene age.
- In Bhogpara structure west of Dikom oil-field in Lakadong + Therria sands of Eocene age and in Langpar sands of Paleocene age.
- In Barekuri, Baghjan, and Mechaki areas north-east of Makum oil-field in Lakadong + Therria sands of Eocene age and in Langpar sands of Paleocene age.

Latest Trends of Crude Oil and Natural Gas Production in Assam

The new discoveries have helped in partially off-setting the decline in production of the older fields which peaked in the year 1989-90. The oil production rate of the Upper Assam basin, which has been declining since early 1990s, has shown marginal increase during last few years as contribution from the new fields has exceeded the decline from the old fields.

Yearly production of crude oil and natural gas from the Upper Assam oil and gas fields since 2004-05 are shown in Table below for ease of reference.

Crude Oil and Natural Gas Production From Assam Oil and Gas Fields

Year	*Crude Oil (M MTPA)*	*Natural Gas (BCM / YR)*
2004-05	4.703	2.249
2005-06	4.474	2.408
2006-07	4.400	2.526
2007-08	4.357	2.598
2008-09	4.674	2.573
2009-10	4.740	2.703
2010-11	4.721	2.680
2011-12	5.025	2.905

Crude Oil Refining

In order to process the additional crude oil available from the Assam oil-fields of Oil India and ONGC, a new oil refinery and aromatics-based petro-chemicals plants (Paraxylene Plant, DMT Plant and PSF Plant) were set up at Bongaigaon in Lower Assam during 1974 - 1990. Indian Petro-chemicals Limited, a Government of India Company, was initially associated with the setting up of the new refinery and the petro-chemical plants. Subsequently, a new company-Bongaigaon Refinery and Petro-chemicals Limited was setup to complete the project and operate the plants.

Based on higher crude oil production potential forecast in the late eighties and in line with the Assam Accord of 1985, a three mtpa capacity refinery was set up at Numaligarh in the 1990s. The refinery was set up in the joint venture by Numaligarh Refineries Limited with equity participation from BPCL, OIL, and the Government of Assam.

In the mean-time, the refining capacity of the Bongaigaon Refinery was expanded from 1.35 mtpa to 2.35 mtpa. in the early 1990s. The control of the Bongaigaon refinery passed onto IOCL in the year 2001 after divestment of the Government of India shares to IOCL.

The old Digboi refinery which was attached to Indian Oil Corporation Limited after nationalisation of Assam Oil Company Limited in 1981, was modernised by IOC with an expansion of capacity to 0.65 mtpa.

Crude throu-put of the four Assam refineries since 2004-05 are as shown in Table below.

Crude Throughout of Assam Refineries

	IOC (G)	IOC (D)	IOC (B)	NRL
Installed Capacity	*1.000*	*0.650*	*2.350*	*3.000*
Year				
2004-05	1.002	0.651	2.311	2.042
2005-06	0.864	0.615	2.356	2.183
2006-07	0.839	0.586	2.067	2.504
2007-08	0.920	0.564	2.020	2.568
2008-09	1.076	0.623	2.163	2.251
2009-10	1.078	0.600	2.220	2.619
2010-11	1.118	0.651	2.008	2.252
2011-12	1.068	0.622	2.188	2.825

The main refinery products can be divided into three groups as indicated below:

Light Distillates : LPG, Petrol, Naphtha;
Middle Distillates : Kerosene, ATF, HSD, LDO;
Heavy End Product : Furnace oil, LSHS, Lube/ Grease;
Bitumen, RPC (Raw Petroleum Coke), CPC (Calcined Petroleum Coke), Paraffin Wax.

Marketing of Refinery Products

Marketing of the products of the Assam refineries is carried out by all the three national oil marketing companies, viz., IOCL (Indian Oil Corporation Limited) including AOD (Assam Oil Division), BPCL (Bharat Petroleum Corporation Limited), and HPCL (Hindustan Oil Corporation Limited). A significant part of majority of the POL products are moved out-side the state after meeting the local requirements.

Company-wise data on retail outlets of POL products, SKO / LDO dealer-ship, and LPG distributor-ship within Assam are given in Table 4 below:

Data on Company-wise Retail Outlets, SKO / LDO Dealership and LPG Distributorship in Assam

Items	*IOCL/AOD*	*BPCL*	*HPCL*	*Total*
Retail out-lets	474	43	72	589
SKO / LDO Dealer-ship	361	—	—	361
LPG Distributor-ship	241	26	17	284

Natural Gas Utilisation

The Upper Assam Basin is a relatively young sedimentary basin, where sedimentation started in the Paleocene age and continued through Eocene, Oligocene, Miocene, Pliocene, and Pleistocene until the recent period. The

basin is basically a clastic basin with limited deposition of carbonates in the Eocene period. Moreover, the temperature gradient of the basin is quite low in view of subduction of the Indian plate below the Tibetan plate.

Consequently, the basin has not attained the thermal stage of large scale gas generation by cracking of liquid hydrocarbons generated in the basin. This is evident from presence of oil reservoirs even at great depths of 5000-6000 m at Mechaki. Accordingly, the natural gas present in the basin is mainly solution gas and gas-cap gas associated with crude oil. There are only limited number of non-associated gas reservoirs whose production could be de-linked from oil production.

The associated gas produced along-with oil is often of low pressure needing compression in multiple stages. Assam Gas Company that transports the gas from the main producing areas to the main centre of gas utilisation at Namrup compresses the gas before transporting the same through their pipe-lines. In addition to generation of electricity and production of fertilizer and methanol at Namrup, electricity is generated at Lakwa by APGCL, and at Kathalguri by NEEPCO (North East Power Company Limited), a Government of India Enterprise.

Natural gas is also used by IOCL at Digboi refinery and by NRL at Numaligarh refinery for meeting fuel requirements. GAIL (India), which was formed by the Government of India in 1984 as the national carrier of gas through-out the country, transports gas from the Assam oil-fields of ONGC to the Lakwa Thermal Power Plant of APGCL.

Additionally, natural gas is being used by a large number (over 300) of tea gardens located in Upper Assam for tea processing in their factories. The tea gardens are connected to the oil-fields with a net-work of pipe-lines laid by the oil and gas producing companies as well as by Assam Gas Company.

Assam Gas Company is also business of city gas distribution at several major Upper Assam towns (e.g., Dibrugarh, Tinsukia, Sibsagar, Nahorkatiya, Duliajan, Digboi and Moran) located in the oil-field areas.

Natural gas is also being used by the oil companies for captive generation of electricity, and industrial fuel. Oil India Limited has also set up an LPG Recovery Plant at Duliajan, which produces about 45000 Tonnes of LPG per annum.

As a result of the multi-pronged approaches, about 96 per cent of the produced gas is being utilised. The remaining associated gas is available in very low pressures that could be used in a commercially viable manner if there are small gas utilisation centres in close vicinity of the producing centres (Oil Collecting Stations).

Consumption of gas in the major utilisation centres is approximately in the following proportions at present:

Power Generation	:	34 per cent
Fertilizer Production	:	24 per cent
Refinery Operations	:	17 per cent
Tea Processing	:	10 per cent
Petrochemicals	:	1.5 per cent
LPG and Internal use	:	9.5 per cent

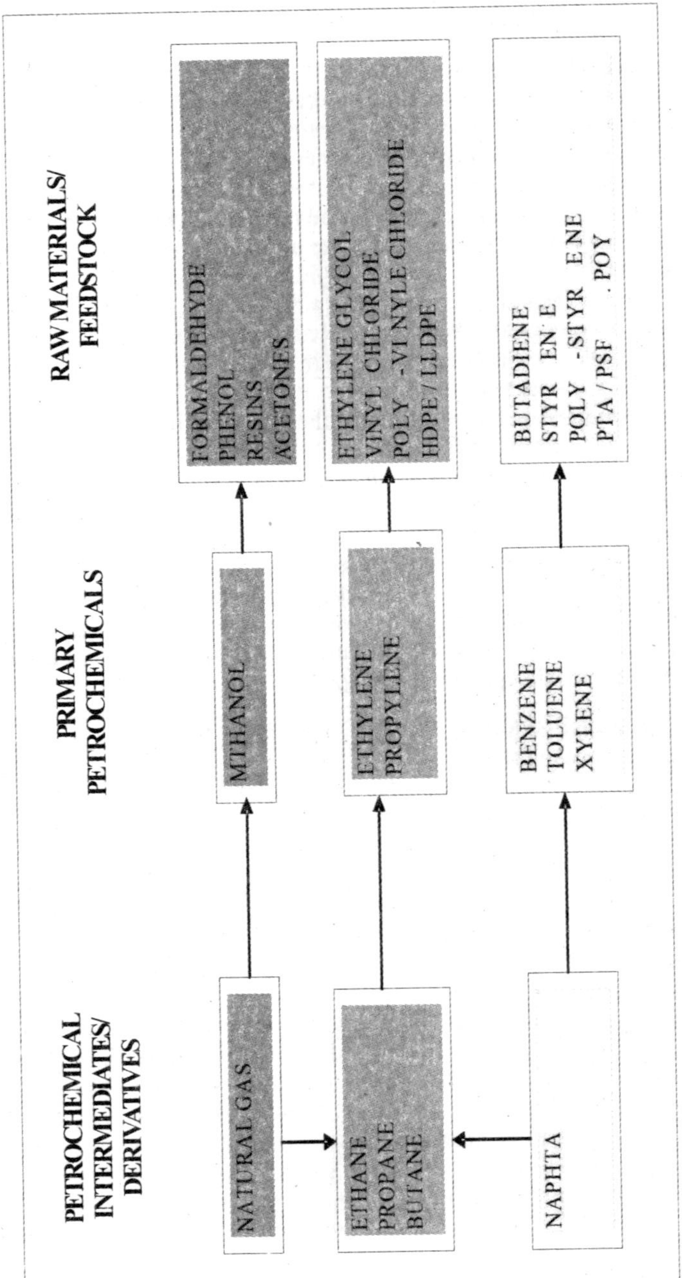

Petro-chemicals Value Chain.

At present a gas-cum naphta cracker plant is being set up near Dibrugarh in the vicinity of the oil and gas producing areas for production of petro-chemical products. The gas cracker plant will utilise about 1.35 MMSCMD of gas.

Petro-chemicals Industry

The Petro-chemicals value chain is very long. In Figure above, the main elements of the chain is presented to provide an insight to the immense possibilities of the Petro-chemicals business.

The petro-chemicals plant of APL (Assam Petrochemicals Limited) at Namrup is the only gas-based petrochemical plant in Assam. The main products of the Namrup Petro-chemical complex are Methanol and its derivative Formaldehyde.

The Assam crude oil is very suitable for production of petrochemicals (Aromatics). Therefore, the BRPL Refinery at Bongaigaon was integrated with petrochemical plants to produce Para-xylene, DMT (Dimethyl Terepthalate), and PSF (Polyester Staple Fibre) using naphta produced in the refinery. However, it is understood that the petro-chemical plants of the complex have been kept shut-in after merging BRPL with IOCL a few years ago after successful commercial operations for over a decade.

The BCPL Petrochemicals Plant at Lepetkata near Dibrugarh is designed to produce Olefins. The construction of the plant is nearing mechanical completion. The main products of the plant will be primary petro-chemical products Ethylene and Propylene, and petro-chemicals derivatives HDPE (High Density Poly Ethylene) and LLDPE (Linear Low Density Poly Ethylene). GAIL India will market the products of the plant amounting to 220000 tpa of HDPE and LLDPE, and 60000 tpa of Polypropiline.

Future Expansion Potential of Hydro-Carbon Industry in Assam

On overall consideration of the Upper Assam Basin being a Tertiary basin with relatively low geo-thermal gradient and absence of oil rich Type I source rocks, the potential for large oil or gas discovery appears to be limited. However, with sustained exploratory activities with adoption of modern technology, it should be possible to make moderate to small size discoveries. Adoption of modern techniques of formation fracturing and horizontal drilling should open up new plays in low permeability sands, silts, and oil shale. Accordingly, while big jump in production rates of oil and gas is less likely, it should be possible to extend the current or marginally higher rates of production for a long period.

As a consequence, it may not be possible to plan large scale additional capacity of oil refining or gas-based industry on the basis of supply of raw materials from Assam fields. However, oil and gas infrastructures built over last several decades and availability of trained man-power for conducting hydrocarbon exploration and production activities (including conducting seismic survey operations, drilling of oil and gas wells, servicing of old wells, designing and operations / management of Enhanced Oil Recovery projects, etc), and operation and maintenance of oil refineries, petro-chemical plants, and thermal power plants, etc are positive factors on which future expansion plans may be prepared.

While production of oil and gas from the Assam fields may have to be limited to a level of about 6 Million Tonnes per annum of crude oil and 4 billion SCUM per annum of natural gas, doubling the refining capacities of Numaligarh and Bongaigaon Refineries may be planned on the basis of crude oil to be transported from Haldia / Paradip after suitably expanding the capacity of the existing pipe-line network.

Similarly, natural gas may be brought to Bongaigaon / Guwahati from Bangladesh and to Numaligarh from Tripura by laying new gas pipe-lines. It should be noted that both the Tripura area and the adjoining areas of Bangladesh have large non-associated gas fields that await development.

Once availability of natural gas and naphta is ensured, large-scale expansion of the petro-chemicals industry can also be planned. Even on the basis of naphtha available from the existing refineries, there is scope for setting up a number of units for production of petro-chemicals as indicated below:

- Paraxylene, PTA, POY, PSF, PET, and PBT Plants.
- Benzene, Styrene, Poly-styrene, Phenol, and MEG Plants.

33

Reflections on Planning and Development

Hiren Gohain

The Chief Minister of Assam has declared time and again that Assam has undergone significant economic development, even though recent press-reports place the State on the 19th spot in the order of the degree of development attained. It is not clear what his criteria are. There have no doubt, plenty of changes in the economic scene, and in comparison with the past the amount of money that has been spent in the name of development seems to be enormous. If one looks around there seems to be more people with money in their pockets, and they are spending it on such consumer goods as cars, fridges, T.V. sets, expensive furniture, and electronic appliances of various sorts and so on. Going by statistics released by government sources, the figures are as follow:

	Percentage in Assam (2009-10)	*Percentage in India (2009-10)*
GDP Growth Rate	7.73	8
Poverty Rate	37	29.80
Ditto among Agriculture and Other Labour	76	80
Contribution of Industry to GDP	13.68	20.16
Contribution of Agriculture to GDP	24.44	14.62
Contribution of services to GDP	61.89	65.22

Source: India Human Development Report 2011, IAMR and Planning Commission.

Even if the record is not compared with that of advanced States in India, it is decidedly disappointing. There is some movement, but not enough to rid

the State of the traditional curse of poverty and lack of opportunities. Even though India is still counted as a developing State, Assam lags far behind the nation as a whole. And the picture has not changed for decades, in spite of the Centre pumping in more and more money.

For one thing, the state government does not seem to have a comprehensive view of the state's economy as a whole. To my surprise I failed to procure from the Directorate of Economic and Statistics copies of statistical handbooks it has been publishing every year since the seventies. It does not have copies for most of the years. The reason seems to be that these statistics are of little use and are not on demand from various ministries, especially the ministry of planning. If the planning department has no idea of the economy as a whole, its weaknesses, bottlenecks, stagnation and potential, gathered from comparative statistics planning will have no role to play in the development of the economy. Then, apart from maintaining law and order, what is the function of the government and its various departments? There are still five-year plans, and massive efforts to stimulate growth in the country. As part of that effort various schemes along with allotted funds come to the state. These schemes are given in outlines and details, complete with guidelines for implementation. The state officials of various departments have to carry out the implementation, maintain accounts, produce utilisation certificates, report on various stages of the work in progress, and explain away lapses. What they are not required to do is to apply their minds and adapt or modify them to suit local circumstances. For example, in some districts, the officials entrusted with introducing the white revolution reared milch cows, looked after them, religiously following directions from above and ended up by producing milk at a higher cost than the market price, and made it available to the public at subsidised price for years before the central ministry woke up to it.

There are broadly speaking two kinds of schemes. One tries to raise the productive potential of the region/community, and the other is part of a new economic order, more or less in the nature of a safety-net. The latter are intended as welfare schemes to help out and protect sections of population that fall behind as the ruthless economic machine of market-led growth roars onwards. These schemes do not by themselves contribute to economic development, and their impact on development is negligible. Further, since their results are either not concretely visible, or only casually monitored these are administered poorly, and are hives of corruption. Their nature is underlined by the Prime Minister's stubborn refusal to grant the officially approved minimum daily wages to the workers under the MGNREGA scheme. Their actual intention therefore cannot be more than prevention of social unrest and ensuring a sort of electoral support for the ruling party, with ruling-party MLAs placed in critical positions in delivery of benefits under such schemes. Scarce funds are thus more or less wasted, as these are not designed to empower the masses in a significant way to improve their standard of living through productive means. These funds could have been used with a visible impact on development had the labour of poor beneficiaries been put to use to build houses under the Indira Awas Yojana and build roads and wells

(for domestic and agricultural purposes) under the MGNREGA scheme, and thus significant social capital might have been built to provide the thrust for 'self-sustained growth'. At best these have helped official and unofficial intermediaries to siphon off at least fifty percent of the funds and purchase luxury consumer goods produced outside the state.

The Assam Government in colourful and elaborate advertisements give frequent and complacent publicity to such schemes, concealing the fact that such centrally sponsored schemes are in operation in different states under different names. As for other central (state or PPP) projects with massive outlay and critical significance for the state's economy – two such projects are the Bogibeel Railway Bridge in an area where the Brahmaputra descends from the hill and joins other rivers mainly rain-fed, assumes massive dimensions, and the Gas Cracker Project at Tengakhat – the state government shows little concern that they take decades to build and commission. Such projects, if and when completed, are bound to alter the economy in significant ways. One suspects the Planning department of the state government has not taken pains to ascertain and project the future impact of these projects on the state's economy and prepare the people for employment opportunities and forestall inevitable destabilising consequences. Already, Bogibeel bridge has displaced people who lived by farming and fishing in large numbers, and the state government has done little to relieve their plight. This is a clear indication that the state government of Assam does not plan for the people under its jurisdiction. Who are the people for whom the state government work and plan, if it does any planning at all? Obviously they are serving powerful interests outside the state. There have been numerous complaints that in accepting passively projects upstream in the Arunachal Pradesh which might have disastrous consequences for lacks of people in Dhemaji and Lakshimpur districts, the state government is serving the caucus of corporates and politicians and bureaucrats with international links.

Planning in India cannot therefore be said to be calculated to further the interests and well-being of the people at large. Perhaps originally, with people like Nehru and Mahalanabis steering the course, fired by the example of the Soviet Union with fabulous growth-rates under planned management of the economy, (which incidentally even impressed J. M. Keynes), there was an expectation of maximising growth with scarce capital. It cannot be said that the decision to regulate foreign and Indian private capital was misguided. Though growth was at snail's pace, surrender to profit-hungry foreign capital might have led to unbalanced growth and a collapse of independent national initiative to shape the economy, as in many hapless African and Latin American countries. The government of India invested with the poor resources at its command pretty heavily in education and scientific research, leading to gradual growth of a respectable force of scientific and technical personnel, indispensable for mastering modern technology and development through industrialisation. (No other model of development was familiar at that time). Nehru of course was committed to socialism of a sort, that is, he wanted the vast rural masses that at that time comprised nearly ninety per cent of the

population to have their due share in the benefits of economic development. But he failed to or did not want to break the monopoly of the landlords on the land, which would have released the suppressed energy of the peasantry, and curb the tendency of private native capital to build monopolies of their own on the basis of borrowed technology and influence on politicians and bureaucrats. Decades of austerity and backwardness in key sectors including agriculture followed. But the elite clung tenaciously to that dream of development and tried to overcome the shortages and bottlenecks by concentrating more and more decision-making power in New Delhi and imposing from above patterns and schemes of development upon the common people. Even the pattern of 'community development' in the countryside was set from New Delhi, regardless of diversity of conditions. With its control over the financial resources of the country the Centre was in a position to arm-twist many of the States into accepting the plans meekly.

As a result, though India as a 'union of states' carried within it seeds of federalism, the Planning Commission with the Prime Minister as the Chairman, planned for the entire nation down to the members of the remotest village. Along with it the Centre grabbed more and more powers from the States by making liberal use of the subterfuge of "the Concurrent List", thus bringing under its control resources that the States could have used to their advantage to forge ahead. Since decisions in planning were concentrated in New Delhi, leaving little room for the States to think and plan on their own, State planning became a charade. And a straitjacket of bureaucratic control with voluminous correspondence, submission of utilisation certificates and vouchers, mechanical supervision on a staggering scale was slipped over the State's administration. The cadre of all-India services detached from all concern for and sensitivity to the problems of local people and conditions on the ground, programmed to think of such people as pieces on a chess board, used to frequent translocations and dealing with such matters with abstract efficiency, become ideal agents in carrying out such "plans". Since they usually wield authority over state cadre, their approach is appropriated by the state cadre too. Such an approach removes flesh and blood people from the calculations of planners. I may be permitted here to cite a bizarre experience of mine. I had been complaining to the Commissioner of the Gauhati Municipal Corporation for years together that money allotted for repairing the road in front of my house had been deftly used on repairing quite a different road, and I produced direct documentary evidence. The injustice cries out for redressal. The Commissioner/s made promises but put off the decision on some ground or other.

Probably a political big-wig was involved. By some accident on one of those occasions I met an Officer from Delhi coming to appraise the progress of the scheme for repair of urban roads. In my desperation I made a strong, emotional appeal to him to inspect the actual conditions of roads and pull up the local administration. The gentleman was visibly embarrassed. He mumbled something about his brief not being physically verifying the implementation. He meets the Commissioner, who reports to him, and that was all. An inspecting team might come later, which I thought was a lie.

If planned development in its actual practice assumes this form it is only destined to cause and conceal massive leakages of public money at every stage of planning and implementation. And some people have used our legal system and administrative norms and procedures to position themselves in appropriate points of the system and the massive hemorrhage of public funds continues, to the immense gain of the classes of people mentioned above. The common people are not beneficiaries but victims. Today, the money and the blueprint come from further afield, with neo-liberal theory underwriting the plunder that ultimately strips the common man naked. The politico-bureaucratic control has become more opaque and elaborate and the leakage of funds enriching swindlers with impeccable credentials has become mind-boggling. Planning in that sense has become a strategy for facilitating the loot. The citizens at large are duped by the *mantra* of development. It is high time we raise our voice against it.

34

North by North-East: Is Assam Back in the Game?

A. Didar Singh, IAS (Retd.)

Assam represents a breathtaking tapestry of history, culture, people, events and nature. The magnificence of the Brahmaputra is as overwhelming as the strength of its immense diversity, the folk tales spun along its river banks and immortalised in Indian literature are as deeply woven into the Indian culture as its powerful and evocative history and the rhythm of the *Bihu* dance is celebrated as much as the musical and cinematic genius of the late Bhupen Hazarika.

In the strategic context, Assam's location in the north-east corner of India bordering two foreign countries Bhutan and Bangladesh and seven states of India makes it undoubtedly the gateway of the entire region. Assam is the largest economy in the north-east region of India and its relatively favourable geographical location and accessibility of infrastructure makes Assam well-placed to consolidate the markets of the other states in the region. Furthermore, it has the potential to become a business hub for not only the entire region but also of the neighbouring countries of Bhutan, Bangladesh and Myanmar.

All that is known.

True, the importance of Assam has never been lost on anyone, but the travesty of the region is that for a good many years in the post Independence period, this glory was shadowed with the snapping of traditional trade and commerce linkages with the state's hinterland that reduced Assam, along with the entire Northeast, into a landlocked cocoon. Assam's progress has since been rather halting and tenuous especially in the 80s' and 90s' but now Assam is back in the game and as Chief Minister Tarun Gogoi puts it across to investors globally, "Assam is the best emerging State of India", a proposition backed by signs of revival and emergence of opportunities that signal a turnaround in the fortunes of the state.

The economy clocked a healthy growth rate of 6.5 per cent in 2011-12 over the previous year. The state has embarked on an ambitious North-East Industrial and Investment Policy (NEIIPP) announced by the Centre in 2007 to boost industrialisation and packaged with fiscal incentives and other concessions to attract investors, Assam's strides in infrastructure development and agriculture has been rewarded with an increase in Assam's annual plan share to Rs 12,500 crore by the Planning Commission and the state is looking at becoming self-sufficient in terms of power generation in the next five-six years.

It is interesting to note that, after the recession of 2008-09, the GSDP of Assam has grown faster than the pre-crisis period. The GSDP of Assam had grown at a CAGR of 7.2 per cent after the recession of 2008-09. The contribution of the service sector has increased considerably from 47 per cent in 2004-05 to 56 per cent in 2011-12. The total number of micro and small industrial units set up in the state from 2007-08 to 2011-12 is 7805, which are a good source of employment. The Government has even taken up a flagship programme for multi-skill development to impart demand-based specialised skills that provide employment in manufacturing and service sectors to the youths of Assam.

A number of major ongoing projects are near completion which includes the Rs 5460-crore Assam Gas Cracker Project, which will generate huge employment with downstream industries, three border trade centres and projects at Darranga and Parvatipur to facilitate trade and commerce with Bangladesh, Bhutan and Myanmar. A mega food Park, a bamboo park, tea park at Chaygaon (Kamrup) and a plastic park in Tinsukia are being developed. In an unprecedented venture for an energy company, state-run Oil India plans to tie up with the Assam government to start a cooperative dairy business along the lines of Gujarat's successful 'Amul' model.

That Assam is on a comeback trail has got a louder endorsement in the organising of a flagship event dedicated to Assam, 'The Gateway of India's North-East' in June this year at Mayfair, London jointly by the Nehru Centre, cultural wing of the High Commission of India, and the Tea Board of India. Last year in December, Assam saw the launch of an American Business Corner (ABC) — the first of its kind in eastern India, which will showcase catalogues and business materials of US companies at the dedicated ABC space allocated by partner organisations. The business corner is designed to assist US companies in promoting their brand and generating business leads from emerging metropolitan cities in the country.

While all this has no doubt put the North east in a different orbit, there are other compelling reasons for Assam to be increasingly seen as a potential game-changer in the region.

One obvious one is the new investment climate that lays emphasis on "Clean Development Mechanism" as an investment proposition. The focus of the growing investment climate today is to build the economy on the core strengths of this region — namely environment, water, agriculture, minerals and other natural resources and geographical location. This finds resonance in Gogoi's strong pitch to attract foreign investments in Assam by highlighting

the availability of assets like oil, gas, coal, limestone and abundant surface as well as ground water. The Government has also invited NRIs living in the US to explore investment possibilities in education, healthcare, biodiversity, and green economy. With these opportunities and developments, Gogoi believes Assam is soon going to emerge as a major investment destination in India.

These prospects are also being complimented by the increasing emphasis on the Look–East Policy being vigorously pursued by the Government, both at the state and central level. With the emergence of ASEAN as a central pillar of India's 'Look East Policy', Assam has acquired a pivotal geo-strategic positioning in the emerging economic architecture of the region. Assam shares a strong cultural and linguistic affinity with the ASEAN region in the form of the Tai-Ahom legacy. Historically, Assam has been a melting pot of various racial stocks, namely Indo-Tibeto-Burmese, Mongoloid, Austro-Asiatic, Aryan, Dravidian etc.

The "Look East Policy" launched in 1992 with the objective of establishing closer economic integration with the South-East Asian states marks a significant shift in India's policy prioritisation and the emergence of a concrete strategy to create an economic hub in its North-eastern region by exploring the trade and commerce potential with its ASEAN neighbours. Among the 13 sectors identified for promoting trade and investment are technology, energy, transportation, communication, tourism, fisheries, agriculture, cultural cooperation, environment and disaster management and public health.

The launch of the Regional Comprehensive Economic Partnership (RCEP) negotiations between ASEAN and its six free-trade partners, including India, will culminate in the formation of the largest free trade zone that will bring enormous benefit to the people of the North-East region. Assam has the unique locational advantage of being situated close to Myanmar, the gateway to ASEAN countries and has the potential to emerge as a strategic base for foreign and domestic investors. It can tap the vast potential of contiguous markets of Myanmar, China, Malaysia, Thailand, Philippines, Cambodia, Indonesia and other East and South East Asian countries which constitute almost half of the world's population.

While the border points at Moreh, Sutarkandi, Mankachar and Dawki have been opened for bilateral trade and commerce, Assam's internal waterways network connects Bangladesh, giving it access to the ports of Chittagong, Kolkata and Haldia. Thus, both the land and water routes are available to investors for re-export to East and South East Asia.

The strategically enviable position that Assam finds itself in today has made the state central to the success of any development plan involving the North-east. There is a growing awareness at the Centre that Assam's development could, in the long term, become a game-changer for the entire North-east. The states in the region can leverage on Assam's proximity to the ASEAN countries, for developing stronger commercial ties with South-east Asian nations and getting access to those crucial markets.

This thinking is being translated into a major exercise of improving road connectivity with ASEAN countries which in turn has the potential to create

new opportunities for India's north eastern region. The Government informs us that there has been significant progress in the area. India has extended assistance for road development projects which include upgradation of the Tamu-Kalewa-Kalemyo (TKK) road (about 160 kms), Kaladan Multi-Modal Transit Transport Project which envisages development of road and inland waterways from Sittwe port in Myanmar to Mizoram and some segments of Trilateral Highway Project (about 1360 km) connecting Moreh (Manipur, India) to Mae Sot (Thailand) through Myanmar. These will prove of great benefit to India's land locked North East.

However, it is not just connectivity to South-east Asia that the Government wants to use to unleash the potential of Assam but an extensive network of roadways and highways connecting Assam with the North-east and the region as a whole to the rest of the country that it sees crucial to lift the prospects of Assam and the North-east. The Centre is expected to spend an additional Rs 2,000 crore in Assam to expand the Pradhan Mantri Gram Sadak Yojana by over 3,100 km to include areas with a population of 250-499 people. The Accelerated Road Development Programme for development of road network in the NE states envisages providing a total 10,141km road connectivity to backward and remote areas, places of strategic importance and neighbouring countries. The Central Government has even accepted an Assam government proposal for a Metro rail project in Guwahati and sanctioned an amount of Rs 25 crore for the feasibility study of the ambitious project and the preparation of a Detailed Project Report (DPR).

The most crucial link being developed between the region and the rest of the country is the upcoming East West Corridor road project in the state which having got delayed due to insurgency, bad weather, delays in land acquisition, etc. leading to cost escalation as well, is scheduled for completion in December 2014. The 3,300 km long four-lane East-West Corridor starts from Porbandar in Gujarat and ends at Silchar in Assam and passes through Rajasthan, Madhya Pradesh, Uttar Pradesh, Bihar and West Bengal. Timely execution could change the face of Assam and the North-East.

Transport connectivity are though only a part of the Indian Government's strategy to reap the rich dividends that Assam's location, resources and assets can deliver. The bigger plan is to cash in on the untapped demand for financial services in the region which would also serve the Centre's larger objective of inclusive growth. The Assam government has sought an expansion of banking in Assam in discussions with the RBI. More bank branches are needed in Assam as the current branches, numbering around 1,110, are not sufficient to meet the growing demand for disbursement of subsidy and other transfers made by the government. There is also concern over the low credit deposit ratio in Assam and flow of credit to micro, small and medium enterprises (MSME). The credit ratio is 37.3 per cent in Assam, while the national average is about 78.1 per cent.

As many as 200 branches of rural banks are expected to be opened in Assam in fiscal 2013-2014. Credit to MSMEs would be extended to Rs 3,800 crore in the next fiscal year from the existing Rs 2,500 crore. The National Bank

for Agriculture and Rural Development (NABARD) and the Assam government have also decided to form one lakh Joint Liability Groups during 2013-14 to encourage credit to agriculture and allied activities.

The MSME sector no doubt tops the pecking order with the highest potential to generate self-employment particularly for the educated unemployed youths, a necessity for Assam where youth unemployment is one of the key underlying causes of social unrest. As per estimation, there are more than 20 lakh unemployed youth in Assam. Prominent industrial houses in the country have offered to help in creating investment at grassroots level for improving rural entrepreneurship, skill up gradation, rural employment and financial inclusion. Among the proposals are a Rs 10 crore Angel Fund for micro enterprises for inclusive growth in Assam which will be operated through financial institutions and a Rs 1.5 crore Special State Capital Investment Subsidy upto a ceiling of Rs 3 lakh per unit for micro units set up by women and first generation entrepreneurs belonging to the SC, ST and physically handicapped categories.

The other big opportunity waiting to be explored is retail. According to CRISIL Research, following the opening up of multi-brand retail to 100 per cent FDI, Guwahati is one of the 21 cities in India that qualify as potential locations where foreign retailers can open retail outlets.

Given the large reserves of Natural gas and coal, Assam has a vital stake in the country's energy security. While government owned ONGC and OIL India are already prospecting for hydrocarbons, Assam Petro-chemicals plans to set up a new manufacturing plant with investment of Rs 1,028 crore. Also, the declaration of the Brahmaputra as a national waterway has facilitated transportation of raw materials and project equipment for growth of the oil sector. The presence of 'associated natural gas' in almost all the petroleum producing areas of the Brahmaputra Valley has spawned important industries like Namrup Fertilizer Factory, Namrup Thermal Power Project, Assam Petrochemicals and Assam Gas Company which provides liquefied petroleum gas for domestic use.

The tourism sector in Assam offers unparalleled attractions like wildlife sanctuaries, adventure tourism, eco-tourism, hill stations, lakes and places of historical heritage. The number of domestic tourist visits and foreign tourist visits in Assam grew at an average annual rate of 5.5 per cent and eight per cent, respectively, during 2006-2010. In 2011, the state received 43.4 lakh domestic tourists and 0.16 lakh foreign tourists.

Investment potential also exists in the agriculture sector which dominates Assam's economy with employment of more than 50 per cent of the rural population. However, improper handling of farm produce leads to huge wastage. There is tremendous scope for agri-infrastructure like modern warehouses and storages as there are only few cold storages (about 10-12) with poor power supply available in the state. Investors can also explore setting up of mini food parks instead of mega food parks.

A lot remains to be done to convert these opportunities into concrete investment flows. There is need for improvement in the infrastructure

development in Assam which is not yet adequate to attract investors. Land acquisition process, environmental clearances, and taking construction permit in the state have to be less time consuming and expeditious. Simplifying the administrative procedures and speeding up the public service delivery mechanism by introducing e-governance in the system will reduce cost, time, delays and unnecessary interference of the government officials thereby helping the investors through a smoother process.

Nancy J. Powell had said in December 2012 during a visit to Guwahati that Assam's future was bright. She was not exaggerating. As a keystone state not just in North-east, but in the broader region, where the countries of South Asia, East Asia and South-east Asia all meet, Assam must seize this opportunity and take the initiative to turn this potential into a reality.

35

Understanding North-East: A Prelude to Development

K.K. Sinha IAS (Retd.)

Most of the time the North-East India is in the news for the wrong reasons. Its pluralism and diverse ethnicity have provided a platform for experiment with political autonomy. But we have yet to get a coherent region bent upon exploiting its vast resources and unique bio-diversity.

There is a fundamental difference between the development of an area or the region and the development of the people residing therein. Even if physical assets are created and these do not mesh in adequately with the requirement, training and ethos of the people the developments are likely to be either underutilised or wasted. It is, therefore, necessary to understand the area really well before seeking physical solutions. This paper is an attempt to understand the area or rather the past experiences and challenges faced by the people and the administrations of the region.

Let us start from the beginning; what had achieving freedom with partition meant to the people of Assam and other parts of the region. Before partition northeast India was a natural extension of the country towards the eastern border; the people of this region had three main avenues of access to other parts of the country—through railways, through road network, and through waterways, either riverine or sea. There was unhindered natural movement of the people and goods through roads, railways and waterways. After Independence with partition, this natural access shrunk to a mere corridor of about 25 km. Through which road and rail networks were built to connect the region with the rest of the country. Waterways have just vanished. This physical diminution of connectivity cast a very profound impact on the psyche of the people and they felt almost cut off and neglected. Chinese aggression in 1962 accentuated this feeling of helplessness when it was realised that how easy it would be to really cut off this region physically from the rest of the

country. The people of this region, including Assam, became more inward looking than ever before. There are a large number of ethnic communities in this area. Each community started erecting psychological barriers around themselves and would make little effort to reach out to other communities beyond these barriers to the required degree not only from other parts of the country but even amongst themselves. This proved to be a fertile ground for fissiparous tendencies and turmoil.

A look at the structure of governance in the region as it evolved this period after Independence is also necessary to understand the situation better for proper appraisal.

At the time of Independence there was the province of Assam, the native States of Manipur and Tripura and the Frontier Tract called NEFT. Even in Assam province there were parts, particularly in hills, which had different pattern of administration and were called Excluded and Partially Excluded Areas. The rest of the province was administered more or less in the same manner as was the rest of the country.

With promulgation of the Constitution a change was introduced in the pattern of administration. Manipur and Tripura became Part C States, Sixth Schedule was introduced in hill areas of Assam under which District Councils were established in Garo Hills, United Khasi and Jaintia Hills, North Cachar and Mikir Hills and Mizo District (Naga Hills refused to have District Councils despite repeated attempts). NEFA came into being to administer the North Eastern Frontier Tract. After prolonged negotiations the State of Nagaland was created in 1962 by carving out Naga Hills District of Assam and Naga inhabited portion of NEFA. Governor of Nagaland was given special responsibility in regard to the law and order situation in the State.

A major change was brought about in 1972 by "reorganising" the North East. Union territories of Mizoram (by carving out the Mizo District of Assam) and Arunachal Pradesh (re-naming NEFA) were set up; States of Manipur and Tripura (by upgrading respective Union Territories) and Meghalaya (by carving out the districts of Garo Hills and United Khasi and Jaintia Hills from Assam) were also created. (Earlier in 1970 Meghalaya was made an Autonomous State). In 1985 Mizoram and Arunachal Pradesh were also made full-fledged states. Though the jurisdiction of the High Court at Guwahati for the whole region was not disturbed, a Permanent Bench of the High court has been set up in each constituent State of the region.

Recognising the organic links of these constituent units with each other in the region, North Eastern Council was established to facilitate regional planning and development.

Even though Meghalaya became a separate State in 1972, the District Councils remained intact one for each major tribe of the State: Garo, Khasi and Jaintia. In Mizoram, the Mizo Hills District Council was abolished and two separate District Councils were set up for Pawi and Lakher regions. The Sixth Schedule was extended to Tripura.

Areas in this region, therefore, have seen many changes, some of them fundamentally different from what it was in the past. How do these changes impact on the local ethos?

The avowed objective of the Central Government at the time of Independence was to permit the local communities, particularly in the hills, to grow and develop according to their own genius. The Sixth Schedule was the chosen instrumentality. But it had a major and self-debilitating flaw. It totally ignored the local ethos and customs. Almost all the Hill peoples have their own traditional functionaries, who are elected on some form of democratic principles. Due to the policy of "hands off" on local administration by the government through the instrumentality of Excluded and Partially Excluded Areas, these functionaries were quite powerful and influential in their own areas. District Councils, on the other hand, were based on the principles of adult suffrage with which the local people were not acquainting. The degree of autonomy which was conferred on the District Council was also unprecedented. But for funds these bodies depended almost totally upon the State governments. As the local elected functionary did not feel themselves up to the task of raising their own resources. As a result, rather than becoming their own leading agencies for development of the people in their own areas, more often than not, these bodies indulged in local political skirmishes. There were at times shining exceptions, but these were the results of political sagacity and leadership qualities of individuals at the helm of affairs at that time.

The second point is the superimposition of the pattern of administration for rural developments as evolved in other parts of countries in these areas. Even in regularly administrated areas the institution of CD Blocks has seen many ups and downs. In these areas, as people's participation was marginal the institution could not become effective. On the other hand, innate self-help attitude and self-reliant instinct particularly of hill communities were severely impaired.

The serious outcome of the District Council was gradual margilisation of the minority ethnic groups. After all. Even in Hill areas not all communities are numerically equal. The dominant ethnic group in area tended to ignore the minority groups in the same manner they were ignored by the State government and the people of the plains. The level of disillusionment therefore, tended to gradually increase. Much of the political developments in the region could be traced to these disillusionments. Self-created barriers around the communities impeded upon free and open discussions and frank discussions, which, intern, tended to increase misunderstanding.

There is a general perception that the Assamese speaking people in Assam, in general always felt a threat to the advancement of their mother tongue. This feeling has tended to make them to an extent, hostile to other people. May be this is due to their own experience between 1829 and 1868. They have naturally always cherished to established primacy of their language by law. It was not totally irrational given the fact of reorganisation of the country on the basis of languages and the fact that the State was called Assam and they constituted, by a good margin, the largest single group in the State. But in a State where the compact parts of the land very largely populated by communities speaking other languages such a feeling of formulation of the law brings in their wake serious disharmony and spiralling tensions. Gradual

waking up of the State of Assam is the direct result of this phenomenon. It could be argued that what is wrong with such advancements! Perhaps it is the destabilisation of the society at large and serious loss of trust among the communities for each other.

As a consequence the Government of India Act of 1955 and rebirth of Burma (Myanmar) Nagas found themselves spread over two countries. They naturally wanted creation of Nagaland comprising of all Naga people in India and Burma. First made their move by petition and discussions. They missed the point that the British not only did not do anything to meet their demands during the period of 1937 to 1946, when they had the power to do something about their demand, but some elements of British Raj incited Nagas to become more strident in their demands before the Central Government after the independence. But by that time the Government of India did not have the power to make any move unification. Their demand and grievances found violent expressions which led to the turmoil in their beautiful but rugged land. There were grievances in the other parts of this region. Protracted violent agitations in Nagaland gave fillip to other disenchanted groups to take to violence and also seek help, guidance and sustenance from this disgruntled group of Nagaland which intern was also getting assistance from outside the country. Actually, the violent group of Nagaland became the umbrella for other such groups of the region.

The causes for agitations in various parts of the region are separate and unique to that area. If it was, as was generally perceived, a lack of trust for those involved with the District Council in Mizo District and the perceived inaction and unhelpful attitudes of the State and the Central Governments besides the immediate cause of bungling in providing relief to the people during "*Mautam*" (famine); in Manipur it was the marginalisation of the Meities, who are in majority but inhabiting in only a small portion of the State and victim of a languishing economy coupled with the spread of Naga militant activities in the hills of the State; in Tripura it was the consistent ousting of the tribal communities from their age old habitat. In Assam the overt cause was the presence of foreigners in large numbers and the demand for their deportation; but one can perceptively discern that what caused an alarm in the psyche of the Assamese people was the fear that they may lose political power if the situation continued. The results of the preceding elections in the State amply hinted about it. In all these cases innovative solutions were possible if constraints, limitations and the real fears of different communities were properly articulated and recognised. But in an atmosphere surcharged with mistrust and lack of frank and open exchange of views only implacable stands were possible which inevitably led to confrontation and violence.

At present only Mizoram has returned to almost complete normalcy, other States including even Arunachal Pradesh are undergoing turbulence within to varying degrees.

The decision to create linguistic States brought in the question of linguistic majority and minority groups giving a potential message to the tribal and ethnic groups that a cultural domination was sure to come. This threat to the

cultural freedom created the fear of losing identity and led to balkanisation of the State of Assam. In Assam, the language movement sought to achieve two purposes, namely, to establish primacy of Assamese and the establishment of a linguistic majority in the State gave way to anti-foreigners movement launched by the All Assam Students Union, one of the biggest movements in history. This movement led to the creation of two divergent groups: one emerging as an organised political movement and party and the other as an organised underground militant outfit.

Tensions in the North East India must be understood in the context of its geographical isolation, economic backwardness and historical separation between hills and the plain. They started in the form of separatist movements. At one level there was the demand of separation of Nagaland from India and the demand for separation of the hills from the plains in Assam. At another level there has been the rivalry between the Assamese and the Bengalis in the plains and the resentment against outsiders in both the hills and the plains. The palpable fear of the microscopic communities of the North East to lose their identities by a deluge from outside must be understood and appreciated in its proper perspective.

From almost the middle of 1970s communal and linguistic riots have, more or less, not taken place in the region. However, a kind of ethnic cleansing has apparently taken place in several States while separatist groups have spread their philosophy throughout the region ethnic minorities' neighbourhoods. External support has strengthened and encouraged such violent movements. A disturbed region with violence, killings, abduction and extortion is not an ideal place in which individual, group or corporate entrepreneurship will flourish nor will the efforts of the State (Governments or District Councils) will be able to achieve a real breakthrough.

The most important steps for finding solution to the ethnic tension and violence or even to prepare an effective roadmap to this end are dissolving the mist of distrust the communities of the region have for each other and for the rest of the country and a solution to their geographical isolation. The people of this region themselves will have to take initiative for the former. The recent initiative of the Central Government of "look east policy' may be of some use for finding solution to the latter.

36

Infrastructure and Public Capital: An Analysis

Amal Kumar Borpujari

Introduction

Good quality infrastructure is a key ingredient for sustainable development. All countries need efficient transport, sanitation, energy and communication systems if they are to prosper and provide a decent standard of living for their population. Unfortunately, many developing countries possess poor infrastructure, which hampers their growth and ability to trade in the global economy e.g., some South Asian and Latin American Countries.

Infrastructure

Most of countries are strongly engaged in supporting infrastructure policies, investment and services in developing countries. The money spent in this area equals to about one-fifth of overall official development assistance managed by individual Governments from loans, assistance, tie-ups, bilaterals etc.

The main sectors of co-operation between the Public Capital Disciples, expenditure are:

- Water and sanitation,
- Energy,
- Information and communication technology, and
- Urban development.

Investment in infrastructure can contribute to the achievement of the Millennium Development Goals, as it leads to improved access to services like health and education, generates employment and enhances a country's ability to trade while reducing the costs of goods and services. Good infrastructure also makes it easier for economic actors to do business and helps to improve environmental conditions.

Making Transport Work

Good quality roads, railways, ports and airports are essential for the smooth running of many key economic sectors in the developing world including agriculture, industry, mining and tourism. Efficient transport infrastructures can also improve the delivery of and access to vital social services, such as health and education.

As sustainable development becomes a more important objective in civil infrastructure planning and policy-making, Quality of Life (QOL) is an increasingly important measure to understand, characterise, and apply effectively in the search for and development of appropriate infrastructure solutions for sustainable development. Let us review the role of QOL in civil infrastructure decision-making. It provides an overview and critique of methodological approaches to defining QOL and explains the significance of QOL in infrastructure decision-making for sustainable development. It is nothing but public capital and our aim is to discuss on this prime issue.

The dominant components in a country's public sector capital stock tend to be related to infrastructure such as roads, telecommunications and energy. Other items include military and structures such as hospitals and schools. Coupled with the network function, which enables interactions between geographically dispersed economic agents, this suggests that public investment and its attendant stock could have a sizeable impact on economic growth, productivity and an economy's ability to structurally transform. Nearly all sectors' production one way or another depends on infrastructure as an input. In short, a country's prosperity may be positively related to public capital.

In 2004, the World Bank in its World Development Report strongly argued for the role of infrastructure in development (World Bank, 2004), a message which was recently repeated in its Growth Commission Report (World Bank, 2011) and also taken up by UNCTAD's Least Developed Economies Report series (e.g., UNCTAD, 2010). For example, the Growth Commission Report states that countries that devote more of GDP to public investment – notably countries in Asia—also grow faster than those that invest a little. Investment in public capital is believed to crowd in private investment. But where does this strong belief in public investment come from?

One argument is that public capital enhances the productivity of private capital, raising its rate of return and encouraging more investment. However, the theoretical impact of public capital to some extent depends on the setting. In a neo-classical growth model, increases in the stock of infrastructure will only have transitory effect, since long-run growth is driven by exogenous technological progress. In an endogenous growth model, on the other hand, steady-state income per capita can increase from investments in infrastructure.

Barro's (1990) seminal endogenous growth paper introduces government expenditure as a public good in the production function and accomplishes exactly this. One could, therefore, say that public capital is the foundation upon which the economy is built, that it is an enabling resource. It acts as a network that connects spatially separated economic agents. To measure its

economic contribution, one would need to account for the full set of interactions that the network enables. As a consequence, the contribution might be large.

Are these arguments supported by evidence? The serious empirical literature on the role of public capital in economic growth essentially started with Aschauer's (1989) work on the United States. He found the impact of public capital investment to be large, actually too large to be realistic. Gramlich (1994) argued that if the return to such investment is as large as suggested by Aschauer's results, everyone should be involved in such investments.

In the case of developing countries Devarajan (1996) found that public capital expenditure had a negative effect on growth. A possible explanation was that expenditures that are normally considered productive could become unproductive if there is an excess amount of them.

It is not easy to empirically assess the impact of public investment and it is problematic to know what the rate of return "should" be. For example, it seems reasonable to assume that the marginal quantities of public capital consumed by firms are "free of charge" and it, thus, becomes an unpaid production factor when maximising profit. McDonald (2008) makes the important point that there is little agreement on what a reasonable rate of return from public investment is. In my opinion it should carry the cost of the investment (that is interest cess, etc). Since the main part of public capital is infrastructure, for example, roads, bridges, and water and sewage systems, etc., and has no market price, its gross return actually cannot be calculated.

Also, it is unclear what the returns to scale of the production function should be. Including public capital in a production function can lead to increasing returns to scale across all inputs, while firms face constant returns to scale in private inputs. Moreover, public investment tends to be lumpy, which could give rise to non-linearities. One could imagine that at low incomes, infrastructure is complementary and has higher pay-offs, while at high incomes, substitutions effects dominate and pay-offs are lower. Beyond a certain optimal threshold, public capital investments may result in a negative net benefit to society as economic and social benefits are exceeded by related costs (Agénor, Bayraktar and El Aynaoui, 2008-2009).

Furthermore, lumpiness breaks the link between capital stocks and capital services. Linking infrastructure and growth through constant coefficients is not sufficient from a policy perspective. The crowding-in effect argued in the Growth Commission Report may well turn out to be crowding-out effects and in other cases maintenance spending could raise budget deficits.

Measuring public capital itself can be problematic. For example, Haque and Kneller (2008) argue that corruption inflates the level of expenditure on public capital projects, while lowering the return to that capital, for example, because of low quality. Corruption implies that a unit spending on public investment does not buy a unit worth of service. Investment may be based on who offers the best kickbacks to officials rather than who offers the best price-quality combination. Public investment-GDP ratios are higher in highly corrupt countries like India compared to low corruption countries, which could

produce large coefficients. Public capital constructed from investment series can be overvalued because of inefficient governments, leading to higher costs of implementation than technically possible. In many developing countries public capital has unproductive uses.

Another source of large estimates may be the composition of public capital. For example, in a road network, the marginal productivity of one link depends on the capacity and configuration of all links in the network. The consequence could be that only the average effect, and not marginal effects, is estimated. Another difficulty is whether capacity is built in advance or as reaction to needs. Investment in infrastructure is likely to lead to contemporaneous growth only if the country is poised for growth, otherwise it only prepares the country for growth, but the effects should show up with a lag.

Suppose there is a link between infrastructure and performance, but that it has an uncertain and variable timing. It could take time for firms to learn how to take advantage of infrastructure improvements, and such timing may depend on the precise type of project and sectors that it affects. The implication is that the relation is complex and it could be too much to ask for a precise estimate given existing data. Level estimations could then be seen as average impacts and not marginal impact. If that is the case, one would indeed expect a large impact.

One cannot help but observe that nearly all of the empirical work concerns aggregate growth. But one may conjecture that sectors that more intensively are dependent on public investment will experience greater benefit, thus, so that a large estimate may be defended. The role of public capital in fostering industrial development. In doing so, several alleged econometric shortcomings are addressed; in particular, reverse causality, endogeneity bias and accounting for omitted state-dependent variables. Another contribution is to examine whether the estimated impact differ according to the stage of development.

The subject article is based on a panel of 57 developed and developing countries and spanning the time period 1970 to 2012. Two principal questions are asked: The first is whether the long-run level of industry is caused by the level of public capital, while the second—more short-term in nature is whether countries investing more rapidly in public capital also experience faster industrial development. And as said, do these two impacts depend on countries' stage of development?

The results clearly indicate that public capital matters. Public capital has strong explanatory power for why some countries have managed to industrialise, while others have not. Public capital matters at all income levels, but largely the impact is diminishing with higher income. Another key conclusion is that growth of public capital not only explains levels of industry, but also how rapidly it grows. Interestingly, the largest impacts occur for the fastest growing countries, i.e., the Asian tiger economies, and the High-income ones.

Another important result is that for all developed countries it seems worthwhile to invest in public infrastructure, since the returns on doing so is

always positive. The rates of return seem to be connected to the rate of development a conclusion drawn because the Asian fast-growers exhibits the greatest rates of return as well as the initial level of development, as suggested by the high scores obtained for the countries with lowest income. In the latter case, investment in public infrastructure pays itself in terms of industrial development in about two to three years. In both cases, the rate of return on public investment exceeds that of private capital. The countries which have already had their growth spurts and accumulated a sufficient stock of public capital the rates of return on public capital is below that of private capital.

37

Wetlands: Dying Eco-systems in a Shrinking World: The Case of Assam

A.K. Bhagabati

Introduction

Wetlands constitute an important component of the earth's natural system. They are geographically significant as they account for around six per cent of the earth's surface. Wetlands include a wide ranging type of water bodies such as lake, marsh, swamp, pond, bog, fen, dead channel, etc. They are known in different countries by many names. In our Assamese also, we have not less than twenty five words to designate different types of wetlands that occur in various parts of the state.

Wetlands are now considered as the last remains of fresh water bodies on the earth excluding the perennial rivers. In spite of their varied positive contributions both in physical and human fields, they are under constant pressure and threat from ever increasing human activities. Like any other parts of the world and the country as well, Assam in the North-eastern region, which is richly endowed with wetlands of various size and shape, has experienced high rate of loss and degradation of wetland environment during the recent period. Therefore, there arises a great need to make people and policy-makers aware of the role played by the wetlands as habitats of plants and wildlife, more particularly as regulators of local eco-systems including micro-climates, especially in the less developed areas where dependence of people on these sensitive eco-systems is diverse and highly pervasive.

Wetland Types

Five major types of wetlands are generally internationally recognised:

1. Marine wetlands: coastal lagoons, rocky shores, coral reefs,
2. Estuarine wetlands: deltas, tidal marshes, mangrove swamps,
3. Lacustrine wetlands: lakes,

4. Riverine wetlands: wetlands along rivers and streams,
5. Palustrine wetlands: marshes, swamps and bogs.

In addition, everywhere man-made wetlands such as ponds, farm ponds, irrigated lands, reservoirs, canals etc., are also there. In Assam, most of the wetlands are of fluvial origin and therefore are distributed mostly along the major rivers of the Brahmaputra and the Barak systems.

Wetlands as Ecosystem

Any land, apart from certain perennial water bodies, which is subjected to submergence for a quarter of the year, qualifies to be considered as wetland. Wetlands generally lie in areas where there is a complicated interplay between land and water. They constitute eco-systems where water covers the ground, or is present either at or near the surface of the ground round the year or for varying spans of time. Thus wetlands are depressions in the landscapes where the precipitation and ground water accumulate providing conditions for the rooted and floating plants and fishes, insects, birds, reptiles and microbial lives.

The multi-level interactions among the members of the biotic community and between the biotic and abiotic elements within the wetland environment form interesting field of interdisciplinary investigation, which has currently created renewed interest among the biologists, geographers and environmental scientists. Like any other parts of the country in Assam also studies have been carried out by scholars on various aspects of wetland environment.

Functions of Wetlands

The functions of wetlands are wide ranging and far reaching in character. However, these are generally clubbed into the following categories:

1. *Regulation functions*: It refers to the capacity of the eco-system to regulate the ecological processes and life support system on the earth.

2. *Carrier function:* It refers to the space or suitable substrate needed for conducting human activities like settlement, cultivation, nature protection etc.

3. *Production function:* It refers to the resources provided by nature for human use.

4. *Information function:* It implies the role played by natural eco-systems in maintaining human health by cognitive development and logical appreciation of the world.

Interestingly, at micro-geographical level, the roles played by the wetlands in the physical and socio-economic conditions of the concerned areas are either overlooked or underestimated because of the long-continued spontaneous relation of the local people to the wetland environment.

Loss of Wetlands

Like any other natural entities, wetlands are also under growing pressure and threat from variety of factors. The factors are obviously both natural and man-made. The human factors are, however, found to be more serious to cause degradation and loss of the wetlands world over. Appreciation of the

ecological and economic values of the wetlands is yet to receive sincere attention of all concerned. It is noteworthy that "a natural area will receive protection only if the value a society assigns to its natural functions is higher than the value the society assigns to exploiting its natural resources". When we refer to natural ecosystems like wetlands we generally place them in an economic setting and while doing this, we often lose sight of their ecological importance.

In a paper published in *Geografiska Annaler* on wetland loss in Lousina (USA), Walker, identified four major processes contributing to the loss of wetlands, which are more or less relevant to all parts and contexts of the world. These processes are: (i) geologic, (ii) catastrophic, (iii) biologic and (iv) human. Among these, however, the human factors have proved to be highly pervasive and destructive during the recent period so far the status and functioning of wetlands are concerned.

In the third world countries also, the wetlands are getting increasingly threatened. The rapid growth of population and resultant expansion of acumen, agriculture and allied activities and infrastructural facilities have been continuously degrading the wetlands and their catchments. The flood control measures, cannel construction for irrigation and fluid (water and oil) withdrawal from the earth's subsurface also no less responsible for the loss of wetlands.

Human activities, particularly farming and grazing around the wetlands create situations quite detrimental to the sustainability of the wetland ecosystems. These not only contribute to gradual shrinkage of the wetlands through accelerated situation, but also sometime lead to eutrophication, a process by which certain pollutants are washed into the water bodies and overload them with organic and mineral nutrients.

Thus wetland loss basically results from the interplay of a large number of physical, chemical and biological processes that operate in the natural environment, and the processes induced by human use of wetlands and their adjacent environment. All these processes operate in both time and space at varying scales and degrees, some of which can be manipulated by humans in favour of conservation, while others are beyond their direct control.

Wetlands in Assam

In Assam, wetlands are locally known as *Beel, Khal, Dong, Jalah, Pitoni, Doloni, Mora Nadi, Hola, Doba, Nala, Pukhuri* and so on depending upon their origin, size, shape and depth. However, the most popular Assamese word used to designate a typical wetland is *Beel.* Thus, in the names of wetlands of considerable dimensions, the word *beel* is associated in most cases like Deepor Beel, Mori Beel, Sone Beel, Bhereki Beel, Urpod Beel, Tamranga Beel, Kayakujia Beel, Chandubi Beel, Ramor Beel etc.

The geographical distribution of beels in Assam reveals that they mostly occur in the riverine tracts of the Brahmaputra and the Barak basins. The flat riverine tracts geomorphologically allow the presence of a large number of beels with inlet-outlet networks. One of the causes behind the richness of these tracts in terms of biodiversity is the existence of the wetlands. Presently, because of intensification of cropping and extension of other economic

District-wise Distribution of Wetlands in Assam

District	Number	Area (in ha)	District	Number	Area (in ha)
Barpeta	97	3301	Karbi Anglong	77	897
Bongaigaon	100	3158	Karimganj	70	5719.5
Cachar	340	7188	Kokrajhar	85	1578.4
Darrang	103	3515	Lakhimpur	151	3033.5
Dhemaji	139	3960	Marigaon	183	11658
Dhuburi	233	6459.7	Nagaon	379	11295.5
Dibrugarh	86	2752.5	N.C.Hills	10	2252.5
Goalpara	165	3832.5	Nalbari	68	1988
Golaghat	330	5467.5	Sivsagar	109	2315
Hailakandi	47	840	Sonitpur	206	3651
Jorhat	109	2108.5	Tinsukia	74	2732.5
Kamrup	352	11407	**Total**	**3513**	**101232**

Source: Assam Remote Sensing Application Centre, Guwahari.

activities to these marginal areas, most of the wetlands have been suffering from severe eco-degradation.

Factors Responsible for Wetland Degradation

A variety of physical and human factors are found responsible for degradation and, in cases, extinction of wetlands in different parts of the world. In the world as whole, the area under wetland has now come down to nearly four per cent from around six per cent in the early part of the last century. The rapid population growth, particularly during the last two hundred years or so (from 1 billion in 1800 to 7 billion in 2012) and its associated developments including infrastructural extensions have put unprecedented pressure on all kinds of natural resources, more particularly the wetlands, as they are close to human habitats and their resources are easier for direct exploitation.

In the Brahmaputra valley, Assam, for instance, the population has increased from only two million in 1901 to about 22 million in 2001 - a ten-fold increase- which is substantially more than the rate of national increase. As a result of this type of growth the hilly areas, the low-lying areas along the rivers and other marginal areas have been increasingly brought under human habitation and intensive use. One of the important consequences of this is the mounting pressure and threat on, among others, the wetland eco-systems of the valley. It is worth mentioning in this connection that most of the wetland areas have been brought under cultivation and other uses including installation of large number of brick industries.

As there has been large scale interference of various forms like expansion of villages and towns, agricultural practices, infrastructural developments like construction of roads, railways, etc., raising of embankments, seriously disturb the eco-systems, mainly their inlets and outlets. Urpad of Goalpara district

with an area of 6 sq km is an important wetland in the floodplains of lower Brahmaputra valley. Jinari, a south bank tributary of Brahmaputra is the major inlet to feed Urpad. In the early 1970s when an embankment was constructed separating the river from the wetland, it adversely affected the natural drainage of the wetland in general and its outlet Jinjiram in particular and above all the biological diversity of the wetland eco-system. Significantly, enough, this kind of unfriendly interference made by humans on the environment is held responsible by many for the unprecedented flash flood of the otherwise mild Jinari river that occurred on 7th October, 2004 killing more than 250 persons within a time span of three-four hours at night.

Development of human settlements and industries around the wetlands can degrade the water quality and decrease the wetland area. Degradation of water quality adversely affects the eco-system of the wetlands. Another important cause of shrinkage of wetlands, in and around Guwahati city area, for instance, is the dumping of huge garbage generated daily in the city. Interestingly, there are three government authorised protected wetlands in Guwahati city area. These are Deepor beel, Borsola beel and Sarusala beel. But except for the Deepor beel, to a certain extent, the other two beels have been almost neglected. As a result they are getting degraded rapidly. Importantly enough, the Borsola beel helps in controlling the occasional flash floods as it is connected with the Bharalu river and many other areas and take the burden of over loaded water of the city during summer.

Deepor beel also bears great importance as aquatic ecosystem. For long it has been an important destination of many migratory bird species. But as the 40 sq.km. wetland has now shrunk to only five sq km, it has naturally lost its past ecological significance.

Similarly, there are many other wetlands in and around the Guwahati city, like Silsako and Bondajan which are more or less heading towards extinction.

Many wetlands in the state are either in highly degraded condition or near extinct form. The changes in the hydrological and geomorphological behaviour of the rivers especially, the Brahmaputra after the great earthquake of 1950 have significantly affected the shape, size and sustainability of the wetland ecosystems. The widening of the Brahmaputra due to lateral erosion has been found to be directly responsible for the disappearance of those wetlands which were located very close to river. However, wetlands which are inside the protected areas like the wildlife sanctuaries and national parks are comparatively safe as they are looked after and maintained under the rules and regulations for the protected areas. But for all those outside protected areas, there is no strict regulation to practically protect and sustainably develop the wetlands. As a result they are getting very rapidly degraded and in cases even completely destroyed.

Conservation Efforts

Conservation of natural element does not imply any use by human society whatsoever; it rather means a kind of management to allow a certain system to recover its loss. The aim of conservation is to manage or regulate use so that it does not exceed the capacity of the system to regenerate itself. The World

Conservation Strategy, a major international initiative launched in 1980 defined three key objectives of nature conservation : (a) to maintain essential ecological processes and life-support systems, (b) to preserve genetic diversity and (c) to ensure sustainable use of species and eco-systems by the present and future generations.

There was a time when wetlands were generally regarded as wastelands which might be useful only after reclamation. But the rapid destruction of wetlands for human use on the one hand and growing scientific knowledge and understanding of them on the other, have encouraged people to work for its protection. Attempts have already been made in different parts of the world to protect the remains of the wetlands. The Ramsar convention held in the Iranian city of the same name as back as 1971 is considered to be a landmark so far conservation of wetlands is concerned. This convention identified around 800 wetlands throughout the world having high potentiality for conservation. Deepar Beel of Assam and Loktok lake of Manipur are two among them in North East India.

Systematic efforts towards scientific conservation of rivers and wetlands are yet to gain notable ground in many of the countries of the world including India. In a growing economy with huge population and subsistence background, haphazard exploitation of natural resources is more common than their systematic conservation. It is more so in India, especially in the states like Assam where the economy continues to remain by and large traditional and pressure of population on the land and water resources in particular is alarmingly high. Wetland conservation is a big challenge before the humanity needing sincere and committed efforts from the people who have historically evolved a close link with such ecosystems and from the concerned governments, the legal custodians of such invaluable but degrading State resources.

For conservation of such kind of wetlands one of the important options is to encourage the local people to join hands with the concerned authority for their systematic protection.

If necessary, people will have to convince the administration to take required steps for the protection and sustainable development of the wetlands. However, the simplest way to manage wetland is not to allow any significant change in the land use type and pattern or hydrologic modifications in and around the wetlands. Government should strictly implement the scheme it has already taken up for the conservation of wetlands. The following points, however, may be noted in this regard:

1. The wetlands which become shallow due to siltation may be dug time to time very carefully and selectively in order to maintain their depth, otherwise they gradually loose their ecological significance.

2. Steps for cleaning the wetlands (wherever necessary), like removal of water hyacinth and other weeds should be taken up from time to time systematically keeping in view the role of all the related aspects of the local environment.

3. Water quality test like salinity, pH, turbidity, dissolved oxygen, arsenic etc. should be done in regular basis to ensure the continuity of habitable condition for the survival of aquatic animals and plants.

4. Constitution of a wetland authority in the State may go a long way in conservation and sustainable development of these aquatic entities, which not only provide valuable resources for human use but also extend a variety ecological services for sustenance of both nature and human society.

References

• A. K. Bhagabati, Wetlands in Assam, in D.C. Baroowa *et al.* eds, *Aspects of Land Policy in Assam*, VKIC, Guwahati, 2013.

• A. Goudie, *The Nature of the Environment,* Blackwell Publishers, Oxford, 2001.

• R.T. Wright, and B.J. Nebel, *Environmental Science: Towards a Sustainable Future*, Prentice Hall of India, New Delhi, 2002.

• H.J. Walker, *et. al.,* Wetland Loss in Louisiana, *Geografiska Annaler,* Vol. 69 A, 1987. pp. 189-200.

• S.J. Brady, and C.H. Flather, Changes in Wetlands on Non-federal, Rural Land of the Coterminous United States from 1982-87, *Environmental Management,* 18 (5), 1994, pp. 693-705.

• C. Park, *The Environment,* Routledge, London and New York, 1997.

• J.M. Rubenstein, *The Cultural Landscape: An Introduction to Human Geography,* MacMillan Publishing Company, New York, 1989.

• D. Sahariah, and A.K. Bora, Wetlands of North-East India, in S. Deka (ed.) *North-East India: Geo-Environmental Issues,* EBH Publishers, Guwahati, 2008, pp. 249-272.

• P. Bhattacharya and A.K. Bhagabati, The Flash of Jinari River: Problems and People's Perception, *Proceedings of National Seminar on Conservation, of Environment,* PANEI, Guwahati, 2005, pp. 42-47.

• B. C. Allen, *Assam District Gazetters*, Vol. 14, Kamrup, Guwahati, 1905.

38

The Potential Impacts of Climate Change in Greater Himalayas

Kanak Ch. Deka, IPS (Rtd.)

High mountain environment in the Greater Himalayas is one of the most complex and sensitive ecosystem on the earth. Due to strong altitude differences and complicated topography, several climatic levels are formed within short vertical distance. Seasonal differences are very conspicuous. The presence of glaciers even complicates the situation. Besides, current climate changes influence considerably the natural processes in high mountains over the world.

Hundreds of millions of people live in mountains being dependent on natural changes of environment, facing the harsh climate, difficult life conditions and various kinds of natural hazards. One of the most important hazards is potential change of water resources due to reduction of glacial mass and change of amount and spatial distribution of precipitations. Glaciers in the Himalayas are melting more rapidly than previously thought. Potential consequences of glacier changes would be unsustainable water supplies from major rivers and geo hazards (glacier-lake expansion, glacier lake out bursts and flooding), which might threaten the livelihood and well-being of in the downstream region.

Climate change is likely to manifest in the greater Himalayan regions by way of increasing temperatures, changing rainfall patterns, increasing aridity and intensity of extreme weather events and climate related disasters (such as droughts, floods, debris flows, glacial lake outburst, landslides and avalanches) indeed, trends over the last few decades. Current climate variability is already adversely impacting development, especially, on sectors such as water, agriculture and energy.

Furthermore, although the region is prone to earthquakes, the majority of disasters are triggered by hydro-meteorological hazards, including drought, floods, extreme temperatures and rainfall related landslides, debris-flows, lake

outbursts all of which are likely to increase under a changing climate. Unless timely, co-ordinated and sustainable Climate Risk Management (CRM) measures are implemented, Himalayan region is likely to experience considerable economic loss, humanitarian stresses and environmental degradation as a result of climate related disasters and incremental change in climate conditions.

The two most deadly natural hazards (earthquakes and volcanic eruptions) are not directly affected by global warming, but most mountain areas in the Himalayas are subject to multiple other hazards and pressures. Globally, climate change is very likely to increase in pressure exerted by non- seismic hazards. Higher temperature will enhance the hydrological cycle and it is predicted that they will alter rainfall patterns and intensity.

However, there is growing scientific evidence that Himalayan regions have become increasingly disaster prone in recent decades, and that a disproportionally high number of natural disasters occur in mountain areas. Entire Himalayan region is vulnerable to rain – induced (torrential rainfall) hazards in the form of flash floods, cloud burst or glacial lake outburst, flood, Flash floods and cloud burst are generally caused by high intensity rainfall followed by debris flow or landslide often resulting into blockade of river channels. The Himalayas is considered to be the youngest mountains on the earth, and is tectonically very active, and hence inherently (geologically) vulnerable to hazards.

Melting glaciers and rising temperatures are forming a potential destructive combination in the deep ravines of Himalayan foot hills. A sustained glacier retreat would increase the volume of water in rivers and also sediments, which could affect agriculture. When glaciers retreat, lakes commonly form behind the newly exposed debris –soil and rocks called moraine which is carried along by the leading edge of the ice wall. Rapid accumulation of water in these lakes could lead to sudden breach of the moraine dam, causing a possible catastrophic Glacial-lake outburst flood (GLOF). In the recent past, Nepal alone has been affected by 21 GLOF events.

Himalayan Tsunami – 2013

From 14 to 17 June, 2013, the North India states of Uttarakhand and Himachal Pradesh experienced heavy rainfall that triggered devastating floods and landslides. One of the worst natural disasters has been seen in Uttarakhand in the Himalayan region when, on June 16, 2013 flash floods caused by a cloud burst and glacial leaks swept thousands of unsuspecting pilgrims away in what scientists are now referring to as a "Himalayan Tsunami". Potted with temples and often referred to as "The land of Gods", Uttarakhand state comprising of both Kumaun and Garhwal Himalayas attracts large numbers of pilgrims from around the country and abroad to its mountainous reaches. Death toll could exceed 1000 still besides the largest temple Kedarnath which is one of the holiest Hindu temples and is located on the Garhwal Himalayas. The temple is at a height of 11,755 feet and at a distance of 223-km from Rishikesh on the shores of Mandakini river, a tributary of Ganges. Countless tourists and pilgrims were trapped for days in pitiable conditions until the

Indian defense forces came to their rescue in aerial sorties one after another. Thousands are still missing and many towns and pilgrimage sites in the Himalayas remain inaccessible, as the raging waters carried away whole strips of roads, along with homes, shops and hotels on the riversides and helpless victims. Barrages of water, mud and rocks have hit the scores of towns and villages in Uttarakhand, inundating homes shrines, roads, and vehicles.

Mighty Mountains Made Fragile : The upper Himalayan territories of Uttarakhand are full of forests and snow covered mountains in Gangotri group of peaks in western Garhwal Himalayas—Kedarnath and Kedar Dome on south of Gangotri and northwest of Kedarnath temple over where cloud burst took place on 15th June. Heavy rainfall for four consecutive days as well as melting of Chorabari glacier at the height of 3800 meters and eruption of the Mandakini river aggravated large flashfloods and massive landslides. As a result. huge boulders broke away from Kedar Dome and ruptured Chorabari lake reservoir, about six-km from the temple. Torrential waters rushed down with tons of debris, slush and hurtled towards the shrine of Kedarnath. Warnings by the Indian Meteorological department predicting heavy rains were not given wide publicity beforehand, causing thousands of people to be caught unawares, resulting in huge loss of lives and properties.

Environmental Issues: Unprecedented destruction by rain witnessed in Uttarakhand state attributed by environmentalists to careless developmental activities undertaken in recent decades and this contributed to high level loss of properties and lives. These are:

1. Construction of 70 hydro –electric projects recently, including 37 in high landslide susceptibility zone which increased instability of slopes. Dams once considered the blessing of mankind are now a days becoming the concern of environments.
2. Roads constructed in haphazard manner.
3. New resorts and hotels built on fragile river banks.
4. Commercialisation of pilgrimage routes with encroachment on river banks, forests and dangerous slopes increased the risk manifold.
5. Erratic rain pattern of intense bursts then slowdown caused loosening of Himalayan rocks, flooding of silted rivers.
6. With the flow of river water restricted, it contributed to higher number of landslides and more floods.

Is It a Man-made Disaster?

1. With the climate change widely acknowledged to be the result of the burning of fossil fuels and emission of excessive carbon dioxide into the atmosphere, it is clear that the ongoing tragedy is human – induced.
2. The glacial lake outburst flood (GLOF) that poured down the mountains bringing boulders and rocks is just another sign that the delicate balance of nature's forces has been disrupted – and Uttarakhand is paying the price.
3. The youngest mountain range in the world, the Himalayas is already prone to erosion, landslides and seismic activity. Development cannot come at cost of the environment in any region of the country, but particularly not in

the Himalayas. Environment experts observed that there had been no credible environmental or social impact assessments of hundreds of projects in the region.

4. *Hydel Projects:* CAG, in environment assessment report, had alerted the Centre and Uttarakhand Government that mushrooming hydel power projects on the Bhagirathi and Alakananda rivers were damaging hills and increasing the possibility of flash floods.

5. Extensive Deforestation, is likely to have worsened impact of flash floods. Scientists also say that construction of dams on the rivers Alakananda, Bhagirathi, Mandakini and other tributaries of Ganga and Yamuna flowing through this mountain region, riverbed encroachment and mining activities are wreaking havoc on the region.

In conclusion, it can be said that casualty and damage due to hazards in mountain regions will increase irrespective of global warming especially where populations are growing and infrastructure is developed at exposed locations. But climate change will definitely increase 'risk' due to the fact that expected increase of heavy rainfall, heat waves and glacial melt will amplify hazards in Himalayas and other mountains worldwide. The International Center for Mountain Development (ICIMOD), in Nepal and the Inter-Governmental Panel on Climate Change (IPCC) agree that global warming will also lead to more storms and floods, especially in tropical and mountainous regions. A report by ICIMOD on the impact on climate change on Himalayan glaciers state, "On the Indian sub-continent, Temperature are predicted to rise between 3.5 and 5.5 degree centigrade by 2100. The change in climate is likely to affect both minimum and maximum recorded temperatures as well as triggering more extreme rainfall events and storms". These heavy storms and floods will jeopardise the economic profitability of hydro-power projects as well as its safety.

A recent international studies indicate that the construction of mega dam and creation of huge water body in seismic sensitive regions on the earth is not advisable, considering complex geological aspects.

Adaptation strategies will need to adopt an integrative approach that covers the whole risk cycle from prevention to recovery. An international co-operation is strongly needed to effectively address the challenges prescribed above in the forthcoming International Conference on "Mountain Hazard, 2013" held in Bishhek, Kyrgyzstan on September 16 to 18, 2013.

39

Safeguarding the Rhinoceros Unicornis

Arup Kumar Dutta

The great Indian one-horned rhino (*Rhinoceros unicornis*) once had a home range across the whole of northern and eastern India and Nepal, from what is now Pakistan as far as Peshawar in the west and Assam in the east. It was extensively found in the alluvial flood-plains of mega-rivers like the Indus, Ganges and the Brahmaputra, as well as the Terai regions of Nepal and Sikkim. There are a host of historical and hunting references to show that it was present in large numbers.

The earliest relic of the animal was discovered by archaeologists at the Mohenjo-Daro excavations. It consisted of a seal bearing the figure of a one-horned rhino. The Mohenjo-Daro civilisation existed around 5,000 years ago and the fact that the animal was used as a seal indicates the significance it held in the popular imagination of that era. The Rhino seal is now preserved in the National Museum at New Delhi. Rhino bones have been also discovered at the Harappan excavation sites.

The fifth pillar edict of Asoka the Great in the 3rd century BC, enumerating the animals that needed to be protected, mentions the Indian rhino, indicating that hunting of this species by human beings had already commenced. Among the fauna to be preserved are mentioned "bats, monkeys, rhinoceroses, squirrels, barasingha stags, brahminy bulls and all four-footed animals which were not utilised or eaten."

From ancient times the Indian rhino was a favourite "game" for hunters, who saw in its intimidating appearance and size vindication of their own prowess. As early as 1398 Timur Beg hunted rhinos at the Kashmir frontier; in 1519 Babur hunted rhinos in Peshawar and in his memoirs he describes how he killed three rhinos on a hunt accompanied by his son Humayun. Abul Fazl records that the Indian rhino was present in the Sambal Sarkar of Delhi during

the reign of Akbar. There are numerous references right to the 18th century of rhino-hunting in the Indian sub-continent, with one Rana of Nepal being credited with 97 rhino-kills in a single month! In the second half of the 19th century the Indian rhino abounded in Coochbehar and the Maharaja there once recorded having killed five rhinos before lunch. In Assam rhino-hide was being used to make shields for soldiers, while later European tea-planters killed them by the dozen, camping around the river Mora Difloo and routinely shooting "two or three rhinoceroses before breakfast."

The absence of historical references points to the gradual elimination of the Indian rhino from the Indo-Gangetic plains by the 18th century, hunting and habitat loss being the primary causes. By the beginning of the 20th century the remnants of rhino population had been wiped out from Uttar Pradesh and Bihar, but in Bengal rhino presence was strong well into the 20th century, so much so that shrinking loss of habitat brought them into conflict with villagers. Believe it or not, the government, holding the animal responsible for damage to paddy, offered Rs 20 per head for its destruction!

Today, an animal that had once roamed in thousands across a huge segment of the sub-continent survives precariously in a few pockets in Assam, West Bengal and Nepal, its number hovering around the 3,000 mark. Sadly, despite its endangered status, the persecution of the animal in the hands of man continues, the difference being that in earlier time it was hunted for pleasure, now for hard cash. It is this lucrative element associated with its horn which makes safe-guarding the *Rhinoceros uniçornis* so difficult a job and remains the sole reason why the animal continues to be killed in these "enlightened" times.

From ancient days man had woven a web of mystical beliefs around the great Indian one-horned rhinoceros. One of the earliest legends associated with the animal was that of the Unicorn, a fabulous animal which ancient accounts portray as having the body of horse, bearded and with cloven hooves. On its head grew a single helical horn, perfectly straight, about 0.5 to 1 meter in length. The Unicorn was an enigmatic symbol and was used by the church as an allegory to interpret Christianity. The Bible compares the Unicorn to Christ, who raised up the horn of salvation for mankind. The Unicorn, especially its horn, was endowed with many alleged magical properties, which tended to reinforce popular superstitions associated with the horn. With the passage of time the legendary attributes of the mythical Unicorn rubbed on to the *Rhinoceros unicornis*, spelling its doom. It is interesting to note that powdered rhino horn is an essential ingredient of traditional Chinese pharmacopoeia, China being one of the countries where the Unicorn legend was widely prevalent.

Hindu mythology also placed the Indian rhino on a highly revered pedestal. According to one popular legend the rhino was created as a *bahon* for Vishnu, one of the members of the Hindu Trinity. At that point of time the rhino did not have a horn on its snout. After saddling the beast Vishnu mounted it, but the animal proved to be obstinate and did not obey commands. The Preserver, in his wrath, took off one of the *kharams* (wooden clogs) he was wearing and threw it at the animal. The rhino, even though beholding Vishnu's

wrath, did not flee but bowed its head reverentially. The *kharam* hit its snout and was transformed into a horn. Since it was made of an object that had touched the Lord's feet, it attained divine powers! Similar legends glorifying the rhino, especially its horn, abound in India, China, Nepal, Myanmar and other Asian countries. The cumulative effect of such myth-making was to invest the animal with a divinity it neither deserved nor desired. Superstitions that sprang from deification have proved to be extremely tenacious and false beliefs remain even today, leading to the slaughter of this animal for its various body parts.

Of all its organs it is the horn of the rhino which is most sought after, being literally worth its weight in gold. Since ancient times magical properties have been attributed to the horn. Like the fabulous Unicorn the horn of its namesake was supposed to have powers of detecting poison. Thus a goblet made from the horn could protect its owner from venom. Medieval rulers being in perpetual terror of being poisoned by their rivals, rhino horn cups were of great demand! Another fanciful belief is that powdered rhino horn can sharpen jaded sexual appetites and restore manly vigour. The rejuvenating property of the horn and its prowess as an aphrodisiac is still widely believed in many parts of South East Asia, and this acts as a powerful incentive for the persecution of the rhino. Various legends apart, two other factors serve to perpetuate the myth of the horn's aphrodisiac properties. Because of its shape the horn was believed to represent the *linga*, or the male sexual organ. At the same time the rhino's period of copulation during mating is inordinately long, in fact far longer than other animals of the bigger variety. These two factors have led to the perniciously false belief of rhino-horn being an aphrodisiac.

Today, the primary use of this horn is as an essential ingredient in a powdered form in Chinese pharmacopeia, both for its presumed "medicinal" value and also as an aphrodisiac. Medicines containing rhino horn are sold all over south-east Asia mainly among migrant Chinese communities, for a wide variety of ailments. In South-East Asian countries the demand for the rhino horn is in proportion to the size of the ethnic Chinese population. If we look at the economics of demand and supply, we can delve into the root cause as to why the animal continues to be slaughtered.

It is interesting to note that legal trade in horns collected from rhinos which had died of natural causes had been permitted till the early 1970s, which had made poaching almost redundant and kept prices down. But once the Convention of International Trade in Endangered Species of Flora and Fauna (CITES) was framed at Washington on 3rd March, 1973, legal trade in the commodity completely stopped. Till the 1970s Singapore was the main centre for legal trade in horn, but all that changed after it adopted CITES. With the sale of legally obtained horns drying up, a black-market for illegally obtained horns through poaching sprang up in countries such as Taiwan and trade centers such a Macao.

Also, the price of rhino horn touched unimaginable heights. When its sale was legal the price fetched in the Calcutta market was around 150-200 pounds per horn, and at the Guwahati sales the price secured was about

Rs 65,000 per kg. But, after CITES, the price rose till it touched around $40,000 per kg in the international market at illicit trade centers such as Taipei. Prices have fluctuated in accordance with the demand and so have cases of poaching. For instance, between 1965-1971, when CITES had not come into being, there were 63 cases of rhino poaching in Kaziranga, but in the post-CITES period, between 1983-1989, the number of poaching cases in Kaziranga shot up to 235.

Similarly, when China signed CITES and enforced a ban on rhino-horn products in the mainland, price of the horn of the Indian rhino witnessed a drop, though demand continued in the migrant Chinese communities of south-east Asia. But recently, as reported in sources such as National Geographic, a rumour sprang up in Vietnam that rhino horn had cured a minister from cancer, which jacked up prices to a fantastic sum of $60,000 per kg or twice the value of gold and even more than the street value of cocaine.

Continued usage in migrant Chinese pockets, resulting in continued demand and escalating prices, lie at the core of the problem of rhino poaching. The exorbitantly high prices the rhino-horn commands ensure that poachers will not hesitate to put their lives at stake, though at the field-level they are paid a pittance compared to what the middlemen and end-level players get. Little wonder that in South Africa crime syndicates have entered the poaching business, while in India it has been taken over by insurgents.

This also means that no matter what protective measures to safe-guard the *Rhinoceros unicornis* are taken, the species will always be open to the danger of being poached upon, as long as the demand for its horn remains. For instance, despite growing conservation consciousness and public outcry, in the year 2012 poachers killed a record 21 rhinos in habitats such as Kaziranga, this high mortality trend being continued into 2013. Thus the only way effective conservation measures can be effected is through a concerted effort to lessen the demand for rhino horns amongst end-users even as more effective measures are taken to protect the animal. Conservation agencies have carried out chemical analysis in laboratory conditions and uncovered the truth that the rhino horn is a compact mass of agglutinated hair and contains no aphrodisiac component. In 1967, the International Union for Conservation of Nature and Natural Resources (IUCN) had analysed samples of rhino horn at Basle, Switzerland — the laboratory analysis confirmed rhino horn is formed of keratin tissues (a fibrous protein, the chief constituent of hair), is inert, has no biochemical or hormonal properties, and possesses no medicinal value whatsoever.

In other words, one might as well eat one's own hair for all the good that it would do! This truth needs to be driven home amongst the end-users if poaching of this unfortunate creature is ever to end. Since the end-users of the horn of the Indian rhino are primarily migrant Chinese pockets in various countries, the endeavour will have to be an international one and involve international conservation agencies under the aegis of the United Nations. Only when the end-users are convinced of the stupidity of using a commodity which has no medicinal value will the *Rhinoceros Unicornis* be truly safe.

It is within such a context that the following recommendations can be made in order to frame a viable and practical strategy to protect the great Indian one-horned rhino in the few habitats that are left.

1. An international endeavour, involving the Government of India, Government of Assam, West Bengal, Government of Nepal and conservation agencies including those associated with the United Nations as also Non-Government organisations, must be launched to educate end-users of the futility of using rhino-horn in order to decrease demand. It is only cessation of demand which will result in fall of prices of rhino-horn in the international black-market, thereby eradicating the incentive to slaughter this innocent animal.

2. While the primary thrust would be to lessen demand, till such an objective is attained, measures to protect the animal within its habitats must be reinforced. The IUCN in its compilation of endangered animals of the earth, ominously titled the *Red Data Book,* had earlier included the *Rhinoceros unicornis*, since the RDB contains a list of endangered species of animals whose number had decreased to below 2000. However, since due to conservation efforts the number of Indian rhino has increased to around 3000, the IUCN has taken the animal out of the RDB. However, it would be unwise to think that it is out of the woods yet, for there have been periodic spurts in rhino deaths which might push down the number of this animal. For example, 235 rhinos were killed by poachers between 1983 and 1989. In the same period 368 rhinos died due to natural causes, which brought the total to 603 deaths, an alarming figure for an animal which then had numbered below 2000.

In the Jaldapara Sanctuary in West Bengal the number of rhinos declined from 88 in 1979 to 39 in 1989. In 1983, when large-scale violence and anarchy prevailed in strife-torn Assam, opportunist poachers took advantage of the situation to wipe out the entire rhino population of Laokhowa Wild Life Sanctuary. In 1988-89, when a section of Bodos agitated for a separate State, poachers made use of the anarchic situation to kill every rhino in Manas.

Thus today the Indian rhino continues to be in grave danger. The problem is compounded by the fact that a bulk of the rhino population is concentrated in just two national parks, Kaziranga in Assam and Chitawan in Nepal. An epidemic or two, or even civil strife, can bring down the rhino population below the danger mark. This is the reason why the recent decision of the IUCN to remove the Indian rhino from the RDB and deprive it of the "endangered" tag is an unwise one, for recent spurt of killings clearly show that the animal is still in dire straits.

Thus, the Indian Government needs to pressurise the IUCN to reinstate the great Indian one- horned rhinoceros in the list of "endangered" species so that conservation efforts at an international level can be sustained and intensified.

3. In recent times there have been a record number of rhino killings in primary rhino habitats such as Kaziranga. What was State Government's response to that? A typical bureaucratic and political one — the Assam Government has ordered a probe by the CBI into all incidents of rhino-poaching

in the last three years. It has also asked for the army's help in combing the Karbi Anglong hills to flush out rebels. But these are merely temporary measures designed to tackle a crisis of the moment. More permanent measures are required to ensure the safety of all wild creatures in all game-sanctuaries of Assam.

Even today Kaziranga, Manas and lesser sanctuaries remain soft-targets for poachers given the inadequacy of existing infrastructure and security apparatus. There is a notable lack of trained security personnel. The area of Kaziranga National Park has doubled in the last three decades but the number of forest personnel has not been commensurately increased and the park continues to be vulnerable, as shown by the spate of recent killings. All that the government does in times of crisis, such as the unprecedented high-floods of 2012, is to employ temporary home-guards without training.

Most of the permanent guards have become aged, over 50 years, and are hardly in physical condition to chase and confront poaching gangs. Moreover, the living and working conditions of the forest field staff are pitiable and they do not get the basic amenities. Also, considering the risks they have to confront, they are not paid adequate wages, which is one reason why black-sheep amongst them occasionally act in collusion with poaching gangs.

There is, therefore, an urgent need to improve the working conditions of the field staff, as also to bring about a thorough overhaul of the security apparatus and infrastructure in our wild life sanctuaries.

4. In the last decade there has been an ominous change in the method of poaching in our wild-life habitats while earlier it had been the pit-system which was used to trap and kill the animal, later methods such as electrocution by laying exposed wires hooked to high-tension electric transmission cables on rhino paths as well as sophisticated weapons have been used. Equally insidious has been the intrusion of insurgent elements into the wild-life habitats armed with extremely state-of-the-art weapons which forest guards with their obsolete rifles can hardly be expected to combat. The latest method of killing ominously warns us of an even greater danger in one of the killings in Kaziranga in 2012 tranquilliser guns were used these shoot tranquillising agents such as Ketamine hydrochloride (also known as Aniket) and also Etrophine tranquillisers into the unsuspecting beasts to subdue them before they are slaughtered. Such attacks are silent and will not alert forest guards as gunfire does. Such development entail that a totally different approach towards guarding our precious wildlife habitats have to be made.

The most urgent need of the hour, therefore, is the creation of a well-trained, well-armed elitist Wild Animal Protection Force devoted exclusively to guard wild life habitats such as Kaziranga.

5. Another negative development has been the setting up of industries within or adjacent to wildlife preserves as well as protected eco-systems. For instance within the Kaziranga "no development" region and other wildlife sanctuaries such as Karbi Anglong Elephant Reserve and Deepor Beel wetland eco-system, industrial units have been allowed to be set up and mining activities carried on. The National Green Tribunal (NGT) has expressed

displeasure with the Union Ministry of Environment and Forests as also the Assam State Forest Department at their failure to respond to allegations of unregulated quarrying and mining.

Given such a scenario, all industries, mining, brick-kilns, etc., within the extended area of wild life habitats need to be immediately declared illegal and removed.

6. It is also necessary to educate the villagers around our wildlife habitats on the inhuman nature of slaughtering innocent animals which are the pride of Assam so that they actively resist poaching activities. It is a fact that some unscrupulous villagers often harbour poachers for money and also act as guides. At the same time, during times of food scarcity within their habitats wild animals occasionally stray out and destroy paddy crops. Similarly, usurpation of traditional habitats have increased man-elephant conflicts and make villagers hostile to the concept of wildlife preservation The government also not only gives poor compensation but also is tardy in making payments.

A sustained campaign is needed on the part of the State Forest Department in collaboration with non-government organisations to educate villagers on the benefits of conservation of Assam's wildlife treasures. The government also needs to enhance compensation amounts in order to mitigate public hostility and ensure that payments are made quickly.

7. Encroachment by groups of migrants of doubtful Indian nationality has become a major threat to survival of wildlife havens like Kaziranga as well as protected forests. Latest arrests of poachers point to the reality that most of them belong to this group of illegal encroachers. As reported time and again in the media due to political considerations the State Government so far have made no move to remove the encroachers from protected land.

The State Government needs to display the political will to evict encroachers and free not only Kaziranga but also other wildlife parks and sanctuaries from their presence. Also, park authorities must ensure that villagers are not allowed to graze their cattle within sanctuaries so that danger of disease communication is minimised.

8. As mentioned before, the presence of the bulk of the population of an animal such as the Indian rhino in just a few habitats poses great danger of sudden mass loss. Thus translocation of animals to other suitable habitats is imperative if the animal is to increase numerically and have enhanced potentiality for survival. New habitats for a unique animal like the Indian rhino must be identified and given legal status before they are occupied by encroachers. In Assam itself there are other areas to which the rhino can be translocated, provided fool-proof security can be provided. The latter aspect has been made more significant with the killing of three translocated rhinos in Manas, primarily because the forest guards there were not used to tackling rhino-poachers. Thus, translocation needs to be attempted with extreme care so that necessary environmental and biotic factors are complied with and there is adequate security.

A concerted, scientific and continuous endeavour must therefore be made to translocate rhinos from optimum habitats like Kaziranga to less populated

habitats so that more rhino populations can be created for better chance of survival for this magnificent animal.

11. A major constraint in tackling the menace of poaching is the inadequacy of existing laws protecting wildlife in general and the Indian rhino in particular. Though of late more stringent laws have been enacted, these are yet not enough because of the huge financial stakes involved. Also, laws by themselves are no good unless there is a sincere attempt to implement them. Also, conventional civil and criminal courts are constrained by certain handicaps — for instance, there can hardly be "independent witnesses" when a poacher is caught by forest guards deep inside a sanctuary, but this is a statutory requirement of conventional courts, and allows many known poachers to roam free.

The need of the hour is creation of independent courts to try cases of crime against wild animals, as also the enactment of even more stringent punitive laws against perpetrators.

These are some of the many steps that can be taken to protect unique species such as the great Indian one-horned rhinoceros. It is needless to reiterate that the most important initiative which needs to be taken is to stop the demand for an item which has no medicinal or aphrodisiac value and is ingested only because of superstition. Safe-guarding the *Rhinoceros unicornis* must be taken as a national issue requiring national and international intervention.

40

Whither Forest Eco-systems

KND Goswami, IFS (Retd.)

During British Raj, reservation of Forests started in the middle of nineteenth century and only the unencumbered forests were taken up for reservation leaving vast areas of forests and wastelands for accommodation of increased population. 1894 Forest Policy of British government also adopted this principle to give more weightage to settlement of people rather than strict reservation of Forests and therefore question of encroachment did not arise then. Towards the later part of British rule however government encouraged settlement of people from across the border under the 'grow more food campaign'. Fortunately, there was vast tracts of vacant lands and government had no difficulty of choosing such lands for settlement and agriculture of these people. These vacant lands included riverine marshes, village forests and other forests which were not classified as reserved forests. Even several deep reserve forests were allowed to be cleared for development of infrastructure like roads and railways and industries like tea, collieries and oil exploration, etc., and establishment of staff colonies thereof. By and large there was not much of public resistance in settling the vast tracts of vacant lands, except in areas adjoined by indigenous population where there was some resistance offered by the local people. However, the government averted any untowards situation by adopting line system in many areas.

Just prior to independence and immediately after independence, there was a spurt of influx of people mostly from the adjoining country and by 1950 the ugly head of encroachment into reserved forests and other unclassified forests started showing up successively to the detriment of the forests of the state. In the aftermath of this, most of the unclassed forests in the plainland, village forests and even some village and protected grazing reserves were gradually opened up to accommodate more and more settlers who thronged in these areas either by migration or by infiltration. To ease out the situation further, even some reserve forests were cleared to settle forest villages in the

manner followed by British government which started in the year 1866 in Sylhet district of erstwhile Assam. Subsequently, more forest villages were created in the districts of Goalpara, Kamrup, Cachar, Nowgong during 1902 to 1920. By 1937, there were as many as 370 forest villages in the state. Even though settling of forest villages was necessary for supplying cheap labours in the interior of forests some villages were created to ease out the situation of increase demands for settlement of people. Nevertheless many of these forest villages thus created overgrew in population and extent, thereby requiring de-notification of part or in few cases full of several reserve forests. Therefore quite a large number of these forest villages got converted to revenue villages as the *"fait accompli"*. After 1950, again the policy of settling forest villages was adopted by independent government and upto 1975 several forest villages numbering 499 were created. It acted as "*a-posteriori*" to perpetuate gradual clearance of forest and posed a severe problem in maintaining all the legal provisions required as per the concerned rules. Even beyond the number of forest villages constituted there remained a large number of people still queuing up to be settled and the flow of stream of batches of people continued. In the process more than 60 reserve forests out of 312 reserve forests of present Assam were completely wiped out by 1970 even though these reserve forests are still shown as reserve forests in the records. Several other reserve forests are also simultaneously denuded of the vegetational cover setting these forests on the path of near extinction sooner or later.

In the initial stage of encroachment for settlement, all the valley bottom lands in the hilly terrain and entire forests of plain areas were taken up as the first charge. After exhausting the areas in the unclassed forests, the encroachers fan out to the nearby reserve forests. These unclassed forests which are under the control of revenue department also contained all the protective elements inherent in a forest ecosystem. These forests within a short span of time from 1947 to 1970 were practically wiped out leaving a meager area of 5800 sq kms in uncultivable hilly terrains as per records of the forest department Similarly, another 3800 sq kms of such forests were proposed to be reserved which remained undecided so far even after four to five decades have since slipped by. Existence of all these forests to that extent is incredulous in view of growing demand for land. In the same analogy the village forests which were created during British rule, were cleared and forgotten by the time India got independence. The village grazing reserves and protected grazing reserves which were set aside prior to independence, were also exhausted under the population pressure after independence leaving only a scanty vestibule of these grounds around the villages of indigenous settlers. This has led to deprivation of proper nourishment to the teeming cattle population of the people telling upon very adversely on health and productivity of these cattle. As a fall out, the cattle had to survive by chance eating and foraging into reserve forests as well as areas protected for conservation. This has posed a serious problem in conservational attempts of these areas subsequently.

It is obvious therefore that the forests of the state are successively cleared by encroachment and making the requirements of energy, raw materials for

cottage-based industries, fodder and fertilizer gradually become unavailable to cater to the needs of the rural population. Whatever reserve forests still remain are facing tremendous pressure to meet these requirements, stretching out the already beleaguered forest beyond its carrying capacity. Even the 1952 Forest policy of India showed up the hang-over of the previous policy regarding accommodation of growing demands of lands for agriculture. Nevertheless, this policy for the first time laid emphasis on setting aside a fixed geographical area under forest cover at 33 per cent on an average of the geographical area and specifically 60 per cent in the hills and 20 per cent in the plains to achieve the ecological balance required for well-being of the country. Constitution of India also provided for preservation of fragile ecology of areas occupied by forests, protection and improvement of environment *vis-a-vis* safeguarding of forests and wildlife and to have compassion for living creatures in the Articles 21, 48(A) and 51(A)g, as the fundamental duties of the government. In spite of policy principles and constitutional safeguards, the forests of the country more so of the state of Assam continuously beleaguered by clearance for settlement through encroachment. Even though all the peace-meal approaches were taken by government to satiate propensity of the increased population as the ill-luck would have it the pressure never ebbed down. Rather it grew both in magnitude and organisational strength of encroachers with the years passed by.

Unfortunately, the forest of the country received the utmost neglect and diversion of forests for non forestry purposes remained the mainstay of the government and the people alike to ease out population pressure. In this respect the state of Assam did not lag behind this perception and up till 1980, huge areas of state forests were de-notified either in parts or in full. By now except some traces left to be seen in the state reserves which were opened up partially they no more exist. As per estimate available about 3700 sq. kms of state reserves were denotified up till 1980 against 48,000 sq. kms in the whole country. Even though the limited areas were denotified with the hope to retain the rest, but in reality all such forests were overgrown with encroachments in a series and 60 Reserve forest out of 312 reserve forest of present Assam were completely occupied in the process without any visible action to curb the encroachment. As per records maintained by the department there is an area of 17,795 sq. kms of reserved and protected forest. The area officially shown to be occupied by 499 forest villages is 538 sq. kms, and 3000 sq kms is illegally occupied by encroachment. Excluding these areas actual state reserve areas will be only 14,250 sq. kms. Even these forests also are severely exploited and opened up giving rise to 65 per cent of the areas as open forest only (as per state report of Government of India in 2001). The areas which were further encroached after 1980 are not included in the above. In fact most of the forest in Sonitpur, Darrang and Lakhimpur are severely encroached thereafter. Under the circumstances the state of the forests of Assam is most deplorable and the state of Assam has earned the notoriety of being the topmost deplorable forest in the country.

Thankfully, Government of India promulgated the Conservation Act 1980 to bring a restraint to this spate of deforestation in the country. Even though

all other states in India left no stone unturned to translate the tenet of this Act in practice, unfortunately the state of Assam could not gear up to rise to this occasion for the state's inherent difficulties. Close at the heels, Indian Forest Policy was revised in 1988. This Policy was not a mere revision of the previous policy rather the policy by taking pragmatic and essential measures to protect the natural heritage of the country is by far the most practical one. This Policy has also clearly stated that no encroachment in the forest will be regularised.

In-spite of the constitutional safeguards and the Policy principles to safeguard the forests they remained at the mercy of the teeming population and encroachment continued to pose a burning problem in conservational attempts of the state forests. In this respect the role of the forest department does not appear to be pro-active one. Honourable apex court of India gave a ruling for ejection of such illegal encroachers in a PIL submitted by *Godavarman* vs *Union of India* in 1995. The department armed with the apex court order could garner the required support from the ccolateral departments of the government and clearance of illegal occupation of forest land could be initiated in 2001-02, but it did not take much time to fizzle out the tempo and position returned to square one again.

At this stage "the scheduled tribes and other traditional forest dwellers (recognition of forest right) Act 2006 was promulgated. Even though the Act is specifically meant for pre-agricultural communities viz., tribals who reside in the forest. These communities have symbiotic relationship for sustenance of ecology and anthoropogenous activities. Such communities are not residing in Assam. But a coterie of people whose main aim is to occupy forest lands is out for agrandisement of personal interest with the alibi of the Act although by misinterpretation. They received a shot in the arm in their activities uder the veil of Tribal population as mentioned in the Act. Unfortunately, the strong action required to quell such antiforest activities does not appear to be exhibited by government departments nor by a larger section of people living outside of the forest through any popular opposition to such a move of antiforest activists. Hence, the movement which already got underway was fortified to occupy most fragile ecosystem of the state. Interestingly, the intervention as required to be taken by the department was clearly negated. It is beyond our comprehension as to how constitutional and Policy principles *vis-à-vis* concerned rules and regulations were all pushed to precariously edged precipice by this act of a section of people. Notwithstanding the subsequent rules framed in 2008 under this Act were moderated by defining period of occupation of the forest land for earning right over land perhaps for justifiable actions to follow yet the harm already got underway did not subside. Resultant movements of encroaching into forest land even bordering Guwahati city can be viewed from this angle.

Assam's map has been successively redrawn along with creation of several north-eastern states. In these hill states valley lands for wet paddy cultivation being scarce the demand on fertile valley lands has grown over the years. As the borders of these states are fringed with state's reserve forests and as there remained a deficiency in permanently delineated boundaries it was an easy

walk for occupying these forests by the people from those states. Most of the reserve forests of the state in the border of Nagaland were already bedeviled by encroachers from Assam's side, the people from Nagaland simply joined the bandwagon from their side and occupied vast tracts of Rengmai, Merapani Doyang, Diphu, Dissoi, Desoivalley, Tiruhills and Galeki, etc., comprising almost 70 per cent on an average of approximately 1000 sq. kms of forests during the later part of sixty's and thereafter of the last century. Similarly, people from Arunachal also started encroachment into several bordering forests of Bhairabkunda, Kalingduar, Ronga, Gali Jiadhol, Kachajuli, Gohpur, Bihali, Chariduar, Na-duar, Singlijan and Balipara, etc., comprising about 30 per cent of more than 700 sq. kms of these Assam forests. People from Mizoram and Meghalaya also opened their doors to occupy smaller pockets in the bordering forests of Assam.

It is therefore apparent that encroachments into reserve forest is neither confined to any type of people based on ethnic variations nor any localised area of the forests. The spate of encroachment is unfortunately not coming to a halt after the conservation Act or even after the Supreme Court's ruling in this regard. Even after 1980 several deep forests were opened and occupied by encroachers and the activities of opening up forests are not showing any sign of hanging up.

The forest ecosystems can be restored if the disturbance perpetrated is within the resilience limit. Unfortunately, most of these reserve forests are repeatedly perturbed due to transformation of these forest lands into open agricultural and habitational purposes. In the early stages of encroachment the forest land is quite fertile due to availability of humus and soil moisture and with the time passing out the humus contents get consumed up without natural process of humus formation followed by. As a result to this the soil moisture and cation exchange capacity of soil get diminished. In addition to this ground water recharge by the forest floor rich with humus gets reduced with the time due to decrease of time of concentration of the watershed yield of runoff. With this the ground water gradually goes down making it unavailable for consumption by man, animals and agriculture alike. This is how a forest land on an eco-fragile area after destruction of the forest cover, the land becomes physically dry and unproductive. Socio-economic conditions of the very people who caused the destruction are set on the path of deterioration. This is a vicious cycle to which the poor encroachers unknowingly or even knowingly get holed up.

Forest ecosystem also provides a natural balance between the consumer animals versus producer plants. The food chains in the great food web of the ecosystem get askewed giving rise to increase of harmful pests which fall upon the adjoining traditional agricultural crop areas. Further the forest lands and agricultural lands of the watershed are suffering from ground water scarcity, flash floods, drought and soil erosion, etc., which we are witnessing every year conspicuously on the northern belt of Brahmaputra. Even the climatic factors like temperature, humidity and rainfall patterns are all effected adversely against sustainable development of large section of rural poor.

Many of our rural enterprises are based on the distinct set of climate provided by the forest ecosystems in eco-fragile areas of our state. Another phenomenon of man's conflict with elephant, monkeys, jungle cats of all varieties and many reptiles is increasing over the years.

To add to the list of woes that we are begetting from the loss of eco-fragile areas is not exhaustive. Loss of forest ecosystems is the primary cause of several species of flora and fauna being pushed to the wall. Occular observation made in this regard reveals that several species of plants viz., Ashok (Seraca indica), Hizol (Barringtonia, acutuangula), Kuhir (Bridelia retusa), Kendu (Diospyrus melanoxylon), Satkura a wild citrus tree (Citrus sp.), Haldu (Adina Cordifolia), Carpinia viminalis (Carpinia), Jutuli (Altingia excelsa), Gineri (Podocarpus nerifolium), Chalmogra (Hydnocarpus kurzii), Gandh Kachu (Homalomena aromatic), Damderuka (Impatient tripetata), Bonada (Zingiber zerumbet), Kola ada (Zingiber perpurea), Jam lakhuti (Costus indica), Satmul (As paragas racemosus), Sarpa gandha (Raulfia canascence), Kalmegh (Andrographics paniculata), Orchids (Vanda cerulis Rhynostylis sp. Vanila assamica, etc.), Pipoli (Piper nigrum), Cycads, Tree ferns, etc., are already in the threat of extinction in the forests. Several species of birds viz. Ulumora, Deohanh, Dawok, Sarali, Kamsorai, Borbog, Hargila, Bortukula, Dhanesh, Raja Sogun, Dhera (Pelicans) etc. are counting their days. Several reptiles like Soonguin, Crocodile, Bonrou (Pangolin), Tortoises (like Durakasa, Borkasa, roofed turtle, leaf turtle), gekkos, snakes (like Ajagor, Cobra, Mosuagum and Bakraj, etc.) are also dwindling alarmingly in our forests. Mammals like Sihoo (Gangetic dolphin), flying bats (Draco norvilis), flying squirrels, several primates like golden Lengur, Loris, Stumped tailed monkey, Rhesus monkey, Holow Bandar (Hullock gibbon), Phery's leaf monkey, etc., are precariously, surviving. So also several ungulates (viz., Swamp deer, gaur, Bison, wild goat, pigmy hog, spotted deer, etc.) are pushed to the wall. Several species of cat family (viz., clouded leopard, civet cats, tigers (Panthera tigris) are threatened with extinction.

Several species of biodiversity of Assam are endemic and once they are lost perhaps they will be wiped out from the surface of the globe. On the other hand, rich biodiversity of the forest ecosystems is a treasure trove which if properly protected and harvested scientifically can bring in a paradigm change to our state of economy in the field of agriculture, scientific research and many rural based industries. The depletion of this rich biodiversity is an alarm to our conscience as to whether we act on now to protect the forest ecosystems before we are acted up. Choice lies with our actions now.

41

The Brahmaputra River, North East India: Its Problems and Prospects

Dulal C. Goswami

Introduction

A river extraordinaire, the Brahmaputra in Assam presents a picture of awesome expanse, enchanting grandeur and immense vigour. It is one of the world's largest rivers with a drainage area of 580,000 sq. km (50.5 per cent in China, 33.6 per cent in India, 8.1 per cent in Bangladesh and 7.8 per cent in Bhutan). In India, its basin is shared by Arunachal Pradesh (41.9 per cent), Assam (36.3 per cent), Meghalaya (6.1 per cent), Nagaland (5.6 per cent); Sikkim (3.8 per cent) and West Bengal (6.3 per cent). Originating from the great glacier mass of Chema-Yung-Dung, south east of the Manasorovar lake in the Kailash range of southern Tibet at an elevation of 5300 metre, it traverses 1625 km in China, 918 km in India and 337 km in Bangladesh before emptying itself into the Bay of Bengal through a joint channel with the Ganga. A unique river, it drains such diverse environments as the cold dry plateau in Tibet, the rain-drenched Himalayan slopes, the landlocked alluvial plains of Assam, and the vast deltaic lowlands of Bangladesh. Flowing eastward for 1625 km over the Tibetan plateau, the Brahmaputra, known there as the Tsangpo, enters a deep narrow gorge at Pe (3,500 metre.) and continues southwards across the east-west trending ranges of the Himalayas viz., the Greater Himalayas, Middle-Himalayas and sub-Himalayas before debouching on to the Assam plain near Pasighat. These different geo-ecological zones have distinctive assemblages of topographical, geological, climatic and floral characteristics. The gradient of the Brahmaputra river is as steep as 4.3 to 16.8 m per km in the gorge section upstream of Pasighat, but near Guwahati it is as flat as 0.1 m per km. Two rivers, the Dibang and the Lohit, join the upper course of the Brahmaputra, known as the Dihang (or Siang) river, a little south of Pasighat and the combined flow, hereafter called the Brahmaputra, flows westward through Assam for

about 640 km until near Dhubri, where it abruptly turns south and enters Bangladesh taking a new name, Jamuna.

In Assam, the Brahmaputra flows in a highly braided channel marked by the presence of numerous mid-channel and lateral bars and islands. An extremely dominant monsoon interacting with a unique physiographic setting, fragile geological base and active seismo-tectonic instability together with anthropogenic factors have molded the Brahmaputra into one of the world's most intriguing and gigantic fluvial systems. In the course of its 2880 km journey, the Brahmaputra receives as many as 22 major tributaries in Tibet, 33 in India- mostly in the Northeastern region (20 of these coming from the north and 13 from the south), and three in Bangladesh. The Subansiri, Jia Bharali and Manas are the major trans-Himalayan tributaries of the Brahmaputra with the first two having their origin in Tibet (China) while the last one in Bhutan. The Dibang and Lohit are two other large tributaries emerging from the extreme eastern flank of the Himalayas. The Jiadhal, Ranganadi, Puthimari, Pagladiya, etc., are major rivers having their sources in the sub-Himalayas, the latter two in Bhutan. Among the south-bank tributaries, the Burhidihing originates at the Nagaland-Myanmar border, the Dhansiri and Dikhow in the Naga hills, the Kopili in the Karbi plateau, while the Kulsi and the Krishnai flow from the Meghalaya hills.

Legends and History

The Brahmaputra has been a subject of great mystery and reverence since the early days of our history and civilisation. The river is mentioned as '*Lauhitya*' in classical Indian literatures like the *Mahabharata, Purana* and *Hasta-Yurveda*. However, *Kalika Purana* and *Jogini Tantra* mention the name Brahmaputra for the first time. According to *Padma Purana (Sristi Khanda)*, the Brahmaputra's birth is linked to Brahma, the creator of the world. Hence, the name Brahmaputra meaning the 'Son of *Brahma*'. The Brahmaputra was referred to as a masculine river (*Nada*) probably because it is a river flowing from east to west, unlike others that flow from west to east, besides being vast and powerful. In the Smriti works, the Brahmaputra is referred to in the following Sanskrit verse: *'Brahamaputra Mahabahu Santanu Kulanandana/Amoghagarbhasambhuta papam Lauhitya me hara'* ('O Lauhitya, the large-armed son of *Brahma*, born as a son in the family of *Santanu*, from the womb of *Amogha*; Kindly remove my sin').

The Brahmaputra remained an enigmatic river all through human history. However, there had been sustained efforts to unravel its hidden mysteries by countless monks, explorers and travellers from India, China and few western nations. The latest, most stunning, and probably the last major discovery in regard to the Tsangpo (Upper Brahmaputra) was made in 1998 when an expedition sponsored by the National Geographic Society and led by two Americans, Tibet-Scholar Ian Baker and Tsangpo-expert Kenneth Storm Jr., ultimately unveiled the riddle of the Tsangpo gorge by surveying and measuring the spectacular 30 meter high Hidden Falls. The Tsangpo Grand Canyon is now the world's deepest, longest and most treacherous canyon of the world with a depth of 5382 meters.

Geo-physical and Ecological Background

The Brahmaputra basin, excluding the Tibetan portion, forms an integral part of the monsoon regime of eastern Asia with a mean annual rainfall of 230 cm having a variability of 15-10 per cent. Distribution of rainfall over the basin shows marked spatial variation, for example, from as low as 175 cm in the Kopili basin located in central Assam to as high as 410 cm in the Jiadhal basin in the northeastern part. Rainfall in the Himalayan sector averages 500 cm per year with the lower ranges receiving more than the higher ranges. Monsoon rains from June to September account for 60-70 per cent of the annual rainfall in the basin, while the pre-monsoon season covering the period March through May produces 20-25 per cent of the annual rainfall caused primarily by depressions moving from the west and by local conventional storms. Intense rainfall activities triggered by cloud burst occasionally cause devastating flash floods and landslides in the region. Snowfall is experienced in the Brahmaputra basin in most areas with elevations 1500 meters and above.

Due to their strategic location in regard to colliding Eurasian (Chinese), Indian and Indo-Myanmar tectonic plates, the Brahmaputra valley and its adjoining hill ranges are seismically very unstable. The earthquakes of 1897 and 1950, both of Richter magnitude 8.7, are among the most severe ones in recorded history. These earthquakes have caused extensive landslips and rock falls on hill slopes, subsidence and fissuring of ground in the valley, and changes in the course and configuration of several tributary rivers as well as the mainstream. The earthquake of 1950, for example, caused rising of the bed level of the Brahmaputra through deposition of sediments at Dibrugarh by at least three meters leading thereby to increased flood and erosion hazard potential of the river.

The Brahmaputra basin in Northeast India belongs to the Indo-Burma biodiversity hotspot, one of the 25 hotspots of mega bio-diversity on earth recognised by the World Conservation Union (IUCN). The outstanding feature of the region is the great diversity of flora and fauna and their enormous variation in both vertical and horizontal distributions. The Brahmaputra basin provides a unique habitat for an exquisite variety of fauna, including many rare and endangered species. Among these, the great Indian one-horned rhinoceros, pygmy hog, hispid hare, Asiatic elephant, clouded leopard, marble cat, golden cat, binturong, hoolock gibbon, White-winged Wood Duck, Bengal Florican, etc. are gravely endangered. All the states in the basin have more than the mandatory forest cover of 33 per cent of their respective geographical area except Assam which has about 22 per cent forest cover. Arunachal Pradesh with more than 80 per cent forest cover remains the greenest state of the region. The Brahmaputra basin in NE India has 59 per cent forest cover, the highest in the country. The flood plain of the Brahmaputra in Assam is dotted with a large number of wetlands or *beels*, which possess tremendous ecological significance as unique habitats for an exquisite variety of flora and fauna. These beels function as flood water retention basins and traditional fisheries. Over 3,500 such wetlands have been identified in Assam. Equally significant

is the cultural diversity of the Brahmaputra basin with its great multiplicity of ethnic, social and linguistic groups occupying their unique habitats in the basin.

Hydrologic Regime

The hydrologic system of the Brahmaputra is characterised by an extremely large and variable flow, enormous rates of sediment discharge, rapid channel aggradations, accelerated rates of basin erosion, and unique patterns of river morphology. With an average annual discharge of 19,830 cumec (m^2/second) at its mouth, the Brahmaputra ranks fourth among the large rivers of the world. The highest recorded daily discharge in the Brahmaputra at Pandu was 72,726 cumec in August 1962, while the lowest was 1757 cumec in February 1968. The mean annual flood of the river is 48,200 cumec. Significantly, the Brahmaputra carries more water from unit area of its basin than any other river in the world. High intensity flash floods with enormous damage potential constitute another significant phenomenon more frequently observed in recent years in the case of some of the tributary rivers of the Brahmaputra.

Brahmaputra is one of the most heavily sediment-charged large rivers of the world. It carries an average annual sediment load of about 400 million metric tons at Pandu (Assam) with an average daily rate of about two million metric tons during the rainy season. Transport rates as high as 26 million metric tons per day are recorded during the peak flood flows. The Brahmaputra river exhibits a classic pattern of channel braiding in its Assam section with repeated bifurcation and rejoining of multiple channels around multitudes of sandbars and islands. The bank lines of the Brahmaputra are extremely unstable and bank failures rampant in numerous vulnerable locations along the river.

Flood and Erosion Hazard

The Brahmaputra valley in Assam have earned great notoriety for the awesome hazards of annual flood and erosion that create mayhem every year bringing misery to a large section of people and shattering the fragile agro-economic base of the region. The valleys of the Brahmaputra and the Barak, which together account for 24.9 per cent of the surface area of NER and 80.8 per cent of Assam, are two worst flood ravaged regions of India receiving, on the average, three-four waves of flood every year. These floods cause extensive damage to agriculture, environment, human life and property, thereby affecting severely the economy of the state. With over 40 per cent of its land surface (3.2 million ha) susceptible to flood damage, which is 9.4 per cent of the country's total flood prone area, the Brahmaputra valley in Assam represents one of the most acutely hazard-prone regions in the country.

Floods in the Brahmaputra are caused by a combination of natural and anthropogenic factors. The unique geo-environmental setting of the region *vis-à-vis* the eastern Himalayas, the highly potent monsoon regime, weak geological formation, active seismicity, accelerated erosion, rapid channel aggradation (deposition), massive deforestation, intense land use pressure and high population growth especially in the floodplain belt and ad hoc type temporary flood control measures are some of the dominant factors that cause

and/or intensify floods in the Brahmaputra basin. The scenario is further exacerbated by a myriad of social, environmental and economic factors that make populations increasingly vulnerable. Assam, the most flood prone and flood ravaged state of the region, has experienced major floods in the years 1954, 1962, 1966, 1972, 1977, 1984, 1986, 1988, 1998, 2000, 2002, 2004, 2007 and 2008. In the aftermath of the Great Earthquake of 1950, the damage potential, intensity and frequency of floods have increased significantly mainly due to aggradation of the river bed. The floods of 1988, 1998 and 2004 were the worst ones in recent history. However, the flood hazard of 2004 broke all previous records of flood damage, affecting 28.5 million ha of land, 12.3 million people, 12.57 million ha of cropland, and 10,560 villages besides claiming 251 human lives and innumerable cattle and wildlife. All the 27 districts were affected by the flood and the total damage was estimated at Rs. 6500 crore. As many as 336 breaches had occurred in the embankments which aggravated the flood, erosion and sedimentation problems. Several tributaries of the Brahmaputra had undergone drastic channel avulsion, thereby causing heavy erosion, extensive sedimentation and severe flooding.

Exceedingly heavy, persistent, and concentrated rainfall in the upper catchments of flashy rivers like Pagladiya, Puthimari, Pohumara, Beki-Manas-Aie etc, synchronisation of flood peaks in the tributaries and the main stream, breach of a natural dam upstream of Kurichu Hydel Project in Bhutan and release of excessive amount of water by the Kopili Hydel project together with long-continued human depredations in the watersheds are cited as the major causative factors of the flood havoc.

Powerful atmospheric systems called cloudbursts that trigger intense rainfall in limited areas causing flash floods of great fury and destruction are being experienced in greater frequency in the Northeastern region especially along the foot hill region and in the immediate downstream areas of the Brahmaputra plain. The situation aggravates further if such extreme climatic events trigger landslide and slope failure in the upper watersheds or temporarily block river courses creating dams that subsequently break sending surging flood waves downstream. During the 1950 Assam earthquake a massive landslide in Arunachal Himalayas blocked the Subansiri river – a major tributary of the Brahmaputra for days together creating a dam which eventually breached releasing a deluging flood that greatly devastated the downstream areas in Dhemaji and Lakhimpur districts of Assam. On 10th June 2000, a massive flood occurred in Arunachal Pradesh reportedly as a result of a sudden failure of a landslide-induced dam in the neighbouring uplands of Tibet. Cloudburst and landslide related flash floods occurred in 2004 in the Manas and Beki rivers of Assam due to failure of a landslide dam upstream of Kurichu hydel project in Bhutan that caused highly destructive flood and channel avulsion. On October 7 of the same year i.e. 2004, a flash flood in the Jinari river of Assam was triggered by a cloudburst over Meghalaya that caused great havoc in the downstream areas in Assam. In the extremely powerful monsoon season of year 2008, there had been several waves of flash flood in the Lakhimpur district of Assam reportedly due to sudden release of excess water

from the Ranganadi hydel project that received excessive rainfall in the upper catchment. The ravage done by the sudden deluge was quite extensive and persistent in the impact zone. There has been repetition of this type of devastation almost every year in recent times. Breaching of embankments has been a major cause of intensification of the flood hazard in this region. These are used so far as the sole answer to tackle the threat of floods. Out of a total length of 15,675 km of embankments built so far in the country, Assam alone accounts for as much as 5027 km, i.e. about 32 per cent of the country's total.

Erosion hazard posed by the Brahmaputra is also extremely severe in several vulnerable reaches like Majuli, Palasbari, Rohmoria, Matmara and Bhuragaon. Majuli, the world's largest inhabited freshwater island and legendary nerve centre of Neo-Vaishnavite cultural heritage of Assam, has already lost as much as 371 sq km of its landmass to the river in the last 50 years with a reduction in area from 1246 sq km in 1950 to 875 sq km in 1998. Erosion is considered nowadays to be a more serious hazard than flood as it leads to total loss of land, especially croplands and settlement areas. Sedimentation caused as a result of flooding and erosion has also become a serious hazard in many riverine areas in the Brahmaputra valley of Assam. Deposition of coarse sediments has damaged large tracts of productive cropland, human habitats and infrastructural facilities causing enormous loss and misery to the public and huge cost to the state exchequer.

Water Resources Availability and Utilisation

The NE Region, drained mainly by the Brahmaputra and the Barak river systems, possesses about 34 per cent of the total water resources potential of the country while it covers only 7.7 per cent of the total Indian landmass. Besides having the highest per capita and per hectare availability of water in the country, the NER carries about one third of the country's total potential for sustainable hydropower use. However, it needs to be kept in mind that the potential for development and proneness to associated hazards is greatly skewed in regard to their spatial distribution across the region mainly due to the highly interactive and dominant highland-lowland scenario. Similarly, as against an ultimate irrigation potential of about 4.26 million hectares, the area presently under irrigation is only 0.85 million hectares. Likewise, only 4.3 per cent of existing groundwater potential has been developed so far although availability of ground water at relatively shallow depth (within 20 m) is very high in the region, especially in the valley areas. River navigation in the 890 km long reach of the Brahmaputra from Sadiya to the Bangladesh border, which is now the 'National Waterway No. 2' of the country, remains poorly developed. Development of other river-based industries like fishery, ecotourism, water sports etc. still remains almost a non-starter.

While it is true that the present utilisation of the colossal water resource potential of the Brahmaputra basin is dismally poor, the policies and practices for the utilisation of these resources in the future need to have a broader outlook and a changed paradigm and philosophy of development. As against the ad hoc, piece meal, short-term structural measures that are being adopted now, an integrated basin management approach for the rivers based on the

principles of soil and water conservation as well as sustainable development needs to be adopted. Proper assessment and reduction of vulnerability, empowering of local populations, and strengthening of existing institutions are essential for this. Especially for the Brahmaputra and the Barak rivers with their rich and diverse background of natural and human heritage, such a plan may contribute immensely towards ensuring food, health and ecological security. As a long-term strategy for resource utilisation and hazard management, a judicious mix of structural and non-structural measures with a greater emphasis on the latter, should form the core of the watershed based regional plan. The water resources of the northeast region must be planned on zonal basis to ensure optimal resource utilisation, hazard management, and welfare maximisation. Networking of hydro-meteorological data centres across state, national and international boundaries can play a key role in the management of water resources and flood hazards in the Brahmaputra basin. Being an international river of immense size, huge resource base and high hazard potential, only effective cooperation and coordination among the basin countries together with persistent efforts at the national and regional levels will be able to create an effective response mechanism to the problems of flood and erosion and usher in an era of progress and prosperity to the region.

Agriculture, the mainstay of most of the basin dwellers, suffers the most as a result of gross under-utilisation of existing water resources and the impact of ravaging flood and erosion hazards. In view of the extensive flood damage to paddy crops, there seems to be an urgent need to adjust the crop calendar by increasing the emphasis on winter (rabi) crops. However, development of sustainable irrigation facilities that safeguard environmental and social concerns is a prerequisite for any such change. Besides, there needs to be significant improvement in the power availability scenario in the state. Presently, there is growing concern about the possible negative impact of the proposed large dams of this region in terms of their viability and sustainability *vis-à-vis* the delicately poised geo-environmental base, ecological balance, ethno-cultural heritage and the extreme dynamism of geophysical processes in the region. In view of the inadequate knowledge base, lack of systematic data over an adequate time span and across diverse terrains and considering the intense dynamism, immense scale and high-order uncertainties of the geophysical processes of the eastern Himalayas, the wisdom behind adopting large structural interventions in the region raises questions that cannot be satisfactorily answered at the present stage of our knowledge and development. Furthermore, given the raging controversies over issues like inappropriate assessment of environmental and social impacts, lack of transparency and public participation in the decision-making processes and displacement of local communities, loss of their lands and livelihoods, the question assumes further complexity. The stakes seem to be too high and risks too great in such ventures of immense dimensions with far reaching consequences. All these aspects naturally call for in-depth and exhaustive investigation, analysis and assessment based on reliable scientific, socio-economic and ecological database spread over reasonable time frames, invariably following an integrated and cumulative basin management strategy.

Looking Ahead

For the Brahmaputra river that flows through three most populous countries in the world–China, India, and Bangladesh, the management of its vast water resources needs adequate regional as well as international cooperation and pooling of resources and expertise at the national and global level. Strengthening of scientific and technical information base, assessment of available technologies *vis-à-vis* the unique nature of the region, and induction of new and more appropriate strategies are other aspects that need to be emphasised. What is most needed, of course, is a strong political will both at the state and national levels and a sustained popular zeal to convert the water resources of the region into a force for sustainable development of the region through an integrated, multi-disciplinary approach that covers not only technological aspects but also social, economic and environmental dimensions. Under the existing circumstances, modest interventions with minimum possible impact on the environment appear to be the safest option for this region. In situations like ours where the stakes appear to be significantly high, risks too great and need for development is paramount, the basin approach is expected to provide us with the most appropriate options that are both socio-economically feasible and environmentally acceptable. On how our country faces up to the formidable challenges posed by the Brahmaputra and use its vast resources as a vehicle of economic change and social transformation will depend the peace and prosperity of the entire region.

42

A Kaleidoscopic View of Assam in the Perspective of Threat and Quandary

Col. (Retd) Manoranjan Goswami

The State of Assam has a distinctive history—history of culture, history of politics, history of ethnicity and a history of peace and conflict. The Assamese people, *per se*, are the end product of conglomeration and consolidation of various ethnic groups. Without going into the historiography, we can say that the Assamese, as a distinctive group of Indian people today, have gone through many challenges history has thrown on it. Unfortunately, the State of Assam is still searching for peace and amity among all ethnic groups—insurgency is gripping the State.

Today, our children, or for that matter the young generation of the country, probably do not know that except for Tripura, the seven sisters of the North East all belonged to Assam elders like me so remember, rather vaguely, how beautiful that map of Assam was with Meghalaya, Manipur, Mizoram, Nagaland, Mizoram and Arunachal Pradesh all being part of the State of Assam. The State of Assam, even after reorganisation in 1956, did have all the hill States to itself. Gradually, with the upsurge of insurgency and political game play, the state of Assam has been redrawn several times since 1970. We shall not go into details of how we, the people of this region, not only got dismembered part by part, and how the original sense of brotherhood and cultural assimilation between plains and hill tribes got disturbed, due to the restrains of space and time.

I have served in Mizoram and Nagaland as a part of the Indian Army while the insurgency movement was at its peak. I have personal knowledge as to how our hill brethren developed mistrust towards the Assamese community as a whole. Unfortunately, the conflict and mistrust is still going on. What I can definitively say is that the self grown ULFA movement has got its genesis

from the insurgency movements of the hill states around. (I must however add that Meghalaya and Arunachal Pradesh were not our mentors of insurgency).

History and Geography always work in tandem, and in the case of North East India we must not try to deal with the problem of insurgency or extremism that has engulfed the region today without considering the geographical location and the history of the region together. The North East, barring Assam and Tripura, is mostly a region with hilly areas and is at the same time an area which holds a separate history from the rest of the country, whether we talk of independent kingdom-ship or cultures of the tribal or semi tribal ethnic groups. Even Assam has a history of its long Independence and autonomous rule with the very least of interference from outside. The modernity of history has touched this region rather late; though the British rule did bring unity and modernisation in administration, the feeling of unity and commonality with the rest of India did take time to sink in-thus comes the feeling of being 'dominated by outsiders'. There is a 'psychological barrier' particularly among ethnic groups in Assam and it requires deep understanding of the politics and history of the people of Assam in particular, before the State machinery puts all its might and force as a measure of control on those who rebel. I will partly blame the bureaucracy and intellectuals who could not understand and appreciate the feeling of alienation that grips a large section of the Assamese population. Talking about the Assam of the present, not only is the State engulfed by the states gripped with the hill-based insurgency groups, but it also has Bangladesh, Nepal, Bhutan, China and Myanmar as its foreign neighbour, each having an envious eye or unfriendly attitude from the heart (the outward friendliness may be a delusion sometime). Assam is also connected to the mainland of India with a 20 km wide 'neck', which too gives a 'feeing of separation from the rest'. Over and above, the Government's present policy of appeasement towards the ethnic groups, not by integrating with the main Assamese society, but by granting greater autonomy to the agitating groups, the blob of mistrust between the Assamese plain populace and the hilly or plain tribes in the state is thickening. Giving 'autonomy' does not solve problems in any way it only spills a short and deceiving sense of achievement. The State Government loses its grip, giving way to greater degrees of lower rung corruption which ultimately hampers social welfare.

To some extent it is true that the Central Government has shown apathy towards Assam for a long time and it is a fact that insurgency did get some support initially from the Assamese people. However, people's support to ULFA was short lived and today ULFA cannot claim that it has the backing of the general people of Assam. Their support base is waning and their institutional framework and agenda is turning obsolete in the socio-economic context of present day Assam. However, it is the duty of the Government, both State and the Centre, to ensure that the basic issues of dissatisfaction and frustration that the people had or still have are addressed. The communication problem, the unchecked infiltration from Bangladesh, unemployment among the youth, the drought in industrialisation or the indigenous people's right over the land are some of the problems that still

plague the state. The ULFA's pro-talk group is doing some talk to bring peace, but truly speaking, many like me do not know really how the talk process is going on and whether the whole process is a political one which has to be sustained till the next elections. People of Assam are more disenchanted about the fact that this talk process is going on without producing concrete results and maybe also with no real voice from the people of the State. We must not forget that with the backing from Pakistan and Bangladesh (till recently) and active association with the Bodo militant group nearby, Assam is still in the danger zone of extremism more so with the immense of Maoist militancy dawning upon Assam.

We have intelligent groups of exuberant youths who are on the wings to bring the State to new heights, given the opportunity. We have a strong history of culture and education, and above all, we have a strong sense of patriotism. Our youth needs proper direction. Let the feeling of alienation not go so deep that it impacts our sense of identity and association with the region. We do not need large and gigantic industry, we need more medium and small industries where young entrepreneurs get a chance to use their talent and be 'masters' than just employees. Handloom, textile, horticulture, fruit processing etc have immense scope. Our economic fundamentals have the capacity to thrive in terms of employment and growth, given the population of the region and its geo-political dynamics.

We cannot, at the same time, neglect the necessity of upgrading and modernising our Police force, both from the Human Recourse point of view as well as the technological. The Police Force, dealing with terrorism or extremism must be separately trained as a special group. Army should not be called at the drop of a hat, because that is diminutive to the image of the state as well as the Army. Regional aspiration should be appreciated, but as stated earlier, giving autonomy is not the only answer. Wining hearts through a genuineness of feeling and understanding is more important.

I would expect that the people of Assam understand themselves better and that the Government in Delhi appreciate the roots of mistrust between mainstream India and the North East. North east as a whole and Assam in particular must not be given a feeling that India's east ends at Kolkata.

Index

B

E

F

G

H

N

R

S

Y

Z